The Flaming Womb

BARBARA WATSON ANDAYA

The Flaming Womb

*Repositioning Women in
Early Modern Southeast Asia*

University of Hawai'i Press   Honolulu

LIBRARY OF CONGRESS CATALOGING-IN-PUBLICATION DATA

Andaya, Barbara Watson.
    The flaming womb : repositioning women in early modern
Southeast Asia / Barbara Watson Andaya.
        p. cm.
    Includes bibliographical references and index.
    ISBN-13: 978-0-8248-2955-1 (hardcover : alk. paper)

    1. Women—Southeast Asia—History. 2. Women—History—
Modern period, 1600– . 3. Women—Southeast Asia—
Social conditions. 4. Sex role—Southeast Asia—History.
5. Southeast Asia—Social conditions. I. Title.
    HQ1745.8.A683 2006
    305.40959'0903—dc22

                                    2006012670

Designed by University of Hawai'i Press production staff

To the memory of my mother, Loloma,
a truly exceptional woman

Contents

Acknowledgments

IT IS MORE THAN ten years since I began research for this book, and in the process I have accumulated many debts. I would like to express my gratitude to the John Simon Guggenheim Memorial Foundation for the financial support that enabled me to extend six months' leave into a year and to include some time in Southeast Asia. The Humanities Research Centre at the Australian National University provided me with a home for three months in 2000 as part of its Law and Humanities program, and chapter 5 was essentially written there. I thank the Centre's then director, Iain McCalman, Deputy Director Caroline Turner, and Anthony Milner, Dean of the Asian Studies Faculty, for arranging my stay in Canberra. The Asian Studies Program at the University of Hawai'i paid for the maps, which were drawn by Bill Nelson. Staff members in the archives and libraries where I have worked have all been unfailingly helpful, but I wish to make specific mention of Rohayati Paseng, Southeast Asian librarian at the University of Hawai'i.

My greatest debts are owed to my colleagues, who over the years have listened to my ideas, attended my talks, and answered innumerable questions about a multitude of matters. In particular, I would like to thank Malcolm Mintz, Li Tana, Peter Xenos, Norman Owen, Merry Wiesner-Hanks, Michael Aung-Thwin, Nora Taylor, Elizabeth Guthrie, Ann Kumar, Andrew Metzner, Wendy Doniger, Trudy Jacobsen, Nhung Tuyet Tran, John Miksic, and Peter Skillings for their prompt replies to queries that undoubtedly interrupted busy and productive lives. Other colleagues took on the even greater task of reading individual chapters. In this regard I am extremely grateful to Nola Cooke, Michael Feener, David Atwill, Leonard Andaya, David Ludden, Harriet Zurndorfer, David Hanlon, Patricia Martinez, Anand Yang, Barbara Ramusack, Nola Cooke, C. Pat Giersch, Geoff Wade, Terence Wesley-Smith, Steven Collins, Juliane Schober, Rosemary Gianno, and Ian Wendt. Amazingly, some courageous souls were willing to read the entire manuscript and give very detailed comments; here I remain permanently indebted to Liam Kelley, Helen Creese, and especially Eloise Van Niel, as well as two anonymous readers for the University of Hawai'i Press. Kennon Breazeale not only worked through the text but also over the years has been unstintingly generous in supplying me with information that is linguistically beyond my reach. I would also like to offer special thanks to Jeffrey Hadler and his graduate class in Southeast Asian history at the University of California, Berkeley, who critiqued an earlier draft. The generosity of friends and colleagues has saved me from serious errors, but I take full responsibility for any mistakes and oversights that remain. Wise advice from readers and my editor at the University of Hawai'i Press, Pamela Kelley, has restrained my enthusiasm for adding yet another intriguing example, although I regret that page limitations prevented me from citing all the many stimulating publications I have read.

My family has lived with this book for a very long time and will undoubtedly be glad that my frequent pleas for "just five minutes more" can no longer be justified. I can only thank them for the years of patient and unquestioning support.

Abbreviations

AAS	Association for Asian Studies
ANU	The Australian National University
B and R	Emma Blair and James Alexander Robertson, *The Philippine Islands 1493–1898,* 55 vols. (Cleveland: Arthur H. Clark, 1903–1909)
BAVH	*Bulletin des Amis du Vieux Hué*
BEFEO	*Bulletin de l'École Française d'Extrême-Orient*
BKI	*Bijdragen tot de Taal-, Land- en Volkenkunde van Nederlandsch-Indië*
BSOAS	*Bulletin of the School of Oriental and African Studies*
EFEO	École Française d'Extrême-Orient
EIC	English East India Company
IAHA	International Association of Historians of Asia
ISEAS	Institute of Southeast Asian Studies, Singapore
JAS	*Journal of Asian Studies*
JBRS	*Journal of the Burma Research Society*
JESHO	*Journal of the Economic and Social History of the Orient*
JIAEA	*Journal of the Indian Archipelago and Eastern Asia*
JMBRAS	*Journal of the Malaysian Branch of the Royal Asiatic Society*
JRAS	*Journal of the Royal Asiatic Society*
JSBRAS	*Journal of the Straits Branch of the Royal Asiatic Society*
JSEAS	*Journal of Southeast Asian Studies*
JSS	*Journal of the Siam Society*
KITLV	Koninklijk Instituut voor Taal-, Land- en Volkenkunde
MBRAS	Malaysian Branch of the Royal Asiatic Society
MEP	Missions Étrangères de Paris
TBG	*Tijdschrift voor Indische Taal-, Land- en Volkenkunde*
TNI	*Tijdschrift voor Nederlands-Indië*
VBG	*Verhandelingen van het Bataviaasch Genootschap van Kunsten en Wetenschappen*
VKI	*Verhandelingen van het Koninklijk Instituut voor Taal-, Land- en Volkenkunde*
VOC	Vereenigde Oost-Indische Compagnie (United Dutch East India Company)

Introduction

If Southeast Asian history were recast so that "women of prowess" received even a fraction of the attention accorded their male counterparts, the individual known as Ken Dedes would certainly assume greater prominence.[1] A shadowy figure in modern textbooks, she is endowed in the Javanese *Pararaton* (Book of kings) with sexual powers that are both mysterious and formidable. The *Pararaton* recounts an episode in Java's legendary past when Ken Dedes, a local governor's wife, is out riding in her carriage. As her sarong falls aside, a gleam of light is visible between her thighs. This catches the attention of a young man named Ken Angrok (seemingly a low-born peasant but in reality the son of the god Brahma), who has taken service with her husband. A sage tells him that this "glowing secret part" marks Ken Dedes as *ardhanariswari,* an embodiment of the perfect balance between male and female, and that the man who obtains her is destined to be king. Accordingly, Ken Angrok kills the governor, marries Ken Dedes, and succeeds as ruler. Already pregnant by the governor, Ken Dedes gives birth to a son, Anushapati, to whom she later reveals the story of his origins and his father's fate. A vengeful Anushapati subsequently murders Ken Angrok and becomes king himself. Although he too is eventually killed, his son (and thus the grandson of Ken Dedes) goes on to establish a line of descent through which rulers of the kingdom of Majapahit (thirteenth–fifteenth centuries) claimed legitimacy. The quiet confidence suffusing the splendid fourteenth-century statue of Prajnaparamita, goddess of transcendental wisdom, may have encouraged the popular Javanese belief that it is actually a portrait of Ken Dedes, "the princess of the flaming womb."[2]

Suitably bowdlerized, the story of Ken Dedes—at once the victim of unbridled male ambition and the catalyst for the founding of a new dynasty—does occasionally appear in Western-style histories of Java. She is nonetheless an exception, since the standard accounts of Southeast Asia rarely permit females more than a minor historical role. This absence occurs despite a succession of commentators who, over many centuries and with varying degrees of censure or approbation, have remarked on the independence displayed by "Southeast Asian" women. In 1944, even as the concept of Southeast Asia was evolving, the French scholar George Coedès listed "the importance of the role conferred on women and of relationships in the maternal line" among various factors contributing to the cultural unity of the region he termed "Farther India."[3] More than four decades later, historian Anthony Reid carried this line of thinking even further, proposing that women's relative autonomy and prominence in marketing, agriculture, and ritual "represented one aspect of the social system in which a distinctive Southeast Asian pattern was especially evident."[4]

The idea that "female status" helps define a Southeast Asian culture area has met a more guarded response from other disciplines. Foremost among those reluctant to assert a regional pattern, anthropologists would prefer to see gender—the cultural system of practices and symbols by which male and female roles are historically produced—as subject to constant negotiation in specific environments.[5] Whether focusing on female health in northern Thailand, the entrepreneurial skills of Javanese batik sellers, aging women in Singapore, prostitution in Bangkok, or factory workers in Malaysia, an array of finely honed studies has demonstrated that contextual particularities will always temper the applicability of translocal generalizations. Unlike their colleagues in history and political science, anthropologists rarely frame their research questions in terms of "Southeast Asia." The contention that such an approach is unhelpful and even "distracting" implicitly challenges historians to reconsider the extent to which extrapolations from separate instances can support wider conclusions regarding "Southeast Asian women."[6]

Anthropologists have, however, been deeply involved in the generalizations and comparisons generated by development studies. Within this framework, research on women's concerns in Southeast Asia has been primarily concerned with the effects of economic and cultural globalization. Yet whether investigations concern practical and applied issues or theoretical and symbolic meaning, the historical dimension is rarely emphasized. As a result, critiques that locate Southeast Asian women in a "world economy" lack the evolutionary roots necessary to reach an adequate explanation of contemporary gender relationships. The proliferation of "women and development" studies has simply accentuated the disjunction between our familiarity with the present and our lack of knowledge about the past. It is clear that the relentlessly globalizing forces of the contemporary world have had far-reaching effects on millions of Southeast Asian women, but any assessment of change and its ramifications demands a much stronger historical base than currently exists.

Although premodern specialists are beginning to address this conspicuous gap, the small body of publications on women's history in Southeast Asia still concentrates on the nineteenth and twentieth centuries. Supported by an expanding corpus of sophisticated literature developed largely in relation to India, scholars have examined the way in which colonization redefined the place of women, whether indigenous, European, or "mestizo." Yet because all Southeast Asia except Thailand came under colonial control, we find that, as in India, a preoccupation with the interaction of gender and race has tended to strengthen the historiographical separation between "modern" and "premodern" history. In other words, by emphasizing the changes resulting from European domination, we risk underestimating the ways in which earlier developments had already affected women's lives. The value of a diachronic approach is well illustrated in Jean Gelman Taylor's pioneering examination of the social changes that occurred in Dutch-ruled Batavia as the creole element became less evident among the governing elite.[7]

Opportunities to employ the longitudinal view occur only rarely in Southeast Asian studies, because of the dearth of research on women prior to the nineteenth century. Given the continuing endorsement of "female status" as a distinctive regional feature, this neglect deserves some explanation. In some respects it is a simple matter of catch-up, since histories of women in other areas of the world have been produced only over the last thirty years or so. However, advances are unlikely to be rapid, because the investment required to master relevant languages and scripts means that the number of specialists working on pre-nineteenth-century Southeast Asia will always be small. Investigation of a female past has been further shackled by long-standing expectations that history will reconstruct the antecedents of modern nation-states and thus help justify contemporary political and territorial realities. Though these expectations are receding, it is not easy to find a place for women when a country's metanarrative is anchored by the lives of individuals (usually men) to whom evolution or liberation from foreign control is attributed. Even in the hands of a sympathetic writer, the nature of "national history" almost inevitably means that efforts to incorporate women will become an uneasy exercise of insertion rather than integration. In the majority of cases, those who have earned a part in the nation's drama have done so by demonstrating their success in "male-like" roles, notably in battle against the enemy. In this capacity several heroines have been incorporated into the patriotic pantheon, such as the Trung sisters, who led the Vietnamese against the Chinese in 43 CE; Thao Suranari, who repelled Lao forces advancing across northeast Thailand in 1827; and Cut Nyak Dhien, the Acehnese woman who joined her husband to fight the Dutch.

The hegemony of the national epic in Southeast Asian historiography has fueled demands that more attention be accorded previously marginalized or silenced groups, including women. Happily, this has coincided with an expanding interest in what has been conveniently termed the "early modern period," roughly spanning the centuries between 1400 and 1800 and previously located uneasily between the "colonial" and the "classical." In Southeast Asia the appropriateness of the term "early modern" (implying an inevitable impetus toward a European-style modernity) is the topic of continuing debates. Although historians generally agree that this period is distinguished by the increasing penetration of a global economy, the spread of the world religions, the growth in the power of the state, and changing notions of how "femaleness" and "maleness" should be constituted, periodization across a region is problematic. Victor Lieberman, for example, has contended that polities on the mainland developed rather differently from those of most areas in island Southeast Asia. Urging a more global approach, he has pressed for a larger framework that would look beyond "area studies" borders and treat Eurasia as "an interactive, loosely synchronized ecumene." By contrast, Anthony Reid has argued that the long-term effects of "early modern" economic, political, and religious changes justify generalizations across Southeast Asia as a whole.[8]

The idea of a period characterized by change should place a historian of women on immediate alert. Because outside ideas are so often appropriated through new or modified formulations of gender, conjectures about representations of femaleness and female response to change may be particularly useful. More than twenty years ago Joan Kelly posed the question, "Did women have a Renaissance?" and more recently European historians have interrogated the rationale for female participation in "early modernity."[9] In Southeast Asia, recognition of new influences, both economic and cultural, should similarly lead to questions about the effects on women, and the extent to which these differed according to locality, ethnicity, and socioeconomic status. Such questions can be answered only by evaluating and measuring change in different contexts, itself a challenge in the Southeast Asian environment, where historical work has been characterized by prudence rather than boldness. Because academics value language facility so highly, most scholars are reluctant to move outside a linguistic and cultural area they know well, with the result that a strong tradition of comparative thinking in the classroom is not reflected in published research. It is therefore ironic that claims of regional distinctiveness in regard to the position of women have become so embedded in the literature.

The Origins of This Book

Debates regarding the legitimacy of the term "Southeast Asia," the possibility of constructing "autonomous" history, the acceptability of historical periodization, the use of sources, and the perils of generalization have dominated academic conversations ever since I entered graduate school in the mid-1960s. Issues related to women, gender, and sexuality are a later entry, especially among historians, but it is evident that their inclusion can imbue even well-worn topics like nationalism and the revolutionary struggle with a new relevance.

In 1993, against this background, I began to formulate plans for a new research project. In accordance with my Cornell training, which had always stressed the need for a "case study" approach, I initially thought of continuing my earlier work and focusing on another little-known area of the

Malay-speaking world. Such a project would allow me to use my knowledge of Dutch East India Company (VOC) and Malay sources to further explore the ways in which local societies were affected by the economic and political changes of the seventeenth and eighteenth centuries. Yet somehow the idea did not excite me, partly because I felt that in terms of methodology and research strategies I would be traveling paths I already knew reasonably well. It was at this point that I began to think seriously of entering the field of women's history.

My interest was not, I hasten to add, a completely new development. Nobody working on premodern societies needs reminding about the critical role of family relationships (and, by extension, the place of women), but during my research on east Sumatra I had been particularly struck by the vigor with which the kinship theme emerged even in the VOC's commercial records. In this case I had found the challenge of working across two hundred years exhausting but nonetheless rewarding. I also remembered the mixture of apprehension and excitement with which my husband, Leonard Andaya, and I had approached the prospect of writing a general history of Malaysia in the late 1970s. While this joint effort proved to be something akin to a mental triathlon, we enjoyed the intellectual venture of moving outside our own area of expertise and thinking about historical processes over many centuries.

As I looked ahead to the shape of my next book, my teaching and interaction with students, especially at the graduate level, also played a part. Like many of my colleagues, I have found contemporary critiques of the "area studies" concept unsettling, given our awareness of the role historians have played in the construction of Southeast Asian studies as a scholarly field. Again, like others, I have seen the heavy weight of national historiography as an impediment to research in this part of the world, limiting curiosity and discouraging inquiries beyond political borders. Increasingly, I came to believe that studying women in the premodern period might be a useful means of reaching outside the parameters academia has helped create. From the very inception of this project I therefore worked from a belief that "the human experience is sufficiently similar to make comparison possible," and that by exploring both resemblance and divergence we can learn more about the histories of the cultures in question. Like my mentor, O. W. Wolters, I believed that "a gender-oriented study should do more than put women into history" and that "it should also throw light on the history—male as well as female—into which women are put."[10] While accepting that I risked overreaching my capabilities, I also hoped that my temerity might nudge the field ahead by provoking others to pursue or contradict my arguments. Indeed, I was encouraged in this belief by observing that in women's history a pattern has been established whereby detailed analyses are often a response to conclusions presented in more general studies.[11]

My inquiry began with what I initially thought was a rather straightforward question: to what extent did changes associated with "the early modern period" reshape the lives of "Southeast Asian women" and affect their relations with men? Although the implications soon proved daunting, I felt I could draw some support from the academic climate in the late twentieth century, sympathetic as never before to the historical study of women in non-European societies. In 1892—a century before I embarked on my research—the Pali scholar Mabel Bode read a paper entitled "Women Leaders of the Buddhist Reformation" to the Ninth International Congress of Orientalists in London. Yet though the movement for female suffrage was then gathering force, and the social and legal advances since that time have been considerable, the emergence of women's history as an academic field is very much a product of the last thirty years. It is intriguing to recall that the initial conference of the National Organization of Women held in Washington, D.C., in October 1966, dedicated toward "true equality for all women in America, and a fully equal partnership of the sexes," was convened only a month after I entered graduate school.

While positioning myself in this research, I have often felt intellectually and emotionally jostled by my personal engagement with the topic, my commitment to "Southeast Asia," and my training as a historian. In this situation it was helpful to envisage the audience who I hoped would read (and enjoy) this book. I will of course be gratified if it proves useful to my fellow Southeast Asianists, but I will be even more pleased if it interests colleagues working on women's history in other parts of the world.

The Argument

Chapter 1 approaches the problematic issue of "Southeast Asia" by considering the ways in which topography helped mark off a geocultural zone and contributed to a claimed regional distinctiveness in gender constructions. Although the political boundaries that demarcate Southeast Asia were largely nonexistent until modern times, the highlands that reach from Vietnam across Laos, northern Thailand, and Burma did act as a buffer against control from centers in India and China. This often inaccessible terrain meant upland populations were less susceptible to domination by lowland cultures informed by political-religious assumptions about female subordination. To the distant east and to the far south, I argue, the seas created "borderlike" zones of a somewhat different kind, so that sustained interaction between "Southeast Asia" and "Oceania" did not extend beyond the eastern Indonesian archipelago and the coasts of western New Guinea. Notwithstanding similarities that connect Polynesian societies with their Southeast Asian kin, Oceania also throws up some striking differences, notably in the sexual antagonism so often described in Melanesian cultures.

With some qualification, chapter 1 concludes that there is a "Southeast Asia" where the history of women can legitimately be investigated. Chapter

2 moves on to consider the historiographical considerations I confronted because of the nature of the project, my own limitations, and the variety of sources I was using. Although I believed that approaching even very familiar material with new questions was potentially fruitful, I fully understood that the pitfalls involved in writing any regional history would be exacerbated by the diversity of Southeast Asia's cultures and the vast range of languages of which I had no knowledge. I was always aware that I would be highly dependent on other specialists, particularly in tapping indigenous material beyond the Malay world, my own area of expertise. I was conscious, too, of other historiographical problems. The phrase "reading against the grain" may be a cliché, but it encapsulates a necessary approach when written evidence privileges elite men. Like other historians of premodern times, I had to decide when a lack of information justified reading backwards from more recent data. Although offering potentially invaluable insights, a retrospective methodology must always be used judiciously. Burmese land surveys from the eighteenth century, for example, demonstrate that women could sometimes hold the position of village head, but in 1953 upper Burmese villagers told one investigator that they considered such an idea ridiculous.[12]

In essence, then, chapter 2 reiterates the message that although the history of women in Southeast Asia must remain at best partial, a cautious yet creative approach to the sources may produce surprising results. In chapter 3, I place myself directly in the line of fire by turning to consider the vexed question of the degree to which the world religions have been instrumental in (re)constructing conceptions of gender. This issue is especially pertinent to Southeast Asian societies because in many areas women and sexually ambiguous individuals played a leading role in indigenous ritual and in communication with the spirit world. From the fifteenth and sixteenth centuries the advance of Islam and Christianity in island Southeast Asia introduced new articulations of messages stressing female spiritual and intellectual weakness—the same messages that Theravada Buddhism and Confucianism had so vehemently promoted on the mainland. Across the region it is possible to track the slippage from "sacral danger" to female impurity, and to document the ways in which women were excluded from the most prestigious areas of religious praxis. Nevertheless, though their field of operation was more circumscribed, the sources suggest that women could still acquire a reputation for spiritual authority, whether as the pious donor of a Buddhist monastery or as a gifted healer who could summon supernatural forces to her assistance.

In any society, economic change is almost always a catalyst for social change, and this is particularly applicable to early modern Southeast Asia. Chapter 4 explores the ways in which the regional position of women was affected by the expansion of long-distance trade, the incorporation of the region into a global trading network, the beginnings of cash cropping and wage labor, and the massive increase in slavery. Growing numbers of Chinese and European traders helped confirm a dual economy where women continued to dominate local markets, but where overseas-oriented commerce was the domain of men. As mediators in the transcultural exchanges underlying the early phases of commercial globalization, the role of women deserves particular historical attention, but as always there is a bleaker underside. In the new urbanized ports, where thousands of manumitted slaves without kin eked out a living, the growing visibility of prostitution signaled a grim trend toward the feminization of poverty.

Chapter 5 draws its inspiration from recent work that stresses the need for historical contextualization of interactions between women and "the state." Despite a lack of agreement as to what constituted a "state" in Southeast Asia, most historians would accept that the obligations and responsibilities embedded in kinship relations provided the template for indigenous governance. Because enforcement of any overarching authority so often relied on the metaphor of family hierarchies, ruling elites became committed to gender regimes that both reflected and influenced the wider social order.[13] Regardless of a state's military or territorial strength, the regulation of appropriate roles for men and women was subsumed in the dynamics of population control. In the sixteenth century the relationship between "state" and "subject" became more complicated with the arrival of Europeans, especially in the island world. Whether in the Philippines, where Spanish imperial ambition laid the basis for a full-blown colony, or in the port cities controlled by the Dutch East India Company, European officials elaborated indigenous ideas of the state as a guardian of moral values. Like their local counterparts, they became deeply implicated in the maintenance of a political order where the superior position of men was persistently affirmed.

Chapter 6 expands on this idea by considering how gender constructs in elite households were inflected by class priorities. The manner in which upper-class women behaved and the lifestyle they adopted became an index of high status not only for females themselves but for their menfolk and families too. Whether in Vietnam or Burma or Java, wellborn women were subject to a battery of representations, ranging from art and literature to moralistic texts, all of which extolled remarkably similar hierarchies in female-male relations. In arguing against the imposition of "Southeast Asian" boundaries, Sanjay Subrahmanyam has pointed to similarities between court life in seventeenth-century Arakan and Bengal and to their mutual difference from Vietnam.[14] Nevertheless, as in western Europe, the exchange of high-ranking women in marriage was fundamental to regional diplomacy. The perceived ability of a Cham princess to adapt to life in a Vietnamese court, or a Khmer lady to adjust to Siamese protocol, suggests that status values were often an effective mediator of cultural or linguistic differences. In specific contexts it is certainly possible to provide instances of wellborn women who rejected or negotiated the gender hierarchies associated with their class. On the other hand, they were still far more exposed to state-promoted didactics than were their lower-ranking sisters. Representations of the ideal might be contested, but it would be unrealistic to ignore their consistency and ubiquity or to assume that these representations were without effect. Because elite women were so closely associated with the world of power and influence, they stood as the village's distant "other," setting standards for female behavior that were variously emulated, navigated, or repudiated.

At the beginning of the twenty-first century we have long passed the point where "women" are depicted as an undifferentiated category. Chapter 7 responds by arguing that a core of shared experiences does come about simply by virtue of occupying a female body and living with the ambivalences that menstruation, marriage, childbirth, menopause, and aging can provoke. Inextricably tied to a woman's reproductive capacity, regardless of ethnicity and class, these experiences provide a site for comparative discussions of "being female" where ambiguity becomes a leitmotif. Despite the received wisdom that asserts a relatively high status for Southeast Asian women, fears of uncontrolled female sexuality thread through the record from very early times. Though male-female interaction remained typically complementary, state structures and religious teachings endorsed gender inequalities. The knowledge of senior women was respected, but malign magic was often associated with female intrigues and there is a disturbing trend toward widow dependency.

The conclusion should be regarded not simply as an overview of my general argument but as an invitation to others to continue the conversation. The evidence has persuaded me that one can approach Southeast Asia as a region where attitudes toward gender, though subject to constant renegotiation, were historically favorable to women. However, I also believe that differences and similarities in women's comparative position stem primarily from socioeconomic environments rather than some "traditional culture." I carry no brief for regional uniqueness, since cross-cultural comparisons commonly associate female independence with communities where women's work is valued, where due attention is accorded maternal descent and inheritance does not exclude daughters, or where the influence of world religions and state ideologies is weak or nonexistent.[15] Despite this disclaimer, in the course of my research I have repeatedly felt myself bumping into manifestations of "Southeast Asia"—amorphous, porous, ill-defined, but somehow persistently there.

Over the last decade, as I have worked on this book, I have been made constantly aware that the process of research and writing forms part of a personal journey. It comes as something of a shock to hear myself called a "senior scholar," for I often feel I have only just started on that journey. Although I remain at once a committed area specialist and a historian with a historian's curiosity, I realize that the current project has also been shaped by the simple fact that I am a woman. More particularly, I am writing at a time when questions about women's history have become legitimate and relevant in a way that they were not when I was a graduate student. Despite my initial misgivings, I have found this coalescence of professional and personal interests emotionally engrossing and intellectually rewarding. I hope that something of my engagement will come through in the text that follows.

CHAPTER 1

Women and "Southeast Asia"

In 1944, the same year in which George Coedès published his pioneering history of the Far East's "Hinduized states,"[1] the National Geographic Society issued its first map of Southeast Asia as a guide to developments in the Pacific War. Nonetheless, despite the confident perimeters drawn by the society's cartographers, the demarcation of postwar Southeast Asia remained a matter for scholarly debate. While some authorities preferred a broader "monsoon Asia" that would include Sri Lanka, southern India, and southern China, others favored a more restrictive approach. D. G. E. Hall, one of the founding fathers of Southeast Asian studies, even omitted the Philippines from his monumental *History* (1955) because he could not detect strong historical links with the rest of the region. Hall's change of heart, evident in his second edition (1964), was legitimized by a growing consensus that global zones were best mapped along national boundaries (often, in fact, the result of colonial jurisdictions). Evidence of "institutional and intellectual inertia" this may be, but after fifty years a "Southeast Asia" defined by political borders is firmly entrenched in academic and diplomatic usage, even as specialists assert its linguistic and cultural diversity.[2] Yet for those who work in periods that predate the formation of contemporary states, the influence of world regions in determining research trajectories is a source of some unease. Charles Higham, for example, has argued that comparisons of prehistoric societies from Yunnan to Vietnam's Red River valley, as well as possible connections with Austroasiatic groups in eastern India, have been seriously impeded by the "intrusion" of China's southern boundary into archaeological studies.[3]

Approaching "Southeast Asia" by reference to human interaction rather than political configurations is fundamental for the viability of a "women's history" that is both regional and comparative. The highlands and oceans that have helped delineate Southeast Asia as a world area are also borderlands (or in some cases, border seas) where the geographer's concept of the ecotone—an interactive area between different physical and botanical environments—can also be applied to cultural overlap, including notions of gender.[4] The tendency to essentialize China and India as Southeast Asia's Others must surely be modified when we consider how officially promoted ideas about relations between women and men were adapted at the margins and in the interstices of state authority. Extending the ecotone model to include a human dimension can be equally helpful in thinking about the rationale behind the "Oceania–Southeast Asia" division, especially as it relates to male-female interaction. In short, even as we deploy "world areas" as a convenient organizational device, comparative vigilance remains essential as we evaluate the received wisdom that sees "relatively equal gender relations" as somehow distinctively Southeast Asian.

"China," Gender, and Geography

The borderlands between China and Southeast Asia are defined by a highland system radiating out from the Yunnan plateau. Southward, mountainous flanks extend to northern Burma (Myanmar), Laos, Thailand, and Vietnam, while eastern ranges give way to the irregular terrain of the Chinese provinces of Guizhou, Guangxi, Hunan, and Guangdong. Forming a natural geographic obstacle in the path of Han migration from northern China, the south and southwest were never fully incorporated into the imperial system. Because new settlements were largely confined to the coastal plains, the interior uplands remained the preserve of tribal groups whose languages and lifestyles resembled those of their neighbors in contemporary Southeast Asia. For the Chinese authorities, these communities were not merely inaccessible but also culturally obdurate; as one Ming emperor put it, "The roads are long and dangerous, the mountains and rivers present great obstacles, and customs and practices differ."[5]

Ongoing efforts by successive dynasties to assert control over the south and southwest merit historical consideration because "Chineseness" came to be intimately associated with notions of how men and women should interact. As imperial power was consolidated under the western Han (206 BCE–9 CE), the teachings of Confucius (551–479 BCE) and his followers were incorporated into the principles of government. Though Confucius himself rarely addressed male-female interactions, his stress on deference and "virtue" directed attention toward women because correct family relationships were increasingly seen as the foundation of the sociopolitical order. With the revitalization of Confucianism under the Song (960–1279 CE), Chinese officialdom became ever more involved in overseeing matters such as betrothal, marriage, and inheritance, while the promulgation of specific law codes affirmed the paramountcy of paternal descent and the legal authority of male heads over wives, children, and junior men. Precepts hitherto loosely observed were now enforced more rigorously, and didactic works advocating female humility and obedience, like the "lessons for women" by a wellborn widow, Ban Zhao (ca. 48–117 CE), and Madam Zheng's *Book of Filial Piety for Women* (ca. 730 CE), acquired unassailable standing in the canon governing the lives of elite females. The influence of such teachings not only in China but also in Korea, Japan, and Vietnam has led one scholar to argue that "in the span of world history few intellectual traditions . . . have had a more telling impact on women than Confucianism."[6] The message that female propriety was a measure of a society's moral virtue was patently evident when the Emperor Yongle (r. 1402–1424) ordered ten thousand copies of "Biographies of Outstanding Women" to be distributed to barbarian countries, including those of the "southern seas" (i.e., Southeast Asia).[7]

Of particular significance in the evolving ideas of gender is that family practices among peoples regarded as Chinese displayed a "relatively high level of standardization . . . across regions, classes, and dialect groups."[8] Male-female relationships may have been conceptualized as complementary, but they were also strictly hierarchical. As patriarchal principles were reinforced, women's marital rights became more restricted, their inheritance of property more limited, and their links to their natal families more tenuous. In the Ming period (1368–1644), the acceptance of foot-binding, a mark of beauty as well as social standing, imposed real restrictions on the physical mobility of wellborn females as they became status symbols for their husbands and relatives. Support for the cult of female chastity and widow fidelity was especially pronounced during the Qing dynasty (1644–1911), and regulations in the eighteenth century sought to enforce a uniform standard of sexual morality across all classes.[9]

Stereotypes about female subordination in Chinese society always require qualification. Social compliance was not without benefits, and access to education enabled some women to gain a position of considerable respect. Although Confucian scholars deplored female influence in political matters, individual women could exploit their personal connections as wives, daughters, and sexual partners. The concept of filial piety invested the mother-son relationship with heavy obligations, and older women exercised real authority in the household, with dowager queens among the most formidable figures in China's political history. State-promoted agendas underwent considerable modification at lower socioeconomic levels, where the stakes of property and inheritance were lower and female support to the domestic economy indispensable. Yet a struggling family could hardly rejoice at the birth of a daughter, whose contribution to household maintenance would be relinquished or substantially diminished on marriage, and female infanticide became a shadowy presence in rural society.

Like Confucianism, Daoism and Buddhism also privileged men, but their rituals were more tolerant of female participation and more willing to recognize women as religious adepts. Gaining pace in China around the fifth century, village Buddhism allowed substantial space for the honoring of motherhood; and the transformation of the (male) enlightened being, the bodhisattva Avalokitesvara, into a Sinicized Guanyin, goddess of mercy, is an intriguing development. Ordination as a Buddhist nun offered elite women some alternative to marriage or sequestered widowhood, and

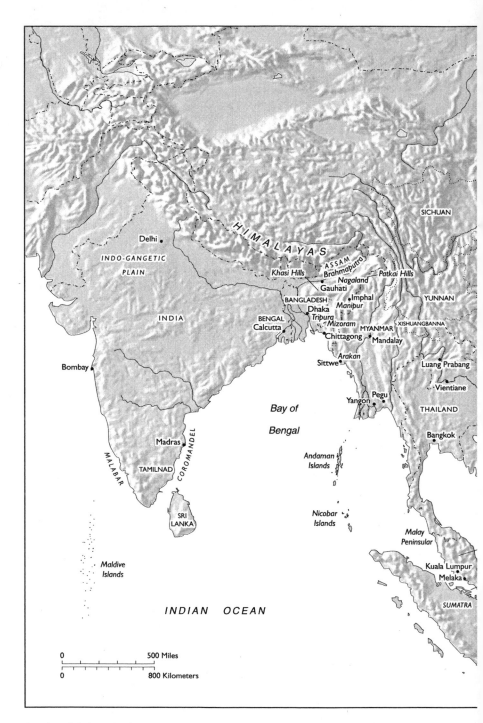

Southeast Asia in its Asian context

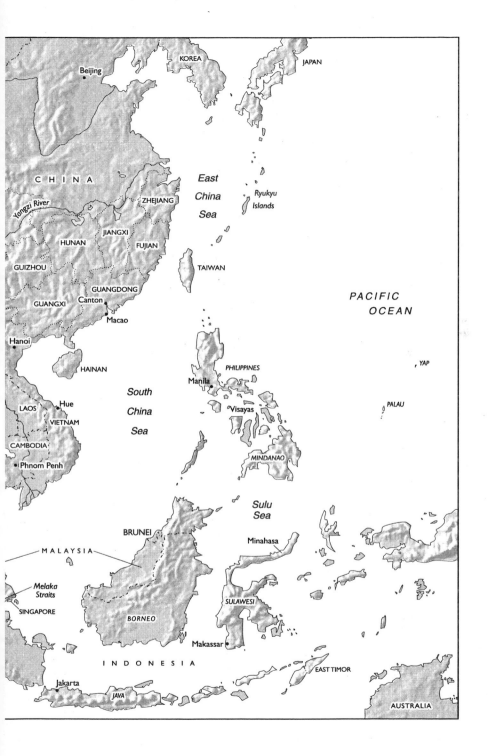

Empress Wu (r. 690–705), the only example in Chinese history of a female monarch, was a major patron. As in Sri Lanka and Southeast Asia, Buddhism was tolerant of shamanism, and communication with powerful spirits remained an integral part of life-cycle rites. Similar comments apply to Daoism, which enjoyed considerable patronage during the Song. The high place accorded goddesses like the Queen Mother of the West in Dao rituals does not guarantee recognition of female religiosity, but the prominence of spirit possession in popular practice permitted female mediums to assume leadership roles.[10] This expertise could then be incorporated into Buddhist and Daoist rites and even influence ceremonies dominated by male masters and monks. Yet the opposition of Confucian scholars to Daoist and Buddhist practices, articulated at the highest levels of the state, was both persuasive and sustained. Subjected to continuing accusations that their exponents promoted immoral behavior and failed to honor family obligations, Buddhism and Daoism both fell from official favor.

The connections between the maintenance of moral order, state surveillance, and "Chineseness" acquired further significance as Chinese moved south of the Yangzi and came into direct contact with non-Han peoples. Speakers of Tai or Austroasiatic languages, these groups were subsumed in Chinese thinking under a variety of imprecise names such as Zhuang, Miao, Yao, and "the myriad Yue." By the sixth century, despite periods of disorder and dynastic collapse, migration into the southern provinces of modern China, the island of Hainan, and Vietnam's Red River Delta was well in train. The Sinicization process of peoples once seen by the imperial court as living "beyond the realm of civilization" is well demonstrated on Hainan, which, after continuing Chinese settlement, had been administratively incorporated into Guangdong. As a result, the "assimilated" indigenous population, the Li, had taken on numerous aspects of Chinese culture, and by the mid-thirteenth century half could reputedly speak "the Han language."[11]

Gender in China's Borderlands

The inculcation of moral virtue—including correct relations between men and women—was integral to the spread of Chinese authority because of the conviction that social decay was a prelude to state downfall. Efforts to change or modify existing customs, however, were often thwarted by cultural norms, economic realities, and the geographic environment. In the rice-growing communities of southern China, for example, a higher premium on women's participation in agricultural labor mitigated gender hierarchies associated with the wheat-farming north. It is not just that irrigated rice farming is labor-intensive; certain essential activities, like transplanting young seedlings from the nursery to the flooded fields, were seen as "women's work" because of the parallels with human gestation and birth.[12] Although little is known of early agricultural deities in southern China, such analogies would have mandated female involvement in the rituals required to guarantee a successful harvest. It was presumably in this environment that the ancestors of peoples who later trickled down into the plains of central Thailand first began to imagine Mother Rice and conceive of the rice grains as her children, who must be carefully nurtured.[13]

Despite some dilution of the state's gender priorities, the Sinicization of the southern coasts and lowlands moved inexorably forward. In the more accessible areas, where Chinese migration had displaced or absorbed local populations, the cultural hegemony of northern models was not easily contested. This hegemony was graphically demonstrated in the acceptance of female foot-binding. Notwithstanding the pain and physical restrictions this practice entailed, the aesthetics of feminine beauty promoted by Han culture and the demands of social status were compellingly persuasive. By late Ming times elite classes in the Canton region, for instance, were routinely compressing their daughters' feet.[14] In the seventeenth century the new Qing dynasty repeatedly forbade Manchu women to follow the Chinese practice, but tight socks and high heels could still be used to simulate the "golden lotus feet" regarded as a distinguishing feature of a refined civilization.[15] Such perceptions help explain the generally disparaging attitudes toward Hakka groups from the Fujian and Guangdong interior. Descended from northern migrants, Hakkas had intermarried extensively with local populations but were relegated to the margins of Chineseness, in part because their women had large feet, worked beside men in the fields, and unashamedly "showed their faces" in the marketplace. In this they resembled the women of upland groups such as the Zhuang (today the most numerous of China's southern "minority peoples"), who were "everywhere in the markets of the towns and cities, trading and selling, pursuing profit."[16]

The Southwest

As Ming authority extended over the southern lowlands, the colonization of Yunnan also gained momentum. Much Chinese migration was spontaneous, but by the sixteenth century an officially directed program had resettled around a million people, mostly soldiers and their dependents, and had equipped them with tools, seed, and draft animals. In this ethnic frontier, however, efforts to transpose "Chinese" values met formidable obstacles, foremost among which was a physical landscape dissected by deep forested valleys, turbulent rivers, and virtually impregnable escarpments. Although eventually forced to accept protectorate status, the resistance of the Yunnan kingdom of Nanzhao (ca. 649–902) and its successor Dali (ca. 937–1253) was a testimony to the protection the terrain offered. The Mongol leader Kublai Khan, whose conquest of China led to the short-lived

Yuan dynasty (1271–1368), lost nearly half his forces in Yunnan during invasions of what is now Burma.

Whereas earlier Chinese texts drew only vague distinctions in a patchwork of Tai, Tibeto-Burman, Yao, and Miao peoples (called Hmong in contemporary Southeast Asia), the colonizing impetus of the Ming and subsequently the Qing is evident in the trend toward more detailed classification of local populations. The term "Miao," initially applied indiscriminately to a range of different tribal groups, was rendered more specific, with appellations such as Red Miao or Flowered Miao referring to the dominant colors or motifs of female dress. In 1741 the Guizhou provincial gazetteer identified thirteen separate Miao groups.[17] Despite a growing awareness of difference, the Chinese believed that communities in these remote southern areas were alike in manifesting certain regrettable cultural traits, foremost among which was animal-like lust among their men and lack of sexual restraint among their women. These stereotypes persisted even as a strengthening Qing control brought greater familiarity with non-Han societies. Stories compiled by the well-known poet and official Yuan Mei (1716–1797), for example, include titles such as "The hairy men from Guangdong use humans as bait" and "A big hairy man abducts a girl."[18] Illustrations in the so-called Miao albums, based on the Guizhou gazetteers and dating from the early eighteenth century, presented tribal groups as quintessential manifestations of "un-Chinese" behavior. Drawing on cultural clichés rather than direct observations, they projected an image of "Miao" societies as indifferent to appropriate gender roles and unconcerned with female modesty. Men are thus depicted caring for children, while women with unbound feet work in the fields, their skirts barely covering their buttocks.[19]

It is significant that one recurring image in the Miao albums shows young men and women unrestrainedly dancing to flutes, for official accounts were particularly critical of premarital sexual freedoms and of the "degenerate" manner in which young couples "pair off whether they are of marriageable age or not."[20] As a Ming commentator lamented, "They do not distinguish between clans and no importance is assigned to a woman's virginity. Before a girl reaches maturity, she is permitted to stay privately with a man, and to go to his house. The man's mother will wash her feet and the girl will stay five to six days. She is then sent back to her mother's house. Only then is an agreement reached through a matchmaker, after which the property and ceremonial arrangements are completed and they are married."[21] These societies were further distinguished by a failure to observe filial piety, as married sons left their natal home to live independently or with their wife's parents. Like the common practice of marriage between maternal cousins, such arrangements were deplored because they upset "the hierarchical principles of kinship" and signified moral decadence. The casual attitude toward the marital bond and the perceived infidelity of married women supplied yet another example of the incorrigible immorality of "barbarian" society. "If a woman's husband is away for even a short time, she will strike up an illicit liaison with another man, and subsequently she will marry him."[22]

Spirit propitiation and the involvement of women as ritual leaders also attracted disapproving comments from Chinese officials, unsympathetic toward ancient beliefs that likened the fertility of crops to the human reproductive cycle. Figurines from Yunnan showing women carrying rice and agricultural implements provide evidence of the female contribution in farming tasks and suggest that women were prominent in rites supplicating the spirits for good harvests. Among mountain-dwelling groups, where soils were less fertile, the major grain crop was millet rather than rice, but we can assume that female participation in agricultural rituals applied here as well. Still in modern times Wa women in southwestern Yunnan assume a leading role when the souls of maize, buckwheat, sorghum, millet—"you who feed us"—are invoked.[23]

For the imperial government this communal mediation with the supernatural was a matter of concern because of official antipathy to individuals acting as spirit mediums. In provinces with a large non-Han population, such as Guizhou, prohibitions were notoriously ineffective, and eighteenth-century observers still commented on female participation in local ceremonies like those propitiating the spirit of the soil. Some women, regarded as receptive vehicles for communication between humans and the spirit world, exercised unusual power.[24] According to a Song account, for instance, a matriarch from a Zhuang community not only wielded authority as a spirit medium in her own right but maintained her influence over her son when he became ruler. Officials stationed on Hainan Island similarly noted female prominence as leaders, commenting that although the native population was "very fierce," quarrels could be instantly resolved when a woman mediated between two hostile groups. From the Chinese perspective this was hardly praiseworthy, and negative views were reinforced by reports of "black magic" practiced by Li sorceresses, reputedly potent enough to entrap Chinese men.[25]

Chinese rhetoric was adamant that recasting gender roles would lead to greater public virtue while addressing economic deficiencies. In Yunnan, for example, one official claimed that female dominance in agriculture meant the productive potential of the land was not fully tapped. The prominence of local women in trade and marketing was similarly a measure of the "laziness" and apathy of their menfolk. In practice, Chinese officials were often willing to make some compromises with local traditions, and in southern Sichuan, Guizhou, and Yunnan they were initially willing to recognize women as native chieftains.[26] Qing attitudes were less accommodating. Increasingly insistent on patrilineal descent and a Confucian-style education as a qualification for public office, authorities now required local leaders and their retainers to send their sons to Chinese schools. By the mid-eighteenth century, arguments that these "savages" could be "civilized" had come under attack. As colonization of non-Han territories gathered momentum, older policies of peaceful assimilation were set aside, and local chieftains were replaced with Chinese officials.[27]

The reshaping of gender embedded in the Sinification process had far-reaching results. As Robert Geddes has remarked, patrilineality is now so widespread among the Miao that any adaptation from the Chinese must have occurred a long time ago.[28] Since there were considerable rewards for those who adopted Chinese language, dress, and modes of behavior, local people were often willing participants in the colonizing project. A seventeenth-century scholar who married the daughter of a Miao chief in Yunnan recalled that "she was expert in painting flowers, plants, birds, animals and landscapes. She understood Chinese. . . . After our marriage, she studied daily with her mother-in-law the *Analects, Mencius,* the *Book of Filial Piety for Women,* and other works. . . . After a year's study she understood the thought of these works and could compose essays." Yet in other contexts the Chinese model was less persuasive, and the same scholar noted that "the daughters of [Yunnan] chiefs sometimes bind their feet, but the girls of ordinary families seldom do it, because it is more convenient to work with natural feet."[29] Furthermore, the movement into "Chineseness" was frequently reversed, and Chinese officials were distressed to discover that migrants were adopting indigenous funeral and marriage practices. Intermarriage was accordingly outlawed in the 1720s, although new edicts in the 1770s suggest that this ruling was often ignored. Despite their best efforts, officials found the effective implantation of Chinese attitudes and practices extraordinarily difficult. Even in the nineteenth century a Guizhou gazetteer noted that "since half [the Miao] do not understand [our] language or script, it is hard to unify attitudes and customs."[30]

The human ecotone of China's southwest and far south thus served as a buffer against the gender priorities of the Chinese government. By the early seventeenth century, tens of thousands of migrants and soldiers had moved into northern Yunnan, but these regions remained essentially non-Chinese. Despite imperial efforts, Sinicization was never more than partial. Although it proved impossible to maintain a cultural boundary between settlers and tribal societies, Chinese settlers and traders mingled with, rather than overwhelmed, local peoples. The linguistic and economic interaction between Tai *muang* (settlements) such as Xishuangbanna (in modern China), Keng Tung (in Burma), and Chiang Mai (in Thailand) were strengthened by local adherence to Theravada Buddhism, with its stress on the links between laity and monkhood. Far from mentioning China or the Chinese, local Thai chronicles dating from the late eighteenth century conceive of a common Tai culture that stretched across the northern hills—a culture to which, claim several modern scholars, the favorable position of women was intrinsic.[31] One must obviously be wary about generalizing across this ethnic mosaic, since patterns of kinship, marriage residence, and inheritance can differ markedly. In one small area of northern Laos, for instance, around 250 kilometers in diameter, there are at least twenty-five different groups, each with its own language and identity.[32] Nonetheless, the centrality of male-female relations in the process of identity creation is evident in Ming references to Chinese men who married tribal women, shaved their hair, and did not return, a process of acculturation termed "getting on the stilted bamboo" (a reference to the pole houses of upland communities).[33]

Emblematic of the persistence of older male-female relations even as social patterns were being reshaped are the Akha (called Honi in China), who speak a language belonging to the Tibeto-Burman family. Today their numbers are estimated at 500,000, and their settlements straddle the boundaries of southern China, northern Thailand, and Burma. Regarded as "patriarchal," Akha society favors male descent, observes patrilocal marriage, appoints men as ritual specialists, considers polygyny to be normal, and excludes fertile women from many public ceremonies. Nonetheless, guardianship of the sacred rice is a female task, and certain ancestral rites are also performed by senior women, who wear a white skirt as an indication of their high status. Ritual chants remember the women who have left the home as well as the sisters of fathers and grandfathers; at a man's funeral it is his daughters who jointly present an ox as a sacrifice. Paid in silver, the bride price testifies to a woman's social and economic value to her family, and although she has supposedly left her clan, she can return to her parents if her husband mistreats her. The role of women as identity markers among minority groups is also evident among Akha subtribes, who are distinguished from each other by the female headdress style.[34] In a similar mode, although men now dominate agricultural and household ceremonies, the Lisu of northern Thailand (recent migrants, probably from Yunnan, and linguistically related to the Akha) still invoke a distant past when women served as ritual specialists and even chiefs.[35]

Taiwan and Vietnam

Although women hardly surface in a recent volume that sees Taiwan and Vietnam as part of a "Pacific world," the two places provide contrasting but telling examples of the effects of Chinese colonization on gender relations.[36] The mapping of world areas has offered little support for accommodating any "Southeast Asian" claims by Taiwan, even though its indigenous languages are members of the great Austronesian family that stretches from Easter Island to Madagascar. At the beginning of the seventeenth century, Taiwan (then home to around twenty "aboriginal" groups) was on the outer edge of Chinese consciousness, being visited mainly by fishermen and pirates. However, the linguistic similarities with Malay that caught the attention of Dutch visitors can be seen as merely one aspect of a larger web of connections linking Taiwan to other Austronesian societies and to non-Han cultures in southwestern China. Particularly striking are the parallels in the female position. When employees of the United Dutch East India Company (Vereenigde Oost-Indische Compagnie, VOC) arrived in Taiwan to establish a base for the China trade, they were surprised to see that "women do not obey or reverence their husbands." Such comments were echoed by their Chinese contemporaries, who noted that the custom of bridewealth placed a high value on daughters. As in the Philippines, priestesses, "old women," played a significant role in indigenous religion, notably in ceremonies connected with head-hunting and death.[37]

By this time, however, more Chinese migrants from Fujian and other areas of South China were arriving in Taiwan, and their numbers increased substantially after 1644 as refugees flooded in after the Ming collapse. The Chinese introduced new attitudes toward the position of women, which reinforced other influences derived from the short-lived presence of the VOC (1622–1662) and Christian missionizing efforts that emphasized male authority. The Chinese hold strengthened after the Dutch were expelled, and in 1684 Taiwan became a prefecture of Fujian Province. Following policies adopted toward non-Han groups elsewhere in China, officials sought to change local practices to conform to the approved mode of gender relations. Customs that permitted free choice of partners, residence with a bride's parents, easy divorce, female economic independence, and widow remarriage were roundly condemned, while other developments like the introduction of Chinese farming methods lessened the importance attached to female agricultural work. In 1715 one official (presumably disregarding the hardships of peasant life in China itself) bemoaned the "suffering" state of aboriginal women, required to labor in the fields for the sole benefit of their husbands. Ironically, it was the physical abuse of such women by Chinese men that precipitated aboriginal rebellions in 1731 and 1732, in turn leading to an intensification of Sinicization efforts. As in Hainan and Yunnan, the "civilizing" of aboriginal youths through instilling Confucian morality and Chinese culture became a major priority. Although many customs that affected women, such as matrilineal inheritance of land, changed slowly and though foot-binding was never adopted, the "assimilated barbarians" occupying the lowlands were frequently commended by Qing officials for their loyalty to Chinese interests.[38]

The case of Taiwan demonstrates that the process of creating political boundaries exerted a profound influence in the shaping of local cultures and the formation of self-identity. Vietnam, located at the periphery of the Middle Kingdom, and under Chinese control until the tenth century, provides another telling example of the borderland experience. Vietnam's immense biodiversity makes it an archetypical ecotone, but in linguistic terms it is also a transitional zone. Although the inclusion of the Vietnamese language in the Austroasiatic complex is now generally accepted, the acquisition of tones and shifts in vocabulary displays the effects of long contact with the Chinese. Indeed, the overwhelming political dominance and cultural assertiveness of this northern neighbor has made comparison with China the most common gauge in measuring Vietnam's Southeast Asian credentials.[39] As a result, the scholarly literature on Vietnam offers intriguing evidence of the ways in which a society at the borders of Chineseness accommodated a cultural ideology that often conflicted with indigenous mores, in gender as in other matters.

Around the beginning of the Christian era, when Han emperors were viewing the newly established prefecture of Jiaozhi (the Red River plain) as a candidate for incorporation into the imperial ambit, its population was regarded as displaying the same "uncivilized" characteristics as other Yue societies, most notably in regard to relations between the sexes. A Chinese prefect stationed in the south early in the first century CE, for instance, complained that men and women chose their marriage partners at random and thus lacked "conjugal morality." Admitting that official prohibitions were quite ineffective, another Chinese administrator deplored the Vietnamese custom whereby a man would take the widow of a deceased brother to wife. Most of the blame for this "immorality" was attributed to the conduct of women, and over the next thousand years the exotic but seductively wanton female projected in the writing of Chinese bureaucrats became inseparable from imagery associated with the south.[40] "Wearing floral hair-ornaments of gold," lyricized a Tang official, "her bosom is snow white, her face like a pink lotus, golden rings hang from her ears, pierced for lapis-lazuli studs, her rose-tinted dress clings tightly. She laughs confidently by the river bank, and beckons to the stranger come from afar."[41]

In the tenth century, Vietnamese leaders were able to evict Chinese forces and establish an independent state centered on the Red River Delta. Yet China's cultural and political tutelage had been highly effective. The frontier, established in 939, was unique in Southeast Asia because it transversed a highly varied ethnic zone of "noncivilized" people but yet recognized the territorial sovereignty of two separate states. It may also have encouraged a tendency to identify cultural difference, and in recording local folklore one early Vietnamese scholar remarked that in "our country" there were no "ancient fox-spirits" like those in China which were so "calamitous to women."[42] Yet a millennium of Chinese influence did have profound effects, notably on relations with non-Vietnamese. It is understandable that local elites, descended from Sino-Vietnamese marriages, looked on the highland-dwelling "savages" with disdain, while the Lao to the west and the Cham and Khmer to the south were at best inferior cultures who should acknowledge Vietnamese overlordship. In 1407 the Chinese reoccupied Vietnam, but the challenge of maintaining control over such a distant and recalcitrant area forced their withdrawal twenty years later. The defeat of Ming forces laid the ground for the emergence of a more self-assured Vietnamese state whose neo-Confucian orthodoxy helped justify the successful attack on an "immoral" Champa in 1471.

The fifteenth century is usually seen as a turning point in Vietnam's gender history because of efforts by the Sino-Vietnamese elite to replicate the neo-Confucian world order, which they admired and of which they believed themselves a part. Central to this order was the conviction that male-female relationships must be regulated because deviance from prescribed norms could be the cause of a state's downfall. Inculcating these values, however, was never easy, and Confucian scholars constantly bemoaned the neglect of correct behavior even at the highest levels of society. Beyond the capital, existing patterns of interaction between men and women were even more resistant to change. This is not to say, however, that change did not occur. Although Tai groups across northern "Southeast Asia" and southern China have been placed in "a single culture area," social organization and ritual practices that were previously more female-centered are thought to have changed under the influence of China and lowland Vietnamese models. For example, some "Black" Tai of the Vietnam highlands (named for the black blouses of their women) apparently view earth deities and the spirit of rice as male, whereas Tai elsewhere almost invariably conceptualized the soul of rice and the earth goddess as female.[43]

"India" and the Borderlands

The borderlands between "South" and "Southeast" Asia also originate in the Yunnan plateau, from whence a labyrinth of thickly wooded mountains extends up to the snow-covered ranges of Tibet and down into the region that in colonial Indian parlance became the "northeast frontier." This hilly, forested terrain is dissected by the wide expanse of the Assam Valley, through which the mighty Brahmaputra River flows into the Bay of Bengal. Between the Assam plains and Burma lies a tangled mass of mountains whose peaks can reach well over 3,500 meters but which also enclose valley tracts where independent states like Manipur could develop. Eventually these ranges fall away to form the Chittagong Hills, separating modern Arakan from eastern Bangladesh. "Hills" is perhaps deceptive, for in 1629 a Portuguese priest, speaking from personal experience, emphasized that this was "a most difficult mountainous region, rendered still more dangerous by the wild animals" and that "the mountains are inhabited by a certain tribe . . . very wild and uncivilized."[44] Although there were certainly well-traveled mountain paths along which traders moved, military access from Bengal into the Irrawaddy Valley was possible only though Manipur, Assam, or Arakan and was difficult even here. Maritime superiority enabled Arakan kings to extend their control into Chittagong in the fifteenth century, while a high range known as the Yoma protected Arakan itself from Burmese attacks. In the eighteenth century, Burmese armies finally pushed through this barrier and conquered Arakan, precipitating hostilities with the British in India that led to war and the eventual demarcation of the India-Burma boundary.

However, as the British began conceptualizing "India" in the 1780s, the status of the borderlands was ambiguous, and swaths of uncharted territory still "disfigured" colonial maps a hundred years later. The northeast had never been incorporated into the Mughal empire, and from the late eighteenth century Burmese kings were claiming Arakan, Manipur, and Assam as vassal states. Early British surveyors spoke not only of their unfamiliarity with the rugged terrain but also of the many tribal societies, which, though "imperfectly known," represented the northeast's most distinguishing feature: "There are few circumstances more calculated to arrest attention in considering this chain of mountains than the number and variety of the tribes by which it is inhabited."[45] Names such as Hkamti, Kuki, Palaung, Lisaw, Singhpo, and Lushai pepper the pages of nineteenth-century accounts, which single out details of dress, ornamentation, and female hairstyle to identify groups that were quite different from each other and distinct from the more familiar populations of "India."

Since most of these groups speak languages belonging to the Tibeto-Burman and Tai families, migration into the northeast would seem to have a long history. For instance, though now separated by the India-Burma border, the diverse peoples collectively termed "Chin" by the Burmese and "Kuki" (Bengali, meaning "highlanders") in India probably began trickling into Burma's Chindwin Valley from western China between the fourth and eighth centuries CE. Subsequently they moved westward, evidently to escape the exactions of expanding Shan and Burman populations, and in the contemporary Indian states of Manipur and Mizoram legends still recall migrations from China and "Siam" sometime in the distant past.[46] The tenuous tribute relationships that linked numerous chiefdoms across the northeast to the Ming court did not survive beyond the sixteenth century, but the region remained an integral part of the great trading network that fanned out from Yunnan. To the rulers of lowland Burma, however, the region remained as remote and exotic as it was to later Mughal officers. A fifteenth-century inscription talks about the "Palaung who grow tails," the "heretic kingdom of naked Nagas," and the upper areas of Assam as a land "where they kill people and turn into spirits." In a similar vein, later Burmese kings referred to their territories as ringed by lands of fire and water inhabited by people with "big ears."[47]

For early British observers, alarming accounts of the "ferocious" inhabitants of Assam and the hilly ranges in eastern Bengal were tempered by reassuring reports that upland peoples were also cultivators, growing rice and maize in semipermanent swidden plots. Hill cultivation was nonetheless distinguished from lowland practices by the absence of the plow, a factor of some importance to the female position. Dr. Francis Buchanan (1762–1829), whose geographic surveys were highly regarded by his contemporaries, indicated that swidden farming was always a joint operation in which men and women had very specific roles. While men cut down and burnt the trees, the women removed small branches, planted the seeds, and harvested the crop. Buchanan pointed to other ways in which women contributed to the domestic economy; in the Chittagong Hills, for example, they wove cotton into "coarse cloth" and were also visible as petty traders. In India the bazaar was already becoming a place that good Hindu and Muslim women should avoid, but in the hills, said Buchanan, "the women go to market like the Burmese."[48] When describing one Chin community east of Chittagong, he noted that monks were not as respected as they were in Burma, in part because of the importance placed on spirit mediums. Only through "certain women, called *deeraree*," could the spirits be consulted. Through communication with the supernatural, the *deeraree* could protect a swidden plot from the depredations of tigers and wild elephants and could inform people about the appropriate sacrifice to offer in times of sickness and death.[49]

Bengal, "Hinduization," and Gender

As influences derived from the core region of Hindu culture spread out from the Indo-Gangetic Plain, the highland areas were increasingly seen as marking a cultural boundary. In Buchanan's words, "All tribes east of Bengal are considered to have no caste, and are therefore highly contemptible."[50] Relaying the derogatory remarks by Mughal chroniclers, another Englishman repeated a common Indian belief that the Kuki of the Chittagong Hills could marry "any woman" they chose, the only exception being their own mother. At the same time, he remarked, "the whole management of their household affairs belongs to the women."[51] Although lowland influences were long-standing, a sociopolitical order justified by Brahmanical texts was never established in the hills, and the transmission of gender constructs that had evolved on the Indo-Gangetic Plains was consequently weakened. This is highly relevant to the position of women because the maintenance of Hinduism as a social system required close control over marriage as a means of preserving barriers between separate and ranked groups (castes). The preoccupation with ritual purity among those of highest status—the Brahmans and the Kshatriya, or warriors—fostered a heightened awareness of the polluting tendencies inherent in some aspects of femaleness, like the blood associated with childbirth or menstruation. The Laws of Manu, apparently compiled between about 200 and 400 CE, reflect a perceived need to regulate female sexuality by affirming the moral subordination of wives to husbands, mandating female chastity before marriage and absolute fidelity thereafter, and restricting women's legal independence and property rights. The first millennium CE saw a growing preference for young brides, the physical seclusion of women, and prohibitions against widow remarriage. Though subject to considerable negotiation, especially at the lower levels of society, these high-caste ideals exercised a commanding influence over the population at large. They were forcibly exemplified in one of the great epics of Hinduism, the *Ramayana,* which revolves around the ideal couple, Rama (an incarnation of Vishnu), and his wife, Sita, who is extolled for her fidelity, even in the face of unjust accusations.[52]

Although relatively uncommon even among higher castes, the ultimate statement of marital loyalty was a widow's willingness to accept self-immolation on her husband's funeral pyre. Like foot binding in China, the sati ritual was regarded by early modern Europeans with a fascinated horror and was described or illustrated in virtually all accounts of Indian life. Certainly, widows who sacrificed themselves in this manner brought great honor to a family, and in some places one even encounters *mahasati,* hero-stones set up to honor women who followed a husband in death. More typical of Brahman society, however, was the widow who lived out her days in a state of permanent mourning, self-denial, and austerity. Even a child-bride whose husband had died could be expected to shave her head and eschew self-ornamentation when she reached puberty. Nonetheless, perceptive Europeans noted a greater toleration of remarriage or cohabitation among lower castes, since female labor was vital to household production and poor families could not support an unproductive widow. In environments where their work was valued, women had greater marital rights and more options in the case of widowhood or a failed relationship.[53]

Because of caste and regional variations, scholars working on India often complain of ahistorical generalizations regarding the subordination of women. They have also stressed the ambiguity of Hindu ideas about "femaleness." Although the primordial and creative force is still male, the spiritual power, or Shakti, of great gods like Shiva and Vishnu is usually personified as a female consort who could be characterized by fertility and compassion but could also exhibit darker and more destructive aspects. The most obvious examples are the various manifestations of Shiva's wife, the benevolent Uma/Parvati and at times the bloodthirsty Kali/Durga.[54] However, because the panoply of Hindu goddesses often incorporated ancient female deities who had dominated indigenous cults, popular Hinduism was always amenable to the continued elevation of the female principle so crucial in agricultural societies. In eastern Bengal, for instance, Durga might be depicted as a bundle of plants wrapped in a sari, resembling the small trees dressed as pregnant women by which hill-dwelling Naga sought to guarantee the fertility of their crops.[55] Vaishnavite Hinduism, with its devotional focus on the love of Krishna and his consort Radha, and the emphasis on singing and dancing as steps toward ecstatic communion, was always sympathetic to female participation. Tantric Hinduism, which developed out of older practices of yoga, medicine, folk magic, and local goddess cults, also thrived in the Bengal environment. Though the effects of Muslim expansion were felt here as early as the thirteenth century, there is no indication of Islamic influence among the peasantry for another three hundred years or so.[56]

Assam and Manipur

Bengal thus served as a prism through which Hindu ideas filtered eastward into the Brahmaputra Valley of Assam, where copper plates pay tribute to the wives of Brahman donors, praising them for their chastity, their devotion to their husbands, and their ability to bear sons. The intermingling that typified this ethnic and cultural borderland is well illustrated by reference to groups speaking a language now called Tai-Ahom, who apparently migrated across the Patkai Hills from upper Burma around the thirteenth century. From a base in the upper Brahmaputra they spread across the lowlands, reclaiming marshes and forested areas for wet rice cultivation. The significance of the term "Ahom" is still debated, but it probably refers not to an ethnic identity but to a status group associated with rulers (*swargadeo*) and those who served them.[57] As successive *swargadeo* and their officials intermarried with local tribal peoples, the territory they arrogated reached further down the Brahmaputra Valley, incorporating Assamese speakers and their more Hinduized culture. The Indo-Aryan language of Assamese eventually replaced Tai-Ahom, which was retained only in ritual texts, with a hybrid form of Hinduism overshadowing practices like ancestor worship. Yet despite active *swargadeo* patronage in the seventeenth century, the Hindu caste system was never fully adopted, and the retention of older traditions reflects a continuing interaction with the surrounding "tribal" peoples. Invoking a familiar Southeast Asian theme, *swargadeo* themselves were said to descend from Indra's union with a heavenly princess who had taken the form of a tribal woman.[58]

Among hill communities, female status was conditioned by women's contribution to rice production and their importance in agricultural ritual. At times of drought or crop failure, for example, their dancing might pleasure the angry spirits, and priestesses known as Deodhai (literally meaning "god's midwives") were consulted to prophesy future events.[59] The temple dedicated to Shiva's consort, Kamakhya (Mother Earth), located near the central Assam city of Gauhati, is an example of how religious traditions could coalesce. Rebuilt after its destruction by Mughal armies, the innermost sanctuary of this temple enshrines a stone representing the yoni (vagina) of the goddess. It is kept moist by a natural stream that runs red during the annual ceremony celebrating the divine menstruation (apparently because of an increase in red hematite during the rainy season). According to some, the original temple priestesses at Kamakhya came from the matrilineal Garo tribe, which inhabits the hill area about fifty miles away. Among this community, land was passed through the female line, and in the eighteenth century one observer noted that Garo women seemed to enjoy considerable privileges and to have as much to say in village debates as men.[60]

A similar amalgam can be seen further south in Manipur, where around the seventh century incoming peoples linguistically categorized as Tibeto-Burman and now known as Meithei had begun to cultivate irrigated rice. Existing tribal groups were absorbed into Meithei society or retreated to the less fertile hill slopes and flood-prone lowlands. The culture that evolved from this interaction was characterized by traditions of matrilineality found among several tribal societies and by an indigenous belief system in which priestesses (maibi) dominated fertility festivals. Female devotion was thought to be especially pleasing to the deities of the Manipuri pantheon, and a priest possessed by a god usually wore the clothes of a maibi and could even be termed a "male maibi."[61]

In the fifteenth and sixteenth centuries, expanding trade routes and migration from Bengal and Assam helped spread Hinduizing influences, although specific effects on Manipuri women are unclear. A shift toward greater privileging of men has been traced to the 1730s, when the ruler embraced a reformed sect of Vaishnavite Hinduism. While the Hinduization of Manipur was always modified by local priorities, new conceptualizations of gender were deeply implicated in a hierarchical social system that involved elite self-definition as Kshatriya. Proponents of reform were outspoken in their efforts to prohibit divorce and widow remarriage while encouraging the taking of child-brides as a guarantee of female chastity. The first recorded case of sati occurred in 1725, and although the practice was by no means common, Manipur chronicles indicate that (as in India) the immolation of a wife on her husband's funeral pyre was a mark of high status; in 1776 three royal widows who fled to escape sati were arrested and exiled to an outcaste village.[62] The prominence of women in ritual was also a target of the reform movement. Worship of the old Manipuri gods was proscribed, and Brahmans were appointed in place of indigenous priests and priestesses. By the eighteenth century the Rice Mother deity had been Hinduized through her association with Durga and the north Indian Mother Goddess. As elsewhere, however, the localization process often subverted imported agendas, and the maibi tradition survived the hardening of patriarchal tendencies. Because Vaishnavite Hinduism encouraged female devotionalism, the ritual centrality of women's dance was maintained, with great honor accruing to those who participated. To ensure a successful harvest, the opening of a swidden plot was preceded by dance rituals in which the maibi enacted intercourse, birth, and the growth of a child.[63] As in many other rice-growing areas, agriculture remained highly dependent on female labor, and nineteenth-century observers familiar with lowland India also remarked that in Manipur "all marketing is done by women, all work of buying and selling in public and the carrying to and fro of the articles to be sold."[64] Female influence was even more evident in the Kuki hill communities, where "the wives of some of the Rajas manage all the affairs of the villages, apparently much to the satisfaction of their people."[65]

Mughal India and the Northeast

Long before the establishment of Muslim rule, Hinduized elites in the Indo-Gangetic Plain had seen eastern Bengal as subject to dangerous and polluting influences because of its proximity to the animist tribal areas occupied by *mleccha* (non-Hindus). Though the nobility had adopted Hinduism, Assam was still seen as a domain of "sorcerers and magicians" who had the power to cast spells over any who entered their country. More than language or unusual flowers and fruits, Assam was distinguished from the Hindu heartlands because its inhabitants did not observe food taboos and were allegedly willing to "partake of every kind of meat," regardless of who had cooked it or how it had been killed. Similar attitudes are found in Mughal chronicles, which also describe the Assamese as sorcerers and record that the word "Assam" was used in formulas to dispel witchcraft. From the thirteenth century, Muslim rulers repeatedly attempted to subdue the Brahmaputra Valley, but in the words of a later Muslim scribe: "In all the past ages no foreign king could lay the hand of conquest on the skirt of this country. . . . Every army that entered made its exit from the realm of life."[66]

The founding of the Mughal dynasty in 1526 led to a renewal of earlier efforts to subjugate the Assam region. In the seventeenth century, battles between the Mughal and Assam armies were commonplace, and in the 1640s one cartographer was sufficiently confident to arrogate much of Assam to the Mughal domains. This confidence, however, was misplaced, for it was extremely difficult to adapt a style of warfare developed on the plains of northern India to a region of "raging torrents and frightful valleys covered with dreadful forests."[67] The tribulations of sustained warfare in this region became painfully evident in 1661–1663, when the nawab of Bengal, Mir Jumla, amassed an army of 12,000 cavalry, 30,000 foot soldiers, and a huge flotilla with the goal of conquering Assam. While some sources explain the campaign as a punishment for past disloyalty or as part of a larger ambition to reach China and Burma, the official chronicle also conveys something of Mughal attitudes, speaking of "a holy war against the infidels of Assam . . . destruction of the customs of unbelief and error." Certainly Mir Jumla showed little respect for Ahom religious practices, sacking the Kamakhya temples and pillaging royal graves, including that of a queen interred some eighty years before.[68] However, continuing attacks by successive *swargadeo* were highly effective, attributed by one historian to a "Southeast Asian style" of organization that could call on all subjects for military or corvée service, regardless of caste, ethnic, or religious qualifications.[69] A

Mughal victory in 1663 came only after months of fighting and enormous loss of life, and almost immediately disputes over the peace treaty led to fresh confrontations. The frontier marshes and dense forests of eastern Bengal remained a turbulent "house of strife," and by the 1680s the Mughal commanders had been forced back down the Brahmaputra to the Manas River, which became the boundary of Mughal-Ahom territory until the British occupation.[70]

Mughal chroniclers leave no doubt as to the alien nature of Assam's population, "very black and loathsome in appearance." It was the unnatural state of the women, however, that exemplified the "otherness" of this "wild and dreadful country, abounding in danger." Stories circulated of a kingdom among the hills inhabited only by females and governed by a woman; any male stranger who unknowingly approached would be struck by supernatural forces and die. Comments by eyewitnesses, though more restrained, are still disapproving. In 1662 a scribe accompanying Mir Jumla's army remarked that although local women appeared beautiful at first glance, they were disfigured by "an absence of proportion in the limbs." His criticisms supply further evidence of how ideas regarding correct female behavior were localized among Assam's Hinduized elite, for the wives of rajas, like peasant women, did not veil their faces "and move about in the market places with bare heads."[71]

This theme of unusual freedom for women and a more privileged position than "the females of Hindoostan" threads through nineteenth-century colonial writings on what is today northeastern India. One of the earliest ethnologists in this region, Edward Dalton (1815–1880), echoed Mir Jumla's chronicler when he noted that even wellborn Assam ladies appeared in public without restrictions. Female independence was especially evident among the hill peoples, whom he and others compared to tribal groups in island Southeast Asia. Among Naga groups of northeastern India and the Dayak of Borneo, for instance, the links between head-hunting and notions of fertility meant women were intimately connected with the ritual that surrounded raiding and spirit communication. Hill women were also active in agriculture, marketing, and small trade and in later life served as ritual specialists and social mediators. Prestige items like gongs often descended through the female line even when inheritance was patrilineal. Premarital chastity was of little importance, and the practice of a groom "buying" his wife through bridewealth or through his own labor was also widespread. In an intriguing contrast to China's widow arches and the *mahasati* of India, a group in the Manipur hills honored women whose fields had yielded a good harvest by erecting a special stone to commemorate the amount of rice harvested.[72] All these cultural features are significant because in combination they enhance the position of women and heighten the value of daughters. In the 1930s one scholar concluded that women "were much better off in the hills than in the plains of India" because of the absence of customs such as purdah, child marriage, and the ostracism of widows.[73]

Arakan and Sri Lanka

Arakan provides another example of the ways in which geographic and cultural factors reshaped imported gender constructions in the borderlands, even as states inspired by Indian models developed. Separated from Bengal by hills that were almost impenetrable during the heavy annual monsoons, Arakan was distinguished by its professed Buddhism, its linguistic heritage of old Burmese, and its strong links with tribal groups. Influences from Muslim India meant that a Bengali notable would have probably adapted more easily to the Arakan court than his Vietnamese counterpart, but local traditions highlight the borderland orientation. One legend, for instance, concerns a Muslim princess from Bengal who is forced to marry the Buddhist king of Arakan but is repelled when she is served *ngapi,* a strongly flavored fish sauce, which, though unfamiliar to her, is found throughout Southeast Asia.[74] The Muslim model may also explain why lowland women were more secluded than in Burma, but in the surrounding hills both sexes worked together in their fields, and Buddhist women enjoyed "great freedom of action, and are unmistakably a power among the people."[75] As Buchanan remarked, the Burmese theft of daughters after the conquest of Arakan in 1784 was a major tragedy, not only because of personal loss but also because the poor were deprived of the resource by which aging parents "most commonly support their infirmities."[76]

Against this background it is useful to reconsider projections of gender in other sources. For example, a fourteenth-century Arakan image of Lakshmi and Vishnu does not follow the conventional Indian style in which the goddess is smaller than her husband, but makes them equal in size and height. This, speculates a modern authority, probably reflects "the more equal status of women in Arakan."[77] It is also noteworthy that the first known depiction of the Earth Goddess in Southeast Asian Buddhist iconography, found in the early Arakanese kingdom of Vesali (seventh–eighth centuries), resembles those elsewhere in Southeast Asia rather than Indian representations.[78]

The Buddhist links exemplified by such images were nurtured by trade across the Bay of Bengal and by a network that drew together southeastern India, Sri Lanka, and mainland Southeast Asia through the regularity of the monsoon winds. Since around the dawn of the Christian era, maritime communications between the Indian subcontinent and Southeast Asia had fostered precisely those transmissions and interactions impeded by the terrain of the borderlands, including Hindu and Buddhist models of kingship and political authority. A historian of gender, however, might well invoke the old concept of "monsoon Asia" to track other affinities, particularly with southern India. Presumably because the indigenous Dravidian culture was less influenced by imported Aryan ideas, gender relations in Tamilnad in many respects paralleled those of northeastern India and Sri Lanka.

Women's agricultural work in the rice fields was more valued than in the wheat-growing north, female fertility was celebrated, matrilocal residence was common, and daughters and wives were more likely to inherit property. One of the pioneers of gender studies, Sherry Ortner, has accordingly remarked that "Sri Lanka and a few south Indian groups" resembled the Polynesian/Southeast Asian pattern rather than "the classical Indian type."[79]

Unlike Taiwan, where indigenous culture retreated in the face of the Chinese advance, Sri Lanka's powerful Buddhist kingdoms withstood periodic Tamil invasions. One aspect of the distinctive Sinhalese identity that developed—the relative freedoms women enjoyed—consistently attracted the attention of early observers. In his well-known description of Sri Lanka in 1681, for instance, Robert Knox noted the female contribution to agricultural work and the involvement of women in harvest rituals.[80] A member of a British embassy in 1782 went so far as to claim that Sinhalese women were distinguished from those of "other oriental nations" because they were in many cases "companions and friends" of their husbands.[81] These patterns apparently tempered more patriarchal influences through a kind of "gender drift," whereby the inheritance rights of Hindu Tamil and Muslim women in Sri Lanka have come to resemble those of their Buddhist Sinhalese neighbors.[82]

The preeminence of the Theravada school of Buddhism in Sri Lanka had important implications for the position of women in mainland Southeast Asia. Although Theravada Buddhism is considered relatively conservative in its textual assertion of male spiritual superiority, it was highly successful in attracting female support, which may have facilitated its rapid spread into mainland Southeast Asia around the eleventh century. The Buddhist connections then established remained an important vehicle for communication, although they were substantially undermined from the sixteenth century as the Portuguese and then the Dutch asserted their presence on the island. While increasing Tamil migration and nineteenth-century British colonialism strengthened the grounds for including Sri Lanka in later constructions of "South Asia," a female perspective might emphasize other connections that shift the focus to Southeast Asia. It is difficult to counter the geopolitical imperatives that have made Sri Lanka, like Taiwan, a Southeast Asian outlier; nonetheless, the conversations between Sri Lankan nuns and their counterparts in Thailand and Burma, and combined calls for a revival of female ordination, are a reminder of older links that are charged with historical significance.[83]

Southeast Asia and "Oceania"

The importance of maritime links between mainland and island Southeast Asia has been central in all efforts to assemble a coherent regional history.

The range of indigenous words associated with riverine and sea voyaging is itself a testimony to the place of waterborne movement in the lives of Southeast Asian communities, which still possess the world's "richest residue" of ancient maritime technology.[84] Early navigation would have been facilitated by a number of factors. Sheltered by a sweeping arc of islands, the region's internal seas are relatively protected from storms, the monsoon winds are generally predictable, and there is a profusion of natural landmarks such as reefs, islands, and coastal mountains. Centuries of seaborne interaction thus make the international boundary dividing contemporary Malaysia and Indonesia down the Melaka Straits as artificial as that separating Malaysia from the southern Philippines through the Sulu Sea. Further afield, the antiquity of long-distance voyaging presents a formidable challenge to "world areas" delineated by national borders. The maritime division of East and Southeast Asia, for instance, ignores the movement of people, goods, and ideas along ocean pathways, and the cultural and ethnic intermingling characteristic of the South China Sea. Japanese scholars, less wedded to Anglo-American conceptions of world areas, have been more willing to see the Ryukyu archipelago as part of a larger world encompassing maritime Southeast Asia and the southwestern Pacific. Winds and ocean currents linked southern Japan and the Ryukyu Islands to Taiwan and the Philippines, and there are claims of linguistic similarities between Old Javanese and Old Japanese that go well beyond coincidence. Specialists in other areas have also detected Japanese–Southeast Asia connections in house styles, music, rice cultivation practices, and mythology. Included in a royal Ryukyu anthology of 1531, the chant of a priestess who summons the spirits of Japan, China, Java, and "the southern seas" is compelling evidence of this wider vision.[85]

Comparative work on the Austronesian diaspora has mounted one of the boldest challenges to the hegemony of world areas. Between 4000 and 3000 BCE, speakers of proto-Austronesian languages moved out from a homeland somewhere in southern China into Taiwan, from thence trickling down through the Philippines, Borneo, Sulawesi, Java, Sumatra, the Malay Peninsula, central Vietnam, and eastern Indonesia and eventually into the Pacific. Early modern Europeans, unaware of what is arguably the greatest migration the world has ever known, were still struck by linguistic similarities. In Madagascar, Spanish priests in the sixteenth century sometimes even referred to Malagasay as "Bugis," and when the Dutch arrived in Taiwan in the seventeenth century they were pleasantly surprised to hear "Malay" words in local languages. As early as 1708 it was suggested that the languages of Madagascar, Oceania (a term now favored over "Pacific"), and the Indonesian archipelago were all linked. Despite its great variety, strong arguments have been advanced in favor of treating the whole Austronesian world as a single "phylogenetic unit" that offers "exceptionally favorable conditions for a holistic and interdisciplinary culture history."[86]

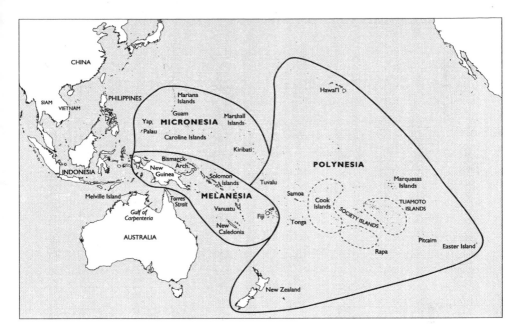

Southeast Asia and Oceania

Although nineteenth-century perceptions of three separate groupings rationalized a still-used division between Melanesia, Micronesia, and Polynesia, any "holistic" study would undoubtedly point to the arbitrary nature of the boundary between "Southeast Asia" and "Oceania." For instance, the languages spoken in "Micronesia" (literally, "small islands," numbering around two thousand, many of which are just coral atolls), like those of Polynesia, are all part of the extended Austronesian family, though this does not necessarily translate into shared cultural practices. While Western Micronesia is linguistically closer to the Philippines, Palau and its neighbor Yap are seen as "less female-centered" than islands to the east.[87] European influence also helped to blur connections among Pacific Ocean communities. Like the Philippines, the Marianas were colonized by Spain, and little remains of precontact life. On Guam, for example, the men's houses were destroyed, and kinship organization came to resemble that of the lowland Philippines rather than other Oceanic societies.[88]

The fuzziness of "world region" boundaries is particularly apparent when we move into the border seas of eastern Indonesia and "Melanesia." The faunal distinctiveness dividing Sulawesi and other islands east of Lombok from western Indonesia marks a transitional zone between the underwater extension of the Asian mainland and a supercontinent comprising New Guinea and Australia. Though New Guinea has much in common botanically and zoologically with Australia, it also received influences from the Malay-Indonesian archipelago because ancient humans were able to move across early land bridges. These links were subsequently reinforced by trading relations, and it is not surprising to find that Austronesian and Papuan languages mingle on several of Indonesia's easterly islands. Indeed, the very fact that "Melanesia" covers an extremely diverse region stretching from western New Guinea to Fiji renders the term meaningless except in a loose geographical sense.

In this context, recent studies have advocated greater attention to conjunctions between "island Melanesia," coastal New Guinea, and eastern Indonesia.[89] Integral to these reconsiderations is the history of the so-called Lapita peoples, named for the distinctive pottery found in these areas. Discoveries associated with the Lapita complex have helped to span the long-held ethnographic divide between Melanesia and Polynesia, as well as that between the larger areas of Oceania and Southeast Asia. It seems clear that during "early modern" times political systems in much of eastern Indonesia resembled those of Oceanic societies rather than the more Indianized states of the western archipelago. Anthropologists still see the clan-based "wife-giving/wife-receiving" marriage systems of the eastern Indonesian archipelago as quite distinct from those of the west, while the taboos associated with female sexuality are similar to those found among many "Melanesians."[90]

An alternative cartography that overrides "world area" divisions obviously complicates any effort to equate "Southeast Asia" with a regional construction of gender. However, ancient maritime connections with "Oceania" were not easily maintained. Prehistorians continue to marvel at the achievements of the early migrants who took advantage of brief but seasonal wind shifts to sail against the prevailing trades eastward into the central Pacific. Return voyages were far more problematic because easterly winds were deflected northward as they approached the Philippines.[91] When Ferdinand Magellan landed in Guam in 1521, local Chamorro told him that the famed "Spice Islands" were a few days southward, but navigation would have been difficult because of the deep waters of the Mariana and Philippine Trenches. Blown off course, boats originating in western Micronesia were occasionally stranded on islands now belonging to the Philippines or Indonesia, but in 1664 a Spanish observer noted that, in his thirty-seven years of residence on Samar, canoes had drifted in from the east on only eight occasions. Although it was possible to reach Yap or Palau from the Philippines (a distance of 1,126 and 724 kilometers, respectively) against the prevailing winds, this voyage was not readily undertaken.[92] Valued items such as beads may have been exchanged between western Micronesia and the eastern Philippine and Indonesian archipelagoes, but commercial incentives were never sufficient to establish regular trading routes that would link "Polynesians" and "Micronesians" with their Southeast Asian cousins. The Malay captain whom a shipwrecked English crew met on

Palau in 1783 had thus not come for commercial purposes but was himself the survivor of a ship lost during a trading voyage between Ambon and Banten.[93]

The Southeast Asia–Oceania divide was accentuated as expanding trade networks and the spread of the world religions fed the growth of new state systems, for the few powerful centers that emerged in eastern Indonesia were not interested in extending their authority beyond the Melanesian fringes. Communities living along the coasts of New Guinea's Bird's Head and the nearby islands acknowledged the overlordship of the kingdom of Tidore, and when the Dutch reached the region in the seventeenth century, a number of chiefs were already nominal Muslims. Farther eastward, however, these influences faded quickly, and none of the small societies in the western Pacific had the capacity or ambition to expand outside their areas of immediate authority. Oceania was essentially unaffected by the great religious, political, and economic influences that swept across Asia during the early modern period, and in this respect the western Pacific Ocean does represent a meaningful boundary for "Southeast Asia."

A similar comment might be made of the southern Indian Ocean, where the Java Trench, more than 7,000 meters deep, curves around the islands of Java, Sumatra, and Nusatenggara. Three thousand kilometers in length and 100 kilometers wide, the Java Trench forms a giant underwater channel from whence the ocean reaches uninterrupted to Antarctica. Between Timor and New Guinea is another such "border," the Timor Trough, where the seabed lies around 3,200 meters below the surface (roughly three times deeper than the regional average). The extent to which this geological formation impeded voyages in early times is not clear, but we know that the Torres Strait was not regularly navigated by Indonesian ships until the eighteenth century, and only then because of the lure of the sea-slug trade. At that time the crossing from Timor to Melville Island —over 480 kilometers—could be completed in around four days, but Australia was never seen as a desirable area for permanent settlement. Certainly, some Makassar influence has been identified among groups in northern Australia; one of the more intriguing suggestions, based on linguistic evidence, concerns the possibility of homosexual contacts between aboriginal men and Makassar crews. Be that as it may, Indonesians apparently saw no need to venture farther eastward, and there is no evidence of early Makassar or Bugis voyaging through the Torres Straits beyond the Gulf of Carpentaria.[94]

The "area studies" border between Southeast Asia and Oceania can also be justified by the common view that the islands of the Pacific Ocean are a coherent and meaningful unit for historical study, despite internal variation. By the end of the first millennium CE, even as new islands were being settled, "Polynesia" is said to have been connected by a "wide community of shared items and ideas."[95] Historiographically, although orally preserved "scripts" such as genealogies, chants, and stories provide revealing insights into early constructs of gender, Oceania is distinguished from much of Southeast Asia by the absence of an indigenous literary tradition and the dearth of European documentation before the late eighteenth century. Though some anthropologists have made admirable attempts to cross academic boundaries, it is difficult to provide any depth to historical comparisons because ethnographic data relating to Oceania has been collected only over the last two hundred years.[96] Even then, European observers—often missionaries—were unsympathetic and sometimes openly hostile toward many of the customs they encountered. For instance, the position of the male transvestite in Tahiti, Samoa, and Hawai'i carries echoes of ritual androgyny found in several Southeast Asian societies, but the earliest European sources were more concerned with condemnations of male depravity than in explaining the apparently privileged positions these individuals held.[97] Rarely does one find any questioning of the view that women in the "South Seas" were by nature lascivious and immoral. A perceptive comment by one writer in 1773 is thus unusual: "All our voyagers both French and English have represented [Tahitian women] as ready to grant the last favor to any man who will pay for it. But this is by no means the case." Sexual relations with married women required negotiations with their husbands, and young women were wary about bestowing favors lightly. In his view, these "prostitutes" were no different from the "nymphs and syrens" who greeted ships docking at Plymouth Sound or Portsmouth.[98]

A broad-brushed consideration of gender in Southeast Asia and Oceania highlights both similarities and differences. On the one hand, features thought to typify Polynesian society, such as the tracing of descent lines through mother and father, inheritance by both sons and daughters, and the authority wielded by high-born women recall the shared Austronesian heritage. The customary inheritance of land rights through the maternal line that occurs in most Micronesian islands will be equally familiar to Southeast Asianists. While the matrilocal residence found in much of Southeast Asia is not universal in contemporary Micronesia, some authorities believe that it was characteristic of the Austronesian-speaking peoples who settled Oceania.[99]

On the other hand, gender constructions in Oceanic societies do assert their own distinctiveness. One striking shift in aesthetics is seen in the relationship between the body and status, which in much of Polynesia was related to physical size. Through increased food consumption combined with massage, high-ranking Hawaiian women became very large; the waist of one renowned beauty in the 1830s measured well over a meter.[100] Other areas of contrast are also pertinent to the position of women. In Tahiti and the Hawaiian Islands, for instance, food cultivation was dominated by males, whereas horticulture in Southeast Asia has always been located firmly within the female domain. Although seclusion huts for menstruating women are rarely found in Polynesian societies, female activities were regulated by elaborated prohibitions subsumed under the term *tapu* (sacred, forbidden). *Tapu* was particularly evident in food restrictions, by which women were precluded (sometimes under pain of death) from eating items such as bananas and pork. Another "Polynesian" element concerns the relationship between sisters and brothers, particularly evident in Samoa and Tonga (but also in Ryukyu) and regarded in Micronesia as the "keystone" of social organization. Men were superior, but they were still expected to respect their sisters, especially the eldest, who was the guardian of the genealogies. If a brother disregarded a sister's wishes in family matters, it was believed that he and his children could incur illness, misfortune, or even death.[101] In sum, in gender as in other matters Polynesians are not "Southeast Asians who happen to live in Polynesia," although the position of women and their relations with men reveal many features reminiscent of Southeast Asian cultures.[102]

The argument that there is a type of "gendered border" around Southeast Asia becomes more defensible in relation to New Guinea and Australia, where an ethnological preoccupation with sexual difference was well established long before gender became a fashionable topic. A succession of case studies has demonstrated that despite the interdependence of men and women in everyday activities, there is a pervasive separation of "maleness" in ritual life. Notwithstanding the mythological space accorded some female figures, men assume all sacral roles, even when these mimic life experiences like the birthing process.[103] The privileged male position is symbolized by the New Guinea men's house, the repository of secret knowledge and sacred objects as well as the focus of initiation rites. If a woman intruded into this domain, even accidentally, she could be put to death. Though men's houses are found in several Southeast Asian tribal societies, they never provided a focus for equivalent male cults that devalued female experience. New Guinea women might act as agents in their own world, but their capacity to harm male potency (especially through the contamination of menstrual blood) meant the husband-wife relationship is often infused with tension, and domestic violence is still common. There are some New Guinea societies where gender relations are more balanced, primarily when descent is reckoned matrilineally, but the indigenous male characterization of central highland women as *korpa* (worthless) is disturbingly typical.[104]

It is not possible for historians to provide these modern studies with more than an impressionistic background, since early descriptions of New Guinea make only passing references to women, almost invariably in derogatory terms. While most Europeans were attracted by the sexual allure of women from the regions we now term Southeast Asia and Polynesia, a seventeenth-century account describes New Guinea females who had blackened their faces with crushed coal as "so ugly that they were more like filthy pigs than humans."[105] Reports compiled from this standpoint can hardly be regarded as perceptive; European perceptions of aboriginal Australian women as chattels, for example, failed to take note of their economic self-sufficiency, the place of females in indigenous mythology, and the nature of family links. Reading back from contemporary material also presents problems, since we cannot assess the degree to which male-female relations were touched by change. As commerce between New Guinea's Bird's Head and the Malay-Indonesian archipelago expanded, for instance, rival chiefs were increasingly willing to force their women into marriage with outsiders in order to obtain valued commodities. In coastal areas items like the rare yellow coral traditionally required for bride-price payments became so scarce that by the late nineteenth century some men were reportedly unable to marry.[106] At the same time, expanding trade opened up access to new resources that clearly advantaged men. It has thus been suggested that male dominance of political and social life in New Guinea was less pronounced prior to the 1930s, when the wider availability of metal tools eased tasks such as the clearance of garden plots and provided men with more leisure time.[107]

Overall, however, it does appear as if the "Melanesian" world was highly gender-inflected. The "black and naked" Papuan warriors mentioned in a Spanish report of 1606 who wore *koteka* (penis shields), necklaces of wild boar teeth, and the bones of swordfish through their noses were simply affirming their sexual virility, their physical strength, and their prowess in war. In the matrilineal communities of island Melanesia, women today are said to enjoy a relatively higher status than their Melanesian sisters elsewhere, but the excavation of Vanuatu graves indicates that five hundred years ago a chief's widow was customarily strangled and buried with her husband.[108] There is no record in Melanesia of a cognatic society like that of the Borneo Iban (typified by close family units, bilateral inheritance, conjugal ties, and sibling equivalence). Indeed, the differences with neighboring Austronesian societies have been sufficiently marked for some scholars of gender to see Melanesia more appropriately compared to Amazonia rather than to any other part of Oceania.[109]

FOR SCHOLARS of Southeast Asia the division of the globe into macrocultural zones remains intensely relevant since we are, as Sanjay Subrahmanyam reminds us, "condemned in greater or lesser measure to Area Studies."[110] Certainly, alternative constructions are possible; for instance, similarities between China's "cultural minorities" and the highland peoples of eastern India, Vietnam, Laos, Thailand, and Burma could justify a map that sets aside regional borders in favor of a "montagnard domain."[111] A variant cartography could also be deployed to overcome seemingly arbitrary divisions between eastern Indonesia, the coastal areas of western New Guinea, and Oceania. Nonetheless, this chapter has suggested that the mountains and ranges of the mainland and the sweep of the Indian and Pacific

Oceans did help create a Southeast Asian zone that is more than academically convenient. Facilitating or impeding the transmission of religious, political, and commercial influences from beyond and within the region, the geographical environment became a dynamic element in determining the shape of male-female relationships. Relative gender equality may not define a "Southeast Asian" culture area "unambiguously and meaningfully," but the "high status" of women so often touted as a defining characteristic makes the region a useful laboratory in which to explore a wide variety of female pasts. If we accept that comparative studies are "the ultimate justification for regional studies," the correspondences and differences in women's experiences can also contribute to more-nuanced discussions about Southeast Asia's alleged distinctiveness.[112] Any exploration of a regional women's history will always be problematic, however, because the historical landscape is so often only dimly visible. As the following chapter argues, attempts to identify landmarks in this unfamiliar terrain are dependent not merely on the available source material but also on the ways in which that material is approached and interpreted.

CHAPTER 2

Early Modernity, Sources, and Women's History

If we agree that "Southeast Asia" is a region in which the history of women can legitimately be explored, the fifteenth century becomes the primary gateway because an increase in source material coincides with the periodization commonly adopted in Southeast Asian historiography. Though some historians are uneasy with the term "early modernity," most would agree that from about 1400 the region witnessed a growing involvement in global trade, greater religious coherence, and increased political centralization. However, they would generally accept that this pattern is more evident in the mainland. During the course of this study, for example, frequent reference will be made to Ayutthaya, the capital of Siam, and to Ava, which became the royal center of Burma. Both were beneficiaries of expanding commerce, and both were actively involved in promoting the Theravada form of Buddhism. Nonetheless, there is a significant counter-narrative. Regarded as a golden age, the fifteenth century in Vietnam was followed by three hundred years of civil war and internal division. In neighboring Cambodia the great temple complex of Angkor still draws tourists in the thousands, but the country's subsequent history is associated not with "fruitful growth, trade and cultural exchange" but with "loss, defeat, retreat, instability."[1]

Developments in the island world also make generalizations problematic. The Malay entrepôt of Melaka was captured by the Portuguese in 1511, but other states—Aceh and Palembang in Sumatra, Banten in western Java, Mataram in central Java, Makassar in Sulawesi, Brunei in Borneo, Ternate and Tidore in the east—emerged as centers of commerce and Islamic leadership. European intrusion, however, exacted a heavy toll. The Spanish conquest of Manila in 1570 set in place a process of colonization that Christianized all the Philippine Islands apart from the Muslim south. By the end of the eighteenth century the Dutch VOC, Europe's most successful trading venture, controlled virtually all of Java as well as most key ports in the Malay-Indonesian archipelago. These developments laid the basis for intensified economic and political pressures through the entire region. The early nineteenth century is commonly seen as marking the end of "early modernity" and the beginning of a new period characterized by European dominance.

Approaching a History of Women in Southeast Asia

The nature of the sources available for the early modern period bears directly on any effort to supply Southeast Asian women with a larger historical space. At this stage any attempt at regional comparison must be regarded as preliminary because few studies have used primary and archival sources as a basis for writing female-oriented histories. Additional challenges are posed by Southeast Asia's cultural and linguistic diversity. Many societies have no literary heritage, and research methodologies used in world areas with stronger documentary traditions have only limited applicability. At the same time, the very need to look beyond written evidence can foster the interdisciplinary conversations that have long been a hallmark of Southeast Asian studies.

These conversations are already opening up new avenues for researching a more female-oriented past. Archaeologists have traditionally been wary of making statements about gender in prehistoric times because mortuary data in tropical climates is so often compromised or incomplete.[2] Of late, however, specialists on Southeast Asia have given more attention to finds like the grave of a woman in a southeastern Thailand site occupied from about 2000 to 1500 BCE. Dying in her mid- to late thirties, this so-called princess, apparently a senior woman in her community, was buried with about 120,000 shell-disk beads and other ornaments. A clay potter's anvil and two burnishing pebbles were by her side, and the fine vessels that covered her ankles may have been her own work.[3] This burial assumes greater importance because a relatively equal style of funerals for men and women correlates positively with female status. Other excavations in northeastern Thailand have yielded "no indications of overt sex preference," and women in this sample outlived men, with an estimated 7 percent surviving beyond the age of fifty. Future determination of the sex of skeletal remains should provide some indication about female health in these early societies, especially relating to osteoporosis, iron deficiency, and anemia.[4]

The dialogue with archaeologists is useful for premodern historians because it supports research frameworks that transverse the boundaries of contemporary nation-states.[5] For instance, artifacts found in Yunnan and dating from the last centuries BCE can illuminate our understanding of culturally gendered practices in the borderlands between China and Southeast Asia. Decorated lids of bronze cowry containers discovered in burial grounds celebrate the success of warriors in head-hunting raids, while women are depicted carrying sacks of rice, baskets, and agricultural tools. High-ranking females in sedan chairs are sometimes shown presiding over ceremonies that link human sacrifices with harvest rituals.[6] Implicit messages tying female fecundity to agricultural fertility open up opportunities to explore how seemingly universal ideas are translated into different cultural contexts. Statues of heavy-breasted and seemingly gravid women discovered in prehistoric sites from Egypt to Turkey and India find parallels in Indonesian images that depict female figures with swollen bellies and women suckling their young. What should we make, then, of a collection of apparently pregnant bronze goddesses unearthed at a site in upper Burma, some of whom display four or even six breasts and two or three bellies?[7]

In terms of women's history, exchanges with archaeologists can also be helpful in exploring the evolution of domestic production and the implications for male-female relations. For instance, in Thai rock art, women are depicted in agriculture but are never shown hunting, and although prehistoric art is difficult to interpret, it seems that certain tasks, like the making of textiles, were already idealized as gender specific.[8] Various excavations in Southeast Asia have uncovered female skeletons buried with bark-cloth beaters and weaving tools, reflecting beliefs that a woman would need her skills in the next life. She would also need to grow food, and in northeastern Thailand iron sickles were found in female graves dated to around 500 BCE–500 CE. Women's work also suggests widening trading connections; in the fourteenth and fifteenth centuries an increased number of spindle whorls in Visayan burial sites may be due to greater access to suitable weaving materials. The vocabulary of early Javanese inscriptions provides parallel evidence, showing that growing contact with India led to innovations in textile design, color, and ornamentation.[9] Discoveries of locally made earthenware are of particular interest, since later evidence indicates that women played a dominant role in production. It is thought, for example, that much of the Lapita ware found in New Guinea and eastern Indonesia was produced by women, always remembering that pots themselves are not amenable to gender analysis. Thus, while Javanese pottery that has been dated to around the tenth and eleventh centuries was produced with some type of wheel, it is impossible to determine whether this was men's work or whether Javanese women were using the same method in addition to the paddle-and-anvil technique.[10]

From archaeology we move to the written sources that anchor Southeast Asia's early history. Around the fifth century CE the expansion of Indian influence becomes visible in the growing corpus of stone inscriptions, with the largest number—two thousand or more—from Cambodia. Written in both Sanskrit and local languages, these inscriptions glorify the royal genealogy or record the establishment of a temple, the dedication of rice lands, the fixing of village boundaries, the collection of taxes. They have been fundamental in the reconstruction of dynastic chronologies, but scholars sensitive to shifts in language and context have shown that they can also contribute to a better understanding of changes in the position of women. For example, in the early stages of "Indianization," it seems that nonmenstruating females could officiate in religious rituals and serve as scribes and record keepers. This does not appear to apply by the time the temple complex of Angkor was founded in the ninth century, when "an important class of non-Indic Khmer goddesses," the *kpon*, had been displaced by male Sanskritic deities.[11] Women rarely exercised authority in the public sphere, and in only one Cambodian stele can we confidently identify a woman's voice. Somewhere around the turn of the twelfth century the learned Indradevi, a devout Buddhist and wife of the famed Cambodian king Jayavarman VII (r. 1181–ca. 1218), composed a panegyric in "impeccable" Sanskrit in memory of her sister, the previous queen. Despite this obvious gender gap, it is important to note that the emphasis on kinship and the prominence of maternal descent foreground women in a way that is seldom found in inscriptions from India.[12]

Though the content of surviving inscriptions in Southeast Asia permits only a surface understanding of female roles, it is possible to make some general comments. For instance, Javanese village women in the tenth century negotiated contracts, incurred debts, and took an active part in ceremonies connected with the granting of land for freehold domains. Women could either inherit property or acquire titles in their own right, and senior village females were involved in communal decisions. Occasionally a particular case affirms situations well known from later times. While the economic independence of ordinary Southeast Asian women has become a truism in the literature, as early as 907 CE a Javanese edict rules that a husband ignorant of his deceased wife's debts was not responsible for repayment. At times, too, we catch glimpses of an underlying male fear of female powers. Composed in the seventh century, Old Malay inscriptions from Sumatra make passing reference to women who might have access to spells that could drive their husbands insane.[13] On the mainland, the spread of Theravada Buddhism from the eleventh century encouraged elite donations as a merit-making activity. Recorded in stone, these mention women in a range of activities—as wet nurses, slaves, religious teachers, witnesses, traders, and supporters of the monkhood.[14] Yet the same inscriptions can also include women's formulaic acceptance that they occupied a lower position in a religiously based gender hierarchy. Because "the status of wife is inferior," a Burmese queen longs for the time when she will become "a man and a spirit [*nat*]," while a pious queen mother in the Thai kingdom of Sukhothai hopes that by founding a monastery she has acquired sufficient merit "to be reborn as a male."[15]

Few inscriptions have been found in Vietnam before the tenth century, and prior to the fifteenth century our information is based largely on Chinese sources or histories compiled retrospectively by Vietnam literati trained in the Confucian tradition. The preoccupation with correct behavior and the observation of "morality" means that such writing often dwells on the relationship between men and women. From 43 to 939 CE, when modern-day Vietnam was considered part of successive Chinese empires, educated visitors from China were unanimously disapproving of what they saw as southern indifference to moral standards. Chinese forces were finally evicted in the early fifteenth century, but over the next hundred years Confucian influence in the Vietnamese court strengthened considerably. Echoing the views of their Chinese counterparts, Vietnamese scholars were highly critical of the ways in which palace women of former times had intervened in government, and of the perceived impropriety of past kings, who maintained numerous women as wives and were guilty of "incestuous" marriages with their cousins.[16]

In addition to inscriptions, historians of early Southeast Asia draw heavily from the Chinese material that becomes available from around the fifth century as maritime trade and religious travel in the Nanyang (the "southern seas") expanded. Despite their undeniable value, comments about women in these descriptions reflect the views of Chinese men predisposed to view "barbarian" cultures as innately amoral. In an account written after nearly a year's residence in Cambodia, the thirteenth-century envoy Zhou Daguan thus called attention to what he saw as a lack of sexual restraint among local wives. "When a husband is called away on matters of business," he remarks, "they endure his absence for a while; but if he is gone as much as ten days, the wife is apt to say, 'I am not a ghost; how can I be expected to sleep alone?'"[17] Another aspect of the Nanyang's "otherness" was female prominence in the marketplace. Zhou Daguan observed that it was "the women who take charge of trade," and more than a century later another envoy recorded that in the country of Xianluo (Siam) men from the king down entrusted "all trading transactions, light and small," to their wives.[18]

In a sense, then, Chinese emissaries and pilgrims become the region's first foreign ethnographers, and despite preconceptions that gender reversal typified all "barbarian" societies, their writings provide a provocative background for later material. One of the most cited references comes from the middle of the fifth century, when two envoys to a "country" called Funan, apparently located in southern Cambodia, recorded a local myth of origin. It tells of a Brahman called Hundien (thought to be a Chinese rendering of the Sanskrit "Kaudinya"), whose ship is directed toward Funan by a powerful spirit and who brings with him a magical bow. The daughter of Funan's dragon-ruler, Willow (or perhaps "Coconut") Leaf, celebrated for her "virile force and her exploits," paddles out to confront him. When Kaudinya fires an arrow that strikes her ship, the princess surrenders and agrees to marry him. Kaudinya gives her a cloth to cover her naked body and makes her tie her hair in a knot. He subsequently becomes ruler of Cambodia (here termed Kambuja).[19]

Sixty years ago academics were inclined to interpret the Kaudinya myth as evidence of Cambodia's matrilineal past, and some modern historians have also proposed a superior female status that declined as Hinduizing influences took hold among the Khmer elite.[20] However, the legend is now commonly read as a metaphor for the process of "localization" by which

Southeast Asian societies selectively absorbed and adapted Indian influences. The trope of the stranger-king who establishes his authority through union with a native princess is well established in Pacific studies, but it is equally pertinent to Southeast Asia, where it is a frequent motif in foundation myths. The legend of a Malay trader who arrived in Perak (on the west coast of the Malay Peninsula), took an aboriginal wife, built a house, and planted fruit trees is just one of innumerable accounts that tell of a foreign male who gained access to land and resources through his relations with a local woman.[21] The marriage of Willow Leaf, the personification of Kambuja, also speaks to recurring indigenous allegories tying communal well-being to sexual unions of extraordinary potency. Even in translation the intensity of such relationships infuses the panegyric extolling Cambodia's Jayavarman VII, who "took the earth to wife and gave her his glory for a necklace."[22] Praise poems recorded across Southeast Asia in more recent times similarly celebrate the male-female union that will ensure the land's fecundity. In a traditional chant of the Toraja (highland Sulawesi), a great ancestor thus intones his intent "to enter into a marriage in the edge of the field / I shall unite myself with the richness of the earth."[23]

Although Willow Leaf is not yet a mother, her story carries the implicit promise of a child-rich future, an assurance of fertility inextricably associated with the symbolism that parlayed imported images of femaleness into local idioms. The Indian goddess Hariti, originally a child-eating demon persuaded by the Buddha to abandon her evil ways, attained a particular status in Southeast Asia as a protector of children who would assist barren women to conceive.[24] Another venerated figure brought from India was Prajnaparamita, the mystical mother of the buddhas, and statuary found in Cambodia suggests that a cult in her honor emerged as early as the tenth century. The indigenous Cham mother-deity known as Po Nagar became amalgamated with the Hindu deity Uma, consort of Shiva, and later, under Vietnamese rule, with the Daoist Queen of Heaven.[25] This localization of "femaleness" is also apparent in statues of the Hindu goddess Durga slaying the demon buffalo, sufficiently numerous to suggest that she had a particular following in Java and pre-Angkorian Cambodia. Yet unlike their Indian counterparts, sculptors in Southeast Asia rarely chose to depict Durga's ferocious aspects. In Javanese sculptures, for example, her wrath is typically directed toward the demon in human form, while the buffalo lies placidly under her feet, perhaps an acknowledgment of its essential role in the cultivation of rice.[26]

In Southeast Asia's Theravada Buddhist societies this reshaping of imported motifs is especially evident in the figure of the Earth Goddess who witnessed Buddha's enlightenment. Around the ninth century the Earth Goddess became popular in India, where she was credited with helping to defeat Mara, ruler of the Buddhist realms of hell. Her subsequent progress into Southeast Asia saw the addition of a significant detail largely unknown in India. From Arakan to Cambodia, stories attached to the Earth Goddess relate how she achieved her victory over Mara by wringing a flood of water from her hair (itself emblematic of fertility). Although this does not appear in the canonical writings of Theravada Buddhism, a young woman washing her hair became a widespread motif in Southeast Asia's Buddhist iconography.[27]

The legend of Willow Leaf can also be read in ways that sit less happily with the male-female complementarity so often cited as "typically" Southeast Asian. Initially defiant, she does not enter into her marriage willingly, and Kaudinya's insistence that she wear clothing and tie up her hair can be construed as legitimizing a husband's authority and the male right to enforce new standards of female modesty. Even when the fertility theme is reiterated, Southeast Asian evidence attests a preoccupation with men's virility, men's strength, men's authority; in Indonesia, for example, male ancestral representations in stone outnumber those of females by three to one, and their sex can be emphatically expressed. One graphic display of masculine potency is found in two Hindu temples located on the slopes of Mount Lawu (east Java), where the prominent penises on male images have round bells inserted under their foreskins, as was common in early times. On the floor inside one gateway is the carving of a penis entering a vulva, and another bas-relief shows a man masturbating.[28] It is not difficult to locate images that assert female subordination to father and husband or present relations with women as distractions on a man's path to spiritual growth. Reliefs recounting the much-loved story of Sita, the faithful wife in the Indian epic *Ramayana,* can be juxtaposed with others that show the ascetic prince Arjuna achieving his status as a world renouncer by resisting the advances of seductive nymphs.[29] Like the earliest written sources, the messages conveyed in architecture and sculpture are ambiguous and at times conflicting. Against the representations of wise goddesses, benevolent queens, and devout female ascetics are other stereotypes of women whose unrestrained sexual desire can subvert masculinity and impede male attainment of temporal and spiritual goals.

Approaching the Early Modern Period

From the fourteenth century onward, a steady increase in source material renders the examination of a female past more feasible. Inscriptions give way to chronicles, royal edicts expand into elaborated law codes, religious texts are translated into the vernacular; sometimes the writers, members of the expanding literate class, are even known by name. The historian can also be heartened by the documentation left by visitors to the region. From the sixteenth century, accounts by travelers from China, India, Arabia, and Persia are augmented by Portuguese documents and by the more extensive material bequeathed by the Spanish, the Dutch, and the English, especially in maritime Southeast Asia. Conclusions may still rest on inference and supposition, but it is possible to develop a more informed analysis of women's experiences.

Southeast Asian historians are painfully aware, however, that surviving documents represent only a fraction of what was once available. In a tropical climate, bark, palm leaf, bamboo, and paper all have an ephemeral life, and over the centuries untold material, both local and foreign, has been lost through natural catastrophe, warfare, or simple carelessness. Despite periodic recopying, indigenous writings have been a major casualty; the Burmese sack of Ayutthaya in 1767, for example, resulted in the destruction of most of the kingdom's historical records. Only about a hundred or so Khmer inscriptions are known from the fifteenth and sixteenth centuries, and the dearth of chronicle support means the history of Cambodia's "middle period" has been extraordinarily difficult to reconstruct. Many valuable texts from Southeast Asia can be consulted today only because the original or a duplicate was transported to European libraries, but there were still some spectacular losses. Thomas Stamford Raffles, the founder of Singapore, was an avid collector of Malay manuscripts, and we have no way of knowing what was contained in the texts that were destroyed in a shipboard fire during his return trip to England.

Despite these qualifications, an increase in sources means that themes identified in older material, such as the relationship between ruler and the "female" earth, can be tracked in greater detail. A fourteenth-century Vietnamese work, *Viet Dinh U Linh Tap* (Potent spirits of the Viet domain), said to be an "authentic account of doings of spirits," records the account of the ruler Ly Thanh Tong (r. 1054–1072), who, when crossing an estuary during a storm, encounters a beautiful young woman. She tells him that she is the spirit of the Earth of the Southern Realm who has long been waiting, hidden within a tree trunk. The king bestows on her a Chinese-derived title meaning "Imperial Lady of the Earth," and a cult is established in her honor.[30] Religious commentaries that frequently assert the spiritual inequality of men and women also reaffirm the ambiguities inherent in being "female." The well-known *Traibhumikatha*, a Thai Buddhist cosmology attributed to a fourteenth-century ruler of Sukhothai, sees women as corrupted beings born into an inferior state because they were consumed by material and sensual desires in their past lives.[31] Nonetheless, apparently misogynist attitudes were always modified in transmission, most notably because the deference accorded age and status applied to both men and women. Another fourteenth-century text, the Javanese *Nagarakrtagama* ("Description of the Districts"), thus describes a ritual combining indigenous and Hindu-Buddhist elements held to liberate the soul of a dowager queen, enabling her to achieve union with Prajnaparamita. It serves as a reminder

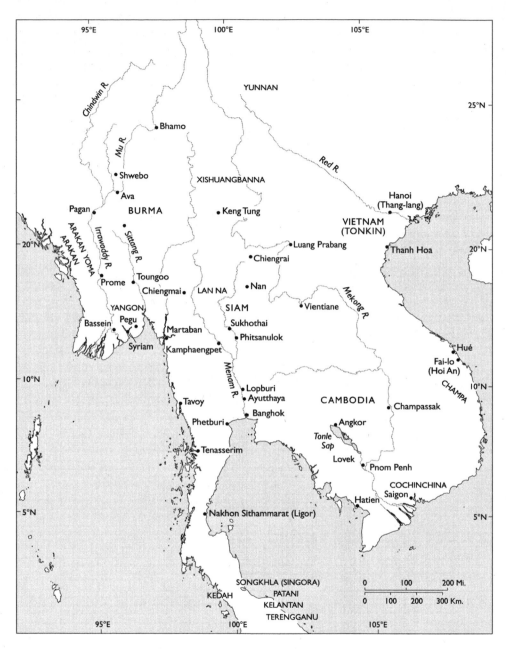

Mainland Southeast Asia

of the special place accorded senior and high-born women, whose relationship with their children and grandchildren may well have served as models for society at large.[32]

Linguistic Access

Exploiting written sources in a multilingual region like Southeast Asia raises the question of linguistic access, as pertinent for women's history as for any other field. Interpreting European material produced more than three hundred years ago can present its own problems—illegible handwriting, idiosyncratic punctuation, archaic word usage—but these pale beside the difficulties that even a specialist can encounter in reading indigenous texts, composed in little-known scripts and employing arcane words or grammatical structures. Regional and comparative conceptualizations are fundamentally hampered when only a handful of historians possess the skills to exploit more than one or two Southeast Asian languages and when an individual like myself (trained in the use of courtly Malay) depends heavily on the work of others and on the textual translations they provide.

One needs to be forthright about this kind of dependency because language can provide valuable insights on social relationships and because the adoption of foreign terms usually occurs within a semantic field where words can take on new meanings as they interrelate. Indonesian *suami* (husband) comes from the Sanskrit *svamin* (master, lord), but it was incorporated together with other Sanskrit-based words such as *isteri* (woman, wife) and *putera/puteri* (son/daughter). It may be that these clusters of words, considered more refined than their indigenous equivalents, encoded new ideas about household relationships and gender-related matters such as sexual modesty. Old Khmer *kupen* and modern Malay *kaping*, meaning a cover for the genitals, are both derived from the Sanskrit *kaupina* and thus entered the region as part of a much larger Hinduized package.[33] Because such connections are usually evident only to specialists, the implications can be daunting. In her study of ancient India, Stephanie Jamison contends that a researcher unable to read Vedic literature in the original is deprived of "a powerful tool" in exploring gender because of the "associational semantics that native speakers had in mind when they heard certain words." Mention of a chariot in Vedic texts could thus have connoted far more than a simple vehicle, since a chariot journey, fraught with danger, indexes ideas of "male" activities. An authority on Sri Lankan Buddhism has been quite blunt; more than historians of South and Southeast Asia would like to admit, she maintains, our historical scholarship has been limited by the languages we fail to engage.[34] Even reliance on the work of colleagues can present pitfalls, since without explanatory notes liberal translations of unusual words or concepts may be misleading. A modern scholar, for instance, has rendered one of "the three causes of barrenness" in an early compilation of Burmese laws as "the destruction of the semen by microbes." While this may convey something of the text's intent, the Burmese word given as "microbes" is *puiw*, which in fact means any tiny creature (such as an insect or even a silkworm).[35]

In Southeast Asia, cross-disciplinary conversations about linguistic nuances are essential in any exploration of evolving ideas about women. For instance, anthropological studies of communities that trace kinship through both maternal and paternal lines have buttressed other research that detects genealogical attention to females in even in proto-Austronesian vocabularies. In a similar vein, the distinction between "mothers" *(moe)* and "lords" *(cao)* discerned in a Thai inscription points to the existence of a hereditary elite whose descent was traced bilaterally, endorsing hierarchies of age rather than gender.[36] Since an insistence on widespread competence in indigenous languages would impose severe limitations on a regionally based history of Southeast Asian women, collaborative work and continuing collegial exchanges provide an obvious and congenial solution.

The Female Voice?

While written documentation inevitably privileges certain groups, it is not easy to locate individual voices in Southeast Asia, because so many texts were anonymous and formulaic. The greatest challenge to "women's history," however, is the near absence of female writing, given the differences with which men and women can perceive the same situation. Working on the border between Dutch New Guinea and Papua in the 1930s, the ethnologist F. E. Williams regretted (unusually for his time) that he was unable to gain greater access to female viewpoints. Nevertheless, he felt that in the coastal region at least "women . . . are generally happy . . . they are not overworked . . . they do not find life too hard." By contrast, conversations with female informants led his wife to a quite different conclusion: "they say they have a hard life; young women have no time to talk."[37]

Mrs. Williams at least had the advantage of personal interaction, but a historian must accept that most evidence about women is transmitted by men, who do not ask the kinds of questions that might have occurred to a woman. This problem, obviously, is hardly unique to Southeast Asia. In 1791, for example, several British women in the new Australian settlement at Port Jackson assisted at the birth of an aboriginal baby, even cutting the umbilical cord, but their account of events is available only through the journal of a marine lieutenant.[38] Twenty years earlier the report supplied to a Dutch governor on *melenggang perut*, the court ceremony held during the seventh month of pregnancy, was similarly compiled not by the royal midwives, those most intimately involved, but by a Malay official. In the late nineteenth and early twentieth centuries some Europeans did compile insightful accounts of previously isolated groups, with the study of Toraja priestesses by the missionary Nicolaus Adriani a significant contribution.[39] However, a striking example of the "male gaze" occurs in the diary of W. W. Skeat, an administrator in British Malaya in the 1890s who jointly led a scientific expedition to the northern Malay states. On one occasion, when his party came across two abandoned panther cubs, a local *penghulu* (district official) sent over a woman whom he said would be able to suckle them. Skeat was apparently persuaded that she was well qualified for the task, his journal noting without further comment that "she had formerly breast-fed a bear."[40] Quite frankly, the mind boggles.

This paucity of "female" documentation in Southeast Asia is underscored by the impressive increase in publications dealing with gender issues in East Asia. As in Europe, the output of memoirs, diaries, and commentaries from upper-class women means gender issues on a range of social and economic contexts can be addressed with considerable confidence. In China there was a veritable explosion of printed material between the late sixteenth and late nineteenth centuries, including more than three thousand works composed by women, although they came mainly from the Yangzi Delta elite. Despite a "silent period" in female writing, historians of Tokugawa Japan (1603–1868) have also demonstrated the subtle perspectives made possible when analyses draw on the views of women themselves. In India, research on folk poetry written by Sufis and on bhakti devotionalism has also opened up insights into the concerns of ordinary women that would otherwise remain closed to view.[41] For Southeast Asianists, however, the opportunities to explore similar themes are rare before the end of the eighteenth century; documentation pertaining to women is limited and is largely the work of men.

This indisputable fact brings us to the issue of female literacy. Based on the observations of Spanish missionaries, Anthony Reid has made a strong case for the ability of women in the Philippines to read and write an indigenous script, an argument that could possibly be extended to other societies.[42] Throughout Southeast Asia, however, oral expressions of experience and emotion were always paramount, even when texts were available. Batak women of northern Sumatra, though usually illiterate in the Batak script, were expected to be skilled in "the language of lament," the traditional chants delivered by a widow at her husband's funeral or by a bride leaving her natal home for that of her groom.[43] The situation Reid describes in Southeast Asia is reminiscent of that among Yao groups in the southern Chinese province of Hunan, where women continued to use a script apparently retained from pre-Han times. With a limited number of syllabic notations, a small vocabulary, and stock phrases, this script could be easily mastered and was employed to embroider lament songs on the fans or handkerchiefs that women exchanged as tokens of affection when (for instance) a bride left home to marry.[44] In a context where formulaic writing is employed for very specific purposes, "reading" is more properly seen as memorized recitation, revealing much of culturally appropriate emotions but little of individual interiority.

On the other hand, literacy among wellborn women is by no means unknown, even though the adaptation of scripts from India, China, and Arabia advantaged Southeast Asian men. In Vietnam, where the ability to read and write was an elite norm, a well-known name is that of Doan Thi Diem (1705–1748). The daughter of a Vietnamese scholar-official, she was educated with her brother, but when both he and her father died, she was left to support her widowed mother and sister-in-law. Because of her education she was appointed tutor to the women of the imperial palace, but she eventually left to open her own school, where her students included girls as well as boys. At the age of thirty-seven she married an eminent mandarin-scholar, dying childless when she was forty-four. In Confucian terms Doan Thi Diem can be seen as a model woman who may have failed to bear a son but whose loyalty to her husband and family was paramount. However, Diem was writing at a time of mounting challenge to Confucian-based values, and her biography of a popular goddess can also be interpreted as a statement of female independence, possibly inspired by her own life.[45]

Though their names are for the most part unknown, there were certainly other Southeast Asian women who achieved local eminence as literary specialists, especially in high-ranking households where largely female audiences were well acquainted with the legends that provided the stuff of elite entertainment. Knowledge of genealogies and memories of court events were more likely to be preserved in the women's quarters, and female courtiers were often primary sources in the compilation of court chronicles.[46] Boys may have been the major beneficiaries as literacy was extended beyond elite circles, but as adults they were also inclined to educate their daughters. In the late eighteenth century, Peri Aceh, the daughter of a Melaka imam, managed a Malay Qur'an school attended by around two hundred children, including her own grandson, Munshi Abdullah (1796–1854), later scribe to Stamford Raffles.[47]

Nevertheless, throughout Southeast Asia there was still a persistent view that writing and reading were inappropriate skills for women. Even in Christian areas, where education was integral to the missionizing project, expectations for female performance were not high. When the VOC established control over Ambon in the seventeenth century, Malay-language schools were opened to girls up to thirteen or so, but the best pupils would only have been able to write a simple letter and compute basic mathematics.[48] Although sources from Bali and Java frequently mention women writing and reading, *kakawin* and *kidung,* the two most important poetic genres, were normally composed by men who projected masculine ideals of female behavior and appearance into the literary universe that they themselves created. This ventriloquism is also found in Vietnam, where elite men sometimes wrote as women, using the female condition as a metaphor for their own grievances or for criticizing contemporary affairs.[49]

In the Southeast Asian context we should thus be grateful for any surviving example of female composition. While this does not necessarily guarantee a woman's perspective, even the strictest genre can be manipulated in the hands of a skillful wordsmith. For example, in sixteenth-century Burma a court lady adapted the regular beat of the poetic form known as *edjing* not to extol the achievements of the king, as was customary, but to describe the fifty-five hairstyles used by the maids of honor.[50] Given the dictates of convention, however, personal emotions are normally expressed in stylized phrases, and it is difficult to identify expressions of individuality even when written material can be confidently ascribed to a woman. In many respects, it seems, community approbation rested on the degree to which such women promoted and projected accepted gender models. The *Memoirs of Lady Nophamat,* apparently written sometime in the Ayutthaya period, presents not so much a personal account of the author's own life but an anthology of "good advice" to noble ladies.[51] Nor is the eighteenth-century report of court activities compiled by a member of the female guard in the central Javanese court of Surakarta an expression of personal feelings. Over a ten-year period the author witnessed many events of note. However, there are disappointingly few revelations about what it meant to be "female" in Surakarta's hierarchical court structure, and it is worth noting that when one of the Sultan's unofficial wives *(selir)* gives birth to a boy, his name is recorded, while that of a daughter is not.[52]

By the late eighteenth century, as more girls acquired a basic education, a faint "female voice" is at least more audible, although clever counterfeiting can still occur. There can be no doubt, however, about the authenticity of work by Vietnam's most well-known female writer, Ho Xuan Huong (1775?–1821?), whose comments on relationships between the sexes are redolent with irreverence, innuendo, and bitterness. Composed in *nom* (Vietnamese written with modified Chinese characters), an oft-quoted poem graphically conveys the humiliation that was the lot of many a concubine: "Screw the fate that makes you share a man. / One cuddles under cotton blankets; the other's cold. / Every now and then, well, maybe or maybe not. / . . . If I had known how it would go / I think I would have lived alone."[53] Nonetheless, while further research may uncover new examples, the autobiographies and letters that have provided insights into women's experiences in "East Asia" are as yet unknown in any Southeast Asian country.

Written Texts and Oral Traditions

Reading indigenous texts as sources for a gendered past raises the question of the Western tendency to separate "literature" from "history," a distinction singularly unhelpful in the non-Western world. Petrus Zoetmulder, one of the great authorities on Javanese literature, has argued forcefully that although texts may ascribe Sanskrit names to people and places, the characters themselves "are essentially Javanese, acting like Javanese, thinking Javanese and living in a Javanese environment."[54] The same comment could be applied to other Southeast Asian societies, where the retellings of ancestral lives, often incorporating legends derived from India, China, or the Middle East, were accepted as a true historical record. Although Western feminists reject the notion that narratives composed in a "phallocentric" tradition can yield reliable information about women's experiences, Southeast Asian historians have been conditioned to see literature as a valuable entry point into earlier mental worlds. They are also more willing to believe that idealized representations of male-female interaction could exercise a powerful influence on a society's attitudes toward sexual behavior and the *imaginaire* of gender. From this perspective, what some have seen as merely the "first stage" of feminist analysis, the categorization of female images, may yet prove fruitful. Heroines of Vietnamese historical legends, for example, certainly resemble their Chinese counterparts, but a recent study suggests that they display more autonomy in making decisions and in negotiating their marital destinies.[55]

Even so, formidable problems confront historians seeking to access this potentially rich mine, because there are so are few scholarly analyses of Southeast Asian literatures. Material in Malay and Indonesian languages are the best-researched, but the written heritage of many areas is still underrepresented in published translations. Linguistic expertise remains essential for any appreciation of the ways in which Indian, Arab, Persian, or Chinese prototypes were adapted and "localized," since there can be intriguing differences between "original" and "variant" texts. For example, while the *Ramayana* spread out from its Indian origins to become the most wellknown epic in Southeast Asia, the motif of the restorative power of mother's milk evident in Thai and Lao versions is absent in Indian counterparts. Elsewhere, too, maternal milk is emblematic of the special bond between mother and child, and a Malay account of the Rama story relates how milk flows from Sita's breast when she learns that the monkey-king, Hanuman, is her son.[56]

If the representation of women is to become incorporated into Southeast Asian historiography, it must involve some discussion of the complex relationship between written and orally transmitted sources. Because so many communities were nonliterate, the cultural codes that justified and explained male-female relations were often contained in the oral archives of chanted myths and sung legends. Historians typically find such material difficult to use, partly because the strength of the spoken tradition lies in its ability to slough off details no longer relevant to the present. Ancestral actions recounted and recorded, say, in 1650 may justify new social demands or practices rather than reflecting customs handed down from some distant past. For the same reason, collections of proverbs and "traditional" sayings are usually approached cautiously because they can so rarely be assigned to any particular period. Folk poetry compiled by Vietnamese literati in the late eighteenth and early nineteenth centuries can be reliably dated, but doubts have been voiced regarding the historicity of other oral material; a work supposedly compiled by Nguyen Trai (1380–1442), for instance, may be the work of a poet born in 1785.[57]

Ultimately, a scholar's ability to tap these records depends on linguistic abilities and sensitivity to the context in which sources are transmitted. Regardless of how "oral legend" has been logged—in a court manuscript, a colonial document, an academic monograph, an anthology of folklore— methodological obstacles are exacerbated by mediation through a third party and via another (written) language. Witness, for instance, one origin story collected among the coastal people of the Visayan island of Panay, which the Spaniard Miguel de Loarca included in his 1582 *Relación de las Islas Filipinas*. While Loarca's valuable account is especially informative about sexual behavior, it was intended to highlight Spain's success in civilizing Filipinos and rescuing them from "barbarity."[58] The basic elements of this myth, describing the emergence of the first man and woman from bamboo stalks and their incestuous marriage (with the conspicuous absence of any "Adam's rib" hierarchy), contains elements found in many Southeast Asian origin stories. What Loarca heard, however, was something akin to a moralistic tale that recorded the first theft in the world (a pig), the origins of concubinage *(amançebar),* and the result of a woman's disobedience. Lupluban, the granddaughter of the ancestral couple, refused to go back to her husband (also her uncle), Pandaguan, after his return from the dead. She preferred to remain with her new partner, who had invited her to feast upon a pig he had stolen. Angrily, Pandaguan returned to the infernal regions. In Loarca's words, "The people believe that if his wife had obeyed his summons, and he had not gone back at that time, all the dead would return to life." Any description of the "revelries" that Loarca says provided the setting when individuals with "good voices" sang of ancient deeds is as lost to the modern historian as the Visayan version itself.[59]

Despite this partial and distorted transmission, myths that relate how a community came into being can still provide indispensable insights into gender symbolism and the nature of sexual identity. Some of the most intriguing legends are those explaining the origins of the "double-gendered" figures whose potency derives from the unique conjoining of female and male. The oral literature of the Iban, perhaps the best studied in Southeast Asia, makes frequent reference to the *manang bali,* men dressed as women, who occupied the highest ritual position and whose ancestral patron was consecrated by his sister, the supreme healer.[60] In other mythologies the apparent reversal of social norms by outsize figures of legend asserts the inviolability of the moral order. For example, the brother-sister incest threading through Southeast Asian myth compels attention precisely because calamitous consequences were often attributed to improper sexual relations among ordinary mortals. In the world of myth, however, the incest that would otherwise end in catastrophe can result in the conception of legendary beings who become the progenitors of new dynasties. A fifteenth-century collation of oral and written sources from northern Thailand thus tells the story of a sage whose urine is so powerful that when a doe chances to drink it, she becomes pregnant. She subsequently gives birth to twins (a disastrous event for mortals), a boy and a girl, whom the sage rears. Brother and sister eventually marry and are installed as rulers of a kingdom from which later *muang* in northern Thailand trace their origins.[61]

Like core legends in most societies, this text, *The Story of Queen Cama-devi*, was not merely a record of ancestral rulers but also a guide to social relations and a reminder of the consequences of noncompliance. Even a king who commits the heinous crime of striking his mother, and thus ignores the debt that every child owes, will be punished. In this case the Earth Goddess causes the entire city to be flooded, drowning all the unrighteous people, including the ruler.[62] Although the great Malay epic, the *Sejarah Melayu*, contains a forthright pronouncement of the mutual obligations between ruler and subjects, it transmits messages that would not have been lost on its audience. In keeping with Malay custom, which favored marriages where husband and wife were close in age, a legendary queen abandons her plan to marry the youthful ancestor of Malay kings and adopts him as her son instead.[63]

Because sexual relationships and the passions they invoked could be understood across generations and across cultures, mythical love stories could be readily reworked to offer a powerful commentary on present circumstances. Examples that illustrate this point are legion, but one of the most striking comes from the early nineteenth century, when a rearticulation of the Ken Dedes legend enabled Javanese chroniclers to explain and justify the origins of Dutch hegemony. A beautiful princess is taken by the upstart lord of Jakarta as his wife, but his attempt to consummate the marriage is frustrated because of the flames that appear from her genitals. Exiled, she eventually becomes the wife of a Dutch prince who is ruling in Spain. It is their son, Mur Jangkung (i.e., Jan Pietersz. Coen, founder of Batavia, 1619), who attacks Jakarta in revenge for his mother's humiliation. In effect, then, the Dutch become "Javanese" relatives whose territorial conquests are explained in quintessentially local terms.[64]

Transtextuality

Accessing an aural and visual past is of especial concern to a female-oriented history because audiences listening to chanted texts or watching puppet plays and dance-dramas normally included a large number (at times a majority) of women. Despite the strength of Southeast Asia's oral tradition, Western concentration on the structures and content of literary works has encouraged an unfortunate separation of "words" and "writing" from performance and from the physical surroundings and tangible objects by which they were animated. Yet the presence of a written text—on palm leaf, on bark, on bamboo, on paper—was simply one facet of a shifting interplay between art, dance, recitation, enactment, and ritual. Central to cultural expression, this interplay intensified the "wise advice" implicit in even the most entertaining village theater. Such "guidance" might enact episodes illustrating appropriate conduct between men and women or reminding audiences of the punishments awaiting those who flouted established norms or, by contrast, the rewards for the virtuous and faithful. A Burmese puppet play, for instance, relates the story of Ma Mai U, a married woman who attracts the attention of a *nat,* a powerful spirit. When she repulses his advances, he orders a tiger to attack her while she is weaving. Incurring a "green" (violent or premature) death, but acknowledged for her virtue, Ma Mai U herself becomes a member of the *nat* pantheon.[65]

Although similar messages about "being female" are often quite explicit, images of submission and modesty could be countered by forceful characters who took on male roles, such as leading troops in battle, or who openly flaunted their sexuality. In the contemporary water puppet theater of Vietnam, with its presumed peasant origins, the two Trung sisters (leaders of a major rebellion against the Chinese in 43 CE) commonly ride barebreasted on elephants, which performers explain as a combination of proud femininity and triumphant military leadership.[66] Eroticism and insinuation can lurk beneath the most refined court performances, providing a source of amusement and titillation even in ostensibly moral or religious stories. "I beg you to wallow in the soft mud [a figurative term for sexual intercourse]," says the daughter of a Naga king to Laksamana in the Lao *Rama Jataka.* "I beg you to come and eat a white piece of root."[67] Young women were commonly thought to be particularly aroused by this kind of suggestive repartee and therefore vulnerable to the amorous inclinations often attributed to male actors, singers, and storytellers. The very reading of texts by a sweet-voiced performer was believed to arouse emotions of passionate longing, and students of Malay literature will readily recall the scene in which palace women swoon in ecstasy as they hear the seductive tones of Hang Jebat.[68]

The blurred lens of written documents or transmitted memory conveys only hints of how audiences responded to the stereotypes of "male" and "female" that activated recitation and dance-drama. It is difficult to guess, for instance, what motivated the Javanese ruler of Kartasura to stage the ritual dance known as the *Bedhaya Ketawang,* which a Dutch envoy witnessed in 1726. Normally performed by nine women solely for the ruler's gaze, music, dance, and litany combined to commemorate the meeting between Ratu Kidul, the princess of the southern ocean, and Sultan Agung (r. 1613–1646). Its potency was such that Ratu Kidul—who could harm mortals and destroy crops when annoyed—was thought to be present when it was staged. If a dancer was ritually pure (i.e., not menstruating), Ratu Kidul might even enter her body, and she would then be taken by the ruler as his sexual partner.[69] In the Malay state of Perak the *Misa Melayu,* a text celebrating the reign of Sultan Iskandar (r. 1752–1765), records the presence of Dutchmen from the VOC post at a royal wedding, but they left no record of this or other court festivities. The chronicler assures us that the crowd favorite was a dance-drama *(manora)* ordered especially from a more northern state, but we do not know whether this was because of the skill with which boys and men played the female roles, the wit and levity of the clowns, or the love story that provided the customary plot or simply because *manora,* associated with the border area between modern Thailand and Malaysia, was rarely seen farther south.[70]

The historian's hesitancy toward accepting "performance" as part of a textual amalgam can be partially explained by the absence of a fixed temporality. Whereas a written document is locked to a historical moment that can usually be ascertained, even if approximately, performance is by its very nature ephemeral. Yet when shifts in dress, choreography, and deportment can be identified, it may also be possible to locate changing messages about gender. For instance, contemporary presentations of Javanese court dances are unlikely to include boys dressed as females, which was customary in performances of the elegant *bedhaya* in eighteenth-century Surakarta. Similarly, in central Sumatra, Minangkabau youths noted for their beauty and grace are no longer singled out to be trained as *bujang gadis* (boy-girls) for female roles in the combination of martial arts, dance, and recitation known as *randai.* This development is noteworthy because, like the male Kabuki actors of Tokugawa Japan, refined impersonations by men were often thought to represent the ideals of feminine appearance and deportment. The displacement of female performers may be equally revealing. In Thailand, women skilled as dancers were once prominent as spirit mediums in the *wai kruu* ceremony, which honors teachers of music and dance. By the early twentieth century, however, there was a greater emphasis on male officiates and on men as conduits to the supernatural.[71]

The visual arts provide another example of cultural texts that have been reshaped by changing consumer demand, even as they retain some elements of older styles and preferences. Across Asia the distinctiveness of "early modern" art derives from expanding audiences whose concerns extended well beyond the religious subjects that had preoccupied earlier artists. Perhaps the most striking demonstration of the new consumerism is the erotic art that blossomed in Japan and China, but a growing interest in everyday experiences opens up other windows through which to view female lives. The magnificent miniatures surviving from Mughal India (some of which were painted by women) concentrate on the imperial household but can at times include glimpses of the mundane. Interspersed among the glittering illustrations of the emperor's court, for instance, are others that show dark-skinned women working on construction projects, carrying mortar, pounding bricks, and making lime.[72]

In comparison with other parts of Asia, Southeast Asia offers fewer visual resources, especially for women's history. The woodblock printing that fostered textual production in China only gathered pace in Vietnam from the late seventeenth century, and illustrated books remained rare. The tropical climate militated against survival of early manuscripts, and in the island world Islamic prohibitions against representation of the human body were apparently more influential than in Mughal India. Though the symbolic representations of ancestral males and females in tribal art are significant cultural statements, it is impossible to reconstruct the mental links between such figures and lived experiences. Arguably the best examples of "real life" in courtly art come from mainland Southeast Asia, where wealthy Buddhist donors gained merit by contributing to the decoration of a *wat* or a teaching hall. Although this genre flourished across the Buddhist world, it has been most extensively researched in Thailand. From the seventeenth century, greater public access to religious buildings and a new expansion of wall space encouraged artists to embark on larger murals in which depictions of *jataka,* stories of the Buddha's former lives, also included scenes of ordinary men and women. Nominally subservient to the deities, heavenly beings, and royal personages who occupy the major portion of the mural, the "pictures of the dregs of society" *(phap kak)* project a vigor and lustiness that has its own appeal. Historians of gender will surely be intrigued by the portrayal of Ayutthaya women serving in the "male" occupation of elephant drivers, and by explicit illustrations of sexual intercourse (or possibly rape). Even so, some illustrations are not easily explained. Is the homosexuality depicted between two male monkeys intended as a comment on human relationships? Are the two women suspended in a basket undergoing an actual form of punishment for immoral behavior, or is this simply a reminder that sexual mores should be observed?[73]

Despite the privileging of written sources, a more liberal interpretation of texts can open up alternative pathways for exploring the ways in which gender difference was displayed. Because (as a historian of Oceania has remarked) the past can be "sung, danced, chanted, spoken, carved, woven, painted, sculpted," the documentary dominance of men can to some extent be countered by attentiveness to other receptacles for historical memories.[74] Early Spanish observers commented on the tattoos that distinguished the great Visayan warriors, but in numerous tribal communities across Southeast Asia and the Pacific the biography of a woman could equally be etched on her body. The permanency of this mode of recording, nicely captured by a European man who visited the island of Pohnpei (eastern Micronesia) in the early nineteenth century, could equally apply to Southeast Asia. Following his explanation that writing was "the English method of tattooing," local women responded by tearing out pages from a book he had brought and weaving them into their bark-cloth shoulder wraps. When the writing washed away in heavy rain, they made the obvious point that tattooing was a more lasting means of recording the past.[75]

In this vein one might also consider Southeast Asia's rich fabric tradition, perhaps most renowned for the time-consuming *ikat* (tie, bind) technique, by which yarn was wrapped and dyed prior to weaving according to a predetermined pattern. Absolutely the work of women, the complex designs that symbolized genealogies, legends, and memories could be "read" in relation to individuals, families, and clan or tribal groupings. The role of textile motifs as markers in an indigenous record meant that female knowledge could incorporate not merely skill in execution but also a huge pool of cultural codes. Whether in a small eastern Indonesian island or among tribal societies in the mainland *masif,* cloth woven by women identified the wearer with a village or a particular clan or located him or her in a social hierarchy. The steplike design featured on certain Iban blankets thus remembers the ancestor who erected a tall ladder to meet the gods, while the boat motif on skirts worn by women on Sawu Island (eastern Indonesia) encodes the story of an ancestress unjustly accused of black magic.[76] Fabrics could equally stand as personal statements of achievement or of entry into a new life phase. On the eastern Indonesian island of Flores, for instance, certain textile designs were reserved for older men who had shown great courage by submitting to a ritual known as *nuwa,* the vertical incision of the penis, while only women of child-bearing age were entitled to incorporate the *mamuli* motif, symbolizing female genitalia, on their betel bags.[77]

The idea of a multidimensional field where texts can be present in many forms opens up alternative perspectives on the processes by which femaleness (and maleness) was understood in different settings. For example, the symbolism attached to spatial organization can reflect cultural conceptions of gender, and Roxana Waterson proposes "several distinctive patterns" connecting indigenous definitions of space to the symbolic correlations between the womb and the "Southeast Asian" house. A whole range of architectural practices—special houses for men and boys, menstruation huts, the allocation of sleeping places according to marital status—thus became cultural analogues for ordering interaction between men and women.[78] Through the gendering of objects—drums, pots, cloth, arrows, daggers, beads—male-female interactions could take place at many different levels and in many different circumstances.

One particularly enduring text, the physical environment, is of special relevance to women's history because sexuality is so often projected through metaphors derived from the natural world. Throughout Southeast Asia's courtly literature, male desire for the female body is commonly conveyed through allusions linking the landscape and plant life. The breasts of the typical heroine are compared to coconuts, her shapely calves to the pandanus flower, her slender arms and waists to delicately trailing vines. The genre of Thai love poetry known as *nirat*, which flourished during the Ayutthaya period, expresses the poet's ardent longing for his beloved and the poignant reminders he encounters in the landscape. Nature and female beauty are so closely linked in Javanese texts "that the mere mention of an element of either in a line or stanza subtly conjures an image of the whole."[79] It was in part her bitter reversal of this imagery—the "deep, deep cleft" around which moss grew, or the "sore-kneed gentlemen" who climbed to reach the "cherry-crimson cave"—that makes the poetry of Vietnam's Ho Xuan Huong so shocking and yet so compelling.[80] In other contexts the landscape could serve as a mnemonic device that enabled communities to recall not only the deeds of great ancestors but the actions of ordinary men and women who rarely figure in written histories. Fleeting, elusive, and largely unrecoverable, such recollections invoke unanswerable questions about the ways in which the condition and circumstance of "being female" may have differed from that of being male. A rock in the shape of a woman's body on a mountain east of Hanoi, for instance, recalls a peasant said to have met her death during ancient wars against the Chinese; a river bend in Sarawak bears the name of a terrified woman, Indai Jungki, who was captured as she fled from an Iban head-hunting raid.[81] The knowledge that myriads of other lives have disappeared without trace is a salutary reminder of how partial our understandings of a female past must remain.

Women in European Sources

The expansion of Southeast Asia's "early modern" sources is most dramatically demonstrated by the surge of European documentation. This material—Portuguese and Spanish chronicles, the accounts of Christian missionaries, the huge corpus generated by the Dutch East India Company, the growing pool of travel literature—is highly significant for reconstructing a female past because it is often the only evidence available when indigenous texts are limited or nonexistent. Yet trolling archives in search of information far removed from the minds of their compilers demands enormous patience. Although Christian missionaries often appear preoccupied with sexual relationships, specific references to women in European administrative records are incidental and unsystematic. Nor is this material evenly distributed. While documentation from the Philippines, Vietnam, and VOC-controlled areas can be voluminous, there are many areas where the touted "global encounters" of early modernity either never occurred or else took place only in a very pale form. Daniel Beeckman, who visited southeast Borneo in the early eighteenth century, assured his readers that while other travelers might furnish "fictions and improbable stories," he himself had tried to adhere to the truth. His detailed description of the Dayaks of Borneo, intended to acquaint other sailors and traders with local cultures, is refreshingly honest: "As to their women, I never saw any of them, and so can give no account of them."[82]

As Beeckman implies, travel writers of the period had already established "women" as one of several categories—religious practices, trade products, house construction, dress—by which knowledge of "the other" could be organized. It was, however, a category where the universal truths espoused by European males—that women were unable to keep a secret, for instance—were complicated by stereotypes about the inferiority of non-Christian peoples and the effects of climate on morality.[83] Perceptions of "native women" as wanton, lascivious, and "given to love" were affirmed by the allegedly provocative manner in which they dressed. The loose sarong worn by Burmese women often parted—deliberately, implied the Scottish sea captain Alexander Hamilton (ca. 1668–1734?)—to show a "pretty leg and a plump thigh." Other accounts noted that female clothing often seemed designed to leave "a great deal of the bosom exposed." The dancing that was a feature of most celebrations was also viewed as a flaunting of the body, while frequent and public bathing provided further evidence of moral laxity. Ignorant of the strict codes banning men from places where women were washing themselves, Europeans were reinforced in their opinion that Southeast Asian women, though often considered beautiful, were "immodest" and sexually permissive, if not actually promiscuous.[84]

Although the prevalence of such assumptions means that supposedly eyewitness European sources cannot be treated as gender neutral, no group criticized Southeast Asia's sexual practices more vehemently than those who came to preach the Christian gospel. In the Philippines, Spanish priests were appalled at the penis pins (in Tagalog, *sagra*) that were used by men to enhance their virility, to protect themselves against malignant spirits, and to ensure a safe conception, and that were often inserted at the behest of their lovers. The well-educated Dr. Antonio de Morga, who arrived in the Philippines in 1595, expressed the accepted Spanish view that the *sagra* were simply one manifestation of native sensuality and the "lewd ways of intercourse" devised by women, in this case to prolong the sexual act.[85] Yet despite the entrenched prejudices of early commentators, we remain in their historical debt. The value of the chronicles and reports produced by Spanish priests in exploring male-female relationships is well established, but aspects of gender are subsumed even in their dictionaries and word lists. The elaborate vocabulary connected with warfare in the seventeenth-century, *Vocabulario de la lengua bicol,* can be juxtaposed with other terms related to household tasks, such as the verb *magda'angon,* meaning to smoke an earthenware pitcher or water urn with rice chaff so that it added an aroma to the water stored within.[86] Through their linguistic skills some priests began to appreciate the oral heritage of the Philippines and to argue that an understanding of poetic allusion and symbolic language would benefit missionaries and administrators alike. It might not otherwise be immediately apparent, for example, that a reference to a man taking a bath in a fountain of salty water was a metaphor for sexual association with a woman of common birth. Images familiar to Filipinos, one missionary suggested, could be used effectively as Christian tutelage tried to foster sexual propriety; "good" women could be compared to sweet-smelling plants, to cane, to the stars and moon, but a "loose" woman was like the leaf of a banana tree that could destroy a harp's music.[87]

Though dedication to language study imparts its own authority to missionary writings, there were numerous other individuals whose expertise stemmed from the circumstances of their birth and upbringing. Indeed, the extent to which it is possible to develop portraits of individual writers marks off European material from the largely depersonalized world of indigenous sources. Born in Melaka, the mestizo Manoel Godinho de Eredia (1563–1620?) was the son of a Portuguese who had arrived in Sulawesi in a missionary expedition but had eloped with a fifteen-year-old Bugis princess. Eredia's 1613 description of his birthplace is written in impeccable Portuguese, a product of his Jesuit education. However, his maternal heritage is evident in his listing of ingredients used in indigenous medicines, in his mention of the enchanted princess who dwelt on a nearby mountain, in his belief in the special powers of *benua,* or forest dwellers.[88] Another individual well schooled in local cultures was Rijklof van Goens (1619–1682), who accompanied his family to Batavia in 1629 when he was only nine years old. Spending virtually his entire life in VOC service in Ceylon and the Indies, Van Goens ended his career as governor-general.[89] Other men wrote with unusual discernment because of their own training and academic background or because they acquired privileged information through their personal life, like George Rumphius (1627–1702), whose botanical compendium apparently drew on information provided by his mestizo wife, Susanna.[90] Yet, as always, there are caveats, for views about desirable female behavior influenced even the most acute observer. Eredia thus talks of "immodest" women who "think it a fine adventure to have lovers whose conversation they seek the whole of the day and much better still, during the night."[91]

Male attitudes, of course, were not frozen in time, and it is possible to track a growing sophistication in European observations. In the sixteenth century, medieval fantasies of a female-ruled domain periodically surfaced; Antonio Pigafetta (1491–1535), the chronicler of Ferdinand Magellan's circumnavigation, unquestioningly records the traveler's fable of an island (here placed south of Java) where women became pregnant from the wind and where male babies were killed.[92] By the 1780s, however, "scientific investigation" was already well in train, like the "description of an albino negro from the Papuan Islands," a medical-style report of treatments for the skin diseases common among tribal groups.[93] Stamford Raffles (1781–1826) and William Marsden (1754–1836), both employees of the English East India Company, were products of this "enlightened" tradition, and despite the passage of two hundred years Marsden's survey of marriage customs in the Sumatran interior still stands alone. Nonetheless, old ideas about the influence of the humors died hard, and Marsden could still speculate that the small size of Sumatrans, "especially the women" could be attributed to early sexual relations, an inevitable result of the appetites fostered by a tropical climate.[94]

In essence, then, the historical descriptions left by European men always require qualification, no matter how informed their observations. Simon de la Loubère, the French envoy whose account of Ayutthaya remains a primary source for Thai history, remarked that the only "nuns" he saw were old women living in bamboo enclosures beside the monasteries. He was unaware that female renunciants could also be women of high status who wielded considerable authority. According to the Ayutthaya chronicles, as lord mother of a monastery, the former nurse of King Narai (r. 1656–1688) mediated disputes between leading members of the nobility and was actually invited to share the royal mat.[95] François Valentijn (1666–1727), the Dutch missionary whose work on eastern Indonesia has also provided material for generations of researchers, was convinced (like most of his peers) that Ambon women were more inclined to "superstition" than were their menfolk. However, despite Valentijn's perception of the cultural distance between the Netherlands and Ambonese society, his examples of native credulity, such as the protection believed to reside in garlic, could have easily applied in most of Europe's peasant communities.

The early modern period provides no female equivalents to men like Valentijn or de la Loubère. The few surviving letters written by Dutch women in Batavia are primarily concerned with details of their own lives— betrothals, weddings, births, illnesses. As the daughter of a prominent VOC official remarked to her cousin, "I can't write much about this country because it's not familiar to you, but the climate is quite different from the Netherlands, as is the way the people interact. Here one only has blacks as servants, and they are extraordinary people to deal with, being very murderous and lazy. They don't work as hard as Dutch maids, and that's why it's necessary to have a large household with ten slaves."[96] There is no earlier counterpart to Sophia Raffles (1786–1858), whose unpublished letters refer to treks "all over Sumatra," where she sometimes walked as much as "240 miles in fourteen days." Remarkably, her description of a visit to the Minangkabau highlands in 1818, where mothers implored the first white woman they had ever seen to touch their children "as a preservative from all future evil," is also documented in a Malay poem.[97] And while seventeenth-century gravestones from Dutch Melaka demonstrate the tragic extent of infant mortality, Sophia's letters provide a rare glimpse of the grief of a mother who had lost four of her five children. She felt, she wrote to a close friend, as if she was "wandering in regions of desolation & woe . . . to see your child perish in all the bloom of health & beauty . . . & yet have no power to save it."[98] When more complete memoirs by European women appear later in the nineteenth century, they serve as a reminder that female experiences and perspectives were "importantly different" from those of men. There is little doubt, for instance, that a list of taboos observed by Iban women when husbands were absent on a head-hunting raid is the more detailed because it was compiled by a missionary's wife.[99]

Europeans also recorded their impressions of Southeast Asia in art, although here too the prevalence of stylistic clichés calls for historiographical wariness. A detailed account of the burning of women in Hindu Bali was included in the report of the first Dutch voyage to the East Indies in 1597, but it was based on hearsay rather than eyewitness observations. The accompanying drawing of Balinese women leaping into a pit that contains a burning funeral pyre is reminiscent of contemporary Dutch biblical illustrations, with little resemblance to anything Balinese.[100] Similarly, the women portrayed in a sixteenth-century Portuguese manuscript illustrated in Goa (probably by an Indian under Portuguese direction) appear identical, regardless of whether they are from Malabar, Goa, Bengal, Sumatra, Java Melaka, or Maluku.[101] Artists included in VOC missions usually made relatively simple sketches that were developed later by the engraver. The resulting pictures were also highly selective, since publishers or translators often chose examples they thought would interest the reading public. The English trader Thomas Bowrey (ca. 1650–1713), for example, illustrated his manuscript on the countries around the Bay of Bengal with "exotic" features—an Acehnese cripple, elephants, tigers, dancing women, a widow being burnt alive, fakirs, dancing snakes.[102]

The records left by European administrations, though much more prosaic than travel accounts, can be highly relevant to women's history because of the space given to counting and classifying local populations and the concern with maintaining settled households. Registers of births, deaths, and marriages in the Philippines have enabled demographic historians to graph tentative population trends, and court documents and notary testaments surviving from Dutch-controlled towns, notably Batavia, preserve details about common lives not found in other sources. Generated by a nascent European bureaucracy, this material acquires added importance because no indigenous government in Southeast Asia offers anything similar to the legal archives now available for China, even though expanding state control was reflected in greater documentary efforts.[103] Conserving written material in a tropical environment is always difficult, and the idea that official records should be organized for later consultation developed relatively slowly. A historian can hardly be heartened by a Burmese decision to collect only royal orders after 1633, since previous ones were "ambiguous," or by learning that eighteenth-century taxes in northern Vietnam were calculated according to population numbers dating from 1664.[104] Because indigenous demographic figures are often notional, cabalistic, or emblematic, they are rarely amenable to a gender-based analysis. For example, there is no way of assessing the criteria by which a woman in a Burmese land register was classified as "old" and therefore eligible for lower taxes.[105] Sources such as family wills in Vietnam or temple donations in northern Thai inscriptions have the potential to yield new information about (for instance) household composition and family structure but demand high standards of linguistic competence.

For the most part, issues basic to women's history, like sex ratios, age at marriage, fertility rates, and life expectancy will remain speculative in Southeast Asia before the nineteenth century. Even when European material supplies some quantitative data, the context is usually limited, and in many cases the information itself disappointing. Portuguese documents from Southeast Asia cannot match those available for Brazil, and the letters written by English factors from their Indonesian posts are meager when compared with the voluminous VOC correspondence. In addition, there are several irreplaceable losses, as in Melaka, where the pre-1740 records of the Dutch administration and the family registers of the Reformed Church have disappeared.[106] In Batavia the Gong Goan, the Chinese Council, oversaw matters such as marriage, divorce, tax collections, donations, and land grants within the Chinese community, but all that remains from the eighteenth century are three "marriage books" (1775, 1778, and 1783–1785). The gap in this judicial record is especially regrettable, since Chinese women were more likely than men to take complaints to court, presumably in connection with marital inheritance and domestic rights.[107]

Words of caution are in order even when European categories appear quite explicit, like those relating to ethnicity. In 1730, for instance, Dutch officials decided that a woman who married a man from another ethnic group would be included with her husband, as would their children. Accordingly, because the VOC assigned ethnicity according to the father, the mother of a woman from "Bima" could in fact have been a "Bugis" from Sulawesi.[108] Philippine parish records must also be used warily. Although the documentation of baptisms, burials, and marriage of Filipino Christians was largely in place by the end of the seventeenth century, little early material has survived, and there was no standardized procedure for maintaining lists until the nineteenth century. We are thus left to speculate about sometimes marked sex discrepancies, as in one Ilocos village where there were only 180 young men to 400 young women.[109] Had men migrated or concealed themselves to avoid corvée or military conscription? Perhaps the explanation is simply due to inconsistent categorization of age groups, since a girl's designation as "young adult" is more easily identified than for boys, especially when menstruation is publicly noted through rituals and changes in dress.

Historians of Southeast Asia have long grappled with methodologies that can both amalgamate and respect the divergent orientations of European and indigenous material. This is especially true of the island world, where Dutch and Spanish records can easily drive the historical narrative. Yet for women's history, as for any other topic, the insights of outsiders often mesh with local sources, providing a richer picture than would otherwise be available. For example, genealogies from southwest Sulawesi certainly make mention of Daeng Talele, wife of the great Bugis leader Arung Palakka (1635?–1696). However, it is only in Dutch sources that we learn of the numerous occasions on which she mediated between her husband and VOC officials and of her contribution to the successful Bugis-VOC alliance. Alternatively chiding, persuading, castigating, and applauding, Daeng Talele appears as the epitome of the strong, confident Bugis woman. The details of Arung Palakka's will, again found only in the VOC archives, testify to his recognition of the loyalty and support she had rendered for so many years.[110]

THE GOAL OF THIS chapter has been to establish the context for the discussion that follows. While there is real potential for research on women in Southeast Asia, all historical projects will be restrained by the sources, and a lack of case studies complicates any attempt at generalization. In many ways Southeast Asia's historiographical heritage mirrors its geographical location between the text-rich areas of East and South Asia and the orality of Oceania. The ability to compose a chronicle or record a poem in writing was limited to a small minority, and hundreds of languages have no literate tradition whatsoever. Sources left by Europeans and by foreign Asians offer some compensation, but these rarely deal with remote areas and are largely concentrated on the island world. Yet despite undeniable frustrations, the interplay between sources that are inscribed, spoken, performed, woven, painted, or carved can promote fruitful cross-disciplinary conversations. In establishing an environment sympathetic to female skills, attention to nonwritten material should also lessen the tendency for well-documented areas to speak for the whole. Ultimately, however, the selection, organization, and interrogation of such material will reflect the historian's personal inclinations, so that any reconstruction is open to challenge or reconsideration. In the revised edition of what will stand as a classic work, O. W. Wolters speculated as to whether a "female historian" might accept his interpretation of women's influence on court politics in Vietnam during the thirteenth and fourteenth centuries.[111] One can only respond that Southeast Asian history needs and deserves the kind of debate that any disagreements might generate.

CHAPTER 3

Women and Religious Change

The advent of "early modernity" in Southeast Asia is usually linked to expanding international trade, but a more significant development for women was the arrival of Islam and Christianity, which joined the other state-supported philosophies of Buddhism and Confucianism in deeming females intellectually, emotionally, and spiritually inferior to males. Although it is possible to track a steady retreat (but not displacement) of the spirit propitiation where women were so often prominent, many areas distant from trade routes and far from royal capitals were barely touched by the currents redirecting religious beliefs in so much of the globe. More particularly, an acknowledgement of women's ritual skills persisted even in societies where hierarchies working to female disadvantage were openly endorsed. Southeast Asia can thus be treated as a cross-cultural laboratory for comparing women's acceptance, negotiation, and contestation of socioreligious agendas that privileged men in new and significant ways.

Indigenous Religious Systems

The survival of so many "traditional" customs, albeit in modified forms, offers a more nuanced context for considering historical sources that often provide only glimpses of indigenous beliefs. For instance, the symbolic fertility in the discharge of rockets is readily detected when descriptions from eighteenth-century Pegu are juxtaposed with modern accounts of the "rocket ceremony" in Laos and with folk epics depicting the sexual explicitness that infused such occasions.[1] Early Austronesian associations between illicit intercourse and supernatural punishment resonate in later references that attribute disasters, disease, and famine to sexual transgressions, and in the specter of unwitting incest with an unrecognized mother or sister that haunts the legendary world of many premodern societies.[2] Recurring mythical motifs ascribing the origins of human, animal, and plant life to union between the female earth and the male sky or rain may still be celebrated in ritually sanctioned copulation, or symbolically elevated into dances and other ceremonies. A striking instance of the belief in the earth-as-womb comes from Minahasa (northern Sulawesi), where the name of one group, Tongkimbut ("people of the vagina") is mentioned in seventeenth-century sources.[3]

The most sustained accounts of women's place in indigenous religions are concentrated on the Philippines, where Spanish missionaries began to work in the late sixteenth century. The Philippine archipelago had been relatively isolated from external influences, and we know much less about practices in areas where Indian and Chinese ideas had been more pervasive. Yet despite entrenched prejudices regarding women, sexuality, and the place of non-European societies in the global hierarchy, the Spanish material provides a number of valuable entry points for thinking more generally about "femaleness" in Southeast Asian religious systems.

The first of these entry points concerns "religious" vocabularies. The Catholic experience in South America had demonstrated the importance of proficiency in local languages, and Spanish descriptions of the Filipino spirit environment consequently incorporate much indigenous terminology. Because cognates of many words invoking the supernatural (*anito, asuang, baylan, patianac,* to name a few) are found throughout the Malay-Indonesian archipelago, Filipino beliefs can be placed in a wider Austronesian context that also reveals similarities with early mainland cultures. In the Philippines, as in so many premodern societies, the natural world was animated by a vast array of deities, ancestors, and spirits whose pleasure or anger could have far-reaching effects. Unexpected tragedy or unforeseen events—drought, earthquake, epidemic, a child's death, a shipwreck, a tiger attack, defeat by an enemy—could all be attributed to supernatural ire. If approached correctly, however, these powerful forces could respond by an outflow of fortune, good health, and well-being for individuals and community alike.

The Philippine data also invite discussions on animist beliefs that saw women as equally advantaged as men, if not more so, in reaching the trance-like state necessary to establish lines of communication with powerful spirits who were often male. Missionaries thus described how female mediums (*baylan* in the Visayas, *catalonan* in Tagalog) called up deities at healing sessions, chanting aloud "with many posturings" and assuring the patient that the *anito* (spirit) would give him strength.[4] References to women's spirit dances in eighteenth-century Pegu match priestly accounts of the beating of drums and the dancing by which female mediums in Vietnam, the "ba dong," fell into trance, relayed messages from deceased relatives, and carried out rituals to cure the sick.[5] In Taiwan, Dutch East India Company (VOC) officials likewise reported that the *inib,* the senior women who communicated with the spirits, were thought capable of controlling the rain and wind. Such examples slide easily into a larger framework that looks across "area studies" boundaries to include the female mediums (*mudang*) of Korea, the priestesses (*noro*) of the Ryukyu Islands, chiefly sisters in Polynesia, and the *maibi* of Manipur.[6]

A third avenue of inquiry opened up by Spanish descriptions of the Philippines concerns the relationship between age, gender, and ritual sta-

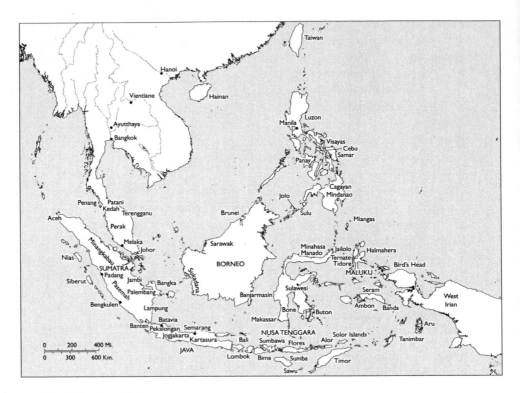

Island Southeast Asia

tus, since missionaries persistently characterized the priestesses, or *aniteros,* as "old." Although the onset of menstruation was an occasion for celebration rather than embarrassment, the Philippines resembled many other premodern societies in seeing female fertility as a powerful and potentially dangerous force. Of all the bodily fluids, menstrual blood had the capacity to work the greatest magic, and the relationship between a Tagalog girl and her community entered a new stage when she experienced her first menses. During the ceremony that ushered her into womanhood, she was forbidden to speak to anyone except the spirit medium, and "it is their custom to enclose her with mantles and cover the windows, such that where she is becomes very dark."[7]

By contrast, the bodies of postmenopausal women no longer emitted the blood that signified the mysterious forces of reproduction, and their place on the male-female spectrum moved accordingly. Female in anatomy and life experiences, and yet biologically more "male-like," they embodied the coexistence of sexual opposites that underlay so much Austronesian symbolism. The prestige thus garnered was buttressed by their longevity, their knowledge of communal lore, and their mastery of genealogy and ritually related skills like weaving. In the Philippines, women designated as *aniteros* were often charged with ceremonies usually delegated to men, such as ceremonial bloodletting; according to Pigafetta, who chronicled Magellan's arrival in the Visayas in 1521, "only old women" could kill the pig offered in sacrifice. Similarly, an English description of Java in the early eighteenth century remarked that the "pagans" (i.e., non-Muslims) usually chose older women proficient in "witchcraft" to be their "priestesses." Such individuals might themselves become great ancestors, and on the small island of Nusalaut (off the coast of Ambon) the Dutch minister François Valentijn mentioned the worship of Tanihale, the spirit of an old woman.[8] Modern studies of northern Thailand, showing how the ritual authority of senior females flows into the domestic sphere, have parallels in seventeenth-century Vietnam, where the Jesuit Alexandre de Rhodes remarked that older women, commonly viewed as religious adepts, exercised unchallenged influence in the household.[9]

Spanish sources on the Philippines open up a fourth arena for discussion, for an early Tagalog lexicon notes that a fertility god was represented as a hermaphrodite or, as a modern anthropologist might put it, a "double-gendered deity."[10] Religious rituals often included sexually ambiguous individuals, "Indians dressed as women," who "applied themselves to women's tasks" like weaving, embroidery, cultivating, and pottery. A Jesuit priest who had spent thirty-five years in the Visayas wrote of one such figure: "All the things that the women did, he performed. . . . He danced also like they did, never like a man. . . . In all he appeared more a woman than a man."[11] In the nineteenth century, descriptions of similar individuals who acted as mediators between the community and the spirit world were recorded in numerous Austronesian societies, notably Borneo. These individuals were ritually potent because they represented the male-female combination that characterized indigenous cosmologies, a two-gender, two-sex division reflecting a range of other dualisms—mountain-sea, earth-sky, upper-lower, light-dark, right-left. In mainland Southeast Asia, where transgender is currently attracting more research, an origin myth from Thailand mentions a sexually neuter figure who stands outside the male-female spectrum while occupying a symbolically equal position.[12] In the mainland, however, Europeans provide only tantalizing glimpses, like Alexander Hamilton's reference to "numerous hermaphrodites" present at a ritual in Pegu, who "danced like mad Folks" and then fell into trance, offering predictions regarding the harvest and the general health of the community. The Vietnam references are equally perfunctory, with one priest simply noting men who acted as spirit mediums and who wore "women's clothes and completely pull out their beards": "They want to be called Ba po, that is, *mistress.*"[13]

The best documented case of a "third gender" is found in southwest Sulawesi, where androgynous beings known as *bissu* were once attached to every Bugis court as advisers to the ruler and as guardians of the regalia.

According to textual accounts, the *bissu* originally descended from the Upperworld to accompany the first rulers to earth, but in the earliest references they are commonly described as older women. One manuscript recounts how a small Bugis kingdom, threatened by its powerful neighbor Bone, sent out about a hundred female *bissu* to meet the advancing army. As they chanted and swung their weaving beaters, their "swords," their supernatural powers made them invulnerable to Bone weapons. However, by the time the Europeans reached Sulawesi in the sixteenth century, most *bissu* (or at least those more easily identified) were male. In 1545 one Portuguese described the *bissu* as "priests of the king," who wore their hair long, dressed like women, and adopted the voice, gestures, and habits of women. Since intercourse with a female was thought to lead to calamity, the *bissu* were permitted to have sexual relations only with men.[14] While the native American berdache and the *xanith* of Oman may offer parallels, one can only speculate that the *mahu* of Hawai'i and Tahiti, and the *fa'afine* of Samoa occupied a ritual position similar to that of their Austronesian cousins. Although the *mahu* were said to live as women and to spend their days making tapa cloth, in dancing, and in other "female" occupations, the ambiguity of early European references makes differing interpretations possible.[15]

A final point is more contentious. Carolyn Brewer has argued that female dominance in Philippine animism was mirrored in relations between wives and husbands and in community attitudes toward sexual expression. The "immorality" deplored by Spanish missionaries allowed young girls to experience different partners before marriage and enabled a wife to discard an unwanted husband or form a temporary liaison with another man. However, although relatively relaxed attitudes toward premarital sex can be found in villages throughout Southeast Asia and women could often initiate divorce, one should be cautious about seeing a ritual role for females as some kind of norm, since the evidence is insufficient to support more than subregional generalizations. On the island of Ambon in eastern Indonesia, for instance, VOC employees saw few signs that women participated in local ceremonies, noting that they were involved only if unseen powers were petitioned for a good harvest.[16] Nonetheless, it is still reasonable to conclude that the expansion of the world religions substantially reduced female opportunities to gain status as communicators with the supernatural. The monotheistic faiths, Islam and Christianity, were especially antagonistic to interaction with uncontrolled, "evil" spirits (while tolerating veneration for saints or "good" jinns), but similar attitudes were found in Confucianist thinking. Like their Chinese counterparts, Vietnamese rulers forbade petitioning "devils, spirits or ghosts" for favors and were hostile toward "witches and fortune tellers" who operated outside imperial authority. Theravada Buddhist authorities also opposed spirit propitiation when malevolent magic was suspected, and an eighteenth-century Thai text warns its audience that those who believe in sorcery and request favors from spirits will become *peta* (hell-beings) and demons.[17] Yet even as monks, priests, imams, and male shamans strengthened men's ritual authority, older women could remain the guardians of sacred objects, and ordinary Southeast Asians continued to see the female body as an effective channel for conveying messages from the nonhuman world.

Theravada Buddhism

The process of adaptation by which imported ideologies and deities were localized is central to Southeast Asia's religious history. In Bali, where Hindu-Buddhist traditions withstood Islam's steady advance, the powerful figure of Durga became interlaced with stories of the Balinese widow (Rangda) Calon Arang, so frighteningly powerful that, if angered, she could destroy the entire country. Ancient patterns of male-female complementarity have also survived, despite the prominence of men in Hindu ritual. It was necessary, for instance, for Balinese priests *(pedanda)* to be married, since a wife assisted her husband on ritual occasions. Unmarried women could even become *pedanda* in their own right.[18]

Cultural adjustments proceeded most smoothly in Buddhism, primarily because Buddhist philosophy does not rest on a monotheistic base and is not opposed to localized supernaturalism. In the ninth century, Mahayana Buddhist texts inspired the great monument known as Borobudur in central Java, although only fifty kilometers away and built around the same time as the Hindu complex of Prambanan. In Cambodia, where kings had previously venerated Vishnu and Shiva, Mahayana Buddhism also gained favor in the late Angkor period (twelfth–thirteenth centuries) and, through Chinese influence, acquired a strong following in Vietnam. In both cases the sources point up Buddhism's attraction to women.[19] Meanwhile, continuing connections with Sri Lanka strengthened the influence of the Theravada school. By the fourteenth century, Theravada Buddhism was dominant on the mainland outside Vietnam, while in island Southeast Asia the Hindu-Buddhist heritage was overwritten by the arrival of Islam.

The spread of Theravada Buddhism in Southeast Asia has been largely explained by its appeal to kings who were drawn to the concept of the *cakravartin* (the world-turning monarch), and to the perception of royal power as a reflection of merit accumulated in past lives. Because all written sources from this period emanate from the courts, the world of the village remains largely unknown. Wary of imputing motivation to people in distant times and distant cultures, historians of Southeast Asia, unlike their anthropological colleagues, have not been tempted to discuss the reasons behind Theravada Buddhism's attraction for ordinary men, much less women. In this regard, the history of Buddhism in Southeast Asia is ripe for reevaluation, especially since lay female support has been a critical element in the monkhood's survival.

This support is intriguing because Theravada commentaries are confident that being born a woman rather than a man is evidence of inadequate merit in former existences. Unlike Mahayana traditions, where numerous bodhisattvas (those who have postponed their final liberation for the sake of other living beings) are female, the core Theravada commentaries contain relatively few "role models" and are more forthright in depicting women as consumed by greed and animal passion.[20] Similar attitudes can be detected in later texts from Southeast Asia, the best-known example being the *Traibhumikatha,* reputedly composed by a fourteenth-century Tai prince but recopied during the Ayutthaya period (ca. 1351–1767). Depicting sexuality and copulation as indisputable signs of lower merit, this comprehensive cosmology declares that any individual who manifests excessive sensual desire will enter the next life as a female. The proper relationship between husband and wife is exemplified by the *cakravartin* and his queen, who is totally attentive to his wishes, fanning him, massaging him, and obeying his slightest wish. Since a woman is effectively the property of her husband, a man who commits adultery with another's wife will undergo rebirth in a fiery hell, where he will endure unspeakably painful punishments. Already signaling a downgrading of the "third gender" role, the text also notes that a guilty man will also be rendered "more female" by being reincarnated as a person of "indeterminate sex" for a thousand generations. Even if he is subsequently reborn as a male, he will retain female characteristics for a number of rebirths.[21]

Despite this apparent misogyny, Buddhist praxis in Southeast Asia provided an environment where the disadvantages of being female were far from insurmountable, even when men were clearly privileged in gaining access to religious knowledge. As part of the passage to adulthood, boys normally spent time in a monastery, where they acquired basic literacy as well as some familiarity with sacred texts. Nonetheless, we should not overlook a long Buddhist tradition of female study and meditation. Full ordination for women in Sri Lanka disappeared around the twelfth century, but although the term "nuns" may not be strictly correct, a cloistered life remained an option in Southeast Asia.[22] A female renunciant shaved her head and eyebrows but observed fewer precepts than a monk, and in Ayutthaya her white rather than saffron robe indicated her lower status. In the seventeenth century, nuns were typically older women who lived near the *wat,* receiving support in return for spending their time in preparing food for the monks, listening to sermons, and visiting the poor and sick.[23] However, the ascetic life was also considered appropriate for a wellborn widow. High-ranking women were appointed heads of religious foundations, and "the monastery

of the white-robed nuns" was sufficiently prestigious to provide accommodation for King Boromakot (r. 1733–1758) while on a royal tour.[24]

Although few girls received instruction equivalent to that of their brothers, Buddhist teachings still infused the environment in which women operated. Their religious education was primarily acquired in village gatherings
where they listened to the sermons of monks, to texts recited in local languages, and to the stories of Buddha's life and his previous existences. It has
been suggested that such occasions typically attracted large female audiences, and in 1720 a French missionary described a group of Thai women
so engrossed by a monk's reading from "a book of fables" that they did not
even notice him enter the teaching hall. By contrast, their "less assiduous"
husbands whiled away the time outside.[25] Women may have been less likely
than men to read and write, but performances that drew from the *jataka* or
used popular legends to impart edifying lessons could provide effective
"teaching texts" for nonliterates. Recitations of the Lao *Rama Jataka*,
chanted by monks during the Buddhist Lent, were replete with admonitions on how women and men should behave, cautioning audiences that "if
a man abandons [his wife], there cannot be family life," while simultaneously presenting an entertaining narrative of romantic love and sexual
adventure. The Earth Goddess protects Sita's wifely fidelity so that Ravana
cannot dishonor her; equally, however, the daughter of a Naga king entices
Rama's brother. "I am a grown woman," she says beguilingly, "with many
years [of experience]."[26] The (to us) unexpected bawdiness of Buddhist
texts is reflected in the murals decorating the walls of *wat* and teaching
halls, some dating from the seventeenth century, which can be quite
explicit in their depiction of nudity and sexuality, even among the heavenly
beings.[27]

Any understanding of the ways in which "texts" helped shape ideas
about femaleness in Buddhist Southeast Asia is complicated by the lack of
a baseline from which to measure change and by the dearth of evidence
regarding popular interpretations of Buddhist teachings. Like other world
religions, Buddhism was infused with messages concerning appropriate
male-female relations. For example, the unquestioning obedience that a
wife owes her husband is implicit in the much-loved Vessantara Jataka, the
story of the Buddha's penultimate life. In displaying his generosity and disdain for earthly ties, Prince Vessantara gives away his belongings, his children, and even his long-suffering wife, Maddi. The idea of the nurturing
woman was reinforced in several *jataka* narratives like the story of Sujata,
daughter of a village chief, who presented the fasting Buddha-to-be with a
dish of rice and milk and thereby attained a privileged position in Buddhist
iconography.[28] Yet these images of virtue, fidelity, and kindness can be juxtaposed with other *jataka* stories that portray women as sexually voracious,
a constant prey to material desires, and a hindrance to the male spiritual

journey. They are therefore more likely than men to be destined for the tortures of hell, often graphically depicted in murals and other religious illustrations. A frightening local addition to the canonical Nimi Jataka shows a woman whose extended and enlarged tongue is eternally pecked by a bird as a punishment for eating before her husband.[29]

The ambiguities between religious practice and textual reservations about female spirituality were often reconciled by Buddhism's relatively comfortable coexistence with spirit propitiation. This negotiation is nicely exemplified in an Arakan ceremony witnessed by a Portuguese priest in about 1630. A man had fallen ill, and his wife had made a vow to perform a special ritual, hoping to gain the favor of the spirits. Dressed in her finest clothes, she gyrated in a frenzied manner, urged on by the playing of loud music. When she could dance no longer, she seized a cloth hanging from the center of the room, twisting herself round repeatedly until she fell breathless on the ground. For eight days the same dance-trance ritual took place, with female relatives taking her place when she was exhausted.[30] After the patient had recovered, the group went on to pay their respects at local "temples," thus incorporating into Buddhist praxis the very old custom of communication with spirits through the swinging ceremonies found in several Southeast Asian societies.

Female prominence in this curing ritual is of interest because across Southeast Asia women were drawn to the world religions as a source of new and powerful protection against family sickness and mortality. Haunted by the possibility of their own death in childbirth and consequent existence as a wandering and dissatisfied spirit, women were offered the example of Buddha's mother, who had died seven days after his birth but occupied an honored place in Tavatimsa Heaven (second in the Buddhist hierarchy of six heavens). One of Buddha's disciples, Angulimala, was commonly solicited by pregnant women who hoped for an easy birth, and certain Pali texts with which he was associated were "specifically sanctioned" to assist in a difficult delivery. It is not surprising that Angulimala's image at the eleventh-century Shwezigon pagoda (in contemporary Yangon) became a focus of veneration for pregnant women.[31] In the never-ending search for the protection of accumulated merit, women could also exploit their own gender-specific skills; for example, Buddhist symbols and lines from well-known texts could be woven or embroidered into the fabric, fans, cushions, and other items offered to monks or reserved for ritual use. In this sense, acts of piety represented a kind of contract with nonhuman powers; a pregnant woman or her family might therefore commission a copy of the Theravada canon in the expectation that she would not suffer in childbirth and that her baby would be healthy.[32]

The liaison between the laity and the *sangha* (monkhood) also goes far in explaining Buddhism's appeal to women. Females may have been relegated to a lesser spiritual level, but Buddhism honored the lay devotee who demonstrated her piety through donations of food, textiles, jewelry, money, and other items to the monastery. Those who performed these meritorious acts clearly anticipated future rewards in recognition of their good deeds. Presenting lands to a temple, a thirteenth-century Pagan queen thus prays that in future existences she might have "happiness, luxury and wealth, better than the average person."[33] One of the most public occasions for merit making was the *kathin* ceremony at the end of the rainy season, when robes that women had woven were presented to the monks. Locally composed *jataka* reminded listeners that householders who offered *kathina* cloth would never be reborn into a low-ranking family and would be assured of happiness, riches, and fame. It is not difficult to understand why a poem composed by a Burmese court lady, Ma Khwe (1781–1836), remembers the festival of the "monks taking robes" as one of the most important seasonal rituals.[34]

Male-female relationships were central to the ongoing dialogue between monkhood and laity. By the seventeenth century the custom whereby young men entered the *sangha* for a space of time, usually during the rainy season, was well established, but this ordination was virtually always temporary. Told of celibacy among Christian monks and nuns, people in Laos expressed amazement at the notion of "perpetual chastity," a practice quite foreign to their own experience.[35] Women had a vested interest in supporting the circulation of young men in and out of the monkhood. In the first place, a mother acquired merit through presenting a son to the monastery. Even today preordination chants proclaim the debt a Thai youth owes the woman who gave him life. Her selflessness in enduring the pain of childbirth and nurturing him thereafter is extolled, and her son's entry into the monkhood acclaimed as *kha nom,* the price of milk.[36] In the second place, the monastic experience became a rite of passage thought to equip youths with the status and maturity necessary for marriage, and from this standpoint, ordinands were husbands-in-waiting. Despite Buddhist strictures, the village environment was generally tolerant toward any dalliance between novices and young women, who could well be their future wives.[37] A retrospective reading of literary evidence suggests that tensions between the ideal of celibacy and the reality of physical desire could be resolved without great heart searching. A poem ascribed to King Rama II (r. 1809–1824) describes a youthful monk who is able to slip away secretly from the monastery to spend time with his beloved and then, after a temporary release from his vows, seeks a preceptor "to admit him to the Order once again."[38]

Ordinary women may well have been able to locate themselves in this ostensibly male-ordered world because a variety of female figures served as anchors for local histories of Buddhism's arrival. The small Buddha image enshrined at a *wat* in Chiang Mai, for instance, reputedly belonged to the first ruler of the kingdom of Haripunjaya, Queen Camadevi, whom a fifteenth-century work presents as the "fertile progenitor" of a royal dynasty, as a Buddhist sage, and ultimately as a most powerful spirit.[39] Other tangible mnemonics—statues, artifacts, religious buildings—could be associated with ancient female spirits who had been absorbed into Buddhist cosmologies or even embedded in sexually ambiguous Buddha images. One such statue in Cambodia, made of lacquered wood and said to be about three hundred years old, is popularly known as the "black lady." According to colonial officials, it represented the country's most formidable and most respected spirit.[40]

While a pattern of vigorous localization counters any perception of Southeast Asians as passive recipients of outside influences, the alliance between Buddhism and state authority did help justify new scripts for male dominance. This collaboration also encouraged a sharper definition of "acceptable" religious practices and greater oversight of ritual observances. In 1635 the royal orders of Burma thus warned a lady that she would acquire no merit from the construction of a monastery if she had permitted spirit propitiation during the building process, since this was the preserve of the monks.[41] In the same mode, a description of "hell-beings" in an eighteenth-century Thai version of *Phra Malai*, regarded as one of Southeast Asia's core Buddhist texts, mentions "a hideous-looking woman" whose decaying body, completely covered with pus-filled boils, is constantly attacked by vultures and crows. She suffers this punishment because in her previous life she had claimed to be a spirit medium and had taken money and gifts from people in return for relaying messages from their deceased relatives.[42]

Women were also affected when Theravada Buddhist kings took steps to purge religious practice of alleged accretions and to reform monastic life of practices that conflicted with basic teachings. Seventeenth-century Ayutthaya saw greater attempts to enforce celibacy within the *sangha,* and a French envoy reported that any monk found with a woman would be burnt to death; about the same time the Sri Lankan ruler proscribed certain village ceremonies that were apparently explicitly sexual.[43] A reforming trend in Sri Lankan Buddhism (probably stimulated by renewed links with the Thai *sangha*) is evident in a manuscript written around 1740 that warns young monks against accepting food and clothing from families who are probably little concerned with piety and are merely seeking a husband for a marriageable daughter.[44] Some Buddhist leaders were critical of the inclusion of the Earth Goddess ("the female guardian-angel of the earth," as a Jesuit missionary termed her) in Buddha's biography and of her prominent place in Buddhist temples. In mid-seventeenth century Burma an Earth Goddess image was erased from a hill cave near modern Mandalay, on the grounds that she was not mentioned in the Pali or Sanskrit canon. In some cases she was transformed into a male deity, or her breasts and other female characteristics were de-emphasized or removed; in others, her statue was moved away from the Buddha's throne to someplace outside the *wat*'s consecrated boundaries.[45] These largely unsuccessful attempts to reconfigure representations of women are key elements in evolving perceptions of femaleness, but a consideration of developments in Vietnam suggests that they are hardly unique to the Theravada world.

Vietnam

Because the case for Vietnam's inclusion in Southeast Asia rests partly on the claim that female status was higher than in China, the position of women has generated considerable debate. It is apparent, however, that despite the persistence of ancient customs and domestication of the Chinese heritage, the study of Vietnamese women cannot be detached from an "East Asian" context. In early Japan, for example, female sovereigns were drawn to Buddhism's great Lotus Sutra, which held that sex was no impediment to either rulership or the attainment of Buddhahood. It is surely no coincidence that a powerful dowager queen in eleventh-century Vietnam engaged as her teacher a monk who advocated meditation through the Lotus Sutra, or that this sutra became popular in court circles.[46] Eminent nuns in Song China and pre-Tokugawa Japan also have their counterparts in Vietnamese women like Dieu Nhan ("Wondrous Cause," 1042–1113), who was raised in the imperial palace but renounced the world after her husband's death, eventually becoming head of a convent and a renowned spiritual adept.[47] On the other hand, one cannot ignore the localization by which indigenous "holy mothers" of rain, thunder, clouds, and lightning were transposed into four buddhas (Tu Phat), said to have been born of a union between a local girl and a monk. Sanctuaries dedicated to these Holy Mothers were frequently incorporated into pagoda complexes.[48] Similar processes occurred in Daoism, which percolated into Vietnam from southern China but never received the official patronage accorded Confucianism. Since relatively few Vietnamese were schooled in Daoist intellectual traditions, localization encountered few restraints. In addition to the "eight immortals" listed in Chinese texts, for instance, the Vietnamese added at least twenty-seven others, several of whom were female. All had deep roots in indigenous history, like the thirteenth-century general, Chen Tran Hung Dao, who had repelled the invading Mongol army. Often summoned by mediums, he had a particular appeal to women because he was reputedly able to cure female sterility and relieve difficult or protracted labor.[49]

The space that Daoist and Buddhist praxis opened up for female participation assumed greater importance from the fifteenth century when the Le dynasty embarked on a campaign to inculcate Confucian teachings as the fundamental basis of government. A reformed examination system qualifying men for official posts affirmed male prerogatives, with the state ethos succinctly captured in a poem by the long-lived emperor Le Thanh-tong (r. 1460–1497): "The superior (male) is strong and enduring / The inferior (female) is obedient and without force."[50] Long-standing customs whereby young men lived in the house of their bride's parents were proscribed; other edicts forbade marriage with the matrilineal Cham of central Vietnam, since inheritance should descend from father to son; widow remarriage was discouraged, although less vehemently than in China and Korea. Yet in keeping with the Confucian vision, the Vietnamese elite also saw female education as an essential element in the cultivation of social morality. As one poem attributed to the fifteenth-century scholar Nguyen Trai put it, "I think that with strict discipline anyone can become a decent person / Women also must be trained / For they too have human hearts wherein lodges righteousness."[51] Replicating an "East Asian" pattern, female learning was best manifested by the private study of Buddhist scriptures as well as Confucian classics. In consequence, court women were frequently known for their patronage and knowledge of Buddhist doctrine, despite official hostility toward practices associated with popular Buddhism.[52]

The seventeenth-century division of Vietnam into two fiefdoms, with the north controlled by the Trinh family and the south by their rivals, the Nguyen, saw a revival of elite support for Buddhism and a reaffirmation of the opportunities for female attainment largely denied by Confucian patriarchy. When Alexandre de Rhodes arrived in northern Vietnam in 1627, for example, he found that the widowed sister of the Trinh lord, learned in classical Chinese, was termed "teacher" *(thay)* by Buddhists.[53] Princesses and concubines are frequently recorded as generous donors to Buddhist pagodas, their statues serving as public statements of their generosity. The influence of court ladies probably explains a continuing Buddhist involvement among wellborn Vietnamese men as well as women; this was especially evident in the south, where it was apparently customary for Nguyen dowagers to become nuns. Elite patrons welcomed reformist monks coming from China, and in 1695 the abbot Dai Shan "converted" the Nguyen lord and his wife.[54]

The perception that Buddhist saints and sages had joined an army of supernatural deities to whom people of any social rank could turn in times of trouble or personal need was a potent magnet in attracting female devotees. Frequently located near hills or caves long regarded as the residence of ancient spirits, Vietnam's Buddhist sanctuaries were places where a woman could plead for a son to carry on ancestral rites, for an easy birth, for the recovery of an ailing child. A deep cavern in the mountains southwest of Hanoi, for instance, became renowned for the veneration of Quan Am (or Guanyin, as she was known in China). As the female transmogrification of Avalokitesvara, the compassionate bodhisattva, she was popularly regarded as the savior of the infertile with the power to grant sons, protect pregnant women, and assure a safe delivery.[55] Her status as a bodhisattva placed her in the Buddhist mainstream, but the cultural archives that recalled her extraordinary life extended far beyond the written word, encompassing, for instance, theatrical performances like the much-loved story of her reincarnation as Thi Kinh. Unfairly accused of infidelity by her husband, Thi Kinh enters a monastery disguised as a monk. However, she inadvertently attracts the attentions of a wealthy young woman who, when rejected, turns to a farmhand by whom she becomes pregnant. Although disgraced because of accusations that "he" seduced the woman, Thi Kinh adopts the child and because of her forbearance and good deeds, ultimately attains nirvana. An eighteenth-century traveler who commented on the number of female images "holding a child" affirms the common depiction of Quan Am / Thi Kinh as a mother with a baby in her arms, a symbol that she would assist her devotees to produce an heir.[56]

The meshing of Buddhism with indigenous spirit beliefs was especially evident in the south, where the Nguyen lords were more accepting of local Holy Mother cults than the Trinh and more ready to reward female deities when they provided protection. In 1601 the founder of the Nguyen regime erected a seven-story stupa dedicated to Thien Mu, the Heavenly Mother, on a site already sacred to Po Nagar, the powerful Cham goddess.[57] Albeit reluctantly, the northern court was also compelled to ratify the authority of certain local deities, most notably that of the Lady Lieu Hanh, whose popularity had grown from the late sixteenth century. Her father was said to be the Daoist Jade Emperor (in China he has no daughter), but she also possessed a human biography, which records that she was reincarnated in 1557 as the child of pious and charitable parents. The extraordinary circumstances of her birth, her early accomplishments, and her intervention in the lives of ordinary people were transposed into legendary accounts that identified her with the Holy Mother of Heaven and the Queen of the Soil and made her a disciple of the Buddha. Confucian literati, however, were not sympathetic to Lieu Hanh veneration. In 1662 Daoist sorcerers were even recruited to expel her, but the epidemics that followed the destruction of her shrines persuaded the Trinh to accord her official recognition as a "Golden Princess, a Terrestrial mother." Preeminent among Vietnam's numerous indigenous female deities, "holy mothers," and formidable "dames," she was thought to heal the sick, drive away evil spirits, reward the faithful, and punish her enemies.[58] As her cult spread, it absorbed aspects of local deities like the Cham goddess Po Nagar, and Lady Lieu Hanh was subsequently incorporated into the Daoist pantheon as the highest-ranking immortal of Vietnamese origin.[59]

Women's participation in the mediumship, ritual songs, dances, and music that were integral to the propitiation of these powerful deities was an important component in a cultural order that asserted male superiority. Recourse to spirits and saintly figures considered responsive to the plight of ordinary people must have strengthened during the political and economic disruption that characterized the eighteenth century. Lieu Hanh's legendary generosity to the poor would have held out comfort in these stressful times, and her popularity may have prompted the biography written by Doan Thi Diem. Even Christian missionaries regarded Lieu Hanh as a formidable spirit, and in 1782 one priest admitted that she had proved impervious to exorcism and that his efforts to drive her from the body of a young woman had been unsuccessful.[60] Economic uncertainties, the weakening of political structures, and the questioning of Confucian convictions ensured that individuals regarded as conduits to supernatural forces did not lack for clients. The Le Code prescribed specific punishments for officials who failed to report women claiming to speak for a bodhisattva, but such prohibitions were not easily enforced. Attending a spirit possession ritual sponsored by the local mandarin, a Vietnamese doctor was told that the medium, the "holy mother," was very efficacious and that "if you give her money, you will make a profit."[61] Yet despite state opposition toward occult practices, there was no attempt to adopt the kind of policies employed, for example, in Ryukyu, where the government organized indigenous priestesses into a strictly regulated hierarchy.[62] In a restatement of Confucian antagonism to "magic," the elimination of spirit mediumship emerged as an official preoccupation when Vietnam was reunited in 1802. That an Englishman then traveling in southern Vietnam could still comment on the number of "priestesses" he encountered is a tribute to the strength of indigenous beliefs.[63]

Islam

Of all the world religions, Islam is arguably the most concerned with relations between men and women, although Southeast Asian historians have traditionally been more interested in the date and provenance of its arrival in the region. After decades of debate it is now accepted that permanent Muslim communities in Southeast Asia began to develop only around the thirteenth century, with the expansion of maritime commerce. A major impetus to Islam's advance came with the conversion of the ruler of Melaka, on the west coast of the Malay Peninsula, around 1430. From this great Malay port, Muslim teachings radiated out through the archipelago to the "spice islands" of the east and up to the northern Philippines. While trade links to the Middle East fostered the movement of Muslim scholars and students, a primary channel for Islamic influences was India, where there was a long history of Muslim adjustment to local customs and interaction with Hinduism. Chinese Muslims in port cities along China's southern coast also played a role in promoting familiarity with Islam via trading routes, notably in the Philippines, in Borneo, and along the north coast of Java.

Examples of powerful courts, the ambitions of proselytizing kings, and the desire to attract Muslim merchants are generally seen as sufficient explanation for Islam's expansion in island Southeast Asia. A more gendered interpretation might be attentive to the ways in which male-female relations helped transmit Islamic beliefs. Located near the north-coast Javanese town of Gresik, one of the earliest Muslim graves in Southeast Asia is that of an unnamed "daughter of Maimun" whose death is recorded as 7 Rajab in AH 475 (30 November 1082 CE). Since Muslim merchants did not normally travel with their families, she was probably a local woman who had married a foreign trader and become at least a nominal Muslim. Legend elevates her to a princess, one of the first converts, and throughout the archipelago the role of royal marriages as purveyors of Islam is a recurring theme. In the sixteenth century, for instance, a Portuguese in the spice-producing kingdom of Ternate was told that local people had accepted Islam for the sake of their king's wife, a Muslim woman from Java. Such unions were critical in creating new Islamic elites in commercial centers as Chinese Muslim men married local women or as daughters of Hindu merchants in Melaka, ordered to become Muslim, became brides of Malay nobles.[64]

The motivations underlying the process of self-identification as a Muslim (often encoded as "becoming Malay") are also amenable to a gendered analysis. Though there can be no doubt that real or putative links with Muslim potentates in Persia, Arabia, Turkey, and India augmented the standing of local Islamic courts, the status gained through conversion was by no means confined to men. Indeed, in some ways it was easier for a Muslim woman to display her piety and her links with this prestigious faith. The Qur'anic injunction that "believing women" should conceal their bodies is quite explicit, and clothing thus became a public statement by which Muslims were distinguished from the unconverted. Although full face covering never became a standard feature of female dress, seventeenth-century accounts do report veiled women in Makassar, where one chronicler stresses that this was the custom in the holy city of Mecca.[65] The revelation advising that a *hijab* (curtain) should shield the Prophet's wives from male gaze had specific implications for women in positions of authority; Sultana Taj al-Alam Safiyat al-Din Syah (r. 1641–1675), who succeeded her husband as ruler of the strongly Islamic court of Aceh, spoke to men only from behind a screen.[66] In areas where Islam had been parlayed through the Malay trading network, the "Islamic" manner of dressing adopted in Melaka and its successor state, Johor, provided the most appropriate models. In the northern Sulawesi area of Minahasa, for instance, women announced their conversion by allowing their hair to grow long, in the "Malay" style.[67]

In accordance with the Qur'an's stipulation that the Prophet's wives should remain in their homes, wellborn Muslim women could also mark off their status by a self-conscious withdrawal from public spaces. An already-existing tendency to see "inside" as the appropriate female domain was reinforced by the example of models from India and the Islamic heartlands. European observers themselves noted that while lower-class women performed outside work and sold goods in the markets, those of high birth remained inside "in the Islamic manner."[68] The Qur'anic teaching that respectable females were distinguished from their social inferiors by retreating into the confines of domestic space was emphatically reiterated by a sixteenth-century Muslim treatise from Java: "A free woman who does not stay in her house is like a slave."[69] A striking example of the way in which these attitudes helped change female behavior comes from the Philippines, where the situation in the Visayas in 1565 can be compared with that of Muslim Mindanao a hundred years later. In the former case, "many of the wives and daughters of the chiefs come to the [Spanish] camp along with the other women" to mingle with the foreign men. In Mindanao, however, ordinary women were free to approach European sailors, but those of noble birth remained in their homes, looking out at the strangers from their windows.[70]

For ordinary women, invariably alert to new sources of supernatural aid, issues of status were less important than practical benefits such as the assistance Islam offered against sickness and disease. Some suggestion of this comes through in the famed Javanese text *Babad Tanah Jawi,* where an Islamic saint cures a princess of a disease that no Javanese doctor had been able to heal.[71] Still today a grave in Makassar (Sulawesi) said to be that of Siti Aminah, the mother (or, popularly, wife) of the revered imam Sheikh Yusuf (d. 1699), is much venerated, particularly by pregnant women and mothers of small children. The healing aspect of Islam was accentuated because a well-developed pharmacopoeia of medicinal remedies was supported by innumerable hadith (precepts and actions of the Prophet) telling of miracles and testifying to the efficacy of prayers. Stories related how Aisyah, the Prophet's most loved wife, acquired medical knowledge by tending her husband during his frequent illnesses, and the inseparability of spirituality and healing made Muslim teachers a potent source of aid in societies where human life was fragile. The introduction of special birth rituals —the recitation of the *azan* (call to prayer) in a newborn's right ear, and the *ikamah* (exhortation to prayer) in the left—symbolized Islam's perceived capacity to protect infants from illness or misfortune. Equally, Muslim teachings offered pledges of support in life-threatening circumstances that were uniquely female. A text drawn up for Filipino Muslims, for example, classifies maternal death with others that deserve special treatment, a direct counter to the prevailing belief that the spirit of a woman who died in childbirth was condemned to an eternally restless and tormented existence.[72]

In any discussion of religious shifts, a major consideration is always the manner in which doctrinal teachings are conveyed. In the largely illiterate societies of Southeast Asia, Islamic-inspired stories of fable, romance, heroism, and supernatural events became a primary vehicle for imparting understandings of what it meant to be Muslim, particularly in relation to female behavior. Admonitions that the faithful would derive "merit and improvement" by listening to accounts of the Prophet and the great teachers fostered a tradition of storytelling that provided innumerable examples of correct conduct as well as reminding audiences of the punishments in store for those who defied Islamic tenets. A popular Malay collection known as the *Hikayat Bayan Budiman,* the oldest fragment of which is dated 1600, describes how a woman whose husband is absent on a trading voyage is warned by a mynah bird (the source of wisdom) to remain faithful. According to the Qur'an and the hadith, he tells her, married women who commit adultery will be impaled by the angels in hell for a thousand years.[73] In societies where marital infidelity had long been thought to result in catastrophe, this stress on sexual propriety was a powerful enforcement of existing mores. The Qur'anic episode relating Joseph's rejection of lustful advances by his master's wife was often recounted at weddings, and a Malay version of the *Hikayat Yusuf* (the story of Joseph), copied for a Dutchman in 1604, similarly reminds readers of the terrible punishments that await the adulterer in hell.[74] Reinforcing the message of constancy, the heroine of another Malay manuscript explicitly states, "We women believers should be devoted to our husbands, in the hope that we shall obtain the mercy of Allah the Exalted in the hereafter."[75]

Islam's ability to reach out to women is particularly apparent in relation to Sufism (mystical Islam) and the links it created between religious philosophy and religious praxis. Although Sufi influence was probably most influential in Java, trading connections ensured that a network of brotherhoods spread through the archipelago. The spread of Sufism had significant implications because it was generally sympathetic toward women's spiritual ambitions. The saintly Rabi'a al-Basra, born around 717 CE, stands in a long line of respected female teachers and devotees like those praised by the renowned mystic Ibn Arabi (1165–1240). In fifteenth-century Cairo, where the scholar al-Sakhawi (1428–1497) compiled a biographical dictionary of learned women, some Sufi preachers apparently addressed their sermons—best regarded as a dramatic performance—specifically to female audiences, often using the symbolism of the nurturing mother.[76] Despite debates about the propriety of some Sufi practices, it was quite permissible for women to be initiated into mystical ways. Through incoming Muslim teachers, Aceh's Sultana Taj al-Alam may have learned that Fatima (1614–1681), daughter of the Mughal emperor, Shah Jahan (r. 1628–1658), was a member of a Sufi order. The religious views of Taj al-Alam herself are not known, but Sumatran-born Sufi scholar Abd al-Rauf (1615–1693) wrote under her patronage and was also favored by the two succeeding queens. It is hardly surprising to find that Abd al-Rauf was not averse to female rule and even endorsed the eligibility of women as judges.[77]

In the wider Islamic world the willingness of Sufi masters to recast a complex theology so that it was comprehensible to unschooled audiences was a significant element in its appeal to women.[78] Local teachers in Southeast Asia proved to be equally skilled in exploiting Sufism's bank of family-related analogies, especially those that likened the believer's relationship with Allah to that of a husband and wife. The mystic Ibn Arabi had written, "The most intense and perfect contemplation of God is through women and the most intense union [in the world] is the conjugal act," and early Sufi poetry from Sumatra also speaks of the devotee "drunk with love," of flirting and "making eyes" at the Lord of the Universe," of being "captivated" by the beloved.[79] In the Indian subcontinent, Sufi poetry sung by women as an accompaniment to their household chores used images associated with female work—the grinding stone, the spinning wheel—to explain the special relationship between Allah and the devotee.[80] In a similar vein, texts from Java tapped cultural metaphors that women would have readily appreciated, comparing the acquisition of mystical knowledge to steps in the weaving process and Allah to a woman waxing and painting the batik cloth: "At the full moon, the beauty takes up the making of batik. Her frame is the wide world; her pot means 'the Lamp'; . . . the wax pen is God's pen and the material which is batiked is the Table of the Word; the patterns are the fixed essences. . . . If you are stiffened with rice water when being dyed blue and when the *soga* [a red-brown dye] is added thereto, you must not be afraid. It is the will of God that you are made red and blue."[81]

For the most part, Islam's expansion in Southeast Asia underwrites a narrative of amicable localization rather than abrupt change and dislocation. The Portuguese apothecary Tomé Pires, whose account of early sixteenth-century Melaka is one of our most valuable sources, thus commented that "when heathens marry with Muslim women and a Muslim with a heathen woman [they each follow] their [own] ceremonies."[82] Restrictions on male-female interaction were more pronounced among the emerging Muslim elite, but at lower socioeconomic levels it does not seem that existing patterns were greatly altered. Despite Islam's insistence on female virginity prior to marriage, village attitudes toward premarital sex remained generally relaxed, while in some instances Muslim teachings may have actually strengthened indigenous practices. Islamic beliefs regarding the impurity of menstrual blood, for example, had a particular resonance in areas that maintained menstruation huts, and Muslim women in seventeenth-century Ambon would have had little difficulty in accepting prohibitions against performing the daily prayers during their menses and after childbirth. By the same token, local cultures were well disposed to the idea that ritual cleansing was necessary before a husband and wife could resume sexual intercourse.[83] Customary laws that condemned adultery while countenancing dissolution of an unsatisfactory union and an acceptable division of property were similarly in keeping with Islamic injunctions. When marriages occurred between Muslims in Melaka, said Pires, "the man must give the women a certain amount of gold as a dowry, and if the husband wishes to leave her, the said dowry and the clothes remain in her possession, and each of them may marry whomsoever he pleases." It is even possible that this type of regulation may have encouraged some families to declare themselves Muslim. Later studies of Sumatra suggest that the exchange involved in the Malay *mas kahwin* (marriage money) was less onerous than the heavy payments that a bride's family expected of men in non-Islamic areas.[84] Furthermore, although Indian ideas had infused asceticism and sexual abstinence with a special authority, especially in Java, Islam (unlike Christianity and Buddhism) displayed little interest in the celibate life. The unmarried state of Jesus Christ was obviously puzzling to a later Javanese chronicler, who depicts him as a ruler with a wife, Bani, and a harem of secondary wives and concubines.[85] Nor did Islam present the ideal of a bereft wife forever faithful to her deceased husband, for the Prophet himself had married a number of widows. The attention accorded husband-wife relations in Muslim teachings thus confirmed the indigenous view of matrimony as a desirable state, with the birth of children considered essential for the full attainment of adulthood.

In her survey of Malay culture, Wazir Jahan Karim maintains that pre-Islamic customs, or *adat*, regularly redefined and reaffirmed women's social contributions after the Muslim arrival, allowing a strong role in communal life to persist despite the new privileges men enjoyed. In seventeenth-century Aceh, for instance, the respect accorded mothers, senior women, and nurses in Muslim literature was in complete accord with the customary welcome extended by older palace females and royal wet nurses when the ruler returned from the mosque or from public prayers.[86] A treatise on royal Malay *adat*, compiled in 1779 by a Melaka mosque official, details the role of Islamic officials at life-cycle celebrations such as birth and death but also shows that female specialists maintained a prominent place, especially in rituals related to betrothal and marriage.[87] A similar comment could apply to other areas of the archipelago. Since orthodox Islam frowned on loud displays of grief, authorities in Middle Eastern societies periodically and unsuccessfully attempted to ban professional women mourners. No mention of similar initiatives has been noted in Southeast Asia, where the chorus of female relatives intoning chants of desolation remained a central part of Islamic funerals; in the self-consciously Muslim environment of Aceh, for instance, a succession of selected women maintained the traditional vigil over royal graves.[88] An even more telling comment on the tenacity of older practices was the retention of "third gender" ritual figures found in a number of societies, notwithstanding Islam's abhorrence of transvestism. Banten in West Java was well known as a center for Islamic study, but in 1661, when the ruler's infant son set foot on the earth for the first time, "men in women's clothes" danced for what must have been a very special occasion.[89]

This is not to imply, however, that change did not occur. One significant outcome of Islam's endorsement of remarriage was the demise of the (always limited) widow sacrifice previously found in Hinduized Java. In the early sixteenth century Tomé Pires noted that Muslim women, unlike the "heathens," did not sacrifice themselves on their husband's bier, although it was quite common to retreat to some kind of hermitage in the mountains.[90] These social shifts were part of more extensive developments that gave the ruler—now the Shadow of God on Earth—a greater role in defining and enforcing acceptable behavior. The earliest evidence for this comes from the Malay Peninsula, where a fourteenth-century edict lists a variety of punishments for sexual crimes, including fines, stoning, and flogging. A partially legible section also prescribes penalties for women who "do not have a husband" and who "cause trouble."[91] It was probably in household arrangements, however, that changes associated with Islam made their most immediate impact. One obvious area concerned food preparation, since pigs had provided the most important ritual food and the most valued blood offering through much of island Southeast Asia. In birth rituals recorded in early nineteenth-century Manado (northern Sulawesi), for instance, a newborn baby's right hand was washed in the blood of a sacrificed pig, and an origin legend collected from another Sulawesi group even speaks of an ancient pig-mother.[92] Because the care of pigs was largely a female responsibility, the gendered ramifications of Islamic aversion—even the smell of pork could be deemed contaminating—must have necessitated substantial adjustments in ritual foods and ceremonial preparations.

The domestic sphere also became the arena in which the family displayed its Islamic affiliation through rituals like male circumcision, previously practiced in numerous Austronesian and Pacific cultures as a rite of passage to manhood, and now elevated into a Muslim obligation. Early Spanish dictionaries of Visayan convey something of this enhanced status, noting the displacement of the indigenous word for a type of circumcision, *tuli,* by *magislam,* meaning to perform the ceremony according to the Muslim rite.[93] Since circumcision was thought to guarantee a man's reproductive capacity, it was of intense concern to women; in Ambon the procedure was a prerequisite for marriage, and in its absence a woman would refuse to have intercourse.[94] By contrast, there is little historical information about female excision, which involved a small cut to the clitoris and was apparently introduced to Southeast Asia through Islamic channels. A rare mention is included in a seventeenth-century account of Makassar compiled by Nicolas Gervaise (1662–1729) from information provided by two young nobles. Gervaise, a priest attached to the Société des Missions Étrangères de Paris, was told that girls were circumcised so that they too would have the means of attaining salvation. It was always a private ceremony, and recovery was rapid, since the next day the patient was able to walk about.[95] On the basis of later evidence from Java we can infer that the procedure was more common among high-status families as a sign of their adherence to Islam and of a girl's readiness for marriage. In one of the few references to specifically female rituals in the Surakarta court, the diary of the female guardswoman mentions the circumcision of the ruler's daughter without providing further details.[96]

Perhaps most importantly, the household provided the setting for the negotiation of new understandings of marriage resulting from the encouragement that Islam gave to polygamy. In societies where the possession of numerous women already displayed wealth and power, and where legendary heroes were always possessed of great virility, "being Muslim" was often thought to entail the taking of a second (or even a third) wife. The Prophet's own marriages were an important theme in his biography and would have resonated in the prosperous coastal towns most exposed to Islamic influence. Scattered references, however, also hint at the distaste with which ordinary people viewed the idea of "sharing" a husband. During his visit to Minahasa in 1679, Robert Padtbrugge (1638–1703) noted the growing acceptance of two or more wives but remarked that some men refused to be party to this "adultery," shaving their hair around to the level of their ears as proof they that were true to one wife.[97] A Sumatran law code collected in the early nineteenth century suggests the kind of compromise that could help allay resentments and help maintain domestic peace. If a man wished to marry for a second time, especially as his first wife passed her childbearing years, he had to pay her a compensation, which she divided into two halves, keeping one herself and sharing the rest among the village's older women.[98]

In the cultural negotiations involved in being both Muslim and female, Qur'anic traditions offered a range of models well placed for transposition into newly Islamizing societies. Given the respect for senior women in Southeast Asia, it is somewhat surprising that Khadijah, a wealthy widow who became the Prophet's first wife, receives little attention in vernacular literature. Perhaps, as Leila Ahmed suggests, her autonomy and economic independence were at variance with Islamic ideals, for in Southeast Asia, as elsewhere in the Muslim world, a special place is reserved for Fatimah, the Prophet's daughter.[99] Malay stories such as *Hikayat Nabi Mengajar Anaknya Fatimah* (The Prophet teaches his daughter Fatimah) present her as the ever-attentive pupil, listening carefully to instructions about a woman's duties, including the admonition that she should think carefully before she speaks.[100] As is proper, she is heartbroken when her father dies, and a Bugis manuscript depicts her public display of grief in the traditionally accepted manner. "It is dark for me, not only at night," she intones, "but in daytime too I am in darkness."[101] In her marriage to Ali, Fatimah represents the ideal wife, remaining loyal even when accused of infidelity. In popular thinking, her name carried extraordinary power and could be invoked to lull a child to sleep, to protect an infant from illness, or to foster longing in a woman's beloved. As one poem puts it, "Let me be clothed with the heavenly joys of Siti Fatimah! / Let them spread through my body, / Let the treasure in them enter the brains and limbs and sinews of my love." It was thus quite fitting that a seventeenth-century manuscript should record a pilgrimage to Fatimah's grave in Medina by the Malay hero Hang Tuah.[102]

The image of a loyal and long-suffering Fatimah can be juxtaposed with that of Aisyah, remembered as the Prophet's most loved wife, a virgin at marriage and a devout woman also unjustly accused of infidelity. Although she wore the veil in public, she assumed a prominent role in the Islamic community after the Prophet's death, including her celebrated participation in "the Battle of the Camel."[103] Known for her intelligence and her appreciation of doctrine, she is important as a transmitter of hadith that are especially relevant to women, such as those dealing with reproductive functions and sexual intimacy.[104] She is also credited with asking questions about potentially perplexing traditions, such as the belief that those who rise from the grave on the Day of Judgment will stand naked before God, despite Islam's emphasis on body covering. A Malay commentary attributes Aisyah with obtaining an acceptable explanation: "One day I asked the Prophet of God, 'How will the people appear who are resurrected from the grave on the Day of Judgement?'. . The Prophet of God said, 'All those resurrected . . . will be naked.' So I said, 'Will all the women be naked too?' The Prophet of God replied, 'All the women will be completely naked.' So I asked, 'Won't all the women feel ashamed?' The Prophet of God replied, 'The events at the time will be so important that no one will be concerned with other people, nor will anyone even notice other people. Each will be concerned with themselves; no one will feel any curiosity towards other people.'"[105]

Local cultures assembled their own company of Muslim heroines, who were not merely physically attractive, pious, and faithful but could also display a religious erudition that was equal to that of any man. For instance, a beautiful heroine of the late eighteenth-century Javanese text *Serat Centhini* eclipses her brothers and other Islamic scholars in her knowledge of Qur'anic exegesis and her understanding of the hadith.[106] Nor did such women exist only in texts; Kartasura's queen mother, Ratu Pakubuwana (1657?–1732), sponsored several Javanese works with a Sufi orientation and may herself have been a Sufi disciple, while the mother of the famed prince Dipanagara (1787?–1855) is known to have been an Islamic teacher and scholar.[107] Yet there was never any possibility of such women assuming positions of Islamic leadership, although the Shafi'i school of law, which dominates Southeast Asian Islam, permits women to take part in communal prayers, and initially females were not excluded from the Friday services. However, the mosque soon became the preserve of men, and Muslim women offered their prayers at home or made their offerings and petitions at graves and tombs associated with holy figures. Thus in sixteenth-century Brunei "the women never go [to the mosque] but it is the men." For a female to intrude into this domain disgraced not only herself but also her husband and family. In Makassar a leading ulama accordingly divorced his wife "as unworthy to be the wife of a priest of the Law" because she had attempted to enter the mosque where men were praying. In 1687 Valentijn was told that elderly females or widows in Ambon were sometimes allowed to enter the mosque but were relegated to a separate section.[108]

By the end of the eighteenth century, Islam was far more firmly established in the archipelago than it had been two hundred years earlier. Debates over the religious duties of a Muslim, and the differences between Muslims and non-Muslims, gained added intensity as the territorial control of the Dutch East India Company expanded, and as the Spanish authorities in the Philippines renewed their attacks on the Muslim sultanates in the southern Philippines. Though Southeast Asia's Muslim world remained populated by a multitude of indigenous deities and spirits, and spirit mediumship still provided the means whereby women could gain recognition as healers and seers, a long line of Islamic teachers saw such practices as unacceptable polytheism. A reformist movement that had gathered pace in the Middle East and India could not fail to make its presence felt in Southeast Asia. Writing in the 1780s, the Palembang scholar Abd al-Samad deplored the widespread custom of spirit propitiation, arguing that those claiming to be possessed had simply fallen under the control of evil forces.[109] Further examination of the literature of this period may reveal a growing concern with maintaining the male-female distinction as a heightened sense of "being Muslim" encouraged a more forthright challenge to the accommodations that had long characterized Southeast Asian Islam. A text commissioned by Ratu Pakubuwana, seeing divine retribution behind the destruction of four villages where "evil behavior took place, illicit sex among men who forgot their wives," could well represent a response to the preference of her grandson, the Kartasura ruler, for male partners. The perception of feminized men as somehow subversive to the patriarchal order also gained ground. In translating a well-known Arabic treatise into Malay, Abd al-Samad apparently altered the original slightly to strengthen the condemnation of men who wore women's clothes and did women's work.[110]

Greater awareness of religious practices in the Muslim heartlands, encouraged by increasing communication between Mecca and Islamic Southeast Asia, was reinforced by a rise in the numbers of Arab migrants. Most prominent were descendants of the Prophet, sayyids from the Hadhramaut, where upper-class female seclusion was a fact of life. Indeed, Francis Light (1740?–1794)—a man with much experience in the Malay region— considered sayyid "jealousy" regarding their womenfolk to be "extreme."[111] Marriages between these newcomers and local elites, which resulted in the succession of several part-Arab rulers, buttressed the state-religion alliance and reinforced the trend toward a more assertive patriarchy. This is not to imply, however, that Muslim communities were moving inexorably toward restricting female space, for the particularities of local contexts were always in play, and historical contexts could change. In seventeenth-century Mindanao the seclusion of wellborn Muslim females had been a matter for comment, but in the 1770s when the English trader Thomas Forrest (1729?–1802?) stopped at Jolo in the Sulu archipelago, he remarked that upper-class Muslim women "all over the island" rode out publicly on their horses.[112] Still in modern times visitors more familiar with Islamic societies in the Middle East or South Asia have continued to comment on the "relative freedom" of Muslim women in Southeast Asia.

Christianity

The Portuguese conquest of Melaka in 1511 inaugurated Christian proselytizing in Southeast Asia. Ten years later a Spanish expedition led by Ferdinand Magellan reached Cebu, although the Catholic missionary orders were energized only after the capture of Manila in 1570. During the following century Christianity was established in the Philippines, apart from the Muslim south. In the Malay-Indonesian archipelago the Jesuits had been in the missionary vanguard, but Catholic fortunes suffered a major reverse when the VOC, essentially a Protestant organization, seized Portuguese positions in eastern Indonesia and successfully besieged Melaka in 1641. While the VOC's primary concern was always trade rather than conversion, the Reformed Church wielded considerable influence in towns and other places under direct Dutch authority.

In mainland Southeast Asia the field was left open to Catholic initiatives, with the Jesuits arriving in Vietnam in 1615, to be joined in later years by representatives of other orders. As in the Philippines, internecine rivalry was often acrimonious, especially after the Missions Étrangères de Paris (MEP) set up a base in Siam in 1662 and from there sent priests to Burma, Cambodia, and Vietnam. Despite claims of thousands of converts, missionary activity was always restricted because Vietnamese emperors, like their East Asian counterparts (and occasionally Siamese kings), were suspicious of the new loyalties Christianity demanded.

The most detailed descriptions of the gender order that Christianity promoted in Southeast Asia come from the Philippines, where missionaries had their most lasting success. The MEP archives are providing new insights on developments in Vietnam, but there has been less research on other mission fields like Timor. Nonetheless, it is still possible to suggest several subject areas where meager documentation might be supplemented by regional comparisons. The first of these could focus on Christianity's preoccupation with eradicating "devil worship" and its practitioners. Both Catholic and Protestant authorities were inclined to see women as a potential medium through which Satan could work his malevolent designs because of female prominence in indigenous ritual. Since "witchcraft" was tantamount to heresy, such women must be purged from the community.

In sixteenth-century Melaka, for instance, the Portuguese captured and excommunicated a number of "enchantresses," apprentices of feared forest-dwelling groups, who allegedly transformed themselves into "lizards and other animals and birds in order to do evil."[113]

Without the support of a European administration, missionaries in mainland Southeast Asia were more constrained. Accordingly, any conversion of local "sorcerers" was regarded as a significant achievement. In 1669 an MEP priest thus proudly reported that he had baptized an old "prophetess" who had more than fifty apprentices, forcing her to acknowledge that her rituals were a deception.[114] As a corollary, Christianity could provide protection against female susceptibility to unwelcome spirit possession; another MEP missionary reported that women came seeking "remedies" that would drive off demons in human form who approached their beds at night: "By the grace of God, all those who carried small fragments of the Agnus Dei [medals imprinted with the image of the Lamb of God, blessed by the Pope] were no longer molested by the devil."[115]

Spanish animosity to animist priestesses in the Philippines was particularly unforgiving, since *baylan* were not only ready to arrogate Christian symbols and preach their own form of the new faith but were also leaders in several local rebellions. For those captured, retribution was swift and harsh. In 1663 "a shameless prostitute" who had assumed the title Maria Santisima (Mary Most Holy) died a horrible death, her body impaled on a stake. As European authority became entrenched, missionaries in the Philippines could proceed virtually unchallenged, humiliating ritual leaders and publicly burning their sacred items.[116] The same processes can be tracked in Taiwan, where the Protestant Dutch similarly regarded indigenous priestesses, the *inib,* as an obstacle to the Christian undertaking. In consequence, idols and "pagan" paraphernalia were destroyed, animist rituals were proscribed, and the *inib* were physically removed from their communities. In 1641, 250 *inib* were banished from the core area of Dutch control and resettled in a northern village. When the ban was lifted eleven years later only 48 old women were still alive.[117] In eastern Indonesia the Jesuits had also led a vehement campaign against "devil worship," and after the Portuguese eviction the Dutch followed similar policies. In Ambon, hundreds of spirit houses and effigies were burnt, and individuals accused of maintaining "heathen" statues were threatened with execution. We can only guess at the social and cultural costs of such campaigns. Offended by the sexual explicitness of an erect penis, VOC officials ordered the destruction of a male image, but since it was believed to aid female fertility, where then did childless women turn?[118]

A second area amenable to regional comparisons concerns the perception of Christianity as a "healing religion." Local beliefs that Christian baptism guaranteed either recovery from illness or entry into Paradise were fostered by biblical accounts of miracle cures and missionary willingness to attend the sick in the hope of gaining another convert. In Siam, for instance, most baptized adults were non-Thai (Lao, Mon, or resident Vietnamese), and Christianity was never a serious alternative to Buddhism. Missionary prayers and holy water were nonetheless regarded as a source of supernatural power that could protect individuals in this life or guarantee a happy rebirth in the next. Parents were eager to have infants christened, sometimes two or three times, no doubt receiving comfort when some priests dressed children who had died before baptism as angels, with wings of gold paper and crowns of flowers. Buried in a special section of the Christian cemetery, they were deemed to be safe from eternal entrapment in some frightening limbo. "Small children at death's door," wrote one MEP missionary, "are the greatest fruit of our mission," and another recorded that over a six-year period he had baptized "three thousand of these little saints."[119] The expectation that the Christian gods would honor the obligations incurred when an individual was baptized or made certain vows or performed penitential acts was another inducement to adult conversion. A female medium in southern Vietnam even told an apostate to reaffirm his belief in Christianity because she considered its genie a more appropriate healer for his illness. On the other hand, if the Christian deities failed to honor their contract, or if prayers and propitiation proved ineffective, a convert could always return to the ancient spirits and to the individuals through whom they spoke.[120]

In a period where every conception was a potential death knell, the view of Christianity as a religion of healing contained a special message for women. In sixteenth-century Spain and Portugal, statues of the Madonna in the last stages of pregnancy continued to attract the devotion of Catholic women, despite the Church's view that these were disrespectful or even sacrilegious. Transported to Southeast Asia, the image of Mary, either alone or carrying the Holy Child, introduced a new genre of representational art to a world where depictions of gods and ancestors were highly stylized. As the ideal mother, she remained intimately concerned with all aspects of a believer's life; in Melaka her statue had reportedly wept at the approach of the Protestant Dutch forces in 1641.[121] A compassionate deity who was at the same time human, Mary was also thought to have a greater understanding of female concerns, and it was her statue in a Portuguese church that led a queen of Arakan to inquire further about Christianity.[122] Such images were saturated with memories of the debt owed by all individuals to the woman who had given them life by risking her own existence. In the Philippines the special bond between Mary and her son, her presence at the crucifixion, and her maternal links with the disciples became a core theme in the retellings and dramatizations of the Pasyon, the story of Christ's life. The impact of such stories must have been heightened when the Madonna portrait was depicted with dark skin and with the earrings and long hair of a Filipino woman.[123]

In Vietnam, Jesuit missionaries seized on the idea of filial obligation, delivering sermons remarkably similar to Chinese Buddhist writings that stress a son's indebtedness to his mother. Vietnamese themselves saw other parallels; statues of the child-giving Quan Am closely resembled the Madonna and Child, and one hagiography urges young women to emulate Mary and her devotion to her mother, Anne, in a manner reminiscent of the Buddhist Thi Kinh story.[124] In the same vein, Vietnamese fishermen readily identified Mary with the protective goddess of the oceans, since the swirling veil and the surrounding clouds depicted in statues and paintings were thought to symbolize a small boat riding on the waves. Alexandre de Rhodes himself recorded that he was saved from a storm at sea by throwing a precious relic, a hair of the Holy Virgin, into the ocean. Across Christian-ized Southeast Asia, the belief that the faithful lived under the watchful eye of "the good Mother" is affirmed in recurring stories that relate how a beau-tiful lady, magnificently garbed and wearing a jeweled crown, miraculously appeared to repel some impending danger.[125]

Mary, of course, did not stand alone. While few saints were introduced to Vietnam, a veritable army arrived in the Philippines, all of whom were willing to act as intercessors and to exercise their own powers on a peti-tioner's behalf. The Jesuits were especially supportive of female saints, but Santa Lucia (Grandmother, Apo Bakit, as she was called by Ilocanos), believed to cure disease of the eye, was a special favorite because she could also cause rain to fall. Since the missionary cause was likely to benefit when an individual's return to good health was attributed to Christian rituals, priests did not hesitate to exploit perceptions that their gods were directly concerned with female well-being. In a typical case in 1667 a Vietnamese family of thirty was baptized because they believed Christian prayers had saved a kinswoman who was three days in labor. Even in death, however, missionaries offered comfort by pledging that a baptized woman dying in childbed would find happiness in the afterlife rather than perpetually wan-dering as a dissatisfied spirit.[126] Promoted by the friars, Jesuit founder Saint Ignatius became (like the Buddha's disciple Angulimala) a protector of pregnant women; his help could be solicited to facilitate an easier birth.[127] And while the Protestant Dutch were determined to eliminate the "idola-try" they associated with Catholicism, the ministers of the Reformed Church found that they themselves were sometimes attributed with special powers. In Ambon it was commonly believed that a pregnant woman who had fallen victim to malign magic could be cured by drinking a potion contain-ing dust from the stairs of the pulpit where the minister had walked.[128]

A third area for cross-cultural comparison could focus on the benefits of conversion, which for some women was purely pragmatic. For example, in the Dutch-controlled settlements of the Malay-Indonesian archipelago, Christians had access to Church charity, an attractive option when the cus-tom of manumitting slaves on an owner's deathbed led to a steady rise in female poverty. An indigent Christian woman or a widow was entitled to seek support from Church funds, which helps explain why 67 percent of the 2,300 members of Batavia's Reformed Church in 1674 were female, with around 80 percent of these being former slaves.[129] However, we should not underestimate female perceptions of Christianity as a new arena where spiritual ambitions could be recognized and accepted. The good works and religious study encouraged among Christian women in Vietnam, for instance, were in keeping with expectations already familiar from Buddhism. Wellborn and educated ladies, whose baptism brought "great joy" to missionaries, could also display their literary skills in the Christian environment. In the early seventeenth century one erudite female convert composed a number of poems on sacred themes—the creation of the world, the life and passion of Christ, and the history of Christianity's arrival in Vietnam—which became popular among Christians and non-Christians alike.[130] A favored concubine of the first Nguyen lord, and mother of his last son, is an early entry in a long list of court women who accepted Christianity. Secretly baptized as Mary Magdalene, she became a fervent supporter of the Catholic mission.[131] However, Christian conversion was never an easy choice for Vietnamese women. Official reprisals could be harsh, and even in Siam, converts were at times treated as traitors. Accepting Christianity could close other options, since missionaries were totally opposed to the notion that a widow could transfer property to a village in return for a pledge to maintain ancestral rites in her honor or in honor of her parents. Yet the martyr's crown has a unique status in Christian beliefs, and missionary letters from Vietnam and Siam laud the dedication of women, from slaves to royal concubines, who endured extreme punishment when they refused to abjure their Christian faith.[132]

Because of the Chinese example, associations exclusively for Buddhist females were probably already known in Vietnam, but the idea of a celibate collective where young, single females as well as older widows could seek spiritual advancement was more forcefully endorsed in Christian thinking. No European nuns came to Ayutthaya or Vietnam before the nineteenth century, but MEP priests in 1670 decided to found a religious community for women, in part because of petitions from converts, in part because Vietnamese men were now being ordained. Members of this new community, Amantes de la Croix (Lovers of the Cross), were expected not merely to continue with their prayers and religious duties but also to undertake charitable works, attend to the education of girls, and treat "female illnesses." They usually came from the oldest Christian families, which had already supplied sons and brothers for the priesthood, but although Amantes leaders were normally older widows, many of the devotees were young, in contrast to the typical Buddhist nun.[133] A girl's resistance to marriage arrangements was often cited as a reason for flight to an Amantes house, and youthful fervor probably explains emotional displays of devotion to Christ and his Passion. In one dramatic episode a young woman even pressed a red-hot medallion of the Sacred Heart against her own, "imprinting her body with this sacred image."[134] Though missionaries initially doubted whether celibacy could be maintained (and there were certainly several pregnancies in the early years), the Amantes de la Croix established their own credibility, with some even authorized to baptize infants in danger of death. These Church-sponsored communities (reaching a total of around twenty in northern Vietnam for most of the eighteenth century) stimulated other female initiatives. In 1683, for instance, a Vietnamese priest visited one village where there was a considerable number of Christian converts. Here he found ten women who, though not living together in a community, met to perform pious works, funding their efforts with the profits they earned from their trading activities.[135]

Catholic authorities in the Philippines, unconvinced that "Indians" could have a true spiritual vocation, were somewhat less supportive of female religious houses. The Church's male-dominated hierarchy preferred to see lay piety manifested in donations to Church coffers, in public and regular worship, in participation in seasonal rituals and holy day processions, and in self-mortification and penance. In this context, the establishment of a "third order" for native women was not easily accomplished. Under Franciscan auspices, Mother Jerónima de la Asunción founded Manila's first community for nuns in 1620 but encountered opposition from the authorities when a Spanish-speaking Filipina sought ordination. In 1697 a royal order finally decreed that pure-blooded "Indian" women were eligible for entry into convents. The Jesuits, meanwhile, had taken the lead in founding sodalities for girls, and in 1684 they sponsored the foundation of a religious house specifically for "pure Indias or mestizas." Ignacia del Espíritu Santo (1663–1748), the driving force behind this Beaterio de la Compañía de Jesús, was the daughter of a Chinese father and a Tagalog mother and was known for her extreme asceticism. Though not cloistered, her community of *beatas* (blessed women), or *mantelatas* (veiled women), professed chastity and obedience, spent much time in prayer and spiritual exercises, and carried out charitable works such as teaching girls and caring for the poor, sick, and elderly. Like the other *beaterios* established during this period, La Compañía de Jesús opened up a domain where women were able to organize themselves (in some cases even voting) and to gain recognition for their particular skills.[136]

It is difficult to assess the influence of the Filipino *beatas*, for although they were active as teachers and in charitable work, their numbers were never large. In 1748, not long before Mother Ignacia's death, the congregation she had founded comprised only fifty women. No *beaterios* in the Philippines during this period attained true convent status, and communities were always subject to some religious order or to clerical visitations. In 1715, when fifteen *beatas* in one of the small islands north of Luzon petitioned to live in a cloister, the archbishop dismissed their request as "a simple caprice of young girls inspired by imprudent zeal."[137] As elsewhere in Asia, *beaterios* often became pawns in disputes between orders or with the (male) church hierarchy. The historical evidence is itself open to varying interpretations. In Vietnam, for example, the Amantes communities can be seen as sites of female subversion, where the distinctions of age and class were set aside in ways that challenged the social order. Yet it is also claimed that by the end of the eighteenth century the Amantes houses were largely maintained as residences for priests, where female "charity" was expended in tasks like embroidering priestly robes.[138]

A fourth topic for cross-regional conversations could analyze those areas where the missionary enterprise generated contention. For European Protestants and Catholics alike, the inculcation and maintenance of sexual "morality" and the fidelity of wedlock was a cornerstone of the Christianizing project. However, the demand that intercourse should occur only within a lifelong monogamous relationship formally sanctified by the Church introduced local societies to radically new ways of thinking about marriage and the family. In Vietnam, MEP missionaries constantly lamented the contradictions between local customs and Christian mores, noting that virginity and marital chastity were difficult to police in villages where prenuptial sex was accepted and where movement in and out of domestic relationships was relatively relaxed. Men who had grown accustomed to measuring status in terms of sexual access to several women were loath to accept the notion that monogamy was a requirement for conversion. Secondary wives and concubines eager to convert were similarly told that baptism was contingent on regularizing their marital status. Missionaries aroused considerable hostility when they unilaterally "annulled" existing unions so that a convert could remarry another Christian; between 1687 and 1697 the north recorded about six hundred cases. However, because female converts outnumbered males, it was often difficult to arrange acceptable marriages for Christian women.[139] Nor were Vietnamese parents necessarily pleased with the establishment of religious houses for girls, since a daughter's withdrawal from the world could deny them the grandsons necessary to maintain ancestral rites.

European authorities in the Philippines and other areas in island Southeast Asia were equally adamant that marriage was the basis for a Christian community, but new laws were not easily enforced. Authorities in Manila approved unions between Chinese men and local women only when both parties were Catholic, but many Chinese accepted baptism merely to obtain a wife, whom they deserted on their return to China.[140] In addition, ecclesiastical jurisdiction in regard to "sins" such as concubinage and bigamy challenged many traditional practices. For example, Spanish priests condemned the custom by which a young man worked for his prospective bride's parents, claiming that it was conducive to illicit sexual relations prior to marriage. A campaign to eliminate bride-service launched at the beginning of the eighteenth century empowered priests to marry a cohabiting couple immediately, but in doing so, the Church unwittingly increased the burden of debt that a new husband carried into his marriage.[141] Although officials were instructed to deal lightly with offenders accused of immorality, individual priests (sometimes themselves maintaining "housekeepers" and fathering children) did employ corporal punishment, including flogging and various types of penance. Even if nonphysical, the punishments meted out to those "living in sin" were real enough, for they were denied burial in consecrated ground, and their children were prohibited from receiving baptism.[142] VOC authorities were similarly insistent that marriage was mandatory for cohabiting Christian men and women, and the Dutch Reformed Church became a tireless guardian of morality. In most cases misconduct was handled at the parish level, but between 1677 and 1693 the consistory censured over eight hundred Batavian Christians for more serious offenses, accusing about half of infringing sexual mores or marital norms. Exclusion from communion was a common form of public humiliation, but in the ongoing campaign against concubinage there was still a racial dimension, and a native woman would be punished more severely than the European man with whom she lived.[143]

Finally, a regional overview might consider the extent to which the Christian enterprise contributed to a reshaping of ideas about desirable female behavior, given the patriarchy inherent in the missionary worldview. As the Jesuit Pedro Chirino explained to his superiors in 1604, "one of the greatest fruits" of early missionizing in the Philippines was the promotion of "reticence and modesty" among Tagalog and Visayan women. Previously, he said, adultery and lack of premarital virginity had been tolerated by Filipino society, but he now claimed that women were resisting the advances of those who would "dishonor" them, presumably by initiating sexual relations.[144] Although it is not possible to track the mental processes behind shifts in indigenous constructions of femaleness, Christianity could draw on a battery of tools that both inculcated and enforced "new standards of premarital and marital morality." Foremost among these tools were confession, penance, and the culture of guilt. The intrusive questions listed in a Tagalog *confessionário* specially written for the Philippines ("Did something dirty come out of your body? Did you cause her to emit something dirty too? How many times did each of you have an emission?") indicate the intensity with which the Church developed its sexual doctrine.[145] In Vietnam, Alexandre de Rhodes told aspiring Christians that Eve was to blame for mankind's fall because she had strayed from Adam's side and had not taken flight immediately after the devil spoke to her. "May this example," he wrote, "teach women . . . not to enter ready conversations with strangers, especially when they are alone, so as not to be deceived."[146] When such exhortations failed, an individual should, of course, be punished. In the

Philippines a woman who failed to appear at Mass, or whose morals were considered suspect, could face a beating or have her head shaved. In Ambon the VOC governor imposed fines for "carnal knowledge" before marriage and, in response to complaints from Islamic leaders, forbade Muslim wives to spend nights away from home without their husband's permission.[147]

A primary vehicle for promoting this new gender order was religious education, most evident in the Philippines, where Christianity established an overwhelmingly dominant position. Although functional literacy among Filipino females was always limited, by the late eighteenth century many girls had been exposed to some school experience. The Spanish goal of basic education for both sexes entailed far more than reading and writing, and the ideals of modesty, chastity, and obedience promoted by Christian/Castilian culture could not fail to influence the way in which daughters were raised. A dramatized Tagalog version of the Pasyon thus presents the young Mary and her cousin Elizabeth as modest young convent pupils who spent their time embroidering and observing their devotions.[148] Despite constant complaints of "immorality" from Catholic friars, the impact of missionary efforts is very apparent when we compare the behavior of well-born Filipinas in the mid-eighteenth century with the unabashed sexual advances that their forbears had made to Spanish soldiers two hundred years earlier.

THE EXPANSION of the world religions is not merely a defining feature of Southeast Asia's "early modernity"; it was also fundamental to evolving cultural constructions of being female. In sketching developments over more than three hundred years, this chapter began by tapping data from the Philippines in order to think about women's position in indigenous belief systems. Although this material appears to highlight female participation in ritual matters, alternative examples of male superiority should caution against regarding Southeast Asia as an exception to what some would see as a "global inferiority of women" in sacrificial systems. Among the patrilineal Toba Batak of Sumatra, for example, women frequently acted as *sibaso,* or shamans, but a much higher position was accorded the male priests, the *parbaringin.*[149] Nonetheless, it does appear that the allegories of fertility and reproduction symbolized by the female body allowed women significant roles in ceremonial life even as these same powers necessitated their exclusion from many male activities. Equally significant was the rise in status that transpired as an older woman, no longer embodying emasculating female forces, was welcomed into a larger ritual space.

By contrast, the basis for authority in the world religions—written scriptures, classical texts, and traditions of commentary—invariably privileged literate men. Yet though references to female spiritual and intellectual inferiority were persistent and persuasive, these traditions were always amenable to alternative interpretations, and it would be misleading to assert an unambiguous narrative of declining female status. Women were obviously attracted to the imported faiths and were quick to seize opportunities to enhance their reputation for piety. Ancient beliefs did not disappear, and women were still seen as privileged channels to the supernatural. Yet the ethical and religious systems that became so dominant in early modern Southeast Asia justified and affirmed a new authority for men, and even women who were considered exemplars of piety and virtue could not maintain their reputation without the imprimatur of male approval. Exponents of Southeast Asia's "relatively high female status" have responded to allegations of religious subordination by pointing to the independence women gained through their prominence in the domestic economy and their capacity to generate and control their own resources. Historicizing this economic involvement is therefore central to any exploration of the female past in Southeast Asia.

CHAPTER 4

Women and Economic Change

From the fifteenth century, widening networks of domestic trade and connections with international markets began to transform local economies in many Southeast Asian communities. These developments are most apparent in insular Southeast Asia, where Portugal's conquest of Melaka in 1511 foreshadowed the arrival of other Europeans whose intrusion ultimately undermined indigenous commerce. Following the capture of Manila in 1570, Spanish colonization drained the vitality from the Philippine economy and developed landed estates that exploited peasant labor. Established in Batavia (present-day Jakarta) in 1619, the Dutch East India Company eventually became the dominant power in Java and imposed monopoly contracts throughout the Malay-Indonesian archipelago in an effort to control trade. By contrast, mainland Southeast Asia had only limited interest for European commercial ventures. Without the pressures exerted in the island world, mainland governments were able to exercise greater agency in responding to the presence of foreign traders, whether European or Asian. Despite periodic collapse and recurring warfare, a trajectory of economic growth was generally sustained into the early nineteenth century.[1]

Discussions of economic change in Southeast Asia during this period rarely address questions of gender, despite the touted authority of women in the household, their prominence in local marketing, and their acumen in business affairs. Yet the economy/gender interface is fundamental to "herstory" because contemporary research has shown that a woman's physical welfare, self-esteem, and group standing are directly related to her ability to manage her own resources and the value placed on her work. Offering a variety of environments, Southeast Asia is again an attractive laboratory in which to investigate women's economic roles and how these were affected by global markets, the commercialization of traditional tasks, greater interaction with foreign men, and the growth of urban centers.

Women as Food Producers

The expansion of international trade often disadvantaged Southeast Asian women, but several constants reinforced their economic standing in the household. Limited grazing lands precluded the herding cultures that privilege men, while low population densities enhanced the value of all individuals, regardless of sex. Since the gendered division of work located key activities such as weaving, gardening, and food preparation in the female domain, a wife had responsibilities not easily delegated to her husband. One cannot, of course, generalize too broadly, since these distinctions were less pronounced among nomadic jungle groups and the *orang laut,* the boat-dwelling "sea people" who roamed the coasts and offshore islands. Women paddling small boats were no particular novelty in riverine and coastal villages, but in 1675 Padtbrugge remarked that among the Bajau, the sea people of Manado, female crews navigated deeper waters "as well as the men, moving like heroines of the ocean among the reefs."[2] It has been suggested that the aquatic motifs on female-produced bark cloth along New Guinea's north coast may reflect women's local role as the primary fishers, their skills much in demand when men sought brides. Contemporary descriptions of "female hunters" among one foraging group, the Agta of the Philippines, complement a sixteenth-century Spanish illustration showing a "pagan" woman accompanying her husband, carrying her own quiver and arrows.[3]

Despite their importance as collectors of jungle and sea produce, nomadic and semi-nomadic groups only rarely enter the historical record. Written sources are more revealing about female work in sedentary settlements, with one of the earliest being a 1621 account of Ambon by VOC employee Artus Gijsels. Like later observers, he expressed amazement at how interior women—"beasts of burden"—could negotiate the steep mountain paths down to the markets while carrying loads weighing as much as forty pounds.[4] Writing at the same time, the Dutch cleric Candidus described a coastal village in Taiwan, as yet untouched by Chinese migration. He was similarly impressed by female diligence, remarking that women were occupied "from morning till night"—cleaning the house, cooking, caring for pigs, gathering wild fruits, collecting shellfish, and trapping fish, often by wading out into deep water "without any men attending."[5]

Because these descriptions were still pertinent in many Southeast Asian communities in recent times, a retrogressive but judicious use of nineteenth-century sources and oral material can be methodologically acceptable. In recounting preparations for a celebratory feast, for example, an Iban ("Sea Dayak") chant from Borneo presents quite distinct understandings of male-female responsibilities. The felling of trees, the setting of traps, drugging and stunning fish, hunting with packs of dogs, cutting up wild pigs, participating in enemy raids, the smoking of trophy heads are all men's tasks. But, the chant goes on, "what, in this all-important gathering, will be the part of women?"

> We want to call a gathering to discuss the collecting of bamboo, / even though we've only just done with the making of baskets; / we want to call a gathering to discuss the collecting of ginger / Even though we've only just done with the testing task of dyeing; / we want to call a gathering to dis-

cuss the collecting of fibers for *ikat* tying; / even though we've just done
with our weaving of a splendid fabric *(pua)*. / We want to call a gathering
to discuss the setting up our looms / Even though we've just done with our
weaving of a splendid fabric *(pua)*[6]

In a context where activities like threading a loom or fashioning a pot could
be infused with symbolic meaning, this call to work is a reminder of the
"religious" component embedded in so much economic activity. For example, the Iban word *gawa* means both "work" and "ritual," and the etymolog-
ically related term *gawai* refers to the most elaborate, complex, and prestigious ceremonies.[7] The interlacing of work and ritual is nowhere more
evident than in the planting and harvesting of food crops.

The argument that sedentary agriculture advances the male position is
not easily applied to Southeast Asia, which has sometimes been compared
to tropical Africa in the prevalence of "female farming." Household gardening requires not so much strength as care and attention, and the absence
of heavy agricultural tools and draft animals in much of colonial Indonesia, though exasperating to Dutch officials, is quite normal in societies
where agriculture is largely a female responsibility.[8] Another dimension to
women's involvement, however, was the ritual associated with germination,
maturation, and harvesting. While the perception of the planting cycle as
the equivalent of human conception, pregnancy, and birth is common to
many agricultural communities, the personification of the earth as a woman
and the image of plants growing from the body of some female deity or
ancestor are recurring motifs in Southeast Asian mythology.

Modern studies of women's agricultural work in Southeast Asia have
concentrated on rice cultivation, but there were many areas where crops
such as yams and tubers were the staple diet. Various species of sago palms
growing in coastal swamplands yielded an edible pith that provided another
basic carbohydrate. However, although the processing of sago flour and the
preparation of the dried biscuits that fed crews on innumerable overseas
voyages were tasks for women, the palms themselves were chopped down
by men. Unlike the femaleness surrounding rice cultivation, sago symbolism appears to favor masculinity. The Asmat of West Irian personify sago as
a male culture hero, and men affirm a pact of friendship by exchanging the
larvae from the eggs of the Capricorn beetle, which lives on felled sago
trees.[9] Yet some legends still emphasize links with an ancestress, describing
the palm itself as the metamorphosis of a female body whose sweat becomes
the life-sustaining sago pap. The uncoupling of sago harvesting from the
female role of food provider is explained in a story from the island of
Siberut (off west Sumatra), according to which women lost their function
as collectors when they offended the first sago palms. An intriguing theory
suggests that eastern Indonesia once supported dwarf varieties, which

women could more easily cut but which were gradually displaced as populations grew and larger trees were preferred.[10]

The drought-tolerant millet, another staple when climate or soil conditions were unsuited to rice, was unequivocally personified as female, and both legends and ritual underscore women's nurture in caring for the infant crop.[11] In the sixteenth century, maize introduced by Europeans began to replace millet and was subsequently incorporated into ritual life. In east Borneo two hundred years later only maize was eaten during periods of community mourning.[12] In the harsher environment of Timor, women and girls performed ceremonies that ensured the maize seeds they planted would be successfully born from the earth and attain maturity without misfortune. Should these rituals be ignored, the crop could well fail, leaving a household to eke out its meager food supplies until the dry rice could be harvested.[13]

The allegories that linked plant growth to human conception and birth were most elaborated in relation to rice. The perception of the rice seed as a baby that needs to be "delivered" is nicely captured in one Malay manuscript, which relates how the royal midwife herself plants the community's first seeds. Rain rituals mimicking sexual intercourse, digging sticks in the shape of a penis, and irrigation ditches compared to birth canals all attest the strength of the fertility metaphor.[14] The widespread Southeast Asian personification of the rice deity as a beautiful young woman is reminiscent of grain goddesses in other preindustrial societies (though apparently absent among Han Chinese), but historians are also fortunate in the wealth of ethnographic data relating to female-dominated fertility rituals.[15] Among the Toraja of the Sulawesi highlands, for instance, the seed intended for the next harvest was traditionally released from the husk not by the trampling of buffalo or threshing flails but by the gentle pressure of women's feet "walking" on ears of rice spread on a wooden plank.[16]

Although hundreds of rice varieties are grown in Southeast Asia, a broad distinction is usually drawn between "dry" and "wet" methods of cultivation. In contrast to the more mobile lifestyle associated with rain-fed, or "dry," rice (commonly grown by the slash-and-burn method), irrigated or bunded rice encourages the growth of larger sedentary populations that are more amenable to state demands. The importance of female labor in all methods of rice cultivation meant women were deeply implicated as production expanded during the early modern period. However, there is some debate about the impact of farming technologies. In Taiwan, the plows and draft oxen introduced by VOC officials enhanced the agricultural role of men rather than women, and in northeast India the shift to irrigated rice is said to have demoted Garo women from partners in swidden agriculture to helpers in a male enterprise. Yet in Japan, where rice rituals have been compared to those of Java, the expansion of agricultural land in the seventeenth and eighteenth centuries made the female contribution even more important than before, especially in the "sacred labor" of transplanting rice seedlings.[17]

The Southeast Asian material is open to various interpretations. The development of the plow certainly elevated the male position in some wet-rice areas, although buffaloes or sometimes horses were often used to churn muddy plots prior to planting. A Chinese tutor, Wang Dahai, who spent several years in Java in the 1780s, specifically commented on the absence of both plows and hoes.[18] In areas where dry rice was grown, always in smaller plots and often on steep slopes, plows were virtually unknown. Although the clearance of tree cover was a "male" duty, work assigned to women stretched over a longer period, since they planted the rice itself, tended and weeded the young seedlings, and were essential in harvesting and threshing. The importance of female labor is indicated by the gendering of tools, like the *anih-anih*, the small harvesting knife, and the miniature sickle attached to a thin wooden handle that Chin women used for weeding.[19] In Java, colonial officials estimated that women devoted roughly twice as much time as men to rice cultivation, especially in nonirrigated areas.[20]

The steady increase in rice cultivation provides convincing evidence of its status as Southeast Asia's favored food staple, even though tubers, roots, and sago demand less labor and are more reliable. The versatility, taste, and prestige of rice may account for this preference, but it is intriguing to think of less obvious reasons, like the fact that infants can digest rice more easily than sago flour. Thus, in commenting on the lengthy breast-feeding of Bajau children, Governor Padtbrugge noted that rice was used in weaning as an alternative to sago.[21] Feminist archaeologists have seen shellfish middens as evidence of ancient collection by women, and the same could be said of rice supplements, the bulk of which were obtained by female foraging, small-scale hunting, and collection of wild plants. A modern study among farming families in northeast Thailand notes that "wild foods," largely gathered by women, make up an estimated 50 percent of total consumption. Insects, fish, snails, and small crabs are routinely eaten, and the collection of insects such as grasshoppers and crickets as well as freshwater shrimp, crabs, tadpoles, mollusks, and snails is almost exclusively female.[22]

Women's role in food production, while hardly unique to Southeast Asia, was particularly significant in a region where men were so often absent—as monks, raiders, hunters, fishermen, sailors, soldiers, traders. A case study of several skippers sailing from Java's north coast in the 1770s shows that on average they captained a vessel only twice during a three-year period, but they could be at sea for up to six months or even longer.[23] In many areas protracted warfare contributed toward a persistent gender imbalance; as a Spanish missionary in sixteenth-century Cambodia put it, "women work the soil while their husbands make war."[24] Labor obligations imposed on men also wreaked havoc with gender ratios. Indeed, Nicolas

Gervaise specifically noticed that women in Ayutthaya were left in charge of the family when husbands were called up for corvée.[25] European regimes could be especially exploitative because officials were largely indifferent to unwritten rules that governed labor services. In 1583, for example, Filipino men whom the Spanish authorities sent to work in the gold mines of Ilocos were not permitted to return in time to prepare the rice lands for plant-ing.[26] Despite a subsequent reduction in labor requirements, gender dis-crepancies in the Philippines are evident even when we allow for ambigu-ous census categories. In 1760 the entire count for "young women" in the Augustinian parishes was 32,958, far more than the equivalent male figure (21,926).[27] A comparable imbalance could be found in Java, where the forcible recruitment of hundreds or sometimes thousands of peasants to serve in the VOC army had far-reaching consequences for kampong life. By the mid-eighteenth century, villages around Batavia were drained of young men, and soldiers returning from VOC campaigns were often disinclined to return to agricultural work.[28]

It is impossible for a historian to reconstruct the informal structures by which "women's work" was organized, but the mortar of female collabora-tion was normally ties of blood or marriage, particularly in areas of matrilo-cal residence. Organized around a core of related women, these groups pro-vided opportunities for senior and respected individuals to emerge as heads of joint activities, like the twenty-five "work leaders" associated with a south-ern Thai *wat* who were named in a decree of 1610.[29] Even the closest kin group paid due deference to status and age, as suggested in Edward Dal-ton's 1850 description of Shan women returning from the fields. They had been collecting firewood, he noted, but while "each woman bore an axe and a faggot of wood," the chief's wife carried a small ornamental imple-ment and a miniature bundle of little sticks, "evidently emblematic rather than useful."[30] In lauding the achievements of senior women, like "Grand-mother Jelapi, famous for her pickled pork because she is skilled in the trapping of pigs," the Iban chant recalls not only the hierarchies of the work environment but also the economic visibility of females and their value to the household. In Java, wrote Wang Dahai, "the concerns of each family are managed by women, hence parents consider it of importance to have daughters born, by the marriage of whom sons-in-law are brought into the family; but when a son is born they are less pleased, because at his marriage he goes out to be housed elsewhere."[31] Nonetheless, there were societies where attitudes were undergoing change. In Bengal, for instance, the Mus-lim preference for women to remain near or within the house meant they were less visible as field laborers. The same trend can be found in Aceh, long noted for its stricter observance of Islamic law. By the nineteenth cen-tury and probably before, men had assumed sole responsibility for harvest-ing, a contrast to two other Sumatran societies, the Batak and Minangk-abau, where it was primarily a female task.[32]

Women and Land

The expectation that a woman would stay close to home helps explain why land and houses in Southeast Asia were so often inherited through the female line. Feminist anthropologists have been particularly attracted to the matrilineal Minangkabau of central Sumatra, where adult males were expected to migrate (*merantau*) for extended periods as workers and traders. The origins of this custom are unclear, but from the sixteenth century it gathered pace as new economic opportunities like gold mining and pepper farming lured men out to the Sumatran coasts and beyond. The Minangkabau are often regarded as exceptional, but the passage of land through the female line was more common in Southeast Asia than is normally recognized; in contemporary Laos, for instance, people remember that in the past women inherited or accumulated more land than their brothers.[33] Female inheritance had significant implications for the absorption of male migrants in a region where travel and adventure conferred men with cultural status. In the fifteenth century, Sumatran newcomers in the Melaka area acquired land rights by marrying the daughters of aboriginal families, and despite Ambon's tradition of patrilineal descent, outsiders could gain access to land through unions with local women.[34]

The ease with which a daughter's husband became a son raises questions about the realities of female property rights. Inheritance in Sri Lanka and south India, as in much of Southeast Asia, was matrilineal or bilateral. This could reinforce a woman's economic and social security, but the extent to which she controlled her property is open to question.[35] As yet, the Southeast Asian material is too fragmentary to warrant any generalization, although it would appear that inherited land could not be alienated. In 1769 missionaries in Cambodia attempting to purchase land were told in no uncertain manner that it was a sin for a family to sell "Madam the Sacred Earth," and according to Malay sources, daughters who brought inherited rice land into a marriage had no power to alienate family holdings. Any sale had to be negotiated and approved by men.[36] A text from southern Thailand listing a long line of women—mothers, daughters, and daughter's children—whose maternally inherited lands were dedicated to a *wat* gives only the slightest impression that this bequest resulted from a female initiative: "All these ladies were/are of one kin group."[37] It is also evident that European authorities, who regarded a written document as the new proof of land ownership, favored male descent. Despite an awareness of the Minangkabau tradition of matrilineal land inheritance and the female contribution to agriculture, for instance, English East India Company survey books from west Sumatra list only the names of male cultivators, merely noting whether they were married.[38]

There is somewhat more detail regarding female landownership in Vietnam because of the state's long-standing preoccupation with cadastral surveys. Few early registers have survived, but in 1968 a series of enactments from the fifteenth and sixteenth centuries were found in a cave about fifty kilometers west of Hanoi, with the fingerprints and names of women who had bought, sold, and mortgaged land.[39] Material from the early eighteenth century provides more solid evidence that a peasant woman could become a landowner in her own right, like a certain "Lady Nguyen who made her fortune" by amassing several thousand *mau* (one *mau* = about a third of a hectare). Surviving registers from the late eighteenth and early nineteenth century indicate that in districts around Hanoi about a quarter of all land-holders were women, although their average holding was two *mau*, as against three overall.[40] Whereas the inheritance rights of Chinese women declined after the Song period, Vietnamese wives and daughters continued to enjoy access to the estates of husbands and deceased parents. A will drawn up in southern Vietnam in 1818 shows how this operated in practice. An elderly villager and wife divided their land equally between two sons and three daughters, with the eldest son allotted the rice fields that would support the ancestral rites. If this couple had been without sons, however, such supervisory rights and the necessary land would probably have gone to a daughter.[41]

Nonetheless, we must avoid pressing the Vietnamese evidence too far. The claims of a male heir were always paramount, even when he was an adopted rather than a natural son, and Nhung Tuyet Tran cites several eighteenth-century cases where daughters received no inheritance at all. In any event, women's landholdings were usually smaller than those of men, and they were disproportionately represented among smaller and poorer farmers. At the other end of the scale, female landlords were few in number and their holdings less extensive than those of their male counter-parts.[42] A somewhat similar pattern might be tracked through the Burmese material. A survey of eighteen *thet-kayit* (loan documents) from one upper Burma village shows that although wives are co-mortgagees in eleven instances, they are never mentioned by name. In most cases women are included in the transaction and may have exercised some influence in the decision-making process, but there is no clear evidence showing that women took out independent mortgages or exercised autonomous control over land.[43]

Other customs, however, buttressed the position of Southeast Asian women in the agricultural economy and made a daughter a valued resource. In most communities a marriage ceremony or its equivalent was the culmination of a long period of reciprocal exchanges, but frequently this exchange (which European observers often described as "buying" a wife) favored the bride and her family. Even when a prospective son-in-law mortgaged his own labor in lieu of marriage gifts, bridewealth enhanced household resources and could help a father repay the debts he had incurred by his own marriage. The economic ramifications were immense.

Like Wang Dahai, European commentators in the seventeenth and eighteenth centuries frequently noted the wealth of men who had fathered several daughters. In Timor, "even a common man is considered rich when he has many daughters because on their marriage he receives valuable payments of gold and buffalo," and an Englishman stationed in west Sumatra put the case succinctly: "the more females in a planter's family, the richer he is esteemed." While such comments occur more frequently in sources from island Southeast Asia, a Chinese observer in Vietnam also remarked on the delight with which parents greeted the birth of a daughter.[44]

The circulating heirloom objects often included in the bride-price—old gongs, elephant tusks, certain kinds of cloth or beads—are another indication of the value placed on marriage. However, these precious items were not easy to obtain, and one can track a growing trend whereby coinage became a convenient replacement for otherwise scarce and expensive items. In turn, this could provide the catalyst for other developments, as suggested by later ethnographic material describing the effects of commoditization. Among Burma's Chin communities prior to World War II, for instance, cash was initially used to buy heirloom goods, with monetary equivalents established for the exchange. This introduction of money not only inflated marriage payments and encouraged a tendency to see wives as "bought" but also accentuated status differences as wealthy families accumulated more prestige goods.[45] Elsewhere in Southeast Asia one can locate comparable processes by which the nature of betrothal and marriage relationships changed as "traditional" items were accorded a monetary value. For example, on the island of Selayar, off the Sulawesi coast, the bride-price was once rendered in gold grains weighed against pips of the *nane'* tree, but the increase in monetized trade made it easier to pay the required amount in Spanish reals, proportionate to a girl's standing.[46] By the early nineteenth century, when bridewealth costs had increased considerably, men from the island of Seram were looking eastward for cheaper Papuan brides. Nonetheless, they still had to pay a prospective father-in-law a couple of *lela rentaka* (small cannon), a few copper gongs, and some cloth.[47] Furthermore, as one anthropologist working in the Vietnam highlands observed, ultimately no payments could truly compensate a family for the loss of a daughter's support and labor.[48]

A Changing Commercial Environment

The changes induced by the increased circulation of coinage were merely one aspect of new trade patterns that introduced an enormous range of new products into Southeast Asian societies. Historians have concentrated on bulk imports like Indian cloth and Chinese ceramics, but in local markets the female demand for less conspicuous items could also generate significant profits. A Visayan vocabulary compiled by a Spanish missionary even includes the term *biniyaga,* meaning "to sell notions to women." One could cite, for instance, a casual European reference to the trade in needles, which are listed along with combs, bracelets, glass beads, and "womanish curiosities."[49] It is unclear whether metal needles were used in the embroidery that so impressed Alfonso d'Albuquerque when he captured Melaka in 1511, but in an environment where many women sewed with bones, sharpened wood, or porcupine quills, fine needles were a prized acquisition. The queen of Brunei would undoubtedly have been delighted to receive a silver case "full of needles" presented to her by Magellan's crew.[50] In the early seventeenth century, needles costing about a penny apiece in Macao could be sold for a real in southern Vietnam, and it is understandable that a Cambodian *chbab,* a verse guide to good conduct, should exhort a housewife to put her needles away safely.[51] Further, while Southeast Asian textile collections demonstrate women's ability to incorporate new materials and adapt foreign designs, the acquisition of new skills is also evident in "female work" that has received less attention. Introduced to the lace-making techniques of Europe, for example, women in Melaka developed their own complex patterns, sometimes using as many as a hundred bobbins, boasting names such as *siku keluang* (bat's wing) and *perut lintah* (leech's stomach).[52]

Beads were another import that attracted a highly discriminating clientele, especially among tribal groups in Borneo and northeast India. As heirlooms, beads were a valued item in ritual exchanges and could assume a sacrality that was beyond economic value. Colors or styles in high demand found a ready market, and VOC representatives in Sukadana (western Borneo) used blue glass beads bought from the Chinese to purchase local diamonds.[53] Though beads were worn by both male and female, threading and application to textiles were everywhere the work of women, who were also the primary purchasers and collectors. In the nineteenth century, women in the Chin hills bought beads whenever possible, even coming down to bargain for pieces dug up in the sites of ancient settlements. Among the Kayan of Borneo a rich man's wife could own old beads valued at thousands of dollars and would wear many of them, especially on festive occasions. At her death they would be passed down to her daughter, together with any precious cloth she possessed.[54]

Although the effects of commercial changes could be discussed in a number of "female" contexts, like food preparation, the production of pottery and textiles has been the most extensively explored. Archaeologists are generally unwilling to attribute gender to pot making, but excavations of mortuary sites point to the antiquity of female involvement, perhaps because containers were infused with the symbolism of gestation and death. Secondary burial in jars was once practiced through much of Southeast Asia, and womblike associations may explain why pots placed next to bodies in southern Philippine graves were apparently deliberately broken.[55] As containers for food and drink, pots were also freighted with ideas of maternal nurturing. Indeed, the handleless pouring vessels known as *kendi* found throughout Southeast Asia often have a bulbous spout shaped to resemble a woman's breast. An Assam manuscript describes how a *swargadeo* symbolically adopted a Mughal representative as his son, sending him clothes, food "of the kind produced in my country," and a vessel with a spout that "is like the breast of my wife; drink water from there."[56]

Studies of Southeast Asian pottery have focused on the glazed ceramics produced in various mainland locations. However, despite influences from outside, most obviously China, the ceramic heritage drew heavily from basic skills developed in the making of local earthenware, almost invariably a family enterprise dominated by women. An eighteenth-century wall painting from a Pagan temple, for instance, depicts two women and a flirtatious youth beating pots with wooden paddles, while a man and a woman offer others for sale and men bring armloads of wood to a kiln ready for firing.[57] In areas where the clay was suitable, and where competition from cheap imports was limited, female potters could generate their own reputation. In Minahasa, Padtbrugge reported that the best pots were made by the sea-dwelling Bajau, with women using their hands and thumbs to make the shape and then completing the process with flat pieces of wood.[58] That this paddle-and-anvil technique ignored the potter's wheel, even when it was available, might seem to support claims of an innate female conservatism, but changing designs and pot shapes indicate that women (who were users as well as producers) were alert to possible improvements. On the Khorat Plateau in Thailand, where pottery has been made for hundreds of years, cord marking increased the surface area, allowing for greater heat absorption and more efficient cooking, and perhaps keeping stored water cool. Other potters adapted their designs to accommodate market demands, with villages around popular pilgrimage centers producing specialized products like incense holders or vases for flowers. As mothers, daughters, and sisters worked together with local clays, communities also developed distinct potting styles, for which they may even have claimed ownership. When the island of Banda was depopulated by VOC policies in 1621, women who fled to the nearby Kei Islands took their pottery traditions with them, making their own mark on the bottom of their pots.[59]

For many families the manufacture of "gerabah" (earthenware) so often mentioned in VOC lists of native cargoes, remained an important means of supplementing household income, especially when little agricultural land was available. Ceramics, both local and imported, were treasured for their colors and varied designs, but earthenware pots could still hold a child's umbilical cord, a fetus after a miscarriage, the ashes of a deceased relative, or holy water blessed by a priest. The symbolic capital represented by seemingly mundane containers made pottery production more than a simple economic enterprise and helps explain the persistence of traditional techniques. In parts of Maluku, men are still debarred from clay-collecting areas, and in other places pottery was largely undertaken by old women whose reproductive years were past. In a cultural context where potting was a female occupation, Christianized Visayans even called the Creator "the potter" (mamarikpik).[60]

Though evidence is meager, women probably retained a leading role when communities concentrated on producing glazed ware and ceramics for a commercial market. This seems to be the case in Vietnam, where the introduction of Chinese techniques and a high degree of specialization allowed local industries to survive the influx of imports, especially with the new opportunities offered by maritime trade. Initially it might seem that men would be favored because of their access to the labor and capital necessary to compete in a more commercialized environment. However, although bulk transactions were usually (but certainly not invariably) a male affair, especially as Chinese merchants entered the market, local exchanges relied heavily on a female network. With production based on household/ kinship units, women traders bought pots from kilns managed by their sisters and cousins; ambitious men used the income generated by their womenfolk to pay the poll tax or purchase a rank in the village hierarchy.[61]

It is in relation to the production of textiles that "women's work" in Southeast Asia has established a unique reputation, and the association between weaving and "femaleness" is extremely strong. Indeed, it comes as something of a shock to read that in India magnificent styles were "kept alive over the centuries, passed from father to son."[62] Indian women certainly played a key role in ancillary tasks like warping the loom, but professional weavers were almost always male. This marginalization of women in commercial textile production can be traced in other parts of Asia. Chinese officials, for instance, continued to laud spinning and weaving as a female task, but economic development under the Ming led to a two-tier system, where "woman-loom cloth" made by farming families was considered inferior to the "waist-loom cloth" produced by skilled male artisans and weaver households. As in China, Japanese women also continued to weave cotton textiles, but in the lucrative silk industry they were increasingly relegated to the labor-intensive work of tending silkworms and reeling thread, with the finest fabrics produced on looms operated by men.[63]

The gender specificity of Southeast Asian cloth is of immense significance in assessing community attitudes to women's work. Basic to many local economies, especially in times of food shortages, cloth could be used for all manner of exchanges and in some areas did actually function as a currency. On the island of Buton (near Sulawesi), for instance, small rectangles of rough cloth were woven and sold as a monetary equivalent that circulated in surrounding areas.[64] The increasing commoditization of cloth meant that a female slave who wove well might command around 130 reals (perhaps more than a skilled man) in Batavia's slave markets, while in mainland Southeast Asia hundreds of women were sometimes captured as prisoners of war specifically for textile production. As late as 1832 about four thousand weavers were taken to Bangkok from the southern and largely Malay province of Patani.[65]

The centrality of textiles, however, was less a function of their economic role than their place in the ritual life of most Southeast Asian communities. Long before looms or shuttles entered the region, bark-cloth beaters were buried with women in ancient grave sites, attesting a female-cloth nexus deeply embedded in Austronesian cultures. In the Pacific, for instance, the making of tapa (bark cloth) was everywhere the responsibility of women, a signifier of femaleness that was commonly adopted by male transvestites.[66] Though noting that in some places "women are always working at [bark cloth] very curiously," travelers in Southeast Asia rarely accorded more than passing reference to textile-related rituals. One exception is the perceptive Governor Padtbrugge, who recorded that, in Minahasa, bark was gathered only at specific times, and complete silence was observed until the work was completed. The ritual potency of bark cloth dictated its usage long after other textiles became available, and at the twentieth century it was still standard wear for female shamans in central Sulawesi.[67]

Although an intimate relationship between women, cloth, and ritual can be traced across Southeast Asia, textile production was immensely enhanced by the spread of cotton. Imported from India through expanding trade networks, the cotton plant (*Gossypium herbaceum* and *G. arboreum*) was far more suited to spinning and weaving than the indigenous cotton tree (*Bombax insigne*). Displacement of existing materials such as hemp was by no means immediate, however, and in some markets fabrics made with techniques other than weaving were still preferred. In the 1650s, women along the Sulawesi coast produced bed hangings and blankets of bark cloth "dyed in all colors," which found a ready market in overseas ports. Filipino women made cloth from abaca and other vegetable fibers, and girls in Minahasa split and chewed young bamboo to make it more pliable for weaving, then decorated the finished product with glass and coral.[68] It was cotton, however, that allowed Southeast Asian textiles to reach extraordinarily high standards of beauty and technical skill, even with simple backstrap looms. Initially cultivated in home gardens with other plants or in combination with dry rice, it quickly became a standard crop, generating, for example, the extensive vocabulary in a Spanish Tagalog dictionary.[69] Again, the resulting fabrics were more than simple covering, for a cloth produced in the right circumstances, incorporating certain colors and patterns, could protect a man in battle, assist him in the hunt, instill fear into his enemies, and even incite him to the warpath.[70] Permeated with potent healing and regenerative powers, textiles both wrapped the newborn and shrouded the dead. In this sense, weaving represented the apogee of female achievement. Among the Iban, where it was "the woman's warpath," the highest honors were paid to those who had mastered the designs for the huge ceremonial cloths that received severed heads, and the hands of a great weaver were tattooed as a public statement of her prowess.[71]

The ethnological literature contains few references to rituals involved in the planting and spinning of cotton, but material about other aspects of weaving is rich and informative. As one might expect, the application of dye was traditionally the work of women, who collected the basic plant ingredients like the roots of the *Morinda citrifolia* shrub and the *kombu* tree, both of which yielded a reddish brown dye.[72] The widespread use of this color, its similarity to menstrual blood, and the womblike vats in which it was prepared may provide an underlying explanation for the frequent exclusion of men from the dyeing process and its attendant rituals. In Sumba the menses are even known as *wai kombu* (*kombu* water), and the vocabulary associated with dyeing replicates that used in childbirth.[73] By extension, the act of weaving itself was surrounded by restrictions that took careful note of a woman's personal condition and specified inauspicious times for setting up the loom, such as the appearance of a full moon. On the island of Sawu (eastern Indonesia), weaving was restricted to certain times of the year, and the success of the project could not be assured unless chickens were sacrificed to the appropriate ancestors.[74]

There is a danger, however, of exaggerating the hold of "tradition" over women's economic choices, since cloth production was time-consuming and onerous. In 1780 a Dutch writer affirmed that a Javanese woman needed about a month to spin a pound of cotton thread and that the physical toll of the backstrap loom was particularly harsh. Weaving had remained "women's work," he believed, primarily because the remuneration was so low. A Vietnamese lament conveys something of the entrapment that many women probably felt: "Is this my fate as a young girl in her prime? / Days spent at the market and nights spent spinning and weaving at home?"[75] Domestic resources could certainly be supplemented, and household and ritual needs supplied, but the availability of cheap Indian cloth (itself produced with poorly paid female labor) and more lucrative sources of income presented an attractive alternative. By the early seventeenth century, Banda was just one of several areas where local weaving was displaced as women used money obtained from nutmeg sales to purchase cloth, sago, and rice brought by traders. At this time Eredia said categorically that there were "no weavers" in Melaka and that the textiles people bought came from Coromandel and Bengal.[76] However, when Dutch monopolies caused prices of imported textiles to rise, women returned to weaving, and in the 1690s an envoy to the Sumatran state of Jambi told his superiors that there was a loom in every house. In some areas the VOC attempted to monopolize cloth sales by persuading native rulers to ban cotton growing, but women easily ignored these ill-enforced prohibitions or circumvented them by buying imports from areas outside Dutch jurisdiction.[77]

Commercialization: Cloth and Cash Crops

It is hard to overemphasize the importance of the cloth trade in Southeast Asia's economic history. In Siam alone, annual imports of cloth in the seventeenth century may have numbered around 75,000 pieces, with even more staggering figures for the Malay-Indonesian archipelago.[78] Yet while the rarity and value of imported textiles ensured a supply of elite customers eager for brocade, velvet, and lace, the vast range in prices meant cheaper pieces were also available to people of modest means. Furthermore, despite formidable competition from imported fabrics, female ingenuity and a willingness to respond to specific markets ensured the survival of local production. The spun cotton thread exported from Bali to Makassar, for instance, had apparently been prewashed, resulting in textiles that did not shrink like those in some other markets. In eighteenth-century Palembang the problem of fading had been successfully overcome so that cloth could be washed, while around the same time the development of a more durable sarong in Burma is also attributed to female initiatives. Because Indian dyes were superior, Burmese weavers mixed imported red yarn with their own white and blue thread to produce fabrics that were in high demand among the elite.[79]

These developments should not be read as an unambiguous narrative of economic triumph, for though female weavers in some areas maintained a clientele, commercialization inevitably advantaged men's access to financial resources. The Chinese and Indian merchants who so often acted as creditors were accustomed to weaving guilds or subcastes under male authority, and the operations they financed transformed many women from independent producers into something approaching wage laborers. Virtually the entire female population in Javanese villages that specialized in weaving or spinning could be producing yarn and textiles, which were then engrossed by some creditor, usually a Chinese man.[80] Some entrepreneurs had already begun extending credit to peasant women in return for guaranteed deliveries of cheap textiles, frequently decorated by simple batik techniques. By the 1690s, cargoes of rough cloth "painted" with flowered designs were already undercutting piece goods imported by the VOC along Sumatra's east coast. The seriousness of this challenge (which even prompted the Dutch to consider banning imports of wax into Java) suggests more than a cottage enterprise; indeed, workshops similar to those known from the nineteenth century were already in place. In the Chinese quarters of Java's urban centers, local wives and female slaves provided the labor for an escalating industry where women had largely lost control over production. As slave owners or creditors, Chinese traders supplied the cheap batik textiles that women hawked in the street or sold in market stalls, and as cloth peddlers they moved into an occupational area where indigenous men had rarely ventured.[81]

The shifts in gender roles resulting from the growing commercialization of textile manufacturing are most evident in relation to silk weaving. The chronology of the introduction of the silkworm (*Bombyx mori*, a native of northern China) into mainland Southeast Asia is uncertain, since there was a much older tradition of producing silk from the pupae of indigenous moths like the large *Attacus atlas*. The breeding of *Bombyx mori* was limited because only certain climates were suitable for mulberry trees or acceptable substitutes. Probably because of the connections with India, sixteenth-century Aceh was already known for its silk exports, but despite archaeological evidence of silk weaving in the cooler highlands of northeastern Thailand, the French envoy de la Loubère said categorically that there were no silkworms in Ayutthaya. Both Dutch and Spanish authorities concluded that local silk production would not be cost-effective, and the sumptuous *kain songket* (embroidered cloth) found in Sumatra and the Malay Peninsula were generally made with imported thread and raw silk from China.[82]

There were, however, several areas where *Bombyx mori* did flourish, one of which was Assam. Here silk made from the cocoons of a native moth had once been an important export item, but it fell from favor following the introduction of the mulberry worm, which resulted in finer silk that was easier to work. As in India, the commercialization of production meant male control, with seventeenth-century accounts of Assam even referring to "weaving castes."[83] To some extent a similar pattern can be discerned in Vietnam's silk-producing districts. In the 1770s a Vietnamese scholar wrote a brief history of a weaving village located close to Hue, consisting of thirty households that each included fifteen weavers. According to legend, a "remote ancestor" of these families had acquired weaving skills from the Chinese, a significant heritage because looms in Chinese "weaver households" were normally operated by men, with women rearing silkworms and reeling thread from the cocoons. When VOC officials negotiated silk purchases, they usually dealt with a mandarin or a court eunuch, although an American trader in the early nineteenth century could still refer to women manufacturing "some of their silk stuffs."[84]

Large-scale production also generated a greater demand for dyes, especially indigo, which is easily fixed to cotton. Its antiquity is attested by the indigenous nomenclature found in Austronesian languages (for example, *taum* in Balinese, *tayom* in Tagalog, *tarum* in Malay), and the rituals that continue to surround the dyeing and preparation of indigo in some areas affirm its place in the female cultural lexicon. In recent times the people of Tuban (north-coast Java) still compared the indigo vat to the "womb" of the cloth and placed it under the guardianship of elderly women.[85] Women could also retain a position of authority even when the indigenous state intervened to impose levies and collect taxes. A *sit-tan* (land register) from Burma thus refers to a woman, Mi Win Tha, who was responsible for collecting dues on indigo dye, which she then submitted as crown revenue.[86]

Yet male labor was almost inevitably favored when indigo became an export crop, although it was not easily transferred from women's gardens to large estates. In the eighteenth century new indigo plantations also helped restore some respectability to the VOC's precarious finances, but the company was asked to provide some training because indigo growing was unfamiliar to local men.[87] In less than a generation the number of dyeing "factories" on Java had risen considerably, and European specifications regarding the organization of the labor force, "half-naked [male] native coolies," presents a remarkable contrast to the female domination of indigo production in more remote areas. No commercial enterprise, for instance, could tolerate ritual restrictions like those imposed on Sawu, where the collection of living coral to supply the lime that served as mordant was traditionally limited to only ten days per annum.[88]

The case of *Piper nigrum* (black pepper) offers another example of an increasing preference for male workers in a male-dominated economy. Introduced from India, pepper was initially interplanted with dry rice and cotton, using labor organized around the family unit. Men cleared the land, while women and children planted out the young vines, kept them clear of weeds, and trained them around the prop plants until they matured (about seven years). Picking the berries could be undertaken by both sexes, but women were responsible for sifting and drying the pepper in preparation for the market. Surplus pepper could be included among other garden products traded by women, and in Banten in 1598 female hawkers were selling both food and pepper to incoming merchants.[89]

The nature of female involvement began to change with a rising world demand for pepper and the arrival of eager buyers from overseas. Instead of long hours spent spinning and weaving, women could now use their pepper profits to purchase attractively patterned Indian and Chinese cloth at low prices. However, pressure from coastal chiefs and foreign traders to increase production soon met grower resistance. Women were central to this resistance because the small family unit typical of most upland communities was simply unable to cultivate the amount of pepper demanded by downstream authorities, especially when this meant rice or cotton planting were neglected. For many families the hiring or recruitment of laborers, often through the purchase of slaves, was the only way to support a successful plantation. The clothing and feeding of dependents placed a new burden on the household economy, absorbing much of the surplus income previously available. Despite Dutch attempts to "extirpate" cotton, the area under cultivation fell steadily as poor returns for pepper and the higher prices of Indian textiles encouraged women to return to weaving.[90]

Developments along Sumatra's west coast were similar. Determined to outstrip their Dutch competitors, English East India Company officials at Bengkulen disregarded local pleas to limit the pepper quota to five hundred vines per family. As a result, a married couple and their children could be required to maintain as many as two thousand pepper plants at one time. In addition, the English introduced new methods of cultivation that required the ground to be kept free of undergrowth for most of the year. Such injunctions were particularly onerous for women because weeding was traditionally a female task, and when a young woman married, she and her husband immediately became responsible for a thousand vines. This fell heavily on a new bride, who was expected to take on most of the field work, and may explain why some women preferred to remain single. The requirement that youths as young as sixteen should assume responsibility for their own gardens also ignored the fact that weeding was demeaning for a man. It is not surprising that there are constant English complaints of gardens "choked with weeds" or that many young men simply abandoned their plots and left for the coast. Male migration to areas beyond English jurisdiction reduced the number of eligible husbands, and by the early nineteenth century there was a substantial number of unmarried women of all ages throughout the Bengkulen districts.[91]

In short, then, cash cropping was not easily adapted to existing gender divisions in labor and marketing. The prominence of women in petty trading in most of Southeast Asia was undoubtedly due to the fact that district markets were located close to home and family and thus the transportation of produce was not problematic. According to eighteenth-century records from central Vietnam "it was very common to see women going to market or traveling on horseback." However, long absences from home were difficult when a wife was expected to maintain gardens, assist in planting and harvesting, and supervise household affairs.[92] Men were further advantaged because the distant coastal ports where foreign traders gathered were the most important exchange points, creating an environment in which all the visible links in the commercial chain—agents, buyers, scribes, weighers, captains—were male. In Sumatra the assignment of menial work to women was especially pronounced in the Dutch and English trading posts, where female slaves were used for the tedious task of sifting pepper. The occasional woman who appeared as an independent and prominent trader was usually a widow who had inherited her husband's interests.

Some foreign men, especially the Chinese, realized the value of the female contribution and were quick to obtain "wives" or purchase slaves to assist in pepper transactions and assume responsibilities when a trader was absent. Such women, however, were privileged servants rather than independent agents. By the mid-eighteenth century, farmers in Sumatra had largely abandoned pepper in favor of rice and cotton, as well as new garden crops like tobacco and coffee. The world demand for pepper led to the establishment of new plantations in the 1790s, but they were financed by Chinese or European merchant houses and relied on male labor. Female involvement reverted to the pattern prevailing before the seventeenth-century boom, with women tending a few pepper vines as their "money trees" *(pohon wang),* to supplement the household income.[93]

A rather different example comes from the Philippines, where Spain instituted a tobacco monopoly in 1782, laying the basis for a factory system in which women were the primary employees. Female employment in Spanish and Mexican tobacco processing was already well in train because women were considered compliant laborers whose "nimble hands" were adept at rolling cigars. Similar attitudes were transferred to the Philippines. These new factories were very different from the elite households described by Loarca nearly two hundred years earlier, where a female slave could certainly be victimized physically and mentally, but might also become a trusted servant or even a member of the chief's family. The contrasting nature of the employer-employee relationship in Manila's tobacco factories was evident in the strict regulation of hours worked and, more insidiously, in the twice-daily body searches by a *maestro* (the lead worker) as a deterrent against smuggling.[94]

Despite this commercialization of previously home-based industries, the escalating demand for products from "the southern seas" did offer new opportunities for women's economic participation. In China, for instance, innovations in the Chinese cuisine and the rise of a wealthy consumer class made delicacies like the famed sea slug (*teripang,* bêche-de-mer, or *Holothuria*) much desired. With the search for *teripang* that lured ships as far as northern Australia, local communities in the remote islands of eastern Indonesia, though far from centers of international trade, found a profitable harvest in coastal mudflats. An 1824 account of Aru describes hundreds of women and children walking through the shallow waters at low tide, each carrying a basket on the back and equipped with a pointed stick, searching for *teripang.*[95] For men, too, the demands of the global market fostered new skills; in the 1660s, Dutch officials complained about the lack of divers in Aru, but by the 1730s local mother-of-pearl collection was sufficiently attractive for the VOC to propose a monopoly contract. Over the last three hundred years or so, Aru's economic cosmology has expanded to incorporate a whole undersea world where a diver's success in locating the ocean's rarities depends on his ability to gain supernatural assistance from a demanding but seductive "sea wife."[96]

The monetized exchanges that underpinned the international market also enabled ordinary women to accumulate savings in a more flexible and portable form, an important factor in societies where marriages were often dissolved. Converted into jewelry or sewn to clothing, Spanish reals and Dutch rijksdaalders could simultaneously serve as personal adornment and display personal wealth, like the woman's *senawir* (girdle) decorated with eighteenth-century Dutch coins that is preserved in the Sarawak Museum.[97] Accustomed to calculating equivalencies in barter transactions, women encountered few difficulties in determining the appropriate exchange rate between local goods and currencies and the foreign coinage now flowing into the region, and their money-changing skills were regarded with considerable respect. In urban centers, there were substantial opportunities for an astute woman. In the Dutch towns, for instance, free Christians of both sexes could borrow investment capital from various charitable institutions, and enterprising wives of VOC officials, often Eurasian, were deeply involved in local commerce. Overall, however, the gap between "male" and "female" economic worlds was steadily widening.[98] While men flocked to make their fortune in new gold, tin, and gem mines in the Philippines, in Burma, in Sumatra, women were relegated to river panning or sifting through rejected tailings. Long-distance trading voyages privileged males in the acquisition of knowledge, experience, and the purchase of prestige items. More significantly, increasing numbers of foreign men who arrived in the region as traders saw other men as their natural partners, despite the assistance they may have received from temporary wives or wealthy female patrons.

Women, Commerce, and Foreign Traders

Typically dominated by women, domestic markets were one context where "Southeast Asia" seems to assume a particular identity.[99] The claim by Artus Gijsels that Banda men were not permitted to enter the *pasar* (bazaar) may have been exaggerated, but foreign observers consistently remarked on female involvement in commerce. Because of the possibility of crop losses, failure in some commercial venture, or deepening indebtedness, a woman's daily market earnings were often the most reliable source for meeting household expenses. An eighteenth-century biographical work thus describes how a Minangkabau pepper trader, far from home and in straitened circumstances, sends a message back to his wife to request funds so that he can purchase a boat and cargo to continue his voyage.[100] Despite the female presence in Chinese markets, visitors from China saw the "southern seas" as a region where trade was "the domain of women" and where "even the wives of high-ranking mandarins" were not concerned that "a loss of honor" could result from commercial activities.[101] Indigenous sources articulate the same overlay of femaleness and financial acumen; a village shrine northeast of Hanoi thus venerates the Goddess of the Treasury, the legendary wife of a former king who held the keys to the palace treasury and its military supplies and brought great prosperity to the local population.[102] Literary and visual imagery offer other insights. The Lao *Rama Jataka*, often regarded as a "religious" text, surely mirrors market reality in its description of female vendors teasing the bodhisattva with risqué jokes and aggressively hawking their wares.[103] The depiction of women selling from boats and along the riverbanks in a seventeenth-century Thai mural meshes well with the observations made by foreigners in the same period; in Vietnam, said a Jesuit missionary, women who ferried passengers and goods across rivers carried "everything that one could want."[104]

Reconstituting the female-dominated environment of local markets is impossible for a historian, but useful analogies are provided by contemporary anthropology. Suzanne Brenner's study of batik sellers in central Java suggests, for example, that even tensions resulting from commercial rivalries could be allayed by codes of conduct that governed market behavior. Though written in a very different place, and in a different time, a Mon law code strikes the same note, stating frankly that it is of no concern "if women in the market place fight with each other over goods for sale because they are like husbands and wives."[105] As modern research shows, the market was never an undifferentiated group of female peddlers, for it contained its own status hierarchies and even spatial arrangements, as in Banten, where a separate area was allocated to married women.[106] There were obvious inequalities between women who could advance credit and act as patrons and those whose slim profits depended on sales of fruit and vegetables from their own gardens. Yet when benefits were evident, female traders could, and did, act together. Steles from Vietnam, for example, list women vendors as joint contributors to a number of mutually advantageous ventures such as the repair of bridges connecting markets or the expansion of selling space. While most donations were small, some were quite substantial.[107] As brokers, richer women could be an important link in the chain of patronage and client relationships that connected producers to consumers, like the Burmese intermediary Mi Zan Hpyu, who received one kyat per load of tea from both purchaser and vendor.[108] As managers of domestic finances these wealthier traders and entrepreneurs were often in a position to lend money. In recognizing the shrewd and astute trader, the market environment allowed even a "low-status" woman to acquire a reputation for commercial shrewdness and organizational skills. Most Javanese, for example, looked down on the group known as Kalang, who were associated with occupations such as leatherworking and woodcutting. The eighteenth-century Javanese *Serat Centhini* describes a Kalang divorcee whose wealth is derived from pawnbroking and her *ijo* business, which involved buying the rice crop at a low rate before the harvest and providing the peasant with credit in return for profits from the eventual sale. In depicting her as the organizer of a *tayuban* (dance party), the text remarks that this Kalang woman "has the power of galvanizing many people," for "it is the blessing of the rich that everything they wish comes about and they do not lack workers."[109] Commerce was placed on a low rung in the Confucian hierarchy of values, but in 1746 French missionaries in Tonkin (northern Vietnam) claimed that the wealth accumulated by one village woman so enhanced her position that even the governor prostrated himself before her.[110]

The tentacles of market exchanges could also reach into the homes of wellborn women, who, like their commoner sisters, were quite likely to be direct participants in a trading enterprise. The correspondence of Penang's first governor, Francis Light, records the trading activities of high-ranking ladies in southern Thailand. Members of Jogjakarta's elite female guard grew rich through private trade in gold and precious stones. The sister and niece of King Rama I (r. 1782–1809) drew part of their incomes from a market near the Grand Palace.[111] In Burma, said a British envoy in 1795, "women . . . manage the most important mercantile concerns of their husbands," and it was probably her supervisory role that explains the daily inspections of shipbuilding in Yangon by the governor's wife and her ladies.[112]

At all levels of society, and regardless of the nature of the endeavor, any independent income a woman gained could only contribute to her confidence and sense of self-worth. While female negotiators often linked household producers to prospective buyers, those best placed to seal lucrative deals were probably the sexual partners of foreign traders. Alexander Hamilton, who spent thirty years in Asian waters, spoke with admiration of the commercial skills of "obliging" local wives. Not only did they operate retail shops, but "some of them carry a cargo of goods to the inland Towns, and barter for Goods proper for the foreign markets that their Husbands are bound to, and generally bring fair Accounts of their Negotiations." [113] Such "temporary marriages" had long been entrenched in local economies. As one observer noted in Burma, "These Pegus have a custom that when a stranger appears in their country to trade, be he from whatever nation, he is asked how long he wants to stay. He is then presented with a number of daughters, from whom he can choose, for the time that he elects to stay." By recognizing a woman as the wife of a foreigner, even for a few days, short-lived or intermittent unions helped created the kinship networks critical to the commercial enterprise. In this arrangement a woman served a trader "as slave and housewife," cooking, washing, tending a stall, purchasing supplies, and even carrying goods into the interior. When a trader wished to leave, he paid the parents or her relatives, and she returned to her family "with all honor."[114]

This type of liaison was most apparent among the community of foreign Asian men, notably migrants from China. By the early seventeenth century, Spanish-ruled Manila was described as "largely [male] Chinese," and between 1602 and 1636 the Chinese population rose from 2,000 to 25,000. Dutch-controlled Batavia was another magnet; in 1625 alone, five Chinese junks arrived, each carrying around four hundred men. By the 1730s roughly a quarter of Batavia's population was Chinese, and although the "Chinese" category included women of mixed descent, there were still twice as many males as females.[115] Poor Chinese men, the human cargo of junk traffic, were quick to recognize that they could only operate effectively in commerce if they established connections with the women who dominated the peddling trade. Thus, while influential Chinese frequently acquired women as gifts from rulers or nobles, ordinary men were very ready to enter into arrangements with local females and their families. In 1694 a Chinese monk remarked of Hoi An, on the central Vietnamese coast, "The women were very good at trade, so the traders [from Fujian, southeastern China] who came here all tended to marry a local woman to help them with their trading."[116]

From the female viewpoint, a relationship with a foreign merchant was clearly advantageous in providing access to desired goods either as sole seller or as agent. Critical to the success of the "marriage" was the assumption that the arrangement entailed the same mutual fidelity and respect expected of a more permanent union. If a man left but wanted to continue the relationship, he should give his wife some payment to cover the period of his absence, but if he did not return, she was free to marry again. Indeed, her chances of negotiating an advantageous match were enhanced, for she had almost certainly augmented her economic resources and gained greater fluency in a foreign language. Rather than being condemned as "loose" or amoral, she was "the better lookt on, that she has had several European husbands."[117]

In 1619 the Nguyen ruler in southern Vietnam married one of his daughters to a Japanese merchant, who was given a Vietnamese name and a noble title, and in Tonkin, said English captain William Dampier, even the daughters of "great men" could be offered to foreign merchants. By the end of the seventeenth century, however, such unions with high-ranking women were extremely rare. Because so many foreign men were unwilling to assume the sometimes heavy responsibilities of a son-in-law, their "wives" were often members of an ethnic minority or social outsiders of some kind.[118] The standing of women who cohabited with foreigners was also undermined by the indifference of their "husbands" to marital fidelity, a cornerstone of the temporary marriage arrangement. European contempt for their sexual partners was all too apparent, and VOC employees in Ayutthaya even referred to their "wives" as "whores, sluts and trollops." As early as 1633 the Ayutthaya ruler had in fact forbidden the cohabitation of Thai women and men "who have come to trade from various foreign lands," although this proscription was difficult to enforce.[119]

The concept of the "temporary wife" was further debased because many foreign traders found it cheaper and less troublesome to buy one or two slaves rather than become involved with a "wife" and her relatives. By this means a man could satisfy domestic, commercial, and sexual needs without subservience to family demands, while a slave could be resold should she prove unsatisfactory or if a trader's resources were stretched or he himself decided to leave. Accordingly, Chinese men in early seventeenth-century Banten "bought women slaves by whom they have many children." On their departure, they could sell their wives and take a son back to China to assume the position of heir.[120] These slave-wives were obviously in a more precarious position than women who had negotiated a temporary marriage position through a contract. They had not played a role in choosing their new husbands, they were more likely to be in competition with other women for the favors of their masters, and without the protection of family they were frequently subjected to physical abuse. One Englishman in Banten, describing the pitiable position of a slave-wife from southern Vietnam who had fled from her Chinese husband, remarked that it was "an ordinary thing for the Chinese to beat their wives, especially she being a Cochinchyne woman, which had no friends [i.e., relatives] in towne, for the Javans will hardly suffer them to beat their women."[121]

When circumstances were favorable, women certainly benefited from their liaisons with foreign traders; an inscription in one pagoda near Hoi An records that a donation received in 1640 from a Vietnamese wife and her Japanese husband was nearly ten times more than the average.[122] On the whole, however, the influx of male migrants militated against the interests of indigenous female marketing. In the piece goods trade, for instance, women working as peddlers had little access to capital and were thus unable to carry credit as could Chinese traders. VOC officials along Java's north coast attempted to deal directly with market women by providing them with cloth on consignment, but soon found that timely repayments could not be guaranteed. In some places the VOC also encountered a reluctance to deal with European males, who were notorious for their lack of respect to the opposite sex. Given these attitudes, it was little wonder that the Dutch preferred to deal with Chinese men.[123]

Beyond the Market

The female prominence in Southeast Asian markets so evident in the historical sources represents merely one aspect of "women's work." A careful examination of pre-nineteenth-century Thai murals, for example, has identified thirty-one specific occupations, with eighteen performed by Thai women and eight by women only. These murals also caution against seeing a timelessness in women's occupations; today the mahout is exclusively male, but several illustrations depict female elephant drivers.[124] Peasant women worked in a range of other occupations requiring strength and endurance—Burmese *sit-tans,* for example, refer to taxes collected from female porters, and from female workers in the salt tracts.[125] More particularly, women were deeply implicated in the circulation of household goods and services from which local economies drew their lifeblood. Kitchen work was of little interest to foreign merchants, but the preparation and sale of ingredients used in food preparation underpinned much of village-based trade. Entertainment could be another income-generating (and taxable) occupation, but because it often involved sexual services, commentators tended to equate dancers with prostitutes. State disapproval is especially evident in Vietnam, where singers and actors and their children were not permitted to sit for the civil service examinations.[126] Yet ancient views of dance as communication with the supernatural could infuse a performance by an ostensibly low-status woman with unique powers that had their own "economic" dimensions. In Portuguese Melaka, said Eredia, the "rajavas" who went into trance "through ingesting the sap of certain herbs" could not only look into the future and see occurrences in distant places but also "reveal profits, and losses and theft." According to Wang Dahai, the participation of *ronggeng*, or "dancing girls," was a necessary part of the ceremonies that helped ensure the success of bird-nest collectors as they sought to supply the insatiable Chinese market.[127]

The fledgling nature of women's history in Southeast Asia and the inadequacy of the sources are not sympathetic to the comparative endeavor, but in some cases the data open up possibilities for more cross-cultural research. In their role as healers, for example, women could enjoy a very considerable reputation; a Sultan of Palembang even asked that two renowned "female doctors" in Batavia be sent to attend a royal illness. Still today the medicinal plant trade in a village north of Hanoi is attributed to a woman whose memory is honored in a local temple. Originally from the south, she is said to have established her residence there and passed on her botanical knowledge to the local people.[128] Europeans were often impressed by the effectiveness of local remedies, and some doctors were willing to incorporate them into their own pharmacopoeia. In the late eighteenth century a Dutchman described with amazement a Timorese woman's successful treatment of a slave whose fevers had defied European medicines; an albino girl from New Guinea, brought to Batavia in 1779 with skin so damaged it appeared leprous, was cured in three months with a salve made of finely cut tamarind and saltpeter.[129]

In keeping with their ability to commune with the spirits, specialist female healers typically served as midwives, which throughout Southeast Asia was a valued and lucrative occupation. A Minangkabau saying mentions "the midwife's fee [*upah*]," which any birth entailed, and the shortage of midwives periodically mentioned in missives from Batavia points to a market demand that helped maintain a healthy remuneration.[130] Another area where women could support themselves free of masculine competition was wet nursing, a topic also well placed for comparative study. In China, lactation had long been regarded as a service from which a woman could draw an income, and by the twelfth century some families were already consulting brokers to obtain a wet nurse.[131] In Muslim societies, wet nursing assumes some importance as the only female occupation endorsed by the Qur'an, although Islamic jurists generally agreed that a husband must give his permission and it should be he who negotiated payment with the infant's father.[132]

Although wet nurses were apparently favored by wellborn women who wished to resume sexual activity, and texts advise care in the selection process, there is no known Southeast Asian example of a written contract. Referring to the late eighteenth century, Munshi Abdullah recalled that as a baby he was "sold" to fifteen or sixteen women because his mother had no milk; some nursed him for a week, and others for two months.[133] However, relatives or household servants were normally preferred because any commercialization sat uncomfortably with the mother-child relationship that infused wet nursing. The hero of an undated Makassar manuscript talks of the abiding debt he owes his "milk mother," and Islamic law regarding "milk siblings" reinforced indigenous ideas that there was a special relationship between children fed by the same woman. In Ternate the wives of important nobles even suckled the ruler's sons for one or two weeks, creating bonds that were not easily translated into ideas of contractual employment.[134] Such relationships were clearly undermined when women's bodies were regarded as male property, and in 1792 an intriguing Batavian court case raised the issue of whether a lactating slave could be beaten and simultaneously required to nurse a master's child.[135]

The gradual shifts whereby "female" duties once performed by relatives —nursing infants, acting as a go-between in marriage negotiations, or keeping watch at a funeral—earned a "wage" rather than a gift is an important aspect of the commoditization process. Inevitably, it seems, more lucrative occupations slipped into the male domain. The tendency to cast women in a healing role is almost a universal, but in much of Asia, as elsewhere, men came to be regarded as experts even in "women's diseases." In China, for example, a whole field of medical knowledge was devoted to the female body, and manuals written by men offered guidance on every aspect of the birth process, including the arrangement of the delivery room and the burial of the placenta.[136] In Southeast Asia a shadowy but perceptible process of demoting women's knowledge reflects a growing view that written documents, prescriptions, and incantations embodied the most authoritative information about the treatment of disease.[137] Access to such material was largely closed to women because it required some acquaintance with the Indian, Arab, or Chinese works on which indigenous formulations so often drew. A Thai text providing advice on the choice of a wet nurse thus cites a learned Indian ascetic "who knew about women and their ways, both good and bad." The prestige of foreign learning in dealing with female bodies was evident in seventeenth-century Siam, where European doctors were asked to treat royal Thai women; in the 1640s a Dutch surgeon in Banten was also prescribing for one of the king's wives.[138] Around 1777 a Vietnamese doctor produced a "Treatise on Pediatrics" that drew heavily on Chinese sources, while another medical encyclopedia devoted a separate chapter to female illnesses and the care of women in childbirth. The author, however, complained that he "would rather examine ten men than one [high-ranking] woman," whose body was so covered that he could "hardly hear the sound of her voice, observe the color of her skin, count her breathing, or even sometimes feel her pulse."[139]

Urbanization

The ambiguities of "being female" are particularly evident in the urban centers that developed in the wake of expanding international trade. On the one hand, towns and ports could provide a woman with access to religious teachers, with a range of economic opportunities, with possibilities for an advantageous marriage. On the other hand, it is in this environment where we see the first signs of widespread female poverty, domestic abuse, and abandoned children. A primary reason behind these developments was the demographic shift caused by growing numbers of domestic slaves, especially in European-controlled towns. For example, as many as 10,000 slaves were brought to Batavia between 1661 and 1682; in 1679 they made up 59 percent of the residents in the inner city, and by 1749 this figure had even risen slightly to 61 percent.[140] Though men outnumbered women overall, the demand for female domestics remained high because they were a necessary prop in the maintenance of social status. Christian Eurasian wives of VOC officials routinely required at least ten female slaves as personal attendants, and European households absorbed even more. The well-to-do Dutchwoman Cornelia de Beveren owned fifty-nine slaves, whose duties she described in a letter home in 1689. "Three or four youths run behind me and my husband, if we go out, and the same number of girls, with five or six young men and women who stand behind our chairs at the table." Each slave had an allotted task, be it guarding the buttery, weaving, sewing, shopping, or simply standing in the doorway to collect messages.[141]

Nonetheless, whether European or local, well-to-do residents in the growing commercial towns found that maintenance of large slave establishments was expensive. As one observer in Banten put it, "The gentlemen of this land are brought to bee poor, by the number of slaves that they keepe, which eate faster than their pepper or rice groweth."[142] One way of ameliorating this situation was to employ female slaves not simply as domestics and retainers but in occupations that yielded immediate profits, such as spinning and weaving, or hawking food or cloth. The sale of sex was simply another means by which slaves could subsidize household expenses. Female slaves in Brunei thus paddled through the town's waterways on small boats, singing and playing musical instruments, while calling out, *"orang laki membeli perempuan muda"* (Men, buy a young woman). Although the ruler's women were sacrosanct, upper-class men often allowed their female slaves to solicit customers, on the condition that profits were delivered to them, and those of lesser means were quick to follow their example.[143] A Christian minister in Batavia even complained that female slaves were often kept "merely to deliver the earnings obtained from their bodies." To avoid trouble with European law, which classified prostitution as an offense, women sent out to solicit were given a few pieces of cheap cloth so that they could claim they were peddlers.[144]

To some extent, however, the visibility of the sex trade in European sources reflects the port milieu with which foreign traders were most familiar. In Vietnam, Father Marini censured female traders for their willingness to "sell their bodies," but he also admitted that such practices only occurred "where they were a great many people and where the merchant ships dock." In rural areas "malice and corruption do not reign as much" and people lived in "simplicity and innocence."[145] In refining a picture that attributes commercial sex to a largely foreign environment, Nhung Tuyet Tran argues that the state's promotion of premarital female virginity in Vietnam increased local clients because young elite men, denied access to women of their own class, usually gained their sexual experience from prostitutes.[146] Indeed, throughout Southeast Asia this upper-class preoccupation widened the social distance from lower socioeconomic levels, where sexual exchanges underwrote economic relationships and where adolescent chastity was not a matter of great concern. A law code from northern Siam deems it quite acceptable for a husband or parents to "have [a woman] go and live with another man in order to get money and goods from him, with a limit on the period."[147]

It is axiomatic, however, that the sex trade ultimately depends on customers. By the late seventeenth century, the influx of foreign and unattached males—former slaves, sailors, traders, soldiers, low-ranking officials —into expanding urban centers eroded the idea that the fictive kinship links created by sexual relations attached an outsider to the local community. In east Sumatra a Muslim ruler, while stressing that Dutch men should not "dishonor" local females, also agreed that consenting women should be given some kind of payment as the equivalent of a wage.[148] Without access to women from their own cultures, and often without the means or desire to set themselves up domestically, foreign traders were usually willing to enter into what seemed to them brief, cheap, and uncomplicated sexual liaisons. The availability of potential partners as "temporary wives" fostered a common European view whereby ordinary Southeast Asian women were stereotyped as promiscuous and prepared to "sell themselves for any gain, however slight."[149]

Other factors help explain the growing commoditization of sex. Thomas Bowrey's perceptive comment that poor women in Bengal were turning to prostitution in return for money illustrates the pressures exerted on the household economy when cash revenues were limited.[150] In eighteenth-century Cochinchina, which experienced continued warfare, peasant flight, and disruption to agriculture, "young women dispose of personal favours to procure articles of the first necessity for themselves and their families. . . . Neither the husband nor the father seems to have any scruples in abandoning the wife or the daughter to the gallant."[151] If a family's financial burden was particularly heavy, daughters and wives might be mortgaged as debt slaves, which usually meant they became sexually available domestic servants. In other cases women resorted to prostitution simply as a matter of personal survival. In Batavia, where the statistics are especially revealing, female poverty is often traceable to the manumission of slaves through conversion to Christianity or in the wills of deceased owners. Unskilled and without kin support, such women found that their sexual availability, along with petty trading or domestic service, was one of the few ways to make a living. They and their dependents often drifted to the district known as the "oostervoorstad" (eastern suburb), which had a preponderance of poor females; in 1686, for example, 1,131 males were outnumbered by 1,823 women. Inns, coffeehouses, brothels, and the streets themselves became markets for the sale of sexual services, both by women working independently and by those who delivered their earnings to others. To a lesser extent the same pattern is discernible in other Southeast Asian cities; an area near Yangon, for instance, was inhabited completely by prostitutes.[152]

Official attempts to control the sex trade were largely ineffective. In Vietnam the Le Code forbade prostitution for girls under the age of fifteen and outlawed the "sale" of wives; in seventeenth-century Burma a ruler issued similar edicts forbidding parents from selling their children. A hundred years later, however, prostitutes around Yangon were often girls who had been mortgaged for their father's debts and subsequently sold by creditors.[153] European administrations, which classed prostitution as a crime, also embarked on frustrating campaigns to eliminate "immorality." Yet despite the threat of incarceration in institutions specifically for "loose women," the poor and unskilled had few employment options if they were to avoid indebtedness (also a punishable offense). Most female slaves emancipated by an owner's charity hoped to find a satisfactory partner, and many did manage to begin a new life as a "wife," usually of another ex-slave. Others pawned the notarial act of manumission, redeeming it when they acquired sufficient funds. Female debt slaves selling textiles or food were also a common sight, and it was quite normal for a (free) domestic concubine/servant to be washing, selling, cleaning, and providing sexual services privately and/or publicly because her master had agreed to pay her debts.

The situation was more difficult for a freed but aging female slave. Far removed from her original home, she often faced the prospect of penury or ending her days in the Dutch poorhouse. Reentering the world they knew best, some became human predators, like a certain Nyai Assan, well known to the Batavia authorities as a procurer. Her methods were simple; she befriended lowborn women, slaves, or former slaves, lured them out to the harbor for a pleasure trip, and fed them drugged refreshments. They were then handed over to captains of vessels sailing to outlying ports.[154] Behind

Nyai Assan, however, is a depressing litany of problems associated with urban society: the impermanence and depersonalization of the master-slave relationship, the absence of communal and social restraints, and the abuse of personal and sexual power. Sworn testimonies submitted to the Batavia Court of Alderman log not only recurring cases of male violence toward their sexual partners but also the cruelty of women, especially of mistresses toward their female slaves.[155] Urbanization offers other bleak pictures, not least of which is the growing incidence of sexually transmitted diseases, characteristically reported only in reference to the effects on men. Yet the consequences for women were just as serious because of the gynecological problems resulting from venereal infections and because infertility was arguably the most socially damaging fate a woman could suffer. Destitute mothers, prostitution, and the departure of foreign traders also led to a dramatic rise in the numbers of abandoned children. By the mid-eighteenth century there were more than forty occupants of the Semarang orphan house, "all of mixed descent from a European father and an indigenous mother." This trend, as the VOC governor put it, "will grow like a cancer the longer Europeans are here, but how can we prevent it?"[156]

THE ECONOMIC HISTORY of Southeast Asian women does not readily submit to generalizations. Although it is certainly possible to trace a downward spiral, any arguments about weakening female control over resources and production can be qualified by invoking cases in which women benefited from the opportunities created by changing socioeconomic circumstances. Widespread cultural assumptions that all women, villagers and courtiers alike, should accumulate resources of their own were fundamental in shaping relationships with husbands, with family and kin, with the community, and with the state. Ultimately, a historical and comparative overview provides broad support for the argument that women's prominence in the domestic economy can be seen as a common "Southeast Asian" feature. On the region's western margins—for instance, in Assam, Arakan, and Manipur—observers contrasted the female presence in the market with the Indian situation, while "East Asians" were similarly struck by the commercial acumen displayed by Vietnamese women. Yet there are strong grounds for arguing that this relatively favorable situation was adversely affected by an increasing exposure to global trade. Despite advantageous moments, the economic environment of "early modernity" was informed by the same assumptions of male superiority that were embedded in the power structures of Southeast Asia's evolving states.

CHAPTER 5

States, Subjects, and Households

There is no consensus regarding the historical definition of a "state" in Southeast Asia, but scholars generally agree that the early modern period witnessed the
emergence of more centralized and administratively complex governments,
with an enhanced capacity to marshal demographic resources, extract revenue, and promote distinctive ethnocultural identities. Whatever the rationale for their presence, and regardless of their modes of administration,
Europeans were also attaching primary importance to the control of people
and the resources they represented. Recognizing that governments evinced
similar priorities is useful because it enables the historian to move across
the otherwise distracting divide between "indigenous" and "European."
Although many communities never entered the purview of rulers or governors, or at least did so only intermittently, state authority was still reaching
into the lives of subject populations in unprecedented ways. Gender has
never been to the fore in analyses of political evolution, yet it assumes
greater salience when we focus on the social systems that states were themselves shaping. Ruling elites were acutely aware that the effectiveness of any
government relied on the cooperation of village communities and the
households they comprised. The household, however, was the women's
realm, and the rearing of children and the transmission of cultural values
rested largely in female hands. A shadowy presence in national narratives,
women thus became active participants in the processes of negotiation,
contestation, and compromise through which state understandings of what
it meant to be a "subject" were parleyed into local environments.

Corvée and Warfare

Several factors buttressed the administrative and cultural integration that
accompanied state development in "early modern" Southeast Asia. The first,
an increased ability to exploit human labor, built on a long tradition of
corvée that was village-led and communally organized. As state requirements grew, threats of punishment were increasingly invoked in order to
compel compliance. Even if enforcement was arbitrary, a growing cohort
of officials allowed the larger Southeast Asian states to maintain a closer
watch over core populations and to compel their services if necessary. This
oversight, however, was primarily directed toward the control of men rather

than women, since it was normally male laborers who were impressed to work on canals, on forts, on roads, on royal graves, and on temples or to row boats and cut jungle timber. Burmese and Thai women were not tattooed for corvée purposes, and Vietnamese village officials who omitted women from population registers incurred a lesser punishment than when they failed to record the names of men. At the same time, household relationships could become a useful tool for enforcing male acquiescence; a northern Thai man who failed to fulfill his corvée duties might return home to find that his wife had been allowed to take a new husband more willing to fulfill his service obligations.[1]

European administrations were also quick to subject their male populations to corvée, and in the Philippines the Spanish initially made extensive use of Filipino labor for military purposes, especially shipbuilding. Although many men took flight, those drafted could be away for months at a time and, given the appalling work conditions, might never return. Pressures likewise increased in areas where the VOC had gained the upper hand, as Dutch officials successfully manipulated the lord-vassal concept to make local heads their proxies for the delivery of corvée workers. In Java the burden became particularly onerous as expanding labor needs brought the Dutch into competition with rulers and regents. In a typical case, one VOC resident in central Java gave notice that the entire population in his district, including women and children, would be required for the pepper harvest.[2]

As this mention of women indicates, female subjects, though deemed less valuable to state projects, could still be pressed into service when additional labor was required. The great religious monuments constructed by Southeast Asia's "classical" kingdoms required thousands of workers, and although estimates of numbers refer only to men, many tasks did not require physical strength. Like the female laborers depicted in Mughal court miniatures, Southeast Asian women could have been employed to pound mortar, carry earth, or serve as cooks and porters. Periodically we encounter specific evidence of the duties that might be expected of female subjects, especially in times of war. In the 1770s, when Cambodian men were forcibly recruited as soldiers, their womenfolk were left to mill rice for the army; when a ruler of Palembang constructed a fort, women were employed making rice balls to plug gaps in the walls. Even in peacetime a rotation system regularly assigned women from specific districts to the Palembang palace to haul water and collect wood.[3] Close attention to the sources should uncover other instances of state demands, for a law code from northern Thailand attributed to thirteenth-century Lan Na (but probably a later compilation) exempted women over the age of fifty-five from corvée, implying that female service was commonplace.[4]

Although women were not drafted as systematically as men, cloth production was an obvious target for enforced labor. When the Spanish first reached the Visayas, they noted that some women spent half of each month spinning and weaving cotton in the households of their lords, although others were allowed more independence and were required to deliver only a hank of spun cotton.[5] Elsewhere in Southeast Asia a similar pattern can be found, with peasant women working under the supervision of female courtiers. In Java, those summoned for duty as spinners could be absent from home for up to a week at a time.[6] Recruitment of workers would have been facilitated when certain villages were known for particular skills, but in Burma, army divisions also provided a convenient base from which to organize human resources. According to a Burmese register, wives and female relatives of men in the elite cavalry units were responsible for making jam (palm sugar combined with fruits like banana and mango) for court use, an obligation that held even when they were widowed. Another document notes that women from the Shan cavalry were assigned to apply indigo dye to cotton and send it to the capital.[7]

The expectation that women could be taken to satisfy the sexual demands of rulers and provincial lords can be regarded as another more insidious form of service, and a guarantee of freedom from such exactions was a high priority for those able to bargain with an overlord.[8] Northern Thai villagers still remember the days when girls could be seized as "play wives" by a passing cortege, and across the region a common folklore motif refers to village parents who hide or disguise a pretty daughter (for instance, by smearing her face with fish paste). That such motifs encode real incidents finds occasional support in written sources, such as VOC reports of royal expeditions from Palembang and Jambi (east Sumatra) when rulers seized local stores of pepper from upland communities and carried off their "prettiest unmarried daughters."[9]

The greatest threat to the maintenance of family structures, however, was male military service because of the likelihood that those taken would be permanently lost to the community. Even allowing for the probable exaggeration of indigenous quantification, intensifying warfare between expansionist rulers meant that state levies were steadily increasing. In 1635, after years of conflict with the Thais, the Burmese ruler raised the number of men liable for military service from twenty thousand to around ten times that number. Decades of civil war in Vietnam also drained young men from their villages, and many followed the same line of passive resistance as their counterparts in Burma and Ayutthaya, retreating to monasteries to escape army duty.[10] European demands could be equally onerous. When launching punitive expeditions in eastern Indonesia, the Portuguese and Dutch required their native allies to supply scores of outrigger canoes and as many as three thousand men, a significant burden for sparsely inhabited island communities.[11]

In terms of warfare, however, the internecine raiding between small communities was far more regionally typical than large battle campaigns and provided a favored stage for the display of masculine prowess. Probably the most compelling image of maleness was the "headhunter" returning with his bloody trophy, an image once associated with cultures stretching from Assam to Sumatra, Taiwan, and western New Guinea. Nevertheless, head-hunting quickly disappeared as tribal areas were incorporated into larger polities and as the influence of world religions expanded. The Christian regime in the Philippines provides a striking example. The taking of heads, in full force among lowland Tagalog when the Spanish arrived in the sixteenth century, soon became associated with "un-Christianized" interior peoples. A similar process occurred in other areas of Southeast Asia as bloodletting and human sacrifice were displaced by rituals associated with Buddhism or Islam. A legendary leader's rejection of heads taken by his followers in a Brunei epic has thus been interpreted as symbolically differentiating the evolving Muslim state from its animist subjects.[12]

State opposition to local raiding had far-reaching implications for male-female relations, since many tribal cultures regarded the taking of heads (thought to guarantee both crop fertility and human fecundity) as central to longevity of the community and the viability of the household. Youths joined head-hunting expeditions in the passage to adulthood, while older and more experienced men were able to reaffirm their virility by demonstrating their prowess as warriors. Marriageable maidens sought husbands among men whose proven masculinity would ensure the safe birth of healthy children, and mothers, wives, and sisters acquired status from the achievements of their male kin. It is thus quite understandable that, according to an eighteenth-century Malay manuscript, young Abung women in Lampung should meet the returning raiders with joy.[13] When Governor Padtbrugge was in Minahasa in 1679, he commented that men were tattooed in patterns indicating the number of men they had killed; if a man's chest was already covered with designs, then his wife was also tattooed as a partner in his greatness. Similar honors occurred in other societies; in the Chittagong Hills, for instance, the wife of a Kuki man who brought back an enemy head was entitled to wear "a head-dress with gay ornaments."[14] Though it was in the interests of the women to foster the fighting skills of their menfolk, who provided the primary source of protection against raiding by neighboring groups, their own conduct could directly affect an expedition's failure or success. The Spanish chronicler Miguel de Loarca noted that Visayan women refrained from work while their men were at war, while more recent material from Borneo and eastern Indonesia provides lengthy lists of the taboos they were required to observe.[15] In their role as shamans it was often women who determined when a raid was necessary and who marshaled the assistance of powerful spirits. According to nineteenth-century accounts, Toraja communities in central Sulawesi saw the priestess as the mirror image of the headhunter, since both undertook dangerous journeys that entailed negotiation with supernatural forces.[16]

Practices associated with head-hunting may encourage a reassessment of the female role in more conventional armies. Bugis men, impressive in their chain-mail armor, were highly desired as mercenaries by both indigenous lords and European administrations, but in the ongoing rivalries between various Sulawesi kingdoms Bugis women still contributed to pre-battle rituals soliciting supernatural support and were central to the ceremonies that motivated men for war.[17] Images of female loyalty were also arrogated to support state-sponsored conflict, with "women-warriors"—often dressed as men—presented as staunch subjects and emblems of marital fidelity. It is in these terms that a Vietnamese poem speaks of "a small white pagoda" that "keeps the memory of an heroic wife / who followed her husband into battle / long long ago. / She fell in the war by the side of her husband / defending his fallen body against the enemies. / Who is equal to this woman? This woman-warrior, faithful and fearless. . . ."[18] Even if they did not offer the ultimate sacrifice, mothers, wives, sisters, and daughters could emulate the heroines of legend by willingly relinquishing their menfolk and by remaining faithful during their absence. Several Southeast Asian law codes thus specify the time a woman should wait for her soldier-husband before remarrying, with those from Vietnam applauding lifelong widowhood.[19] The idealization of the mother, wife, or sweetheart who offers up the man she loves to serve a noble cause is already evolving as a literary theme, and an anonymous Burmese song eulogizes the mother bidding her son farewell as he leaves to fight the Thai: "With the army / She has entrusted him / Her dearly beloved son. She must not pity him. / On the way to Yudhaya / Many are the rising rivers and streams / Violent are the rains and strong is the storm. / But his own mother has agreed, 'let him die . . . (if need be) . . . .'"[20]

In extolling loyal and unquestioning service, court chronicles pay little attention to the effects of warfare on family life when significant numbers of fathers, husbands, and brothers failed to return or fled to escape duty. In southern Vietnam, marriage was obligatory for all soldiers, but by the 1670s French missionaries remarked on the number of widows and the lack of prospective husbands, estimating that there were at least three women for every man.[21] The results of protracted conflict are strikingly evident in eighteenth-century Chiang Mai, where it was said that in 1782 only around a thousand men remained,[22] and male absence may have been a contributing factor in the periodic famines reported in various parts of Southeast Asia. Nor do elite sources that laud a ruler's battle triumphs dwell on the fate of thousands of ordinary women and men who were carried off as prisoners of war, to be condemned to perpetual servitude or sexual exploitation. Rituals of grieving for those whose kin had been captured or killed in battle were largely conducted by women, who could even be charged with consoling their own anguished enemies. An account of eighteenth-century Timor thus refers to the "lamenting" that accompanied women's celebratory dances around newly severed heads, and during the great Iban feasts the sponsor's wife often acted as the head's "mother," caressing and feeding it so that its spirit would be appeased.[23]

The State, the Household, and Revenue Collection

A second factor contributing to greater political cohesion was the state's ability to raise revenue and channel it to royal capitals or important administrative centers. Although a considerable portion of this revenue was derived from international trade, the income of rulers, provincial lords, and European administrations was still heavily dependent on taxes and tribute levied on household production, delivered both in kind and in specie. It is impossible, however, to calculate specific amounts or to determine precisely how imposts were applied. Outwardly simple terms like the Javanese word *cacah* or the Thai term *khrua* (loosely translated as "household") are open to different interpretations, and when such ambiguities are combined with shifting categories, imprecise calculations, and notional figures, any attempt at computation is highly problematic.

Introducing gender into an already confused picture might seem an unnecessary complication, yet women were deeply implicated in the revenue-raising process because it was based so firmly on the domestic economy. Taxes could be extracted in many forms, but as the previous chapter noted, woven fabrics and spun thread were among the most favored because cloth was such a versatile commodity. As early as the tenth century, Javanese rulers classified weaving, spinning, and dyeing as taxable occupations, and the word *pacumpleng*, sometimes translated as "house tax," can also be rendered as "yarn money." VOC involvement in the textile trade mirrored that of Javanese kings, and the Dutch soon entered into arrangements with local authorities. By the end of the eighteenth century most Javanese households annually delivered around a skein or two of cotton yarn to their own lords as well as fulfilling VOC quotas.[24] Admittedly, custom allowed for some flexibility in determining what constituted a household, but any concessions were probably insufficient to compensate for those living in straitened circumstances. The Dutch on Java followed indigenous practice in assessing widows half the taxes paid by a family, although the levy of fifteen 10-cent pieces per year, as well as four or five fowls and a quantity of spun thread, must still have been a burden.[25] While less detailed, sources from other Southeast Asian societies also point to state interest in weavers and spinners. An eighteenth-century Burmese *sit-tan* records that looms were taxed at a fixed rate of one hundred cubits of cloth and a packet of tea, while the 1,970 pieces that Bangkok required from northern Thai towns in 1809 encode the assertion of authority implicit in the control of textile production.[26]

Other tax obligations, like the offerings required for special ceremonies or the obligatory gifts for visiting officials, bore directly on the way women organized their daily duties. Burmese peasants may have been freed from taxes if they worked monastery land, but households could still be requisitioned for "oil for lamps and torches and food to the extent of their generosity."[27] Female duties could also be affected by the growth of new urban centers and trading posts that depended on a steady supply of food. In 1766, British officials required each family in the Bengkulen district to rear a minimum of sixty fowls, invariably a female responsibility; around the same time, the Spanish regime in the Philippines obliged all "Indian" households to plant fruit trees and maintain a sow, a cock, and six hens.[28]

The administrative records from seventeenth- and eighteenth-century Burma have yet to be examined in terms of gender, but they have the potential to provide further evidence of state intrusion into the domestic economy. A woman's calculations of profits and losses, for instance, would have to include payments exacted at toll stations when she went to market as well as any compulsory deductions from wages, like those imposed on female workers in the salt tracts of the Irrawaddy Delta. The Burmese material also raises intriguing questions about the extent to which women acted as state agents in collecting revenue from lucrative concessions such as fishing grounds, toll stations, or ferries, especially in villages that paid taxes in lieu of army service.[29] Although females were definitely excluded from higher offices, a number of registers list women as hereditary *myo-thugyi*, or village heads, sometimes acting jointly with their husband, at times assuming sole responsibility as widows or chief householder. As one woman explained in 1767, "My great-grandmother Ma Nyein Tha had charge of this village. When she was no more, my grandmother Mi San had charge. When she was no more, my mother Mi Wei had charge. As she is no more, I have had charge from 1119 [i.e., 1757 CE] until now." In effect, a daughter in this situation served as an apprentice, assuming office as her mother advanced in age.[30] The responsibility for compiling the records for any revenue inquest would have rested with the *myo-thugyi* and her husband or male relatives, although the evidence indicates that it was men who normally submitted the written documentation.

It should not be inferred, however, that women who inherited positions of authority were only nominally in charge. In many marketplaces, for example, they would have been the logical choice as revenue collector, and in nineteenth-century Siam, women responsible for collecting taxes from individual traders were known as *kamnan talat*, a variation of the term used for a subdistrict head.[31] Occasionally one encounters official recognition of a woman's qualifications for assuming a deceased husband's position, and in 1678, VOC officials permitted the Balinese widow of Batavia's Chinese captain to represent Chinese interests.[32] Nonetheless, though women of high rank and those who had gained favor were frequently given villages or districts as an appanage or were granted the revenue from some market, the trend by which rulers "sold" the authority to collect taxes in return for sizable compensation inevitably advantaged men.

Little is known about the history of indigenous tax farms, but their evolution under European control is easier to trace. In Melaka the Portuguese continued the Malay practice of assigning streets and alleys to different officials, who then had the right to collect revenues from the small traders, mostly women, who sold food or vegetables from stalls set up in front of their homes.[33] After taking Melaka in 1641, the Dutch introduced revenue "farms," which were already established in the Netherlands and allowed individuals to bid for the franchise to collect taxes. Melaka was typical of much of Southeast Asia in that tax farmers were commonly Chinese men, while taxpayers were frequently female. In early eighteenth-century Melaka the most lucrative source of tax revenue came from the sale of fish, vegetables, rice, and fruit—all commercial activities where women were predominant or deeply involved.[34] Like other traders, they would at times have been hard-pressed by the tax farmer, who was subject to penalties if he was in arrears, and in Java some Chinese even preferred to pay the Dutch a fine rather than extort more spun thread from overworked Javanese women.[35]

In assessing tax liabilities and monitoring defaulters, European administrations were undoubtedly more efficient than their indigenous counterparts. They were also more insistent that in-kind and labor services should be commuted to cash payments, and when this was enforced, the inflationary tendencies accompanying monetization are readily identified. In the Philippines the tribute payable by a couple and their children initially amounted to about eight reals annually, with unmarried men and women over the age of eighteen considered half tributes. By 1700 the tribute in some regions was raised to twelve reals per family, added to which were other payments to the church and community funds.[36] As household managers, women would have been particularly aware of the cash economy, since a feature of this period is the growing indebtedness of ordinary Southeast Asians as government demands became more intrusive. Serving as an allegory of state penetration into individual lives, a report in the official history of Laos seriously asserts that some French authorities imposed a tax on women's breasts, with the amount due calculated in proportion to their fullness.[37]

The State, Gender, and Identity

Although the beliefs, behavior, and appearance by which an individual could identify as a "Thai" or an "Acehnese" were open to some negotiation, a third element in the consolidation of Southeast Asian states was the assertion of a cultural authority usually associated with the dominant ethnic group. Historians are inclined to track this process through the spread of religion or political models, but for large states, as for the region's innumerable smaller communities, clothing and body decoration were often more conclusive in establishing the boundaries of "otherness" and in designating who culturally belonged and who did not. Imperial Chinese records, noting how different Miao groups could be identified by the clothing and hairstyles of their women, thus tracked the processes by which Miao men became more "Chinese" as they adopted Han dress. In Southeast Asia the sources are less revealing, primarily because the territorial control of most states was limited, and because so many peoples—in the remote highlands, in the deep jungles, on the open seas—remained untouched by state efforts at acculturation. One such group is the Padaung of contemporary Burma, who elongate the necks of their women by brass coils that depress the shoulders and collarbone, a custom that may have originated in rituals associated with an ancestral dragon-mother.[38] Throughout tribal areas of Southeast Asia and northeast India the female body became a particular marker of singularity by inserting large nose plugs, by encasing the legs with rattan, by tattooing the face, by deliberately distending the earlobes. In many cases ornate headdresses and specific styles of embroidery, jewelry, or textiles blended the display of ethnic affiliation with statements of personal wealth. In 1679 Padtbrugge estimated that women from the interior of Manado could be wearing copper girdles and jewelry weighing as much as twenty pounds.[39]

The process of acculturation was also ameliorated because the retention of ethnic distinctiveness could serve practical purposes, if only as a means of identifying inclusion in a specific group. In 1754 Burman warriors in King Alaung-hpaya's army unloosened the long topknots that marked them off from the short-haired Mon, in order to attract the support of fellow Burmans in the enemy forces.[40] Yet there were also perceptible shifts as the influence of Southeast Asian states expanded into areas where their authority had once been merely nominal and as the dress and appearance associated with dominant state cultures were incorporated, adopted, or imposed. In consequence, certain modes of bodily adornment became associated with lesser peoples. Already in the fourteenth century, military leaders in Vietnam (unlike, say, their counterparts in Burma) had decided that tattoos were inappropriate as a display of male courage and warrior status and should not be regarded as a source of invulnerability.[41] In the Philippines the Spanish also condemned tattooing as a "barbaric practice," and Christianized women of rank no longer covered their teeth with gold or allowed their earlobes to become distended by heavy earrings.[42] In other cultures, ideas of female beauty were similarly shaped by elite aesthetics that the state itself endorsed. Malay literary eulogies of women's teeth, "black and shining like a bumble-bee's wings," slowly give way to metaphors of gleaming pearls, although in the mid-nineteenth century, "Malay" (i.e., Muslim) women in Sarawak were still blackening their teeth with antimony.[43] Comparable changes reshaped the display of masculine virility. The penis pins, or *sagra,* used by Filipino males, reputedly to enhance their sexual performance, were banned by Spanish friars, and as elsewhere the decoration or modification of the male genitals became symbolic of animist and "uncivilized" peoples. In the 1880s one observer in northeast India commented on the "scorn" with which the Naga were regarded by "their more civilized neighbors," not least because of customs like those followed by men in the Patkai Hills, where "a little cane crinoline and small strip of cloth passed between the legs" forced the testes into the abdomen.[44]

Covering the genitals was a very old practice in Southeast Asia societies, but the concern with correct dress that infused the state-religious alliance could hardly fail to affect self-representations of gender. Unlike the sexually explicit statues of ancestors among tribal societies, the divinities and sovereigns depicted in "Indianized" statuary are always shown with the lower body covered, and the discovery of small silver and gold chastity plates indicate that the concept of modesty was well entrenched in child-rearing among early elites. Concealing the chest was less important, although in Vietnam the Chinese example of the completely clothed body (including footwear) was a hallmark of the civilized person. Vietnamese standards contrasted with those of wellborn Thai and Khmer women, who used only a loose scarf to hide their breasts; this contrast probably prompted the Italian Jesuit Christoforo Borri (1583–1632) to record that Vietnamese women "cannot endure any part of their body to be uncovered."[45] Islam and Christianity held similar views about clothing, especially for women. Muslim females in Southeast Asia may not have adopted the facial veil, but for those aspiring to social status, some kind of breast covering became absolutely de rigueur.

Because clothing styles were saturated with cultural statements regarding hierarchies of power, any innovation could carry significant messages of allegiance and identification. While praising the Javanese style of dress, the author of the *Hikayat Banjar,* a Malay text from eastern Borneo, predicted that "misery and misfortune, illness, epidemic, unrest," would result if people were to clothe themselves "like the Malays or the Dutch or Chinese or the Siamese or the Acehnese or the Makassarese or the Buginese." In Java a bare male torso was customary in court attire, and the unease aroused by the "donning of Dutch garb" is evident in a Javanese poem describing Amangkurat II (r. 1677–1703), who "looked like the Governor-General of Batavia" and "not at all like a prince of Mataram sitting upon his throne."[46] Women's dress, by contrast, was more likely to conform to "traditional" standards, perhaps a comment on the perception of females as transmitters of culture. In 1681, when the VOC was nearing the height of its power, the ruler of Ternate arrived in Batavia dressed in black broadcloth, "according to the Dutch fashion." His wife, however, wore not European clothing but a "Malay-style overdress or *kebaya* of cotton."[47] Even when wellborn women adopted elements of European dress, like the fans, stockings, handkerchiefs, and mantillas of Christian Filipinas, clothing was carefully monitored because nonconformity was construed as a rejection of the social order. Sumptuary regulations thus became a cardinal signifier for both social differentiation and ethnic classification. In Batavia, for instance, only Christian Indonesians were allowed to dress like Europeans; non-Christians were required to wear their own regional costume. Slaves employed in a European household were not permitted to wear hats unless they could understand and speak Dutch, and Chinese and Arabs were forbidden from wearing Indonesian clothing. At the upper echelons of VOC officialdom, where so many wives were Eurasian, a woman was allowed to dress according to the rank of her husband rather than her father. However, elaborate laws promulgated in the mid-eighteenth century limited the wearing of frocks of velvet, silk, and linen and the use of lace trimmings to the wives and widows of men above the rank of senior merchant and dictated that they could wear only jewelry befitting their status.[48]

The view that dress and morality were correlated is well illustrated in Vietnam, where the Confucian ethos endorsed the state's role in suppressing unacceptable customs, most notable in village communities and in areas inhabited by non-Vietnamese. If appropriate models were needed, the authorities had only to look northward, where the Chinese had undertaken a concerted campaign to persuade or compel Miao men to adopt Han clothing and hairstyles. In 1744 the south's Nguyen lord marked his succession by proclaiming that henceforth his subjects should adopt a more Sinicized style of dress. But although women's costumes now resembled those of men —trousers and a gown buttoned down the front—there was ample opportunity to display wealth and social status. Rather than wearing cheaper cotton clothing, southern women preferred garments made of fine silk, or ramie tunics embroidered with flowers, and round rather than upright collars. Combs, bracelets, and earrings completed the ensemble. It is not surprising that people from the Nguyen domains considered northerners to be "poor" because of their sober dress and preference for cotton or that northern officials were shocked at the "extravagance" of the south. In fact, it seems that governments located at the margins of the Sinicized world, like Korea and northern Vietnam, were far more concerned than China itself about observing the simplicity enjoined by Confucian philosophy. In the Korean court even the queen consort and other wives wore simple ornaments and few jewels, and in 1776 when northern Vietnamese troops seized the Nguyen city of Hue, the Trinh ruler decreed that only officials and their wives could dress in silk and brocades.[49] Foot binding never gained any following in Vietnam, but it would be intriguing to know if elite women used high heels to counterfeit the tiny shoes so popular in China, as was the case in Taiwan.[50]

The concern of Southeast Asian states to ensure that subjects be appropriately clothed highlights a continuing ambiguity toward cross-cultural marriages. While kings commonly took wives from other countries or ethnicities to cement an alliance, and while male traders or migrants frequently married local women to gain access to land or assistance in commerce, the potential for cultural dilution could generate considerable unease. Once more the most forthright expression of such attitudes can be found in Vietnam, where Confucian views on moral rectitude helped create a sharp distinction between the "civilized" Vietnamese and the hill tribes, as well as their southern neighbors, the Cham. Fifteenth-century Confucian literati could thus say little in defense of earlier kings who had exchanged women with their Cham counterparts, and in 1499 all Vietnamese men were forbidden to take Cham wives. Marriages with hill tribes were also proscribed; in theory at least, any government functionary who married into the family of a highland chief would be punished.[51] The rulers of Siam were likewise concerned about the effects of intermarriage. A 1633 law condemned Mon and Thai who gave their daughters to English, Dutch, Javanese, and Malay men, since such women were liable to be swayed by "wrong beliefs" and fall away from "the holy religion of Buddhism." Punishments could range from fines or confiscation of property to execution, although it does not appear that penalties were rigorously applied, since individuals of mixed descent often rose to important and responsible positions in the administration.[52]

European attitudes toward the children of these liaisons were inconsistent, despite alleged concern about the souls of part-European children who might not receive an adequate Christian upbringing or might even be induced to follow the "perfidious" teachings of Muhammad or the Buddha. In Ayutthaya this view led to protracted battles between Dutch authorities, who believed that a European father should have custody of any children he acknowledged, and Thai rulers, who argued that the mother had the superior claim. The Portuguese in Melaka and later in Timor and Flores may have encouraged miscegenation as a means of increasing the Catholic population, but they still allocated native Christians to categories that tied social standing directly to skin color. As in all other European centers, the assumption that the prestige culture should be both Christian and "white" was unquestioned. In 1712 two of the four English women in the tiny post at Bengkulen in west Sumatra were even sent home because their behavior was thought to demean British standing.[53] In practice, however, there was never any prospect of sustaining the ethnic boundaries that Europeans had once envisaged. Forbidden to take up residence in Filipino villages, Spanish men commonly found brides among the urban Christian mestizo community, because of the shortage of eligible Spanish girls.[54] In Java, miscegenation was even more evident. Early efforts to sponsor the migration of young Dutch women to Batavia failed miserably, and although Europeans were under constant pressure to legalize their sexual relationships, concubinage and common-law marriages were rampant. A Christian union with a "native" wife was permitted only if she could speak some Dutch and had received religious instruction, and early treaties between the VOC and Indonesian states even contain clauses where both sides agree to proscribe marriage between Muslims and Christians.[55]

Attempts to divide populations in terms of ethnicity and religion, most obvious in European-controlled areas, were particularly problematic in the Chinese case, and the mothers of "Chinese" women who appear in VOC notarial records, like "Oey-Moeytese van Batavia" were probably Balinese.[56] While every urban center had its Chinese quarters, Manila's Parian district, finally abolished in the late eighteenth century, probably represents the most determined state effort to maintain ethnic separation, at least of non-Christians. Spanish regulations in the mid-eighteenth century also made it illegal for non-Christian Chinese to live in Filipino villages, with offenders subject to two hundred lashes or four years penal service.[57] In a more muted form, similar policies are apparent in measures adopted by the Trinh lords of Tonkin, who forbade their subjects to adopt Chinese dress and laid down that unassimilated Chinese should live in separate areas.[58]

To some extent, this growing tendency to see the Chinese as a separate category was reinforced from within the "Chinese" community itself, and the eighteenth century saw a growing Sinification of mestizo culture. In 1717, for instance, the Gong Goan, or Chinese Council of Batavia, was given permission to register Chinese marriages and divorces, together with other powers that provided for considerable authority over the personal lives of the Chinese community.[59] As the part-Chinese population increased, wealthier men sought enhanced status through marriages to women whose behavior and appearance were closer to Chinese norms. When a retired merchant, Xie Qing'gao (1765–1822), composed his *Hai-lu* (A record of the seas), he noted that the first waves of Chinese males reaching Borneo had readily taken Dayak women as sexual partners. This was regrettable, he argued, because Dayak women "are licentious. They do not know modesty or shame." He was happy to be able to report that "when the population had grown," the Chinese began "to arrange marriages among themselves and then rarely took Dayak women for their wives."[60] A somewhat similar process can be traced in southern Vietnam, where thousands of young Chinese males settled during the seventeenth and eighteenth centuries. Although their brides came from local Cham communities, it seems that the children of these marriages were oriented toward the "high-status" culture of their fathers rather than that of their Cham mothers.[61]

The growing pressure for local wives to act in a "Chinese" way was most pronounced in the expanding urban enclaves, notably Batavia, where the Chinese merchant elite dressed as mandarins for official occasions, and community leaders discouraged Muslim influences in Chinese-Javanese households. New standards were set as men of means brought in wives from China or employed Chinese-born tutors for their children. In 1818 it was even alleged that in Kupang (Timor) some Chinese women were binding their feet. The strong current of localization thus faced a weaker but significant counterstream, prompting Wang Dahai to praise "exemplary women" who demonstrated that barbarian tendencies could be checked. One individual, the wife of a prominent Batavian Chinese merchant, committed suicide rather than marry a wealthy suitor after her husband died in the rebellions of 1740. A second woman cared for her parents-in-law and children following her husband's death. "Alas," wrote Wang Dahai, "this loyalty and feminine virtue are hardly met in China."[62] Such praise, however, was rare. Despite the separate identity that overseas communities were able to maintain, Chinese travelers persistently deplored the bastardization of their culture and the distortion of family values, an explicit comment on the influence of local women.

The State-Household Compact

As states attempted to attach tangibility to abstractions like "authority" and "obedience," the arrogation of symbols and vocabulary associated with the family is almost a universal. Historians have made the case most strongly in Europe, where the household model and its justification of inequities evolved into a formidable instrument of control. The persuasiveness of the ruler-parent/subject-child allegory relied heavily on the notion that the relationship between husband and wife was the pivot of the social and political order. "Marriages," said a French edict in 1666, "are the fecund sources from which the strength and grandeur of states is derived."[63] A similar sentiment was expressed by the VOC governor of Ceylon, Rijklof van Goens, well known to Southeast Asianists because of his detailed description of seventeenth-century Mataram. "How much," he wrote, "depends on good and bad marriages, from which countries and cities must take their rise."[64]

In the non-Western world, understandings of the obligations implicit in kinship and gender interaction were even more significant in affirming the sociopolitical hierarchies that supported "government." In Southeast Asia the perception of "the state" as a family writ large is a recurring theme, since ideas about the relationship of husbands to wives, fathers to mothers, and parents to children were embedded in the power distribution on which authority rested. In the words of a Malay code, "In this world, father and mother and kings must be considered great rulers, taking the place of Almighty God," and the depiction of the ruler as "the father and mother of his people" is commonly applied to other authority figures as well.[65] If, as a Vietnamese code has it, marriage is "the basis of social relations," then male-female hierarchies within the household should mirror those endorsed by what one scholar has called the state's "gender regime."[66] Though, as Tony Day points out, the continuous and ambiguous interplay of "gendered forces" meant the masculinization of authority could never be absolute, the principle that patriarchy was intrinsic to the natural order was rarely questioned. Anthropologists have long been attracted by the special status of women in the matrilineal Minangkabau culture of central Sumatra. Nonetheless, an oft-quoted saying recorded among migrant Minangkabau communities on the Malay Peninsula lays down that "the raja rules the country / The chief rules the district / The headman rules the clan / The leader rules his followers / The husband rules the wife."[67] The Lan Na chronicle likewise notes that "servants respect their masters. Wives respect their husbands. Children respect their parents. . . . Younger brother and sister respect the older."[68]

Assertion of this household hierarchy spoke to more extended relationships of power. While the husband-wife metaphor was frequently invoked in indigenous diplomacy, it was particularly significant in regard to Europeans. The Javanese ruler Amangkurat I (r. 1646–1677), for example, compared his relationship with the VOC to that of a married couple, with the Dutch displaying the quality of *strijdbaarheid* (militancy) and the Javanese in the humble role of wife, "ignorant and lax in discipline."[69] European governors and officials found the same parallels useful in dealing with local rulers, with themselves invariably cast in the male role. The deputy governor of the English East India Company post in Bengkulen openly acknowledged that he treated Malay rajas "as a wise man should his Wife, am very complaisant in trifles but immovable in matters of importance."[70]

The idealized concept of the male as household head—husband, father, or (in matrilineal societies) mother's brother—had important ramifications for marital relations. A principal wife in Ayutthaya was normally worth half the *sakdina* grade (the "worth" of an individual measured in theoretical rice fields) of her husband, and in Vietnam the mourning robe worn on a mother's death was slightly shorter than for a father, a symbolic statement that she was not his equal.[71] Almost certainly expressing an ideal rather than actuality, a Mon *dhammasat* (law code) lays down that a wife needs her husband's consent before she can give religious donations or offerings, since he "owns" her. Rather more serious is the advice that a husband administer "gentle chastisement" by beating a recalcitrant wife on the buttocks "with a cane, split bamboo, or the palm of the hand." This gender differential was also reflected in state pronouncements regarding crime and punishment, for although the murder of a spouse is everywhere a great crime, it is invariably more serious for a woman to kill her husband than vice versa. The Lan Na code, for instance, prescribed a fine of 1,320 pieces of silver for a man who murdered his wife. In the reverse case, however, a wife should be put to death, like a servant who kills a master or a child a parent. In short, whatever the reality of husband-wife relations, the authority of the man was legally paramount. The marital provisions that applied during the Ayutthaya period, many of which were retained in the revisions ordered by Rama I in 1805, indicate that the payment of a bride-price gave a man not merely conjugal rights over his wife but entitled him to sell her or give her away.[72]

Marriage, Property, and State Oversight

The perception of marriage as the bedrock of a prosperous community had wide-ranging repercussions as Southeast Asian governments began to construct the ideal family as a sedentary and male-headed kin group that transmitted approved cultural values, monitored its members, and was responsive to state demands. The view expressed by the Dutch administration in 1808 would have been strongly endorsed by most indigenous rulers:

> One of the most important concerns of the [Javanese] regents must be that the common native will not remain single, but that all young marriageable males and young females must be wed properly, thereby preventing idleness, vagrancy and other mischief, and promoting a regular increase of the population.[73]

The sanctioned union of a man and a woman, in opening the door to parenthood, ensured the perpetuation of kinship structures, guaranteeing a settled and growing community that would fulfill its tax and service obligations. The counterimage, presented in a text from northern Thailand composed in the late eighteenth or early nineteenth century, predicts an apocalyptic time of social chaos when families disintegrate and women find no husbands, which will end only with the coming of the righteous king.[74]

In its fundamentals the state view of marriage was ratified by the cultural pragmatics prevailing in most Southeast Asian societies. Notwithstanding the stories of romantic love that entertained so many village audiences, matrimony was considered the basis for a domestic order that was economically viable, congenial, and cooperative. Official prohibitions of marriage across social borders (for instance, between different castes in Bali or between princes and commoners in Vietnam) were quite in keeping with communal law (most commonly transmitted in short verses and proverbs) that saw a domestic partnership functioning best when husband and wife came from similar backgrounds. In this relationship men and women had specific responsibilities, and again one sees the melding of state and village interests. The rhymed Khmer verses known as *chbab*, often composed by monks, extolled the family and enumerated the duties of its members. A Mon *dhammasat* notes that the ideal wife should not only care for the children, speak sweetly to her husband, and refrain from drinking alcohol and from visiting other men but also "cook, launder, spin cotton, weave, and manage the household."[75] Underlying such injunctions was the recognition that marital breakdown was always a reality and that personal humiliation or disputes over property could generate lasting resentments. In such cases, the task of the community and of the state—and thus of "law"—was to determine the appropriate means for restoring social equilibrium.

At the village level this task was made easier by the general understanding that both bride and groom made their own contribution to the household economy and that this contribution could be evaluated in terms of pecuniary benefits. Written into state codes, customary law recognized the right of parents to exchange their daughters for a negotiated amount or in some cases allowed a husband to "mortgage" his wife in payment for some debt. In fact, the sign given by Filipino parents to indicate they had accepted the promised dowry for their daughter was the same as that following a market transaction, "to signify that the price has been agreed upon and the sale cannot be made to someone else."[76] In the light of state priorities, it is not surprising that the official value placed on a male body was often more than that placed on a female. The Lan Na text, for instance, values a son at 50 pieces of silver, and a daughter 22. Although the worth of a grown woman is equivalent to that of a man (330 silver pieces), this lessens as time goes on because she "gets older day and night, each year, each month."[77] Nonetheless, commoditization of marital relationships did not invariably mean a devaluation of female worth, especially when bride-price was customary and a man's wealth was reckoned by the number of daughters he had fathered. A Rejang law code from the Sumatran highlands recorded by English East India Company employee William Marsden hence provided for a fine of $150 if a woman were killed, but only $80 for a man or a boy.[78]

In societies where documentation was rare and where "contracts" regarding the disposition of goods and property were verbal rather than written, the economic underpinnings of marriage required public and communal witness. A betrothal in the Visayas could take place only after negotiations had established the amount of the dowry and a ceremony had been held in which the intentions were made clear. "While the betrothed pair are drinking," wrote Loarca in 1582,

> an old man rises, and in a loud voice calls all to silence. . . . He says: "So and so marries so and so, but on the condition that if the man should through dissolute conduct fail to support his wife, she will leave him, and shall not be obliged to return anything of the dowry that he has given her; and she shall have freedom and permission to marry another man. And therefore, should the woman betray her husband, he can take away the dowry that he gave her, leave her, and marry another woman.[79]

Significantly, Loarca noted that this type of ceremony did not occur among people who had no property, for whom marriage was a much simpler affair.

The cultural collateral symbolized by wedding and betrothal exchanges supplied the necessary safeguards for ownership and inheritance precisely among those settled communities that the state favored. Accordingly, in their incorporation of customary laws, written documents devote considerable attention to regulations governing the return of gifts should a betrothal be broken or a marriage fail. As in any contract, the failure to deliver or the delivery of damaged goods canceled the arrangements. Presents and money should be given back, for instance, if either partner died or was killed or was found to be deficient (codes often list insanity, handicap, impotence, or disease) or was in some other way unsuitable.[80] The northern Thai kingdom of Lan Na ruled that a family should surrender the betrothal gifts to the value of 11,000 cowries if a girl should reject her suitor, and as in Burmese and Javanese law, these gifts should be returned twofold if the marriage had actually occurred. According to the same code, although a husband who demanded a divorce could reclaim the bridewealth, his wife was entitled to a portion as a "daily wage" calculated in terms of the time she had spent with him.[81]

While the possibility of disputes over the reallocation of property and the consequent threat to communal harmony helps explain the attention given betrothal exchanges by indigenous governments, European intervention had rather different motivations. Dutch and English officials in Sumatra actively sought to eliminate the payment of bridewealth because it meant that a man became indebted to his wife's family, sometimes for life. Instead, they promoted Malay-style marriages, where the gifts to the bride (Malay *mas kawin*, Arabic *mahr*) were much less.[82] As governor of Ternate, the otherwise discerning Robert Padtbrugge (1638–1703) even tried to eliminate matrilocal marriage by encouraging newlywed couples to establish their household in the husband's community.[83] Spanish authorities likewise disapproved of "selling" a daughter and condemned the custom whereby a poor man worked for the family of his betrothed for three years or so in lieu of bride-price. In 1628 Philip IV ordered that no Indian in any part of the Spanish empire should make a bride payment or provide free labor to his future father-in-law, but Philippine authorities did not enforce this legislation with any vigor, and bride service was still a reality into the nineteenth century.[84]

Indigenous preoccupation with the compensation due when a betrothal was broken or a marriage failed attests the need to restore amicable relations so that the cycle by which a household was established could start afresh. The ease of divorce is often cited as a common feature of Southeast Asian societies, and it is certainly true that among smaller tribal communities an adverse omen, such as a dream, might be reason enough for a couple to separate, with little ceremony involved.[85] When property and the division of children were involved, however, marital ruptures could be complicated. The traditional ritual recorded in a Javanese text, which involved breaking a gold piece in the presence of witnesses, bathing the face with special water, and accepting unhusked rice, conveyed an explicit message: divorce was not a casual matter. A number of texts express the hope that a woman who drinks, quarrels with her husband, or spends time with other men or away from her house can be "reformed" through instruction and that an estranged couple can be reunited.[86] Written codes often insist that a woman should remain faithful to an absent husband for a period varying from one to eight years, even if he left her to live with another woman.

There were situations, however, where the authorities would have agreed that divorce was appropriate, and even desirable, especially for a man. A text from Nan (northern Thailand) dating to the late sixteenth or early seventeenth century thus notes that a wife can be set aside if she was inclined to quarrel, if she was not sufficiently respectful, if she was deceitful, or if she frequented "places of amusement and enjoyment." An unassailable justification for repudiation was a wife's failure to bear children or even, according to a 1707 Mon *dhammasat,* her inability to conceive sons.[87] Draw-

ing on the Islamic heritage, Malay law roundly condemns a woman who seeks a divorce without being able to prove any fault by her husband. One text even mandates that she should be sent into the jungle for seven days by herself: "If she returns she is carried round the mosque, so that . . . she may serve as a warning to others."[88]

Yet written laws were not necessarily unsympathetic toward a woman's marital unhappiness. For instance, the conditions under which the rejec-

tion of a Muslim wife is legal are carefully spelled out, and Shafi'i interpretations are more amenable to female-initiated divorce than other schools. Islamic injunctions did not conflict with legal traditions developed under Hindu influence, affirming that it was quite acceptable for a woman to leave a man if he was affected by a serious disease like leprosy or was impotent or otherwise failed to satisfy her sexually.[89] The repudiation of matrimonial bonds in Vietnam was mandatory in seven specified instances, but (as in Chinese law) a wife should not be set aside if she had mourned correctly for her husband's parents, if her own parents were no longer living, or if the couple had become wealthy after the marriage. Vietnamese codes proscribed a wife's return to her natal home, but in most of Southeast Asia the rulings attributed to the Burmese princess Learned-in-the-Law, which permitted a mistreated woman to go back to her parents, are probably more representative of actual practice.[90] In addition, women could sometimes buy themselves out of a marriage: "If a woman wishes to divorce her husband," says the Lan Na chronicle, "let her beg his pardon with 110 pieces of silver; if she is poor, let her pay 52." The "juristic tales" interpo-
into Buddhist law, ranging from Jataka episodes to a folk story or a
n actual decision, provided "precedents" for situations that ordi-
e may well have faced, like the real possibility of being married

to two husbands. The Lan Na manuscript, for instance, tells of a trader who was absent from home for so long that his wife, thinking he had died, married another man. After some time the first husband returned and wished to reclaim his wife: "The two husbands could not come to an agreement, so they went to court. The court ruled that they should not quarrel, that they were both her husbands within the law, as her parents had arranged both marriages. No offense had been committed by either man."[91]

These precedents, however, had no legal standing in a European jurisdiction. Since a Christian couple had vowed before God that they would remain together until death, marriage was indissoluble, and bigamy even worse than adultery. Despite lapses in their own morality, Spanish friars were indefatigable in enforcing the permanence of matrimony and tireless in their condemnation of the casual manner in which Filipinos had previously ended their unions. Separation of husband and wife "from bed and board" for adultery, cruelty, heresy, and lunacy was a possibility, but the parties were free to remarry only if the marriage was annulled. European officials who supported the idea of patriarchal privileges often found that their views of household hierarchies echoed those of local men. In response to male complaints, a VOC edict issued in Ambon in 1680 stated that a Muslim wife who returned to her family without her husband's consent could be placed in the house of correction and a fine levied on those who had sheltered her.[92]

The State and Morality

The attention given to marriage relationships in Southeast Asia's legal texts reflects not merely socioeconomic realities but also a deep-seated conviction that the cosmic order could be directly affected by sexual misconduct. Since earthquake, plague, shipwreck, or other catastrophes could be attributed to human wrongdoing, it followed that written laws, like community custom, should delineate and, if necessary, redefine the acceptable paradigms for social behavior. Vietnamese law followed the Chinese model in drawing a more specific connection between sexual disorder and political anarchy, and it is no coincidence that Vietnamese and Chinese terms referring to illicit intercourse could connote both adultery and treasonous communication with an enemy.[93]

Obviously, there was always a gap between a state's gender order and the actual operation of law. Without strong enforcement agencies, most penalties assigned in "traditional" Southeast Asian codes remained theoretical and negotiable. Nonetheless, the widespread religious message that humans were fundamentally lustful and could not control their own passions strengthened the view that the state should shoulder the burden of maintaining moral standards. Declaring that "a strange man is to a woman as the sun is to the moon; they should be always apart," a Malay text goes on to assert that the parents of a child born out of wedlock should wed "because if there are many unmarried Muslims in the country it is a reproach towards its ruler." In pursuit of the public good, no area of family life was considered "private" or immune to state intervention. Even quarrelling between co-wives might call for officially prescribed penalties, as in Vietnam, where a culpable woman should have her head shaved.[94]

The preoccupation of lawmakers with enforcing sexual restraint deserves particular attention because it is so often asserted that in Southeast Asian societies premarital sex was regarded with some toleration. As Helen Creese has pointed out in relation to Bali, such comments do not apply to the upper classes in socially hierarchical states, where a high priority was placed on virginity at first marriage. In this sense Southeast Asia differs little from marital patterns in comparably complex societies, with expectations of chastity applied to any girl of good birth but being far less pertinent at lower socioeconomic levels. Edicts in Tokugawa Japan, for instance, admonished peasants to withdraw their daughters from male company after the age of ten, but such rulings were ignored whenever surveillance was weak. European statistics also show a high rate of prenuptial births, despite the best efforts of the state and church, and in early nineteenth-century England it is estimated that between a fifth and a half of all brides were pregnant at marriage.[95]

In much of Southeast Asia, village acceptance of adolescent sexual relations meshed easily with the common practice whereby a youth lived and worked with the family of his betrothed as a substitute for bride-price. As early as 1471, *lamre* (acting as son-in-law) had been prohibited in Vietnam because premarital adoption of a "son" created a shocking situation in which a young man and his betrothed wife were effectively brother and sister.[96] Other regimes, however, were more tolerant. French envoys in seventeenth-century Ayutthaya commented on the fact that men lived with their future parents-in-law prior to marriage, and Burmese texts formalize the expectation that a second daughter should be offered to the prospective husband if the woman promised to him should die within this period.[97] The abduction of an unwed girl was frequently employed as a convenient means of avoiding the expensive payment of betrothal gifts, and in this case sexual relations were simply regarded as a prelude to marriage. At times, such practices were endorsed in collations of written law. Thus, while the fifteenth-century *Undang-Undang Melaka* imposes a fine for rape, the text also notes that the crime is negated should the couple follow custom and marry, an interpolation that is not found in Islamic law. It is clear, too, that Muslim codes could be subject to considerable reinterpretation. In the words of one Minangkabau text, "It is a great offence for a girl to be pregnant with an unknown father, but when the child is born, she is free of offence according to custom, but by religious law she is taken to the mosque on a Friday and forty people spit on her."[98]

Even when communities regarded premarital sex with equanimity, they were at one with state authorities in categorizing adultery and incest as the two great sexual crimes, a threat to the well-being of all. Though precise definitions could vary, incest was universally regarded as heinous, incurring customary law's harshest fines and requiring lengthy and expensive rituals of purification. The vocabulary of law codes has the potential to open up interesting areas for comparative discussion. Can other Southeast Asian cultures, for instance, provide parallels to the Bugis term *ripaliq,* meaning "to be expelled after committing incest"?[99] Does the use of foreign expressions, like the Vietnamese Chinese-based word, *loan luan,* meaning "anarchical morals," or the Arabic *wati* (rape) in a Malay text imply new interpretations of incest and sexual violation?[100] To what extent did recourse to religious and legal documents reduce the flexibility of orally transmitted law and the authority of village custom? The Le Code, for example, meticulously spells out prohibited relationships—fornication with the cousin of either parents or with the wife of a cousin, a maternal uncle's wife, the wife of a nephew on the paternal side, his adoptive daughter, his stepdaughter, his sister-in-law—and prescribes appropriate punishments, like decapitation for the man and exile to a distant place for the woman.[101] The possibility of new interpretations was especially evident when Europeans compiled their own versions of "indigenous law," often amalgamating and simplifying several sources. Because the Dutch regarded "Mohammedan priests" as potentially subversive, they were inclined to favor customary or Hindu-based practices while removing what they saw as "absurdities and obscurities." Even so, consultation with Muslim authorities tended to strengthen Islamic elements, notably in relation to marriage, inheritance, and sexual offenses. For example, Muslim teachings supported local condemnation of intercourse between those nursed by the same woman as incestuous, but punishments that were rarely enforced, like branding, forced labor, and imprisonment, were now included in European-compiled codes and classified as "traditional" custom.[102]

Southeast Asian laws and edicts have a great deal to say about adultery, although here again linguistic investigation might uncover a concealed history of how "immorality" was interpreted. Despite the ideals projected in religious teachings and literary images, "virginity" and "marital fidelity" were not rigid categories, even among the elite, and travelers frequently commented on the fact that married women could be sexually available to foreigners as a mark of hospitality. As William Dampier noted, "The offering of Women is a Custom used by several nations in the East-Indies, as at Pegu [southern Myanmar], Siam, Cochinchina, and Cambodia. . . . It is accounted a piece of Policy to do it; for the chief Factors and Captains of Ships have the great men's Daughters offered them, the Mandarins or Noblemen at Tunquin. . . ."[103] However, although in some cases women themselves initiated such encounters, the agreement of husbands and fathers was normally critical in absolving sexual exchanges from the taint of adultery. A Lan Na text even cites the case of a bodhisattva who told his fifty wives to take care of a male guest: "There was no sin by the women, nor by either of the men," for "if two friends like each other, and one says to the other, 'Go sleep with my wife,' and he does, there is no fault, for permission was given." If a woman had merely slept in another man's house, and no intercourse had occurred, says the same code, she only had to beg her husband's forgiveness; though she had been "very bad," her actions were not rated as a serious crime.[104]

By contrast, sexual intercourse that was not condoned or at least tolerated by the husband was an egregious offense, a clear challenge to a man's marital rights. Condemnation was particularly vehement in the Malay-Indonesian world, where even in the thirteenth century a Chinese account of Palembang remarked that adultery was the only crime that merited death. Customary law *(adat)* in the Indonesian archipelago, committed to writing in later times, is generally unanimous that a man found in the room of a wife or a marriageable daughter could be killed with impunity. The very suspicion of indiscretion, such as improper words or gestures or unacceptable proximity, called for action. The *Agama*, a Javanese legal text probably written in the nineteenth century but reflecting older traditions, even sees the crime of violating a married woman as equivalent to someone who slanders the king. One Malay code acknowledges that in Islamic law "he who kills should also be killed," but according to "the custom of the country" there would be no litigation against a man who took the law into his own hands in the case of a wife's adultery.[105] The perception that sexual access to a woman was effectively "owned" by some male relative, and that illicit relations challenged these rights, is also found in legal codes drawn up under the aegis of Theravada Buddhism. Despite religious prohibitions against taking life, such texts generally agree that in principle a husband can kill his wife's lover (and, said Gervaise, the wife as well) if they were actually discovered in the act.[106]

The idea that a wronged man could act on his own cognizance sat uneasily with the emerging assumption that judicial authority was located beyond the family and should be exercised by officials ultimately responsible to the state. Melaka legists hence noted that it was wrong for a husband or father to kill a man found in a compromising situation with a wife or daughter, since no one except the judge or another high-ranking official was authorized to order an execution.[107] In Vietnam, Tran rulers (1226–1400) had permitted a husband to kill his wife's lover, but such acts were not condoned by the succeeding Le dynasty. A person who murdered a man involved "in criminal sexual intercourse" would be condemned to "penal servitude" or corporal punishment according to the rank of the woman involved. The penalties for adultery varied with social status and could include a beating with rattan sticks, exile, facial tattooing, and garroting for women (also used in Malay society). Women found guilty of other sexual offenses could be condemned to menial work such as breeding silkworms, agricultural labor, or paddy husking. Yet the sources also provide recurring evidence that written codes were always prescriptive rather than a description of how "law" actually functioned. In southern Vietnam, claimed the silk merchant Pierre Poivre (1719–1786), a wife found guilty of adultery was put to death by being tied into a sack together with a pig and thrown into the river.[108]

State efforts to close the gap between documentary law and customary practice were most evident in areas under Christian-European control. While the severe punishments prescribed for sexual transgressions were not consistently enforced, monogamy and fidelity were still seen as fundamental to Christian praxis. From a vast range of oral transmissions, an English rendition of Rejang customary law (western Sumatra) specifically included provisions penalizing unmarried mothers or women who gave birth "before the due course of nature."[109] The most hardened attitudes against sexual crimes were probably found among the Calvinist Dutch, who waged an incessant if unsuccessful campaign against "fornication," especially among Christian converts. Finally approved in 1650, the Statutes of Batavia classified adultery, like prostitution, as a criminal offense. The Consistory Council of the Protestant Church regularly reviewed the moral condition of its parishioners, punishing sexual misconduct, adultery, concubinage, and unlawful divorce by excluding sinners from communion. Retribution for those pronounced guilty was unforgiving and often ferocious. Whereas the Javanese normally levied fines for sexual offenses, with mutilation and other types of physical punishment sparingly imposed, the VOC institutionalized punishments such as flogging, branding, and public display. In early seventeenth-century Batavia, for example, a girl of twelve and a boy of seventeen were accused of having illicit relations; he was executed, she was exposed naked and beaten. These penalties were applied with equal savagery in other Dutch posts, especially when adultery had occurred across religious lines. In Ambon in 1672 a Muslim man and a Christian woman, found guilty of sexual intercourse, were condemned to flogging and working in chains (he for two years, she for one year).[110]

Perhaps reflecting the contrast between Dutch and Iberian values, authorities in the Philippines were more sympathetic toward a Spaniard who felt his masculinity had been impugned. In 1621 a governor who killed his own wife when he found her with a low-ranking lover went quite unpunished, although he later died, reportedly "of a broken heart." A Spanish missionary even commented that "after knowing Spanish ways, some of those [natives] who reckon themselves more enlightened have sometimes slain the adulterers." The Catholic Church, however, was intent on enforcing the marriage vow among the native population because the union between men and women was deemed part of "natural law."[111] Hardly inclined to countenance a Filipino taking the law into his or her own hands, Church authorities rarely referred the sins of adultery and bigamy to the secular courts. As the unchallenged agents of the Crown, it was generally priests who determined sentences for sexual crimes.[112] It is thus ironic that although Spanish officials used condemnations of immorality to bring down a rival, it was still common for a friar (the personification of law in the provinces) to maintain a female "housekeeper" with little fear of reprimand and even to initiate or demand sexual relations with married women.

In sum, the criteria by which blame for sexual misconduct was apportioned were hardly neutral. One Mon *dhammasat* even remarks that a man could not be held guilty if a woman made advances to him because her desires were so strong. Husbands were advised to maintain control over their wives and female attendants because they so often tried to entice a man by "letting something fall as if accidentally, and picking it up in such a manner as to show off their figures." In a similar vein, Vietnamese law condemned a man's seduction or rape of a virgin, but a married woman who had been violated bore responsibility for contributing to the offense.[113] Inherent in these pronouncements was the belief in an underlying female weakness for unsuitable men. The motif of ladies swooning over the seductive voice of a male courtier recurs frequently in Malay-Indonesian literature; a central episode in the immensely popular *Hikayat Yusuf* describes the advances of Potiphar's wife toward the slave Joseph.[114] Catholic priests encouraged the view of women as sexual temptresses, and sermons delivered in Tagalog reminded congregations of God's anger should a man "live with a woman who is not his . . . her mouth is as big as a deep well, into which he will fall."[115] The Thai *Traibhumikatha* depicted the ghosts of the Buddhist hells as preponderantly female, including nuns with golden bodies but piglike mouths who had been disrespectful to monks. The great Sufi al-Ghazali (d. 1111 CE), whose name was always invoked with reverence in Muslim Southeast Asia, recorded that the Prophet himself had said, "I looked into hell, and found most of the occupants to be women."[116]

Gender and Legal Codification

It bears repeating that even when written codes existed, the exercise of "law" in most of Southeast Asia remained localized, personalized, and arbitrary. Nonetheless, from the fifteenth century what William Cummings has called "the codification of culture" gathered pace as literate courts compiled collections of ancestral sayings, rulings of ancient kings, or the commands of sacred scriptures.[117] At lower levels, traditional injunctions acquired a new authority as they were recorded in writing. Village morality had long used humiliation as a means of enforcement, but the customary right of an aggrieved wife to pull the ears or topknot of any woman with whom her husband had slept must have been strengthened when it was incorporated into Burmese legal codes. Like Burmese laws, northern Thai texts dictated that a man who had intercourse with an underage girl should have his head shaved and be paraded in the village, while a Malay man discovered attempting to seduce another's wife was required to humble himself before a community assembly. In Ayutthaya, the use of tattoos to identify wrongdoers, including an adulterous wife, became a recognized punishment, and in Vietnam, tattooing of the forehead and face with up to ten characters could also be imposed for moral crimes.[118]

In these environments, the village councils that had been largely responsible for ensuring compliance with local custom fed into an evolving court system where the details of disputes and crimes were heard by legal specialists. An indigenous judiciary was most elaborated in Vietnam because of the Chinese model and the example of Qing attempts to enforce greater sexual morality. However, the corpus of legal codes shows that formalized structures were developing in most literate centers. Foreign visitors to Ayutthaya, for example, observed that court officials were expected to be familiar with established practices and that information about specific cases was recorded in writing.[119]

Given the present state of research, it is difficult to generalize about the ways in which these emerging legal systems affected Southeast Asian women. On the one side, one might cautiously suggest that courts did provide an arena for complaint and reparation, especially when legal rights were officially documented. Ayutthaya's 1614 Law of Inheritances makes careful note of inheritance entitlements, such as the shares that should go to the deceased's surviving mother, his childless widow, and his adopted children. It also makes provision for divorcées and for children and wives who live in another province or another region of the kingdom.[120] We can infer that these laws were actually being applied, since Gervaise specifically commented on the vitality of the courts: "Each party pleads his own cause without dissimulation and in good faith. Since the women are more lively and more articulate than the men, they almost always receive a more favorable hearing, and they know much better how to defend their interests."[121] For those equipped to argue their case, the legal system could provide recourse for perceived injustice. A Vietnamese example concerns a man who contracted a second marriage to the daughter of a wealthy family following his success in the 1757 civil examinations. When his first wife complained about her relegation to a lesser place in the commemorative procession, the judge was sympathetic, and her husband was removed from the list of those recommended for official posts.[122] In European-controlled areas, civil and ecclesiastical courts became a venue where women could publicly air their grievances. This was highly significant in urban settings, where the machinery for community conciliation was largely nonexistent and where former slaves were separated from their kinfolk. Cases commonly involved inheritance and property rights, but courts under VOC aegis were also much frequented by Christian converts petitioning for marriage dissolution. In Batavia, it was said, two-thirds of the cases that clogged the courts were brought by local Christian women seeking divorce from errant and allegedly adulterous husbands.[123]

The expanding textualization of law also provided a vehicle by which specific breaches of sexual norms could be categorized and then matched with penalties that were increasingly commuted into a monetary equivalent. In the northern Thai states, for instance, "grasping the hand or touching the breast of another man's wife" is one of the sixteen categories of contention, for which the actual fine depended on the offender's own marital state and the extent to which the woman's body had been exposed.[124] With increasing circulation of small coinage, monetary compensation as a substitute for other forms of punishment probably benefited women, who (with access to their own income) could buy themselves out of an unsatisfactory marriage or offer recompense for some misdeed. Thus, while one Malay code lays down that a seduced woman should be put in stocks at the door of the mosque and her head shaved, it also provides an alternative by which she could pay a fine and be released.[125]

The great value of reckoning reparation in this manner is that amounts could be finely tuned to the nature of the offense and the status of offenders and victims. In Java a widow or divorced woman with children could receive monetary compensation of ten silver reals [or the equivalent] if she had been sexually assaulted; should she be childless, however, she would receive only four reals, the same as an unmarried woman.[126] It was also understood that any fine should reflect the standing of those accused and the context in which the offense had occurred. According to the Lan Na code, a headman who beat his wife should be required to pay a larger fine than ordinary men, and an official who seduced the wife of another official could pay as much as 2,200 pieces of silver.[127] By the same token, a poor Malay who seduced a betrothed girl should be fined half the amount due from a rich counterpart, and a wealthy Mon man who forcibly untied the skirt of a woman should pay more than a poorer one. The fines for sexual offenses noted in one of the earliest Islamic sources, the Terengganu Stone, reflect indigenous influences rather than classical Islamic law; in this sense, too, Vietnamese law was very "Southeast Asian" in imposing fines and demotion in lieu of physical punishment. Unlike China, the Le Code sentenced offenders to pay reparation for moral as well as actual damage, so that the shame a woman might suffer from adultery, rape, seduction, or a broken betrothal could be given a monetary equivalent.[128]

Suitably adjusted in terms of social status of victim and accused, the remittance of fines could make restitution for virtually any moral fault, even incest and adultery. It is likely, as in early modern Germany, that Southeast Asian authorities favored fines because they were simple to enforce and that offenders also preferred payments in money, kind, or labor to other penalties such as public humiliation, beating, banishment, or confiscation of property.[129] Some texts appear to be self-consciously aware of the advantages of imposing fines rather than physical punishments, particularly when family or individual honor is involved. A Malay code, explaining that a man who inadvertently marries a woman suckled by his own wife can offer retribution by distributing alms in the mosque, continues, "for in this world, provided the parties are able to pay, one can be freed from any offence against *adat*." A similar view was expressed in Lan Na: "Compensation in money should be paid so that people will not be stirred into seeking revenge." In essence, paying fines is seen as a curative process that allays anger and wipes out demerit. The Malay document puts the case even more strongly. "The use of money and the reason for its having been given to us by Allah is so that those who possess it should live in comfort and be free of the consequences of their misdoings. If it were otherwise, what would have been the use of Allah sending it into the world for his servants?"[130] The practical application of such views is evident in a 1708 case from Cirebon (north-coast Java). A part-Chinese woman, Sinio, had physically attacked another woman, a Javanese who later died of her wounds. Sinio was detained in the VOC fortress, awaiting extradition to Batavia. The case was then referred to the Cirebon princes, who found Sinio guilty but imposed a fine and a prison term rather than the normal punishment of death by the kris.[131]

Sinio's case is a reminder that even when clemency was extended, it was men who made judicial decisions and it was men who handed down the penalties. Although Malay law recognized female expertise in assessing virginity and other matters that are "usually only known to women," it accepted the Islamic view of female unreliability as witnesses and unsuitability as judges. Nor are suspicions of the veracity of "female-like men" limited to Muslim and Christian areas, for they surface in Burmese documents as well.[132] The view that women were somehow culpable for lapses in moral standards often helped justify stricter penalties. Makassarese *parakara* (legal guidelines), for example, held a woman twice as accountable as a man for committing adultery; both offenders were wrong, "but the woman was doubly wrong." A man was therefore fined one real, and a woman two.[133] When the Burmese took control of northern Thailand in the seventeenth century, a law was promulgated fining a man for adultery or incest, but "as for the woman, if she knew he had a wife already, let her hair be cut and her ears cut off so that everyone would know she took another's husband. If her hair is cut and her ears are cut, let her also be charged the cost."[134] An increasing preference for documentary proof meant that a defendant who could produce written material to support a case undoubtedly had the advantage. With less access to literacy, women were inevitably disadvantaged. Well before the turn of the eighteenth century, Vietnamese law no longer accepted tokens such as a split coin or a broken chopstick to indicate a mutually agreed divorce, and a signed deed was now required to establish legality.[135] As in Europe, it may be possible to detect a trend whereby a woman's sexual history could influence court decisions. In 1805, for instance, a Thai woman named Pom sued for a divorce from her husband in a provincial court, obtaining restoration of her premarital property. Pom's husband successfully challenged this decision, arguing that his wife's alleged adultery negated her case.[136] The tendency of male officials to support men's conjugal rights, especially when compensation was involved, also militated against formal annulment of marriage. Although the details are not provided, it is worth noting that in 1810 a Burmese woman claimed that she had been forced to ask three times before the headman granted her a divorce.[137]

Yet it was not the judgments of zealous officials or the "cultural codification" generated by literacy that were ultimately the most effective custodians of morality. In guarding against sexual transgressions and regulating male-female relationships, the preoccupations of local communities and the state overlapped. At all levels of society, leaders wished to avoid social disruption and the conflicts that could arise when women were dishonored or property contested. Indeed, embedded in written documents was a recognition of the force of communal oversight. As the statutes of Melaka put it: "Allah has left all human beings to their rulers and ministers; the subjects are like roots and the rulers the trees; roots and trees should stand firmly together. Do not be reluctant to go to the meeting hall [*balai*] to investigate the families who have committed offences so that your trial will be lightened by Allah Almighty on the Day of Resurrection."[138] State regulation of sexual conduct might have only limited success, but it nonetheless placed a heavy load on the community. According to the Cirebon code, should a woman become pregnant by an unknown father, her fellow villagers would be held responsible because they should have informed the authorities.[139] Underpinning this surveillance, the family—itself providing a rationale for the authority of the state—could be recruited as an ally in the realization of state priorities. In the words of another Malay text, "Parents and children, brothers and sisters, share the same family fortune and the family repute. If one suffers, all suffer."[140] And while vigilance was incumbent upon all family members, the greatest burden almost invariably fell on the parents. As early as the ninth century, Khmer inscriptions call down imprecations on the mothers of those who destroy the god's goods, and the idea of parental culpability for the wrongdoing of a son or daughter was in most places culturally axiomatic. Thus, although Vietnamese laws exonerated the wider kinship circle from blame, the immediate family was still answerable for individual infractions. Should a woman flout her husband's wishes, her parents would be held responsible.[141] This shared liability helps explain why appeals might be made to a court when a daughter's honor had allegedly been violated and why village communities could sometimes treat a woman accused of "licentious behavior" so harshly.[142]

Perhaps the most powerful weapon in the family's armory was the self-regulation inculcated by the idea that disregard of sexual prohibitions would incur some kind of supernatural punishment. Thai sources remind men that offenses such as touching a woman's breasts could result in painful hands and feet, diseases of the eyes and ears, or other illnesses; however, some of the *peta* (hell-beings) in popular stories are women who had "lacked reverence for a husband or had been disrespectful to a mother-in-law, or even caused a co-wife to miscarry." Since sexual misdeeds by females were regarded as public offenses that dishonored their families, the agonies suffered in hell by those who flout cultural norms, a favorite subject in temple decoration, are often directed toward women. Carvings at a Taoist pagoda in contemporary Ho Chi Minh City thus depict a netherworld where the stomachs of adulterous women are slit open, their tongues cut out, and their bodies thrown to hungry tigers and dogs.[143] In promoting ideal forms of female behavior, judges, officials, elders, and parents could also draw on a pool of cautionary tales that revolved around religious or semimythical personages who could be recruited as exemplars of the moral order. A story included in the Malay *Hikayat Bayan Budiman* (one manuscript of which dates from 1600) thus cautions a woman whose trader husband is absent that she should not succumb to the advances of a prince. According to the Qur'an and the sayings of the Prophet, says the wise mynah bird, married women who commit adultery will be impaled by the angels in hell for a thousand years. The early seventeenth-century poet Hamzah Fansuri similarly assures his listeners that those guilty of fornication will be assigned to perdition, where they will suffer for their misdeeds into eternity.[144]

THE DEVELOPING ability of political centers to galvanize human resources and extract revenue—always limited by low levels of urbanization, relatively weak bureaucracies, and geographical distance—is regarded as a feature of "early modernity" in Southeast Asia. Whether indigenous or European, all administrations placed a high priority on settled communities, which could be tapped for labor and tribute and through which approved values and beliefs could be transmitted. The matter at hand could concern corvée service, military conscription, the payment of taxes, or the education of children, but the cooperation of the community and its family networks was always essential. Metaphors of kinship relationships remained immensely relevant in societies where images of stern yet loving parents, obedient children, and supportive siblings could be invoked to justify hierarchies in a variety of different situations. In this sense, the family unit, the basis of any community organization, not only buttressed the state-building project but also transformed its members into potential agents of government.

State indifference to a paradigm laid out in terms of familial rights and obligations quite commonly resulted in peasant rebellion, which, notwithstanding the occasional presence of some valiant "woman-warrior," is normally glossed as male. Accepting that the catalyst for revolt almost always was unacceptable state impositions, "peasant rebellion" must be read as the ultimate expression of household anger, the frustration of women as much as men. Invariably the goal of such uprisings was not government by "the people" but the institution of a kinder and more parentlike regime that would mimic the idealized behavior of mothers and fathers. For their part, rulers and governors in Southeast Asia, like their counterparts in Europe, believed that the state's hold over its subjects ultimately relied on the cooperation of the family and on the acceptance of a gender hierarchy controlled by men. Taj al-Alam, succeeding to the throne of Aceh in 1641 as a young widow, was said to have loved her subjects "as a mother does her children," but her nobles, fearing that she would become subservient to a new spouse, successfully dissuaded her from remarrying.[145] Taj al-Alam's compliance is a salutary reminder that women, despite undoubted subversion and counterfeiting of male privilege, were cosignatories to a cultural compact by which a husband-dominated household was elevated as an appropriate model for political authority.

CHAPTER 6

Women, Courts, and Class

The extent to which the sources privilege the rich and powerful has long been a cause of angst among scholars of premodern Southeast Asia, but it does mean that the experiences of upper-class women are more amenable to historical investigation. Even when the focus is on men's affairs, there is a persistent female presence. Women emerge as progenitors of a prestigious dynasty, nubs of a diplomatic alliance, or catalysts for some great conflict, while objects associated with them have survived as symbols of personal status and residues of life histories. A queen or princess might have commissioned a Buddha image or given her name to a batik design; perhaps her sleeping couch or personal chariot is preserved in a museum, or her grave has become a place of local veneration. Shored up by texts and legend, the fragmented narratives encrypted in such memorabilia offer promising material for exploring women's lives at the highest levels of society.

Once again, however, our ability to generalize across Southeast Asia is limited, for a blanket term like "elite" can disguise significant differences between royal courtiers in an urbanizing capital and tribal chiefs in some distant highland village. The early modern period also witnessed the rise of new status groups, like the Sino-Thai aristocracy of Ayutthaya, the mestizo "Topasses" in the Portuguese-controlled areas of Flores and Timor, and the mixed Malay-Bugis nobility in Johor. The uneven spread of the data presents another historiographical obstacle; information about women in the *kraton* (palace) in central Java, for example, is considerably more detailed than that relating to the Burmese Western Palace, "where only females are allowed to work."[1] As yet we know little of the inner workings of high-ranking households in Vietnam, nor the extent to which they replicated those of China. Nevertheless, despite distinctive cultural contexts, the battery of visual, written, and oral representations to which Southeast Asia's wellborn women were exposed extolled remarkably similar ideals of female behavior. These ideals were most clearly articulated in the great courts, which supply the richest historical material and which lesser states and chiefdoms sought to emulate. A juxtaposition of these palace settings can simultaneously accord women greater attention, facilitate the transition from particularity to generalization, and provide opportunities to revisit claims of regional distinctiveness.

Women as Rulers

Trained in the Orientalist tradition, the first generation of Southeast Asian scholars was predisposed to see stories of legendary queens as emblems of a "ruder" matriarchy eventually displaced by more sophisticated patriarchal systems.[2] Though no modern historian would endorse this evolutionary model, one still notes periodic mention of female rulers in datable sources, like a ninth-century Chinese reference to "the kingdom of the queen" somewhere in contemporary Laos. Later inscriptions from Pagan, Pegu, Sukhothai, and northern Thailand record the visibility of royal dowagers and consorts as they honored the monkhood, donated religious buildings, and even accompanied armies into battle. As one authority remarks, "[In Sukhothai] it seems to have been the custom for a Queen Mother, no matter what the king's age, to take an active part in affairs of state."[3] In insular Southeast Asia, respect for senior royal women is likewise a persistent theme; the Javanese chronicle *Description of the Districts* (1365) describes a dowager queen as "the auspicious leader of the world" who "made [members of her family] rulers and watched over all their affairs."[4]

Nonetheless, in Southeast Asia as elsewhere, women installed as independent rulers entered a domain where the vocabulary associated with leadership was quintessentially male. In commemorating a queen's establishment of a religious foundation in pre-Angkor Cambodia, for example, a Khmer poet praises the divinity "who gave to a woman the status of a man [or perhaps masculinity, *pumtvam*] which is difficult to obtain."[5] The phrase *gaga berani*, frequently heard in classical Malay texts, subsumes the courage and daring that are essential qualifications for a great hero but are uneasily applied to women. An eighteenth-century Acehnese poem, describing a female pirate as a "cursed whore," acknowledges that she is indeed brave *(beurani)*, but attributes her victories to magic and the awe-inspiring appearance of the "sixty or seventy men" who followed her.[6] Because male authority was generally seen as inseparable from the natural order, the lives of women who achieved recognition as leaders can reveal much about the extent to which gender boundaries could be acceptably adjusted.

By the seventeenth century, sovereign queens had virtually disappeared from mainland Southeast Asia, and we find no equivalents to the famed Mon ruler Baña Thaw (1453–1470), who among her many titles was known as Mistress of the White Elephant.[7] Traditions of female governance were stronger in the northern Thai kingdoms, and a text from the upper Mekong records several occasions when a queen mother took control because the throne was vacant, or because a ruler had unexpectedly died. At times her position as caretaker could became more permanent, and in 1612 the dowager queen was installed with all the appurtenances used for a king—the crown, the sword, the umbrella, the betel set, the drum, the set of clothing—and ruled until 1637.[8]

Female rulers are more evident in island Southeast Asia, although the nature of their authority is not always clear. One enigmatic figure is Puteri [Princess] Jamilan, a title referring to successive queen mothers in the triumvirate that ruled the Minangkabau kingdom of central Sumatra. Presumably reflecting female status in this matrilineal society, the qualities associated with the shadowy Puteri Jamilan recall the legendary Minangkabau queen mother Bundo Kanduang. Occupying a central position in traditional sung epics, or *kaba,* Bundo Kanduang—whose husband is never mentioned and whose foremost relationship is with her son—exemplifies the strong, wise, and nurturing mother figure found in so much Minangkabau literature. At the same time, references to Puteri Jamilan in both Dutch and indigenous sources remind us that women of authority are often feared as well. In the elevated language of letters sent in her name, Puteri Jamilan is credited with "the highest most supreme dominion and power," and Minangkabau's migrant communities on the Malay Peninsula spoke with awe of her supernatural ability to punish unresponsive subjects.[9]

During the seventeenth century one can find other instances of women who dominated the administration even in societies where traditions of male authority were well established. An example from Sumatra concerns a Palembang princess entitled Ratu Mas, who became the dowager queen in neighboring Jambi following the death of her husband in 1630. Succeeding at a time when pepper profits were at their height, she acted as patron to both Dutch and English factors and until her death in 1665 exercised considerable influence in the affairs of both Palembang and Jambi.[10] On the far side of the Malay Peninsula, from 1584 until about 1688, a succession of four queens reigned over the state of Patani, leading one Chinese observer to conclude that "since olden days only a woman can become the ruler." Although in fact three of Patani's queens were sisters, he believed that even a commoner born "with the auspicious signs of an extraordinary nature which eventually prove to be the indubitable indication of royalty" would be welcomed by the entire population as their queen.[11]

It is the long period of female rule in the northern Sumatran state of Aceh, however, that has attracted most historical attention. After Melaka's fall to the Portuguese in 1511, Aceh emerged as a flourishing trading port and a center of Islamic scholarship. Its powerful ruler Iskandar Muda (1607–1636) extended his control down both coasts of Sumatra and over several states on the Malay Peninsula. His son, Iskandar Thani, who died in 1641, was succeeded by his long-lived widow Taj al-Alam Safiyat al-Din Syah (1641–1675). A devout patron of Islam who only spoke to European men from behind a curtain, Taj al-Alam was the first Muslim queen in Southeast Asia to use the feminized title of *sultanah.*[12] Europeans who attended her regular Saturday audiences reported that she was well versed in commercial matters and alert to any threat to Aceh's interests; their accounts leave little doubt she was an effective and forceful ruler. With several eunuchs "of very acute witt" as her advisers, Taj al-Alam was never the mere tool of powerful nobles.[13] The pomp that had characterized the court during the reign of her husband and father continued, even to the maintenance of a "harem" of over a thousand women. Nonetheless, there is a degree of male condescension in Thomas Bowrey's statement that the queens of Aceh were customarily "old maids" who eschewed sexual relations. We can only regret that the wife of a Dutch factor, invited to Taj al-Alam's inner chambers to explain how European women dressed on formal occasions, left no record of her experiences.[14]

Much less is known about the three queens who followed Taj al-Alam, although Europeans still commented on the splendor of the Acehnese court. Following the succession of Sultana Zakiyat al-Din Syah (then about sixty years of age) in 1678, Bowrey wrote: "She went down the River of Achin in soe admirable a Grandure of Worldly State, that the like I believe was never paralleled in the Universe." Accompanied by courtiers, eunuchs, and her women, the royal procession proceeded on barges decorated with gold, as "varieties of musick, and delicate Voices . . . sange to the great Honor and Majestie of their great Virgin-Princess."[15] It is evident, however, that opposition to female rule was growing, and some people said openly that they wished "to have a Kinge to rule and beare dominion over them." Rebellions may have been fueled by a decline in Acehnese prosperity, but religious teachers were prominent in the opposition. Matters came to a head after the succession of Sultana Kamalat Zinat al-Din Syah in 1688, and local chronicles allege that in 1699 a fatwa arrived from Mecca decreeing that no women should be permitted to rule, since this was against the law of Allah.[16]

In spite of this ruling, Muslim preferences were not rigorously honored even in areas where the Islamic affiliation was most pronounced. In eighteenth-century Banten, for instance, the ruler married the daughter of a respected Arab scholar and a local commoner, installing her as Ratu Syarifah Fatimah. Although she is not treated sympathetically in VOC sources, she was obviously a politician of some ability. At Ratu Syarifah's instigation the Dutch deposed her husband, enabling her to assume complete control and govern as sovereign queen after his death in 1750. The rebellion against her, and her subsequent banishment, were due more to political misjudgment, the withdrawal of VOC support, and the alienation of the nobles rather than the unacceptability of a female ruler.[17]

The most intriguing example of Muslim queens is found in the various Bugis kingdoms of South Sulawesi, where Islam had been adopted at the beginning of the seventeenth century but where women who carried the "white blood" of royalty could outrank and supplant male rivals. Adapting their origin myths to incoming Islamic traditions, Bugis royal families traced their genealogies back through an ancestral queen to a marriage between the queen of Sheba (herself a mighty potentate) and King Solomon (the prophet Sulaiman).[18] Yet the Bugis were unusual in accepting that women of prestigious descent could become sovereigns who wielded genuine authority; for instance, there were no queens in neighboring Makassar, despite the linguistic and cultural links to Bugis society.[19] By the end of the eighteenth century, female rulers were almost unknown in the rest of the Malay-Indonesian archipelago, although the influence of royal women in state matters remained considerable. Indeed, their recruitment as negotiators was sufficiently widespread for VOC officials to issue a warning that in "serious and important affairs" company employees should never use women as intermediaries.[20]

Preferring Kings

Despite some toleration of female rulers in Southeast Asia, two factors ensured that political consolidation privileged male authority and patrilineal descent, even when bilateral or matrilineal inheritance systems operated in the society at large. In the first place, the standing of individual queens did not undermine the general categorization of females as mentally and emotionally weaker than males and more vulnerable to exploitation or manipulation by spouses, lovers, or relatives. Notwithstanding Dutch experience of several formidable queens, a VOC official could still ignore the awe with which Puteri Jamilan was regarded and dismiss her as a "mere figurehead."[21] A number of royal chronicles, notably from mainland Southeast Asia, counter legends of a golden age under female rule by emphasizing problems that may arise when women assume political power. Lao court texts, for instance, detail the tyranny of the long-lived Maha Thevi (Great Queen) who, together with her husband, was allegedly responsible for the deaths of seven successive rulers between 1428 and 1438. Maha Thevi's background is obscure. She may well have been Lao, but some historians believe that she was an Ayutthayan princess who had married the Lao king and that her "brutality" is best understood in terms of the "wicked foreign queen" motif found in popular histories and sometimes in court chronicles. At a more fundamental level, argues Martin Stuart-Fox, Maha Thevi can be seen as the "quintessential scheming woman" whose intrusion into the male realm brings great harm to the state and "serves as an object lesson of the danger of allowing women a role in politics."[22]

Foreshadowing later nationalist debates about women's inability to offer unqualified loyalty to a great cause, stories of female betrayal regularly surface in royal chronicles and local legend. In 1788, in a war between two Lao kingdoms, the widow of a former ruler of Luang Prabang is said to have secretly opened the city gates to admit enemy forces from Vientiane, on the condition that the victorious king marry her and install her as his queen.[23] Assumptions regarding the malleability of women may also explain the support for female rulers given by male courtiers, who expected that they would thereby gain more control over the government. In the early seventeenth century, nobles in the Bugis kingdom of Bone apparently pressed for the installation of a woman, We Tenrituppu, to safeguard their own authority. According to local manuscripts, We Tenrituppu was even compelled to assert her sovereignty. "Remember," she told her courtiers, "that I am a queen."[24]

A second disadvantage of "femaleness" was rooted in the notion that a successful ruler was by definition a great conqueror, who demonstrated his superiority by vanquishing lesser kings and laying claim to their possessions. Queens were certainly not unknown on the battlefield in Southeast Asia and are occasionally celebrated in written sources. A Thai inscription dated to 1400, for instance, describes how the Queen Mother of Sukhothai accompanied her son in a campaign to recover lost territory. "Bold and intrepid," they "led the army forth to fight and marched over the territories of numerous rulers . . . jointly they destroyed the host of their enemies."[25] A favored character in much court literature is the beautiful queen or princess who dons men's clothing and guides her forces into combat, like Srikandi, the archer and warrior wife of Arjuna in the famed *Mahabharata* epic. One version of the Ayutthaya chronicles elaborates on this theme in recounting Thai resistance to Burma in the sixteenth century. In 1549, it is said, Queen Suriyothai dressed herself as the Uparat (the heir, or second king) and, riding on an elephant, followed her husband the king into battle. Hard-pressed by the enemy, the king would have been killed if Suriyothai had not urged her mount forward, losing her own life in the attack. The chronicle affirms her reputation by recording that a Lao ruler specifically requested Suriyothai's daughter in marriage because he considered her lineage to be "of the greatest faithfulness."[26] The periodic presence of queens in battle may also be explained by the belief that some possessed spiritual powers, which would ensure a successful outcome. When William Dampier visited the island of southern Mindanao in the late seventeenth century, he commented that the Muslim regent's consort—"the War Queen, we called her"—always accompanied her husband on campaigns, and in Java the devout Ratu Ageng Tegelraja (d. 1803), a secondary wife of Hamengkubuwana II (r. 1792–1810, 1811–1812, 1826–1828) did the same.[27]

High-status women who followed men into combat, however, were always exceptional. The early modern kings who affirmed their place in history did so largely by virtue of their personal prowess and by commissioning texts to commemorate their achievements, detailing the territory conquered and prisoners seized. Perhaps the most telling affirmation of a ruler's power was the capture of his enemy's women who, as the spoils of victory, were his to take at will or distribute among his followers. Despite examples of able women who ruled in their own name or as regents, the sexual violation of royal females presents a dark subtext in the narrative of kingly achievement, more particularly because such violation often served as a measure of male prestige. The elite ideal of feminine beauty, deference, and modesty was not easily translated into the courage, vigor, and virility associated with battlefield triumphs. Although a popular cult had developed around Vietnam's Trung sisters because of their stand against the Chinese, a fifteenth-century account could still claim that their followers ran away because their leader "was a woman [and they] feared she could not stand up to the enemy."[28] By the same token, a country headed by a woman was perceived as militarily disadvantaged. The comment by a seventeenth-century Chinese captain nicely encapsulates a view many men would have shared: "Patani is a country ruled by a Queen and not a country of military prowess." Despite evidence of continuing Patani defiance, the captain went on to report that the Queen was so daunted by the sight of the approaching Siamese forces that she and her army hid in the mountains and Patani was forced to accept tributary status. Another Chinese was even more dismissive; in his view, government by a woman made Patani "one of the most inferior countries amongst the countries of barbarians."[29]

It is significant that this condemnation of female rule, like the fatwa from Mecca, came from outside the region, for sources from Southeast Asia, carrying echoes of much older attitudes, are more ambiguous. As examples, we can consider three texts, all of which survive in eighteenth-century recensions. The first, the Malay *Hikayat Patani*, describes how the *bendahara,* the prime minister, claiming invulnerability for both himself and his followers, leads a rebellion against the newly installed queen, Raja Ijau. Abandoned by her ministers, Raja Ijau, wearing a green jacket and a yellow *selendang* (shoulder scarf), receives the *bendahara* at the palace entrance. She takes off her *selendang* and throws it to the *bendahara*, who immediately winds it around his head. He then makes obeisance and returns upstream but is never again summoned to appear before the queen.

We can only speculate about how a Malay audience might have reacted, but since yellow is the color of Malay royalty, Raja Ijau's surrender of her *selendang* would surely have symbolized the relinquishment of her authority over the *bendahara.* Yet her name (literally "Raja Green") and the jacket she wears are heavily charged, because green is believed to have been the Prophet's favorite color; it is no coincidence that Raja Ijau receives her defiant minister as the drums are being beaten for Friday prayers. One could thus infer that the queen's status is ultimately derived from Islam, which renders her sufficiently powerful to retain her position as ruler, despite the *bendahara*'s army and his magical powers. In fact, she retains the ultimate victory, since the *hikayat* implies that the *bendahara*'s subsequent death is linked to his *derhaka* (treason).[30]

A second example of this more ambiguous reaction to female rule is provided by a text from central Java commissioned by the dowager queen Ratu Pakubuwana (1657?–1732). In an environment where the implications of being Muslim had generated considerable discussion, the writer employs a female spirit, Ni Donya (Lady World), to deny that a woman should be paid honor by a man, even by her own son: "Authority is not given, / be it known, to a woman / by God the Most Holy. / The earthly community / has been given notice: / it is compulsory to follow a male. / If the ruler is a woman, / for example, there would be injustice / and the state would come to be destroyed." Yet the text also accepts that a highborn and capable woman is deserving of male respect, and a ruler can grant his mother the status of one "freed of obligations." When Ni Donya asks the Prophet if a man can honor a woman who has the attribute of lordship (asifat gusti), he offers the equivocal but appropriately Javanese reply, "She may not be paid obeisance / yet it is partially allowed / to pay obeisance to such a woman."[31]

A third instance comes from Vietnam, where male scholars, like their Chinese peers, were vehement in their condemnation of female intrusion into the "outer" space of male authority. Nevertheless, there could be exceptions, as Le Quy Don (1726–1784) showed in his history of Vietnam. In a section of this work devoted to the biographies of the early Le dynasty, Don stated specifically that women should confine their activities to the "inner" realm. In his view, the intrusion of palace women into the "outer" domain during the tenth and eleventh centuries had resulted in moral anarchy. Although this situation had been slowly resolved, it was not until the fifteenth century that royal women conducted themselves according to prescribed standards. Yet of twenty-eight biographies of Le women, Don devoted most attention to Nguyen Thi Anh, the dowager queen who ruled Vietnam for several years from 1443 during her son's minority. Despite the Confucian disapproval of women in politics, Don acknowledged that Nguyen Thi Anh had held her own in a male environment and had followed established custom in fostering peace and harmony.[32]

Polygamy and the "Women's Quarters"

Among the more notable "traveler's tales" of the early eighteenth century were the published letters of Lady Mary Montague, wife of the British ambassador to the Ottoman court. Her astute description of the lives of wellborn Muslim women was a timely counter to the titillating images associated with the Oriental "harem."[33] Nonetheless, despite caustic comments on the "confused informations" provided by her male predecessors, neither Lady Mary nor like-minded contemporaries unsettled the European conviction that Asian rulers were innately lecherous; polygamy was simply proof of their sexual depravity and vulnerability to female wiles. While modern historians would vehemently distance themselves from such judgments, there has still been a tendency to view the "domesticity of kings" as peripheral to kingship itself, always subservient to the administrative and bureaucratic structures to which courts gave rise.[34] Yet the women's quarters of

Southeast Asian palaces were more than sources of subterranean influences; rather, they were matrixes of the human configurations, political machinations, and cultural mechanisms through which governance in early modern states functioned.

Indigenous cosmologies that linked the land's fertility to the virility of rulers are central in explaining the inseparability of "femaleness" and royal authority. The more women a ruler maintained and the more progeny he fathered, the more he became a manifestation of procreative forces at work. The sequestering of royal women is not difficult to understand in a context where rulers were expected to provide constant proof of their sexual potency, and where kingly authority could be fundamentally undermined if this potency was challenged by other men. Among Southeast Asian elites the acceptance of seclusion can also be explained by pointing to very old associations between "inside" and "femaleness" and to indications that the status of a woman and her family rose in direct relationship to her distance from the more masculine "outside." The impact of the world religions, with their insistence on the modesty and retiring nature of "good" women, merely helped intensify existing attitudes and placed an even higher premium on maintaining boundaries that hid the king's women from the gaze of male commoners.[35]

Because sexual relationships among the highborn were highly politicized, it was a matter of public concern if a ruler was indifferent to women or was attracted to other men. Sultan Mahmud (r. 1685–1699), ruler of the Malay state of Johor, was condemned by Europeans as a sadist and a "sodomite" who had taken the sons of several nobles "by force into his palace." According to port gossip, his mother sent a beautiful young woman to the young sultan's bed, but "he called his black guard and made them break both her arms, for offering to embrace his royal person." In this case, Malay histories resolve the cultural conundrum of the infertile king by providing Sultan Mahmud with a fairy wife who is jealous of any other liaison. Encik Pong, a wellborn concubine, forced to swallow the ruler's semen, becomes pregnant and gives birth to a son, who subsequently returns to Johor to claim the throne.[36] In a case from Java, it was again the female relatives of Pakubuwana II (r. 1726–1749) who were concerned about his homosexuality, and two texts attributed to his grandmother, Ratu Pakubuwana, specifically refer to the punishment God will wreak on men who "turn aside from women." According to a later manuscript, the king was induced to make love to his wife and thus father an heir only through the prayers of religious scholars and medicines provided by those skilled in the occult.[37]

Helen Creese's translations of court writings from Java and Bali illuminate new entryways into the recesses of elite households, but even here it is impossible to locate an individual female voice. Throughout Southeast Asia, it seems, the subject matter of women's compositions—seasonal rituals, flowers, the beauty of nature, the songs of birds, the loss of a lover—is largely formulaic. In Ava, for instance, the genre known as *yedou* commonly invoked images from nature to describe the grief of lovers forced to separate, a popular theme fostered by the absence of so many men during the Thai-Burmese wars. The royal consort Ching Ming (1738–1781) is just one among several royal women known to have been adept in this form. "When I see the multicolored beauty [of nature]," she wrote, "I think of my love, whom I have not seen for so long; and with great difficulty I try to overcome my sadness."[38] However, as yet we have no Southeast Asian equivalent to the writing of palace women in India or anything approaching the volume of women's letters and memoirs from elite Chinese households.

Envisaging life within the women's quarters of Southeast Asia's great courts is also impeded by a lack of physical evidence. In modern Beijing it is possible to glean some sense of an imperial concubine's world through a tour of the Forbidden City; a visit to Delhi's Jahangiri Mahal, built as a zenana, serves the same purpose for Mughal India. In Southeast Asia, however, the deterioration of wooden buildings, the vicissitudes of a tropical climate, and the ravages of war mean that our knowledge of female space is largely based on archaeological reconstruction and on illustrations or written accounts left by travelers. For example, nothing remains today of Lan Xang, the most important Lao kingdom in the seventeenth century. We must perforce accept the account of an Italian Jesuit, who remarked that the royal palace, with its spacious courtyards and "a great series of houses all of brick and covered with tiles, where the second wives usually live" was "so large one would take it for a town."[39] Royal residences built or enlarged in the nineteenth century, like those in Bangkok and Jogjakarta, convey an impression of former times, but others such as Hue and Mandalay are now mere vestiges of past grandeur.

Yet even glimpses of how space was gendered within royal residences can contribute to wider discussions about Southeast Asian adaptations of foreign models. The pleasure gardens of Persian and Indian emperors exercised a strong influence on the *imaginaire* of Acehnese rulers, and Iskandar Thani, the husband and predecessor of Sultana Taj al-Alam, is said to have built a small palace and an enclosed "garden of love" (Taman Ghairah) for a homesick wife. This touching story is probably apocryphal, but the remains of the Taman Ghairah suggest that it did not simply cater to male indulgences and female frivolities. At a deeper level it indexed the Muslim architectural world of which Aceh was now a part, for the bathing pools where court ladies splashed and the gardens where they gathered flowers invoked Qur'anic accounts of the Garden of Paradise and of the houris, the beautiful maidens who waited on the faithful. Symbolically, the "garden of love" also encoded the ideas of fertility and regeneration that lay at the very heart of kingship. Acehnese sources, for instance, mention the *balai gading,* where sultans commonly made offerings when a wife became pregnant, and the pools where a royal couple underwent ritual lustration.[40]

A more elaborate complex is Jogjakarta's Taman Sari ("fragrant gardens"), built in 1758 by Sultan Hamengkubuwana. As in Aceh, a prominent feature is the bathing pools, including two set aside for the royal wives and concubines, and a third smaller one, reserved for the sultan and his chosen partner. Court women and their attendants could relax in the pavilions surrounding the pools, while the sultan's bedroom in a three-story tower overlooked the entire bathing area. Because the women's quarters were heavily guarded, the Taman Sari also served as a type of armory; through the length of the complex were underground tunnels that connected chambers in which ammunition and other weapons were stored. Another feature transformed what might appear to be a royal whimsy into a site of immense cultural significance. It was widely believed that in the deep recesses of the Taman Sari a special room was set aside for periodic meetings between the sultan and the goddess of the South Sea, Ratu Kidul, and as a site for the sexual union that would ensure the longevity of his line and the prosperity of the kingdom.

Perhaps the most valuable description of a Southeast Asian court was written by the VOC official (and later governor-general) Rijklof van Goens. His report of a mission to Mataram in central Java in 1656, while providing a wealth of information about general conditions, is also a unique testament to the women's world of the Javanese *kraton.* According to Van Goens, after nightfall the only man in the entire palace was Sultan Amangkurat I (who was surrounded by nearly ten thousand women, including senior princesses, official wives, *selir* (roughly translated as concubines), attendants, and slaves. The foremost ranks of this hierarchy, numbering about four hundred, included Amangkurat's own female relatives and others of noble birth, usually chosen for their beauty. As a Muslim, Amangkurat had taken four official wives who had been selected from the great Javanese families, but to these were added forty to sixty *selir,* who could also become the ruler's sexual partners. It was customary for the ruler to temporarily marry any *selir* who became pregnant, in order to legitimize the children, while divorcing one of his other wives to maintain the acceptable number of four. Van Goens was particularly struck by the extent to which the *kraton* circumscribed the world of the highborn. After a ruler's death a *selir* was expected to remain faithful to his memory and normally did not take a husband, although his other women could be given out to favorites.[41]

While men could and did enter this theoretically closed world, the perception that only the king should have access to the women's quarters made security a matter of considerable concern. In Burma the Western Court, the area occupied by palace women, was administered by four court officials known as *anauk-wun;* court documents specify that an individual holding this position should display great circumspection, fear and respect for the ruler, and have "the blessing of being content with his own wife."[42] Other courts used women as sentinels, perhaps emulating a model found in Muslim India. For Van Goens "it was a source of great wonder" to discover that the entire guard in the Javanese *kraton* was female. At night, he estimated, about three thousand women were posted around the walls to ensure that nobody left and that no men entered.[43] The elite guard, the *prajurit estri,* was made up of around 150 young women, all skilled in the use of pikes, lances, and muskets. Thirty were chosen to flank the king during royal audiences, with ten carrying the royal paraphernalia such as the water vessel, betel set, tobacco pipe, sunshade, perfume box, and items of clothing for presentation to favored subjects, and the remaining twenty, armed with lances and blowpipes, standing guard. According to later observers, these weapons were not merely ornamental, and in the 1780s another VOC envoy was impressed by the proficiency and accuracy with which the *prajurit estri* handled European musketry and by the fact that they trained daily. They were also expected to be refined dancers and singers, though a guardswoman was rarely taken by the ruler as a sexual partner. Because they were exempt from the strictures of fidelity that required most *selir* to become lifelong celibates following the ruler's death, *prajurit estri* were frequently presented to prominent nobles in marriage. Others might rise to even greater heights. Ratu Ageng Tegelraja, the favorite of Hamengkubuwana II, was a commander of the Jogjakarta female guard and subsequently became a favored *selir.*[44]

The Javanese case may be the best documented, but it is by no means unique. One of the most informative sources on Angkor, a thirteenth-century report by Chinese envoy Zhou Daguan, described women "holding shields and lances" as they marched in the royal procession, and there are passing references to female guards in other areas of island Southeast Asia.[45] Notable among these are the accounts of seventeenth-century Aceh, where about three thousand women—armed with bows and arrows, as well as blowpipes, lances, and other weapons—were employed as palace sentries.[46] In Ayutthaya, liaisons like that which led to a royal widow raising her lover, a common guardsman, to be joint ruler may have encouraged the formation of a similar body of female guards termed *khlon.*[47] However, this corps did not attract Western attention until the mid-nineteenth century and was possibly constituted only after the inauguration of the Bangkok dynasty in 1782. The *khlon* was responsible for ensuring that no male gained illegal entry into the palace, and the vigilance of its members is remembered in royal chronicles, as in 1783 when an alert guardswoman raised the alarm after two men in female dress smuggled themselves inside. The *khlon* were also charged with surveillance over the palace occupants, apprehending and bringing back, for instance, a number of concubines who had escaped following a palace fire. According to a later French account, the battalion of four hundred women was divided into four companies. Recruited at the age of thirteen, they served as guards until they reached twenty-five or so, after which they continued as royal attendants and supervisors. Their leaders were women of proven courage and loyalty, handpicked by the king, and the corps itself was a model of organization and military prowess. A group of such women accompanying a princess into battle is depicted in a temple mural in the northern Thai city of Nan.[48]

In some areas of Asia the use of castrated men provided another answer to the problem of sequestering the ruler's women and safeguarding his sexual monopoly. Southeast Asian societies generally found genital mutilation distasteful, and castration is found only in palaces that self-consciously adopted models from beyond the region. The example of China, where eunuchs were still maintained despite criticisms, explains their presence in Vietnam, although there were significant differences. Mature Vietnamese men, "people of quality," might undergo castration as a path to a lucrative future, but the procedure was forbidden for commoners, and "eunuchs" had normally been born with some kind of genital defect. By law, parents were required to notify the authorities of an abnormal birth, and when such a boy reached the age of ten, he could be sent to the court for training as a guard in the women's quarters or to take up some official position. In return, his family and perhaps his entire village would receive some compensation like exemption from corvée, while the boy himself might eventually gain a position of considerable authority. In the seventeenth century, for instance, eunuchs supervised several weaving villages and largely controlled the silk trade. Some even reached the rank of governor or served as civil and military administrators. Nor were such men denied a family life; it was customary, said French missionaries, "that all eunuchs have their wives," and there was no hindrance to adopting sons who would carry on the ancestral rites.[49]

In Aceh, European references to the influence of *capados* (Portuguese, "castrated ones") are best explained by looking to Persian, Turkish, and Mughal examples. Whereas harems in early India had been guarded by old men and armed women (a practice presumably exercising some influence in Southeast Asia), the demand for eunuchs increased dramatically after the Mughals came to power, despite Muslim ambivalence towards castration. A pale reflection of these trends is evident in Arakan, where eunuchs and elderly women directed court ceremonies, and where a visiting Catholic priest reported his reception by "an ancient hump-backed eunuch." In the Acehnese palace, however, a Chinese report of 1617 remarked that there were "more than one hundred eunuchs, and this is something that other countries [in maritime Southeast Asia] do not have."[50] From 1641, during the reigns of the four queens, the role of the *capados* as confidants and go-betweens was further strengthened by their access to the inner court. Because of their favored position, they came to occupy positions of considerable importance, notably in regard to trade and revenue collection. During her river procession in 1678, said Bowrey, the Acehnese queen was accompanied by around a hundred "eunuchs": "Each of them wore his Turban after the Arabian mode of beaten pure Gold and very large Shakels of beaten Gold quite up their arms and leggs, and bore each of them a lance of beaten gold of 7 or 8 foot longe, and proportionately thick."[51]

Occasional references in other Southeast Asian courts are tantalizing at best, but what a colonial scholar termed "natural defectives" were a common feature in many royal households. In Ayutthaya a mural depicting a group of female musicians includes an apparently androgynous figure, and in the 1680s French envoys said that "eunuchs" were among the inner circle that surrounded Princess Yothathep, daughter of King Narai and wife of his successor.[52] The continuing influence of indigenous priests, the *bissu*, in southwest Sulawesi may be partially attributed to the fact that their "third gender" status allowed them to associate more with Bugis queens and other high-ranking women than was appropriate for male ministers.[53] Yet for outsiders, the presence of such figures in the ruler's residence was emblematic of an "inside" or "forbidden" domain that was both splendid and mysterious. "The women's quarters," wrote one Balinese poet, "seemed to radiate a shimmering light, as if the amazing beauty emanated from heaven."[54] This elegance in language and metaphor, of course, does not address the tangled lines of authority, subservience, and exploitation that inevitably developed in an environment where women spent most of their time in the company of other women.

Servants and Slaves in the Women's Quarters

Within Southeast Asian palaces, female hierarchies normally mirrored the social structures of the world outside the palace walls. Women of high birth automatically assumed a higher position than those of low status, and older women outranked younger women in the same cohort. Occasionally, an individual was able to subvert these rankings because she had been particularly favored by the ruler. One remarkable example from the late seventeenth century concerns a Bugis slave, To Ayo, who became the concubine of the heir to the throne of Jambi in east Sumatra. Against all the dictates of custom, To Ayo was accorded a public place in court ceremonies and raised as the prince's wife in preference to his official consort, a princess from the neighboring kingdom of Palembang. A divorce was the inevitable result. To Ayo herself emerged unscathed, the more surprising since her husband (installed as sultan in 1679) also married two highborn Makassar women, the first being no less than the daughter of the Makassar sultan. Despite clear signs of tension—one queen reportedly referred to To Ayo as a "Bugis whore," and at one point there was a physical confrontation—the co-wives were able to reach a working relationship. Ultimately, To Ayo became part of a female triumvirate that virtually governed Jambi and controlled most of its commerce.[55]

Although personal histories like that of To Ayo provide grounds for seeing the royal household as a meeting ground for commoners and upper classes, there are only glimpses of how village girls were recruited, and it is impossible to reconstruct the experiences of any one individual. The appearance of a royal party en route to a temple festival, or some nobleman on a hunting expedition, could mean that a woman was lost to her family forever. The dishonored female, the bereaved parents, the heartbroken suitor, the vengeful lover, are familiar in many a folktale. Quite commonly, female overseers of upper-class establishments, including wives and concubines, were responsible for selecting village women, and the exploitation of a pretty maiden by an unfeeling queen is also a recurring motif. Such stories, however, are countered by others that tell of romantic love, of a king who is captivated by a commoner and raises her to be his consort, and of the rewards that come to her family and community. All across Southeast Asia one finds areas that still retain a reputation as a source of attractive maidens who became attendants in the homes of the highborn. A girl thus chosen could expect to be well-fed and dressed in some finery, in keeping with the status of those she served and, unlike her superiors, could be permitted to enter and leave otherwise closed establishments, deployed to carry out routine tasks or to serve as an agent for her mistress.

The To Ayo episode serves as a reminder that many of those who worked in elite households were slaves, captured in a raid or transported from some distant land. Historical sources reveal little of the cultural bridges that many crossed, whether forcibly or of their own volition. How, for instance, did the "small savage slaves" in the entourage of Nguyen princesses in seventeenth-century Vietnam adapt to the Sinicized world of their mistresses?[56] In many cases, it would seem, the exotic appearance of such individuals actually assisted their survival in an alien world, since the display of unusual objects or persons was seen as a manifestation of a ruler's mysterious powers. Nevertheless, the inclusion of certain "abnormal" women in royal households calls up other disturbing images. In sixteenth-century Ternate, for example, the female dwarfs who carried the king's sword and betel box were reputedly deliberately disabled as children by having their backbone broken. A few years later a Dutch observer in Bali referred to misshapen people, often women, "who for a long time" had their arms and legs tied in such a way that they appeared like the stylized figures carved on the handle of a dagger.[57] The accuracy of such statements is hard to gauge, but the suggestion that some families were complicit in deforming their children itself indicates the perceived benefits when a daughter or a sister lived in proximity to those of high rank.

In a sense, though, the formulaic "fifty humpbacked women"—as well as cooks and bakers, harpists and drummers—in the retinue of Burma's legendary queens is emblematic of the special character of royal households. On the one hand, it was an economic unit. Van Goens, for instance, calculated that in the Javanese *kraton* there were around four thousand women involved in weaving, spinning, sewing, embroidery, and painting, as well as kitchen duties. A royal order issued in Ava in 1635 lists forty different groups among the occupants of the women's quarters, together with occupations that ranged from bearing umbrellas and arranging flowers to cooking and cleaning copper utensils.[59] On the other hand, the palace community was also a ritualized organism where even apparently menial tasks could be culturally weighted, as demonstrated in the annals of Thailand's Cakri dynasty. In 1782 the founder of this dynasty, Rama I (r. 1782–1800), decided that the problems besetting his predecessors could be attributed to their failure to observe royal traditions and the consequent displeasure of the deities.

Historians have drawn our attention to the rewriting of Thai legal and religious texts under Rama I, but he was equally concerned about laxity in royal protocol. As a result, a kind of revolution occurred in palace management that directly affected the women who served the king and his family. Those in charge of laying out the ruler's clothing, for instance, were ordered to observe strict procedures. Garments worn by the king in the morning should be replaced by a new set before sundown; those used while he defecated could never be mixed with others; night clothing should be distinguished from that appropriate during the day. Women responsible for the royal bedchamber had to ensure that all articles handled by the king were ritually pure. Water used in cleaning his mouth and face had to be stored in a special place and covered so that none could see it, while the cloth for drying should be spotlessly white and delicately scented. Other women were in charge of tending the plants that provided ingredients for the royal toiletries, and for mixing the sandalwood oils, roots, and flowers to make powder for the king's face or to perfume the wax used on his lips. Garlands of flowers should be hung near the bed and replaced whenever they withered. Since any sudden illness could be attributed to poison, the text goes on to stipulate that containers of food should be carefully sealed before being passed to the attendants who would carry them into the royal presence. En route, female attendants inspected the seals several times to ensure that they remained unbroken and that there had been no tampering with the contents. Only then could they be set before the king. After he had eaten, the remains were carried back to the kitchens, where written notations were made as to what and how much had been consumed. Adherence to this protocol should be strictly enforced, and any deviation punished severely. An indication of the penalties that might be imposed is seen in the case of one concubine who was raped by a palace intruder. Though her innocence was acknowledged, she was stripped of her insignia of rank and sent back to her father.[60]

The Bangkok chronicles are not alone in demonstrating that the whim of a master or mistress could turn the life of even privileged slaves or attendants upside down, whether they were gifted to some favorite, sold to defray debts, or simply discarded. Yet the sources also provide glimpses of others who flourished, not necessarily because they held any formal office but because they had gained positions of trust and were thus privy to many secrets. A young woman who stood guard by the ruler's throne, who held his betel box, or who served in a visitor's bedchamber not only heard much but also frequently served as a confidante in delicate matters. The loyal maidservant who carries messages to her mistress's paramour is a recurring figure in court literature, and the role of female courtiers as informants or intermediaries is frequently demonstrated in historical accounts. In the early seventeenth century the Portuguese in Arakan learned of plots against them only because the chief attendant of the dowager queen (herself from Pegu) was the wife of a Christian Japanese, and because other women married to Christians had the queen's ear.[61] A century later the Chinese official in charge of Ayutthaya's trade, the *phrakhlang*, "knowing the ways of the court," sought to strengthen his position by introducing Chinese women and girls into the palace to guarantee both their physical proximity to the queen and princesses and their access to important sources of information.[62] For many such women, disclosing what they knew must have required some calculation as to whether a shift in allegiance would better safeguard their future. In 1790, for example, a slave assigned to one of women in the Bangkok court claimed that her mistress and another royal concubine were conspiring to set fire to the Grand Palace. The chief female officials considered the matter sufficiently serious to warrant calling for the king's attention. A subsequent investigation proved that the accusation was true, and both women were then burned to death, the punishment decreed by law. We do not know the fate of the slave concerned, but if her superiors approved of her action, she presumably received appropriate recognition. In turn, however, such individuals might well have found any expectations of advancement dissolve as female networks were recast following a patron's death or disgrace.[63]

Royal Brides, Mothers, and Senior Women

Throughout Southeast Asia, court sources accord special attention to potential mothers of royal heirs, since the preference for prestigious genealogies made the choice of consorts a matter of enormous importance. In Ayutthaya and in the Lao kingdoms, the purity of the royal line was reinforced by a ruler's occasional selection of a sister or half-sister as queen (a relationship absolutely forbidden to ordinary people). Royal brother-sister marriage also occurred in Cambodia, Arakan, and Burma (where an edict of 1630 legalized the union of siblings born of different mothers).[64] On the other hand, the very notion of sexual intercourse between brother and sister would have been abhorrent to the Vietnamese courts or to a Muslim ruler. In words taken from the Bugis *I La Galigo* cycle, arguably the world's longest epic (and in its best-known version, assembled by a Bugis queen), "It is forbidden to become a couple / For people who are siblings. / Obviously you would call down disaster upon your country." In this case the hero Sawerigading is persuaded to leave his native country to find another wife, thus providing a model for the rest of society.[65] In fact, there is little evidence that sons born of unions between royal siblings were more privileged than others, and most Southeast Asian rulers used the institution of marriage to strengthen their links with powerful families within their own society or to affirm an alliance with neighboring countries.

The exchange of women between high-ranking men raises the question of the much-touted sexual freedom of Southeast Asian females. As we have seen, in most societies the idea of a sexually shared woman was not in itself offensive and indeed could establish a special bond between two men. Around 1755, for instance, the sultan of Jogjakarta presented one of his favorite wives to the Dutch governor of Java's northeast coast. In return, and as an acknowledgement of their mutual affection and friendship, the governor gave the sultan another woman from eastern Java, presumably from his own household.[66] When elite marriage was involved, however, a young bride's virginity could be crucial. It may have been quite possible for a village girl to have several sexual partners before marriage, but this could be disastrous for the marital prospects of a wellborn girl. A major concern of the older women so prominent in negotiating elite marriages was to assure the groom's family that his prospective bride was sexually intact. In a region where ritual deflowerment was still occasionally practiced, the breaking of the hymen proclaimed an overthrow of "the fortress," with the bloodied sheets—carefully inspected and sometimes publicly displayed—a war trophy. In the same mode, court poetry in Bali and Java routinely presents the marital bed as a battlefield where the ravished wife feigns refusal but eventually succumbs to her husband's advances. The adoption of European-style weaponry in Southeast Asian warfare has attracted considerable academic attention, but it could also serve other purposes; in 1609 the ruler of Banten borrowed twenty-five armed men from the English trading post to fire a salvo celebrating the conquest of his wife's virginity.[67]

For common Southeast Asian women, marriage did not usually mean exile from family, since newlyweds usually lived in the same vicinity as the bride's parents, even when residence was patrilocal. A lady of rank, however, was normally expected to move to the home of the man to whom she had been delivered, either as a wife or as a sexual partner. The adjustments would not have been so great within a single culture area, and a shared religion, a common language, and similarities in dress and customs help explain why marriage diplomacy was so prominent in relations between the Muslim courts of the Malay Peninsula and east-coast Sumatra. The situation was subject to greater tensions when cultural differences were more pronounced. The many marriages that sealed alliances between great states or important families must have frequently brought unhappiness and loneliness to women condemned to live out their days far from the familiar world of their childhood. One can only imagine the feelings of a Vietnamese princess, the daughter of "the king of Annam," sent to Cambodia in 1616 as a bride for the crown prince, or of the "Dutch wife" (possibly of Portuguese descent) married to Vietnam's titular ruler, Le Than Tong (1619–1643, 1649–1662).[68] The tyranny of diplomacy meant that an unwilling bride would be unlikely to arouse parental sympathy. For example, in 1560 a treaty concluded between Ayutthaya and the Lao kingdom of Lan Xang was to be sealed by a royal marriage. According to Lao accounts, the Ayutthaya princess initially selected was Thepkasattri, daughter of a queen (the latter identified in Thai texts as Suriyothai) who had distinguished herself fighting against the Burmese. Thepkasattri was apparently reluctant to leave home, and when she pleaded illness, her younger sister was sent instead. However, the Lan Xang ruler refused to accept this alternative, claiming that his honor would be impugned "and it would bring shame to our people." The following year Thepkasattri set out for her new home with a thousand attendants, only to be ambushed by a Burmese vassal and sent to an undocumented fate in Pegu.[69]

Some women, brought up with the knowledge that they could end their days in a distant land, coped remarkably well, despite their vulnerability to the "wicked foreign queen" stereotype. Those who arrived from a prestigious court were clearly advantaged, for they often became a conduit for important religious and political connections or introduced new forms of performance and artistic expression. Yet a royal wife from a minor kingdom could also be attributed with significant innovations, like a sixteenth-century princess from the island of Selayar (near southwest Sulawesi) who married the ruler of Ternate. Her entourage of weavers exerted significant influences on clothing styles in the Ternate court.[70] Nonetheless, it was not easy for an outsider to be integrated into the entrenched hierarchies within the women's quarters. Her title had to be carefully chosen, because it would not only indicate her status and that of her children but also determine the clothes and jewelry she wore, the number of her attendants, and above all her standing vis-à-vis the women who surrounded her. For instance, a non-Thai princess had the lesser rank of *phra-ongchao,* although if favored she could be elevated to the level of *chaofa,* the title given to consorts born of a Thai mother. Wives who could not claim royal descent were accorded the rank of *phra sanom,* or royal concubine; they received the title of *chaochom* if they were childless and *chaochom manda* if they bore children.[71] This affirmation of status was important because a newly arrived woman would have to deal with the veritable army of officials required to oversee the smooth running of these large establishments. Anna Leonowens (whose writings should be used with considerable caution) still captures something of the complex society of the nineteenth-century Bangkok court. It was, she said, "a woman's city . . . as self-supporting as any other in the world: it has its own laws, its judges, police, guards, prisons and executioners, its markets, merchants, brokers, teachers, and mechanics of every kind and degree; and every function of every nature is exercised by women, and by them only."[72]

In time, however, an outsider would normally be able to establish herself, if only by virtue of seniority and the experience that came with longevity. Administrative duties in Southeast Asian courts were generally the responsibility of senior women who had been in the palace since they were young, as was the pattern in many other female-dominated environments. In the Japanese palace of sixteenth-century Kyoto, for instance, the *koto no naishi*, the "imperial matron," held a position of great authority, controlling such matters as palace finances and the drafting of correspondence. Her counterparts, the *darogha* of the Mughal court, similarly served as officers, superintendents, and guards.[73] In Southeast Asia, too, senior palace women were the most mobile, the most outspoken, and the most influential cohort. Freed by age from many of the restraints that governed the behavior of younger females, they often enjoyed greater access to economic resources. An early example comes from Banten, where English merchants described "an old woman who commands the Protector [i.e., regent] and all the rest and indeed is called Queen of the land . . . , although she bee not of the King's blood, but only for her wisdom is held in such estimation among them of all sorts that she ruleth as if she were solely Queen."[74] Some years later, Van Goens reported that in the Javanese *kraton* two old women supervised hundreds of attendants serving the wives and concubines, even deciding who should be permitted outside. Experienced palace women also helped select sexual partners for young princes and might also instruct young couples in lovemaking techniques.[75]

As occupants of the most carefully guarded sections of the ruler's residence, senior ladies quite commonly acted as guardians of important documents, sacred texts, and the regalia itself. When an Englishman entertained by the court of Banjarmasin in east Borneo noted that an old woman "whom I supposed to be their teacher" was in charge of royal music and dancing (which could itself be a sacral act), he was describing a situation found over much of the region. Recognition of older women as authorities on history, genealogy, and custom ensured that their opinions were commonly sought on a range of matters. In the late seventeenth century it was reportedly an elderly female member of the Khmer royal family who provided court officials with the anecdotes encapsulating the rights and obligations of kingship. Similarly, after the destruction of palace documents in the Burmese invasion of 1767, Bangkok palace authorities turned to a senior princess to determine the procedures for a royal hair-cutting ceremony so that the Cakri dynasty could follow the precedent set in Ayutthaya.[76]

Rank among this cohort of older women was normally decided by birth, with precedence usually given to the ruler's mother or, if she were still alive, his grandmother. We can only imagine how status hierarchies were negotiated when such women were of humble origins. Cases where the ruler's mother was a former concubine or an unofficial wife are legion. One of the more interesting, the daughter of a stallkeeper in Jogjakarta, received the title "Ratu Kancana" and became the mother of the future Pakubuwana IV of Surakarta (r. 1788–1820).[77] The uniqueness of the mother-son relationship was a significant counterweight to low birth, for the frequency with which women died in childbirth and the cultural impossibility of full recompense made refusal of maternal requests extremely difficult. The effectiveness of the ruler's female relatives in mediating between quarrelling parties, and their capacity to resolve dynastic or state crises, are mentioned repeatedly in indigenous sources. A fragmentary text from sixteenth-century Cambodia thus refers to several instances where the women of the Khmer royal family, especially the queen grandmother, were instrumental in finding solutions to a political impasse. A particularly striking instance occurred in Lan Xang in 1758, when one dowager queen pledged to fast unto death to force her two rival sons to reach an agreement.[78] The influence of the king's mother was the greater because she usually enjoyed high honors in the royal household and had more freedom than other palace women. This was not, of course, invariably so. In Java, Amangkurat's mother had to request permission from her son to leave the court when she wished to visit the grave of her husband, Amangkurat's father. By contrast, Vietnamese law allowed the widow of a former emperor to live outside the palace so that she could pay regular homage at her husband's mausoleum.[79]

In some cases the inequities of royal favor must have given rise to considerable tension, especially when there were clashes with court protocol. There is undoubtedly an untold story behind the fact that Rama I, founder of the Bangkok dynasty in 1782, ignored traditional practice and did not award a royal honorific to his principal wife, the mother of his four living children. His mother, on the other hand, received an elevated title and was supplied with a retinue of officials in charge of various palace departments.[80] Because the stakes were so high, a key figure in many of Southeast Asia's palace coups was often a minor wife or concubine who was the mother of one of the ruler's numerous sons. If a plot to seize power was successful, she could end her days in luxury and comfort; should a rival prince became king, she might be condemned to penury, servitude, or worse. In Java the eighteenth-century *Babad Kraton* claims that Amangku-rat II (r. 1677–1703) had only one male heir because his wife, Ratu Kulon, sought to secure the succession for her own son by causing pregnant *selir* (secondary wives) to abort.[81]

Another recurring figure in palace factionalism was the ruler's surrogate mother, his wet nurse. In Southeast Asian societies, as elsewhere, it was common to give royal children to another (usually wellborn) woman to nurse, apparently because of a belief that the colostrum produced immediately after birth was too thin and that only rich, creamy milk would guarantee an infant's good health. Historians of China have shown that wet nurses held respected positions in the imperial court, where they were honored by the emperors whom they had suckled as babies. In royal Muslim households, wet nurses were similarly respected, and in the harems of Mughal India they helped create a "foster community" that extended the linkages created by blood, birth, and marriage.[82] Their Southeast Asian counterparts have not attracted the same interest, but even a cursory overview shows that wet nurses were frequently at the center of a web of interrelationships, transforming unrelated individuals into "family" through the sharing of milk. The resulting genealogies could have a decisive effect on marriage patterns, negating even the common Austronesian preference for unions with near relatives. The wellborn female cousin of a Muslim prince, for instance, would normally be a prime marital candidate, but if they had shared the same wet nurse, they became "milk siblings" and, as brother and sister, could not marry.

Already high, the standing of the foster mother in Southeast Asian societies was reinforced by the arrival of the world religions. Muslim biographies supply detailed information about the Prophet's "milk parents," Halimah and her husband, and according to Malay traditions, the great hero Hang Tuah visited Halimah's grave en route to Mecca. It is thus quite understandable that palace wet nurses were among those who formally greeted Aceh's sultan when he returned from prayers on important Islamic occasions.[83] Buddhism provided a similar endorsement because of the unique status accorded the Buddha's foster mother, Mahapajapati Gotami. Given this religious-cultural heritage, it is not surprising that Buddhist kings regularly honored the women who had fed them as infants and that, as adults, rulers often sought their advice. A French missionary in Pegu in 1689 found that one of the most powerful individuals in the palace was the prince's former nurse, and through her he obtained permission for the Christians to finish building their small church. Nonetheless, even in this context we find evidence of the ambiguities that invest any discussion of femaleness. Women from Balambangan in eastern Java, famous for their bluish, or "half-indigo," milk, were forcibly moved to the Mataram *kraton,* where they were used not just as wet nurses for royal children but also for distasteful tasks euphemistically termed "bathroom duties."[84]

Palace Occupations

It was often the economic activities of royal women that attracted the attention of Europeans and thereby secured them a place in written records. Such activities frequently entailed well-capitalized operations, for highborn women usually brought substantial resources with them when they married, which they continued to exploit or tap for further investment. It was not uncommon for whole villages to be part of a princess's dowry, with the revenues from appanages considered her due portion. VOC representatives often commented on the involvement of queens and princesses in maritime trade, and in areas where monopoly contracts had been negotiated, the Dutch regularly complained about "smuggling" by royal women and their agents.[85] These resources could also be augmented by the king's bounty. For instance, an undated letter written by Hamengkubuwana II of Jogjakarta to a certain Raden Ajeng Sulbiyah (possibly his daughter) lists the money, clothing, gold jewelry, and other items gifted to her, evidently prior to her wedding.[86] Favored women could also receive rewards in the form of land grants. In eighteenth-century Vietnam this is particularly noticeable because civil unrest led to the redistribution of communal landholdings to royal clients, including concubines and female attendants, who were then able to amass large estates. Some women in the powerful Nguyen and Trinh families had more than a thousand *mau* of land, and the mother of one Trinh lord owned land scattered through more than fourteen villages.[87] Personal and economic links provided access to rural production. During one reign the royal concubines of Ava even set up scales in the palace grounds, where they sold rice at highly inflated prices, and the palace women in Aceh were said to maintain their own market. Once again, Java's Ratu Ageng Tegelraja provides an example of the benefits accruing to those favored by the ruler, for she owned large estates that produced various products ranging from rice to batik cloth, all of which were sold by an agent on her behalf.[88]

On the whole, however, we are given only glimpses of economic life in the women's quarters and of the ways in which the ruler's largesse was distributed. It is doubtful whether the sources from any Southeast Asian court would permit the kind of reconstructions possible in Mughal India, or in sixteenth-century Kyoto, where historians have been able to calculate the precise salaries and emoluments paid out to the ruler's wives, relatives, harem administrators, and female officials.[89] On the other hand, it is possible to see that royal women in Southeast Asia derived incomes from a variety of enterprises that could be used in numerous ways, including extending their circle of clients and supporting religion. The temples and monasteries built by Theravada Buddhist queens stand as an enduring testimony to their piety, and royal women in Vietnam actively supported shrines and pagodas.[90] Visible evidence of religious expenditure by wealthy

Muslim women is less common, but the activities of Taj al-Alam in Aceh and Ratu Pakubuwana in Java indicate that patronage of religious teachers and the commissioning of texts were typical. In about 1806 a number of Jogjakarta court ladies, including members of the female guard, entrusted money to several respected scholars who were embarking on the pilgrimage. They were instructed to buy camels as an offering and to sponsor a religious feast in Mecca, possibly in memory of Ratu Ageng Tegelraja, who had died in 1803.[91]

The involvement of royal women in the production of texts is in many respects a natural outcome of the skills and pastimes associated with high status. In the Thai court certain ladies known as *nang ham*, for instance, were forbidden from marrying but were renowned for their expertise in religion and history and for their skill in composing poetry.[92] Yet while the travails of lovers and the union of predestined partners formed the core of many compositions, recitation was also intimately involved with performance. The dance-drama that survives today, though undoubtedly altered over time, nonetheless conveys some idea of an important form of court entertainment. When VOC official Johannes Paravicini served as an envoy to the court of Banjarmasin in 1756, he was entertained with a "comedie" about "wars and love affairs." It was performed in a room hung with gold tapestry, with the characters, all richly dressed and bejeweled, played by the leading court women, including the wife of the crown prince.[93] And while visitors were expected to give dancers a token of appreciation, such as a piece of cloth or a few coins, such occasions could be far more than entertainment. Dance had long been used as a conduit to the supernatural, and certain sacred dances performed only by chosen females could serve to summon a spirit audience; at the founding of Bangkok in 1782 the royal troupe thus presented a special dance-drama so that the new city would receive divine blessings.[94]

It is difficult to judge whether concepts such as monotony or boredom had any meaning to women in Southeast Asia's great courts. In such a large "family" there must have been a constant succession of ceremonies for royal births, ear piercings, circumcisions, betrothals, marriages, funerals. As the lingering descriptions in chronicles and literary sources suggest, these were occasions of full female involvement.[95] While reference to entertainment of various kinds—tourneys, recitations, games, quail fights—surface in court writings, it is evident that royal pleasure trips provided a welcome opportunity to move beyond the confines of the palace. Malay records, for instance, refer to the enjoyment of court women in picking fruit and collecting shells and to their participation in boating and fishing parties. One can well imagine that suggestions from royal favorites were often the motivation behind such expeditions. In 1642 a VOC employee in Palembang explicitly commented that the sultan had decided to sail to the island of Bangka to please a new concubine; a century later another Dutchman stationed in the Malay state of Perak reported that a ruler's trip to the river mouth was undertaken at the request of his first wife, who had never seen the ocean.[96] Pilgrimages to sacred sites, ostensibly for religious purposes, might provide unexpected opportunities for court women to interact with male companions. In this vein the court poet of Rama II (r. 1809–1824) used the *nirat* form (often describing the parting of lovers but also hinting at the delights of physical love) to describe a pilgrimage to the Holy Footprint at Saraburi, when "we, of the retinue, [are] exhausted, like the dead. / A-shiver in love-longing I lie, anxious are all my thoughts."[97] The poem's underlying assumption—that a courtier could be involved in a secret liaison with a female attendant—brings us to the question of sexual relationships and their implications in a polygamous household, most notably when the husband and lord was also king.

Wives, Co-Wives, and Sexual Relations

Many of the tensions in royal courts resulted from competition among women anxious to gain a place in the ruler's affections. In order to cement an alliance between males, a high-status lady might be introduced into the inner quarters as a royal wife, but the sexual rivalries thus created were not easily resolved. A Javanese chronicle graphically compares the hostility between two contenders for the throne to that of women "recently abandoned by their menfolk," who have taken new co-wives.[98] By contrast, Burma's *Glass Palace Chronicle* depicts an idealized situation when a king married three sisters who were treated absolutely identically. "Because he loved them equally . . . they were content and felt no envy nor eyed each other askance."[99] This is no idle emphasis, for friction in the women's quarters could have a direct impact on state matters, especially if the relatives of powerful families were involved. Grand titles were of little comfort if a husband demonstrated that he preferred other women, and humiliation could be especially galling if the favored one was a person of low social status.

One way of ensuring an amicable atmosphere was to allow a woman to choose her co-wives, and in Vietnam a seventeenth-century observer remarked that although men had many concubines, "as many as their revenues will maintain," the first wife normally chose the others "according to her liking."[100] The larger the establishment, however, the more likely that a wife or concubine would be superseded by a woman to whom she felt no personal ties, and the motif of the resentful wife and virtuous but victimized maidservant became part of the storyteller's stock-in-trade. The jealousy between Siti Hajar (a former slave girl) and Siti Sarah, both wives of the prophet Ibrahim (Abraham), is thus a significant subtext in the Malay version of the tale of Abraham and Isaac.[101] Another recurring motif concerns the despairing wife or concubine abandoned by a fickle husband, and an eighteenth-century Vietnamese consort, Nguyen Thi Ngoc Vinh, used the lyrical "lamenting song" genre (patterned after the lament poetry of the Chinese court) to regain favor with her estranged husband. Metaphors like the fidelity of a discarded concubine were also exploited by Vietnamese men to draw imperial attention to their own faithful but unrewarded devotion.[102] In the nineteenth century, poems attributed to Burmese court women developed the same theme of unrequited affection, and even in translation these convey something of the plight of the repudiated lover. "On oath you promised never to shun me," wrote Princess Hlaing-Teik-Khaung-Tin (1833–1857). "Always to be loyal to me / Solemnly you swore / If I become King / I shall make you my Queen / Even if a Goddess tried to seduce me / Never would I surrender to her. / In coronation's splendid display / I shall give to you the place of Chief Queen / With eight Brahmins and many pages attending you / And at the time of libation's ceremonial / I shall cause all men to worship you / I believed you and gave you my love / Now . . . how different is your manner, Oh Prince of Kanaung, how stern is your face / Where is the former brightness of your face? Where are the loving caresses / You so fondly showered on me? Oh Prince of Kanaung."[103]

Since so much depended on maintaining favor with powerful individuals, most notably the ruler himself, the sexual politics of polygamous households was always intensely relevant. The selection of those permitted to enter the royal bedchamber could generate extreme anxiety because pregnancy was always a possibility and the potential gains so great. Thai chronicles suggest that Bangkok palace protocol resolved the problem by a rotational system, since one episode refers to a concubine who was sleeping at the king's quarters "as she was scheduled to do."[104] In other places the selection was more arbitrary, and when William Dampier visited Mindanao, he noted that the woman chosen to spend that night with the sultan was entitled to wear a kerchief, an open sign of her preferred status.[105] Understandably, there was a continuing market for exotic products that would enhance the allure of candidates for the lord's bedchamber or that would increase his sexual desire. With his scientific interests, G. E. Rumphius (1627–1702) reported that a special mixture of lead and alum was regularly sent from the island of Banda to Java: "Moorish women use it for themselves in order to make their nature pure and dry and therefore most pleasing to their men. This trick is necessary in such nations where many women are kept by one man and each one seeks to make herself the most comely."[106] Even the most potent concoctions, however, might not be sufficient to allay suspicions if a woman were deemed incapable of reproducing. According to Van Goens, Javanese women who bore a deformed child were usually repudiated, and only four years after her marriage in 1722, Amangkurat IV's queen was evicted from the *kraton* because of persistent leukorrhea (vaginal discharge, perhaps considered evidence of a sexually transmitted disease).[107] In an environment where rumor thrived, an ambitious woman had to be very sure that she did not step beyond prescribed limits or arouse the enmity of her co-wives. According to palace texts, an eighteenth-century Thai queen was put to death because of harem accusations that she had used love philters to entrap the king.[108]

For royal favorites the provision of pleasure to an all-powerful but sexually avaricious man could result in substantial rewards, but it would also be degrading and humiliating. Versions of the Ayutthaya chronicles compiled in the early nineteenth century do not always present past rulers in a complimentary light, perhaps an implicit comment on the perceived reasons for the kingdom's fall in 1767, and several episodes emphasize the moral failings of previous regimes. Of King Phetracha (1688–1703) it was said that he "consumed alcoholic beverages" and then indulged in sexual intercourse with young girls around the age of eleven or twelve, even when they had not reached puberty: "If any girl shoved, struggled and rolled around, the king showed his anger by striking and even killing her in the bed. If she remained still, she was rewarded."[109] According to this text, Phetracha also lusted after the wives of his nobles, and here, as in so many other indigenous histories, the violation of married women and maidens encodes a general dissatisfaction with government.[110] Real or imagined, a royal woman's claims of sexual neglect could have far-reaching implications because brothers and fathers were culturally obligated to avenge her honor. European-recorded stories of a vassal lord who rebels on receiving a bloodstained handkerchief from his daughter, evidence that she has been struck by her princely husband, may be apocryphal, but they do speak to the fact that mistreatment of royal wives could be a genuine reason for interstate enmity.[111] Yet there must have been many women who lacked champions and who were effectively trapped for life. Something of their emotions comes out even in semimythical sources. According to the *Glass Palace Chronicle,* the cruelty of King Narasu (r. 1167–1170) of Pagan was that of a reincarnated demon, and his "queens, concubines and handmaids stood in fear and awe of him, and loved him not, but hated him and cursed him in their hearts."[112] The belief that regicide of an unpopular ruler was the result of a female conspiracy was thus quite explicable, especially as women were responsible for preparing food for men. VOC officials reported that when Sultan Ibrahim of Johor died unexpectedly in 1685, three of his wives, accused of poisoning him, were put to death.[113]

Probably the most common accusations of female disloyalty concerned simple theft. In 1636, for instance, four female attendants in the Acehnese court were found guilty of stealing the silver service; as a punishment, their hands, feet, and noses were sliced off, their stomachs cut open, and their skin torn from their body, after which they were burned alive.[114] In a somewhat similar episode, the Bangkok chronicles report that several concubines were accused of taking a chest of coins from the royal treasury. Those found guilty were whipped and imprisoned, while their leader, who worked in the treasury, was roasted to death.[115]

Sexual infidelity constituted a betrayal of a very different order, even when intimacy was with another woman. In contrast to sources from East Asia, the Southeast Asian material is virtually silent on lesbianism, although it was probably common in households where so many women never caught the ruler's attention, were never given as wives to favorites, and never had a physical relationship with a man. For example, the sexual explicitness in Bali's court literature projects a preoccupation with heterosexual relations, although a somewhat prurient nineteenth-century account claimed that *onanie* (insertion of balls) and masturbation were common in the women's quarters, as were wax dildos and even yams and bananas.[116] Probably Southeast Asian attitudes were generally similar to those of the imperial court in China, where physical affection between women of the inner quarters was generally tolerated, provided that excesses were avoided. However, royal edicts from Ayutthaya apparently forbade sexual relations between palace women (using the term *len phuan*, literally "playing with friends") because this could undermine loyalty to the king. Those found guilty would be lashed fifty times, tattooed on the neck, and paraded around the palace compound. It is thus intriguing to find a scene on Thai temple murals clearly depicting physical intimacy between females.[117] A closer examination of court literature in other parts of Southeast Asia might open additional perspectives, given the frequency with which women dress as men in order to seek adventure. Possibly drawn from a Javanese original, the Malay *Hikayat Panji Semarang* describes how the heroine, disguised as a man, enters the women's section of the ruler's palace. One can imagine that the coy but unequivocal references to kissing, embracing, touching, and flirting must have given rise to giggling and innuendo among the predominantly female court audiences.[118]

Illicit relations with a man were not completely impossible, since the separation of royal women from unapproved males was not easily maintained. As one Balinese poem puts it, "If taken in moderation, dear sister, there is nothing to equal the pleasure of taking a lover. Once I passed nine nights savoring the delights of love-making."[119] Extramarital love and secret affairs provide the stuff of many classical romances, while local chronicles, European sources, and other accounts point to the sexual attraction that could entangle men and women, regardless of the strictures to which they were theoretically subject. Furthermore, it was hard to draw a line between incest and simple adultery in households where men could take numerous secondary wives, concubines, and slave-wives. According to the Ayutthaya chronicles, for instance, Prince Narai's conspiracy against his uncle in 1656 occurred because the latter, despite his fatherlike relationship with Narai's sister, had summoned her to his chambers.[120] In insular Southeast Asia an age-old revulsion to the idea of sibling marriage appears in much indigenous material, but convoluted bloodlines in high-ranking establishments meant it was quite possible for a man to fall in love with his own daughter or a close relative. In some cultures the ruler's special status, and his allegedly divine origins, made condemnation difficult, as suggested in a Malay text, the *Hikayat Raja-Raja Pasai*. A king who "conceived a passion for his two daughters" justified his claim by asking his ministers, "If a man spends his time planting crops, who should have the first claim to eat what has been grown?" The brother of the girls defied his father and spirited his sisters away, but he in turn had an affair with one of his father's *gundik* (secondary wives). Implicitly recognizing that they were guilty of *derhaka* (treason), all three took the poison sent by their father and died.[121]

In addition, because so many women in a ruler's household were young, the normal age relationships that applied at lower levels of society were often reversed. As a result, an adult son could often find himself attracted to some secondary wife or attendant who was in theory the sexual property of his father. The passions thus aroused could be great. Upon discovering that one of his sons had made a woman from the royal harem pregnant, the Burmese king Anaukpetlun (r. 1606–1628) threatened to roast the culprit alive. However, before the sentence was carried out, several princes surprised Anaukpetlun as he slept with a concubine and beat him to death. Though their role goes unmentioned, court women must have been coconspirators.[122]

There are, of course, many cases where highborn men flouted sexual taboos with relative impunity, but the consequences for females were always more serious. Makassarese *rapang* (collections of guides for conduct) even insist that a noblewoman who committed incest or married a slave would endanger the well-being of the entire country.[123] In a royal household such actions could be regarded as tantamount to treason, for which the penalty was normally death. Describing an episode around 1697–1698, the Javanese *Babad Kraton* recounts the seduction of the crown prince's estranged wife who has returned to her father's residence. When she is betrayed by a spy, her father orders her killed, with her brothers carrying out the strangulation traditionally prescribed for adultery.[124] A rather different, but oft-cited example comes from a French account of Ayutthaya, where it was said that a high-ranking woman convicted of adultery was not executed but placed in a kind of brothel together with purchased slaves, where a percentage of the profits went to the ruler. When she died, her body was not cremated; instead, it was thrown aside to become the food of dogs and crows. Though culturally abhorrent, women would have presumably preferred this fate to the gruesome penalty meted out in southern Vietnam, where palace ladies accused of infidelity were reportedly "crushed underfoot" by elephants.[125]

The counterpoint to the heinous crime of sexual infidelity was absolute loyalty and a willingness to follow a husband or lord even into death. It is possible that the sacrifice of wives or female attendants after the death of a chief was common in ancient Southeast Asia and that the practice was reinforced by early Indian models celebrating the idea of a widow's self-immolation as a sign of loyalty. Following the death of a Cham king in 1003, for instance, "all the females of the household, to the number of fourteen, followed him to death."[126] Nonetheless, although Europeans often referred to the ritual suicide (voluntary and forced) of highborn Javanese and Balinese women, it was not only wives who were expected to demonstrate their loyalty in this manner, and in 1633 twenty-two women were sacrificed at the cremation of a Balinese queen.[127] In the seventeenth century a Cham queen was repudiated when she declared that she would refuse to join her husband's corpse on his funeral pyre, although his second wife, a highland woman, ultimately did so. Yet while *sati* was still found in nineteenth-century Bali and was still celebrated in *kakawin* literature, the practice had largely disappeared in the rest of Southeast Asia. Even though Sino-Vietnamese literature abounds with stories of virtuous but unhappy women who take their own lives, usually by throwing themselves in a river, there is no historical evidence for a dramatic rise of female suicide as proof of marital fidelity like that noted in Ming China.[128]

Muslim attitudes were also important in changing views of the obligations of a royal wife or concubine, since all the Prophet's wives except Aisyah had been widows. Writing in 1515, the Portuguese Tomé Pires stressed that *sati* was not found among Muslim Javanese, and there is nothing resembling the *juhar* followed by Mughal officials in Bengal, when wives and children were killed to prevent their falling into enemy hands.[129] A striking example of the marital marketability of a highborn widow or divorcée is provided by the Makassarese princess Karaengta ri Bontojeqneq, who was born in 1628, the daughter of the sultan of Goa and a commoner mother. In 1646, at the age of eighteen, she married the ruler of Bima, but they were divorced twelve years later after she had borne him four children. In June 1658, as soon as the prescribed three-month waiting period was past, she married a Makassarese prince, only to be divorced after two years. Temporarily banished from court, she married the ruler of Sumbawa in 1662, but the union ended less than five months later, and she was apparently reunited with her former Makassarese husband. In 1669 she died at the age of forty-one, having been married and divorced at least four times, twice to rulers of overseas kingdoms under Makassar influence and twice to one of Makassar's foremost nobles.[130]

This outline of Karaengta ri Bontojeqneq's life survives because the Makassarese maintained court diaries. It is also demonstrates how clearly the historical sources favor those of high status, for a similar biography for a village woman would not exist. Yet in an environment where gender considerations have received little attention, elite experiences reveal much about the complex interaction between sexuality and political power. This interaction is well illustrated in the life of Krom Luang Yothathep, daughter of King Narai of Ayutthaya (r. 1656–1688). Narai has assumed an icon-like status in Thai historiography, in part because he actively cultivated relations with outsiders, even appointing a Greek as confidant and adviser. As Narai's only daughter and the most powerful woman in the country, Yothathep is given a relatively large space in the French accounts of the Ayutthaya court. The envoys never actually met her, since she had been secluded since the age of fourteen, but they reported that the "princess-queen" maintained her own establishment and exercised considerable political authority. When a Siamese mission was dispatched to Paris in 1687, Yothathep sent valuable gifts to the dauphine, wife of the royal heir, and her two sons, who been given scant attention in Narai's presentations. Nevertheless, the French envoys in Siam were unanimous in their disapproval of Yothathep's influence. They believed she was a leading figure in the faction opposing the foreign presence, and they did not hesitate to recount stories of her horrifically cruel behavior. She was said to have silenced her talkative ladies by sewing up their lips and to have slit "up to the ears" the mouths of other attendants she considered overly quiet. Yet French sources also indicate that Narai had a high regard for his daughter's capabilities, despite their estrangement and her refusal to marry his adopted son. At one point Narai even left the kingdom under her control for several days, and in laying out plans for future government, he specified that she should become regent and trustee for the crown after his death. In 1688, however, these plans were derailed when Phetracha, whose mother had been Narai's wet nurse and who was thus the king's foster brother, seized power. Shortly afterward Phetracha married both Yothathep and her aunt, Narai's sister.[131]

The picture becomes more complicated when Western sources are juxtaposed with Thai chronicles, apparently composed much later and often critical of Ayutthaya rulers. Here Yothathep is represented not as vicious and scheming but as the victim of her father's sexual exploitation. The chronicles record that one evening, when Narai's sister repelled his advances, he entered his daughter's chamber. The latter, however, refused to accept him, uttering "cutting insults" and even seizing a sword to protect herself. A specialist in love philters was summoned, and subsequently Yothathep became infatuated with her father and consented to intercourse. "Approximately seven or eight months later, she was in the third month of her pregnancy," according to the chronicles, and when her baby son was born, "the earth quaked," by implication reflecting cosmic abhorrence at the circumstances of his conception. Following the death of her husband, Yothathep and her son, together with her aunt (who was also her co-wife), took up residence in a monastery, where Yothathep subsequently died. Ten thousand monks, we are told, officiated at her cremation.[132]

HISTORIANS MAY BEMOAN their inability to offer a subaltern view of early modern Southeast Asia, but sources privileging the wealthy and powerful can be a fertile field for women's history. The belief that masculine virility and royal legitimacy had to be constantly proven through the accumulation of females sexually available to the master alone justified the existence of households occupied largely by women with limited physical access to the outside world. Yet ideas of elite seclusion were always tempered by indigenous imperatives, such as cultural patterns that condoned female involvement in economic activity and permitted older women to step beyond boundaries that their younger sisters perforce recognized. Nor were traditions linking kingship and male status to a formula of "one man/many women" completely unquestioned. While allowing for the bias of European chroniclers, and admitting that there was some dissension, the reported preference of court women in seventeenth-century Mindanao for the "English custom" of one wife is still noteworthy.[133] A royal version of the popular Thai text *Phra Malai,* composed in 1737, even depicts the ideal society that will exist in the life of the Mettaya, the future Buddha, as one where men will only have a single wife.[134] Nonetheless, though it is always possible to locate instances of women who rejected or renegotiated upper-class gender hierarchies, the dominant discourse continued to measure male achievement and social status in terms of sexual prowess. Accordingly, images of courts where one man was served by many women should be regarded not as mere marginalia in the Orientalist archive but as texts of utmost relevance to the cultural order.

CHAPTER 7

Being Female in "Early Modern" Southeast Asia

Though useful for general discussion, broad classifications like "Thai girls" or "Vietnamese women" obviously elide real differences in socioeconomic status and local identity. Nevertheless, while the particularities of context can never be overlooked, the fact that a princess was biologically closer to a peasant woman than to a man of her own cohort is hardly inconsequential. The assumption that all female bodies, regardless of status, shared the capacity to conceive and give birth was central to understandings of gender in Southeast Asian societies. As a Thai medical text has it, "women differ from men in two ways: they have a blood gland [i.e., menses] and breast milk to feed their children." As a corollary, Burmese treatises on medicinal practices calibrated a woman's life in terms of three separate but connected phases: from birth to the onset of menstruation; from the menarche to the end of fertility; and from this point to death.[1] For advocates of a "Southeast Asian" perspective that is at once female-centered and transregional, progression though these stages entailed experiences that can be treated as legitimate units of comparison. Scrutiny of the female life cycle is particularly salient in gender history, since a worldwide tendency to view women's fertility as dangerous or potentially polluting has no equivalent in the generative functions of the male body.[2] Deployed here as an organizational framework, the shifting interaction between biological realities and sociocultural attitudes opens up a critical space in which the recurring ambiguities inherent in the female condition can be replayed.

From Birth to Menses

In all cultures the steps by which little girls learn that they are physically different from boys begin virtually from birth. Despite the perennial problem of locating historical sources, we can probably assert fairly confidently that by the age of twelve or so most Southeast Asian girls, regardless of social status or ethnic background, had internalized the gender system that determined cultural expectations of an adult female. In societies where the domestic economy depended heavily on the work of daughters, childhood was essentially an apprenticeship for later life. Drawing from her research among the Rungus of northern Borneo, anthropologist Laura Appell offers a suggestion of how village girls acquired their expertise in "female" tasks. By the age of five, she writes, a Rungus girl will be feeding chickens and pigs; she has her own weeding knife and is probably already caring for a younger brother or sister. She might even join playmates in mimicking the curing rites practiced by adult specialists.[3] In this type of environment, a girl's primary teachers would have been her mother, her older sisters, and her female relatives, with mentoring occurring wherever women gathered—in the home, at ritual celebrations, around a sickbed, during harvests, at weddings and funerals. Among some Naga groups in northeast India, girls spent the night in special dormitories where elderly women tutored them in songs, dances, and ritual activities, but nowhere is there a female counterpart to the "men's house" typical of numerous tribal communities, as well as several Pacific cultures. Nor is there any Southeast Asia evidence of village institutions like the "needle shops" of Tokugawa Japan, where girls could go in the evenings to learn crafts from older women.[4] The nearest equivalent is the work group, as important in familiarizing girls with family descent lines and thus potential marriage partners as in supplying practical knowledge about wild plant collection or gardening techniques. An Iban chant, for instance, speaks of men with dibbling sticks "making holes in the ground / While we women, with baskets of seed / Walking contentedly on the fertile soil of our hillsides sowing our rice / have time to trace genealogies and locate kinsfolk."[5]

Awaiting further historical research are the written guides for training daughters in wellborn families, like the *nom* poem *Gia huan ca* (Familial instructions in verse) attributed (with some reservations) to the fifteenth-century Vietnamese scholar Nguyen Trai. "Young girls," he wrote, "pay attention to your parents' teaching / Listen to old stories which furnish you with good examples of virtuous daughters-in-law of times long past." When married, a young woman should remember that "though you sleep intimately on the same bed and use the same cover with him / You must treat your husband as if he were your king or your father." Composed in early nineteenth-century Siam, *Words of Wisdom for Women* similarly advises wives to watch for a husband's every need, to prostrate themselves at his feet, and "if he feels sore or aches / give him a massage."[6]

Even in literate circles, however, the most influential guidance was more frequently transmitted orally in the form of proverbs, wise sayings, aphorisms, songs. Khmer girls, for instance, learned to recite *chbab*, verses that date from at least the sixteenth century and that served to socialize women in matters like household management and child care. "Let your house be spic and span," says one, "with no dust rising / Clean, rake and sweep the ground / so that its neatness will cause content." An eighteenth-century Vietnamese adage echoes the same sentiments: "Keep an orderly house, flavor the sauces to pickle the greens / Food must never be lacking and each must be flavorful."[7] Such material could also relay more personal advice ranging from the frequency of hair washing to the choice of a husband and the maintenance of virtue; a Javanese piece recorded by Stamford Raffles thus conveys a mother's cautionary words: "My handsome girl! / In bringing a purchase from the market, / When you have paid the price, cast not your eyes behind, / But move quickly, lest men may seize upon you."[8]

Though appropriate female behavior obviously varied across cultures, compliance was ultimately dependent on an individual's acceptance of a gender assignation based on the sexual organs. Learning to conceal the genital area, even when the rest of the body was naked, was probably the most obvious signifier of this awareness. It was a lesson that girls were expected to learn much earlier than their brothers, regardless of whether the covering was a silver or gold plate, a strip of cloth, a coconut shell, or simply "a piece of string on a straw" like that used by aboriginal women in seventeenth-century Taiwan.[9] Self-classification as "female," initially the result of categorization by parents, relatives, and the community, could be affirmed by physical changes such as breast development, but in most cases it was the onset of menstruation that verified a daughter's readiness for marriage and childbearing. These connections are nicely captured in a Thai text, which explains that a girl will dream of a supernatural being who "comes to admire her and has intercourse with her. From then she has her seasons, such that it is apparent to all, and her breasts develop also."[10] The maturing female body stood as visible evidence of the awesome but potentially threatening energy underlying the reproductive cycle and the monthly discharge. The idea that male strength can be somehow vitiated by contact with female fertility helps explain the legion of taboos that prohibit pregnant or menstruating women from approaching men's houses or touching implements used in hunting, fishing, or warfare. In the seventeenth century the prowess of Makassar warriors was even attributed to the fact that their women, who were responsible for storing the *upas* tree poison used in blowpipes, mixed it with their menstrual blood.[11] Male ambivalence toward menstruation in eastern Indonesia and New Guinea has been the focus of considerable anthropological attention, and the uncontrolled power inherent in a woman's body may have been as significant as notions of "pollution" in necessitating a woman's monthly exclusion from the community.[12]

Subsuming promises of conception, pregnancy, and birth, the menarche could also be a time when families publicly rejoiced that a daughter had survived to maturity. Accounts of celebrations left by Spanish missionaries in the Philippines have already been noted, but occasionally other observers were sufficiently interested to record the ceremonies they witnessed. In Ambon, said VOC minister François Valentijn, a girl menstruating for the first time was required to remain indoors. She was not permitted to bathe and ate only raw fruit. Meanwhile, her family made ready for a feast. While village girls danced, boys cut down a coconut that was taken

to the girl's house and presented to her. When preparations for the obligatory ritual meal were complete, she was accompanied down to the river by
a retinue of women, and there bathed and dressed in special ceremonial
clothes. Returning "with a small cloth used for underwear over her head,"
she was pelted with fruits by her male relatives. The ensuing feast marked
the climax to the celebrations and could last up to three days.[13] Perceptive
though he was, Valentijn's casual reference to a "small cloth" passes over an
important ritual moment: the *cemar kain* (besmirching of the cloth), mentioned with extreme distaste by François Caron, another minister who
worked in Ambon. According to Caron, the explicit symbolism accompanying this ritual was so "immoral and idolatrous" that he could not bring himself to provide his readers with further details.[14]

Because the world religions promoted the belief that menstruation was
shameful, or polluting, or a divine punishment visited on all females, public celebrations of physical maturity largely disappeared in the region's
dominant cultures. Although anthropologists have described various tribal
groups where the menarche attracts little attention, it has also been suggested that relatively casual attitudes in some cultures may be related to a
decline in earlier rite-of-passage rituals.[15] Political and religious authorities
who did not condone blatant displays of sexual readiness were generally
tolerant of other customs signaling that a girl had reached puberty, like the
ritual ear piercing and tooth blackening described by the trader Thomas
Forrest during a visit to Mindanao.[16] Filing the incisors so they were level,
thought to enhance female attractiveness, was a proclamation that adult
status had been attained; population returns from early nineteenth-century Jogjakarta thus include a category of female children, "girls whose
teeth have not yet been filed."[17] In premodern Khmer society the tooth-filing ritual was an important aspect of a girl's "exit from the shade," a period
of seclusion following the menarche when she avoided contact with men
and observed food taboos.[18] Other forms of body decoration or modification could likewise encode statements of sexual maturation and social status, and an eighteenth-century Malay court text depicts the insertion of the
subang, the ear studs denoting virginity, as the ritual highlight of a
princess's betrothal.[19] In mainland Buddhist societies a girl's ear-piercing
ritual, including the ritual shaving of her topknot, was usually held to coin-
cide with (although overshadowed by) her brother's initiation as a novice.
An exception would obviously apply in the case of the highborn, and the
Bangkok chronicle devotes considerable space to the week-long ceremonies
that celebrated the tonsure of the eleven-year-old daughter of Rama I in
1808. It describes how the procession circumambulated the palace walls,
with the princess carried in a golden palanquin and accompanied by Buddhist monks and court Brahmans. Escorted by a noble dressed as Shiva, she
then ascended a representation of Mount Kailasa (renowned in Hindu
myth), an effective reincarnation of the god's spouse. Innovation was rarely

valued in the ceremonies marking an individual's sexual passage to maturity, and the chronicle stresses that the precedents for a royal tonsure established in Ayutthaya were carefully observed.[20]

Though nineteenth-century missionaries, explorers, and colonial officials assumed that the life-stage rituals they witnessed in more isolated communities were rooted in antiquity, no cultural practice was immune from change. Shifting attitudes toward tattooing, an important means of gendering a young body, show that practices sanctified by tradition could be modified or discarded with the introduction of new beliefs or aesthetic criteria. Tattooing in Southeast Asia and the Pacific has been commonly analyzed in terms of male maturation and achievement, but in some cultures it could be even more significant for girls, as among the Kayan of Sarawak. Operating under the auspices of a tutelary spirit, a female specialist began applying carefully selected designs when a Kayan girl was about ten. Since only a small area was covered at any one time, the process continued until puberty, by which time a girl's stoicism and ability to withstand pain demonstrated her readiness for the rigors of childbirth. Yet change was occurring even as early ethnographers were sketching or photographing female bodies. Status distinctions like those limiting thigh tattoos to the daughters of chiefs were no longer strictly observed, and some motifs, their significance forgotten, were already disappearing.[21] As in the Philippines, the adoption or imposition of imported views regarding appropriate female appearance often reinforced ethnic hierarchies. According to Father Vincenzo Sangermano, who worked in Burma between 1783 and 1808, Burmese men were reluctant to take Chin girls as wives because of the "disfiguring" facial tattoos that were an essential marker of Chin womanhood.[22]

Throughout Southeast Asia, puberty rites could be marginalized, reshaped, or displaced, but a girl's life was still conceived as a path that led inevitably toward motherhood. Childhood was essentially a preparation for the next stage in "being female"—union with a male partner, conception, and the bearing of children. As the previous chapter suggested, however, the sexual education of a girl was inflected by class as much as by gender.

From Menses to Menopause

SEXUAL KNOWLEDGE

Western feminists have long railed against the "double standard" by which women are so often expected to come to their first sexual encounter as a novice, apprehensive and chaste, in contrast to male confidence and superior experience. In Southeast Asia, as elsewhere, such expectations were vigorously articulated at higher socioeconomic levels, where behavioral norms were more influenced by the value placed on female chastity. A powerful conduit for such messages was the iconography of literature, with compelling images like that of the beautiful Sita guarding her virtue against the lustful Ravana. It is unclear, however, the extent to which the allusion and metaphor of textuality provided, as Helen Creese has suggested, a training ground for wellborn women. Did Javanese and Balinese maidens connect their own lives and their own sexual experiences to the images of rape and enforcement so prominent in the arsenal of male poets? How would they have responded to metaphors that compared the calls of herons to "the moans of [a maiden], invoking her mother's help, when she was being deflowered?" Were their fears allayed by the comforting words put into the mouths of nursemaids and aunts, who reassured them that "it is just like taking betel—the first time it is bitter, but there is no doubt the next time it is delicious."[23] Did they see any contradiction between assertive female characters, like those portrayed in the *Serat Centhini*, a Javanese text conventionally dated to the late eighteenth century, and its authorial view that in sexual relations a woman should always follow the male lead?[24]

Assumptions that a young woman is sexually innocent are largely absent from the suggestive metaphor and innuendo found in the "courting poetry" common throughout Southeast Asia. Displaying their verbal skills in public and rapid-fire repartee, young women answered male witticisms with insinuations implying that they too were practiced in the game of love. For instance, in answering the male sally, "I shall take aim at the target," a Lao girl might respond, "I wish to ride the buffalo down to the rapids" or "I saw a tuber in the narrow mountain pass."[25] These verbal competitions, blatantly disdaining the modesty and sexual naïveté expected of young upper-class females, maintained their hold at the village level, despite official disapproval or prohibition. Vietnam's fifteenth-century rulers were adamant that fertility dances, drumming, and the singing of "libidinous" music should be forbidden, but the popularity of suggestive dancing and courting poems remained a matter of comment. Even in Portuguese Melaka, European visitors were struck by the enthusiasm with which women joined men in the "amorous" exchanges of rhyming couplets, taking pride in their ability to think and compose cleverly and quickly.[26]

Providing an opportunity for young men and women to communicate a mutual attraction, these oral contests (often descending into unabashed ribaldry) were commonly the prelude to more intimate meetings with a prospective lover. The possibility of conception was rarely a deterrent, despite the elite model of premarital chastity. For the most part, ordinary Southeast Asians regarded a girl's pregnancy with equanimity as long as her relationship with the father was regularized or the infant guaranteed adequate care. Writing in 1621, VOC official Artus Gijsels remarked that an Ambonese child born out of wedlock was normally raised by the mother herself or by her parents. Should the woman then marry another man, he would usually treat the child as his own and accept responsibility for the child's upbringing. Gijsels noted, however, that relatively few undesired pregnancies occurred, in part because women who did not wish to conceive ingested a daily contraceptive made from areca nuts and other plant and root ingredients.[27]

But while many communities tolerated youthful dalliance, there was also a tacit recognition that a girl's coquetry should operate within certain limits. An attractive young woman with an unusual number of admirers might be suspected of using magical charms to bind male affections; it was even possible that she would be judged a spirit in human form, like the *asuang* whom the Tagalog believed could appear as a seductively beautiful maiden and lure men to their death.[28] It also appears that parental concerns about prenuptial intercourse grew greater as a daughter's "loss" of virginity became more serious. Islamic families, for example, became increasingly vigilant custodians of female sexuality, since a Muslim husband who found that his bride had experienced a previous relationship could divorce her with impunity.[29] A widening view that parents should guard a daughter's chastity—"as vulnerable," wrote one Vietnamese scholar, "as a drop of rain" —can be discerned beyond elite circles. The hard-hearted stepmother, invariably hostile to young love, is a common motif in Burmese folk songs, and the mother who punishes her daughter for secret meetings with a lover can be regarded as a comment on shifting viewpoints: "Mother in her fury, picked / A bobbin big to throw at me / And instead with spindle shaft / She lammed me heartlessly."[30]

Given the strengthening of the state-religion alliance, one can only speculate about the effects of socially induced humiliation on an unwed mother and her family in communities where the concept of "illegitimacy" had once been unknown. Official attitudes in the Christianized Philippines, for instance, reflected the European view that pregnancy out of wedlock was self-incriminatory evidence of "premature coitus" and that abortion and infanticide were therefore "female" crimes. Spanish missionaries in the Visayas spoke in harsh terms of women who had specialized knowledge of abortifacients and of those complicit in such procedures. "Woe to the woman," warns a sixteenth-century Tagalog catechism, "who poisons the child in her womb, and kills it so that people would not know about it."[31] In a departure from its Chinese prototypes, the Le Code also includes a paragraph imposing penal servitude on any woman who administers or purchases drugs to induce abortion. By contrast, the majority of Islamic theologians, though disapproving of abortion, condoned termination of pregnancy as long as the fetus was not fully formed, conventionally fixed at 120 days after conception. Yet the protection of sexual honor was always paramount, and a nineteenth-century account from Lampung (south Sumatra) describes a female *dukun* (doctor) who explicitly induces the fetus to emerge before its time lest it "bring shame upon its mother."[32]

Arguments that class was a major consideration in determining attitudes toward premarital sex are complicated by evidence that in numerous communities the breaking of the hymen was treated as a mysterious and momentous event. Because this unique release of blood portended a girl's future fertility, those concerned would be in a perilous position should correct procedures be neglected. Ideas of menstrual pollution were deeply embedded in Hinduism, and Zhou Daguan's description of ritual deflowering by Brahman priests and Buddhist monks in thirteenth-century Angkor suggests influences from India, where similar customs were found.[33] The idea that intercourse with a virgin placed a man in great jeopardy and should be entrusted to those who could access superior powers can also be detected in a report from seventeenth-century Arakan, which mentions that locals were recruiting Dutchmen for the task. According to another account, a Burmese nobleman was honored when a foreigner slept with his bride on the wedding night. While it is easy to envisage Europeans accepting this responsibility with alacrity (they received payment), the experiences of the girls involved are less easily imagined.[34]

These ceremonies surrounding the termination of virgin status provide further examples of how imported ideas fed into much older practices. The role of selected men in a girl's first intercourse was described in less Sinicized areas of southern China, and in the Philippines, said early Spanish observers, Cebuano women also had their vaginas "opened," with those responsible for the first penetration paid for their services.[35] In thinking across the "Asia-Pacific" divide, it is instructive to consider attitudes toward the virginity of highborn women in Samoa. Ancient narratives, we are told, depict the successful marriage of a village princess as one where her *mamalu,* or sacred essence, is preserved for her husband. The blood of the first sexual intercourse was evidence not only of her *mamalu* but also of her family's ability to guard the chastity so important to their status.[36]

A girl's first experience of physical intimacy with a male was surely not easily forgotten, regardless of community attitudes and social status. It is clear, however, that "early modern" attitudes toward premarital sex were changing as elite norms were emulated at lower social levels. The situation of a wellborn Javanese girl may have been more similar to that of her Chinese or Indian counterpart than to that of her father's peasant laborers, but class differences were by no means immutable. The elite and transregional ideal of the apprehensive and sexually inexperienced bride who reluctantly yields to her husband's desires came to exercise a pervasive influence even in societies previously tolerant of adolescent sexuality. Emblematic of these shifts is the counterfeiting of chastity in a modern Rungus marriage, although the bride and her future husband may already be lovers. "Abducted" from her longhouse, she screams out frenzied but formulaic pleas to her mother, begging the wedding attendants to help her escape the awaiting ordeal.[37] In effecting what were often significant cultural adjustments, communities could enlist the supernatural agents that had traditionally policed gender norms to inculcate new standards for female behavior and self-censorship. By modern times Northern Thais came to believe that a woman who offended the clan spirits by engaging in premarital sex would be stricken by some illness that could be cured only after certain rituals had been performed.[38]

MARRIAGE

As chapter 3 has shown, it is quite possible to locate Southeast Asian women who retreated from domestic life, primarily as religious renunciants. In sixteenth-century Java, female ascetics (usually widows) were not uncommon, and it has been estimated between that between 5 and 6 percent of women in the Philippines, Thailand, Myanmar, and Sri Lanka remained celibate, probably through entry to religious houses.[39] Nonetheless, few scholars would disagree with the assertion that, in premodern Southeast Asia, marriage and parenthood were the most significant steps in attaining full adulthood. As a princess in the Lao *Rama Jataka* says, "My lord father, it is really rare that those who are born into this world do not take husbands or wives. Only by taking a husband or wife is [human life] fulfilled."[40] The assumption that conception, pregnancy, and childbirth would soon follow meant that marriage was especially significant for a woman, with public notification commonly made through changes in hairstyle, clothing designs, body adornment, and jewelry.

From simple cohabitation to the elaborate ceremonial of royalty, the multitude of forms that denoted "marriage" in Southeast Asia were almost invariably an affirmation of female expertise in the organization of domestic life. Because the legitimacy of wedding ceremonies rested heavily on the observance of "tradition," older women—so often the accepted guardians of custom—assumed a prominent role in negotiating a betrothal, instructing the bride, determining correct ceremonial procedures, ordering correct food and drink, and confirming the successful consummation. As a guest at a Banten wedding in 1787, a VOC official remarked that although an imam presided, the bridal couple was surrounded by women. One of the most important ritual moments occurred when an elderly woman (chosen because she had lived for many years in marital harmony) fed the newlyweds a little cooked rice to ensure the fertility of their union.[41] At the farthest extremities of "Southeast Asia," similar patterns still held. When a Chinese official in Yunnan married a Miao woman in 1667, the ceremony was "a mixture of Chinese and Miao customs," but an older woman still acted as "the female master of ceremonies," while the bride was accompanied by hundreds of other women. Despite the typical Chinese residence with the husband's family, the official's Miao mother-in-law rather than his birth mother took responsibility for ensuring that he fathered a child.[42]

Though this personal record illustrates how patrilocality (typically thought to diminish a daughter's value by making her a temporary occupant of her natal household) could be negotiated, a married woman was most advantaged when she lived near or with her siblings and parents.

More than forty years ago Manning and June Nash identified the mother-daughter bond as the anchor of the Burmese kinship system, but the same comment could apply to much of Southeast Asia.[43] In Minangkabau the privileged status of a wife in a matrilineal society has been well studied, and proverbs collected by British officials in colonial Malaya point to the husband's alleged subservience as migrants carried matrilineality into the diaspora. In countering the saying that placed raja, chief, headman, and husband in a continuum, the folk wisdom of one migrant community maintains that "the married man must go when he is bid, / And halt when he is forbid. / When we receive a man as a bridegroom, / If is he strong, he shall be our champion. / If a fool, he will be ordered about."[44]

Elsewhere in Asia, historians have suggested that matrilocal residence was formerly more common than in later times. In medieval Japan, for example, a young couple frequently lived with the bride's parents, with the move to the husband's household only becoming the norm from the seventeenth century. In China too, despite state mandates and the exhortation of Confucian scholars, a man who could not afford a traditional marriage sometimes lived with his wife's family.[45] The Vietnamese Le Code followed the Chinese model in favoring patrilocal residence but did permit husband and wife to establish an independent home; in Tonkin, said the missionary Abbé Richard, young women "always choose their husband according to their liking, which the Chinese are not allowed to do."[46] This relative female independence was particularly evident in southern Vietnam, where Jesuit missionary Christoforo Borri reported that "the husbands bring the Dowries, and relinquish their own houses to dwell with their wives, by whose means they are maintained, and by whom all the household affairs are managed." A woman's ability to marshal family support could provide her with allies in marital relations, and again the independence of southern women evoked particular comment. "When a man marries," remarked the experienced merchant Pierre Poivre, "he marries his master. His wife orders him about and the law shelters her from the man's mistreatment. . . . A woman who has been maltreated by a man lies down in front of the doorway or in the middle of the street and covers her face. Then her relatives congregate and go and fetch the mandarin." Even in the north a bride was able to maintain close family links because Vietnamese villages, unlike China, were never organized as single-surname lineages, and endogamy was normal. Although officially proscribed, marriages between cousins remained common. Since exogamous unions were largely a preserve of the mandarin class, most girls did not wed strangers even when residence patterns became more patrilocal.[47]

Overall, the many ways in which newlyweds and their relatives could interpret marital relationships in Southeast Asia still remains frustratingly conjectural. Loarca's description of a Philippine wedding in 1582, when a young woman, affecting coyness, is essentially lured up the steps of her future home, implies that the gifts offered by the groom's family were payment for sexual access. But was bride-price seen as the "purchase" of a wife, as Europeans believed, or was it remuneration to the family for loss of her labor?[48] Do the laments that speak of a bride's unhappiness at leaving her parents speak to a common experience? Or were they largely formulaic, like a Miao (Hmong) folk song from the highlands of central Vietnam that depicts marriage as some kind of sexual ambush? "Attracted by the song of the treacherous decoy," the plaint goes, "the poor forest bird is caught in the trap, shut up in a cage, he looks with sorrow at his companions flying by. Such alas is my sad fate."[49] Yet tradition accepted that a Miao woman could return home if she was mistreated, since it was unlikely that she would live a great distance from her parents.

Immune from the demands of upper-class diplomacy, marriage for most people meant an affirmation of ties between relatives or families well known to each other. When Buddhist convents or Christian *beaterios* were available, they may have furnished a retreat for unhappy wives, but in general the natal dwelling was seen as the first place of refuge. A traditional Ambonese song, for instance, speaks movingly of a daughter's place in parental affections: "Young lady of Ambon / If you marry, may your husband not hit you / If your husband hits you, come home to us / Ah, we enfold you / we truly enfold you."[50] In eighteenth-century Java, echoes of ancient practices can be discerned in references to a custom known as *purik adat*, by which an unhappy wife could flee to the home of an older (female) relative. The latter would then try to effect a reconciliation. If this proved impossible, the couple could be divorced according to Muslim law.[51] In demonstrating that idealized patterns of behavior could always be questioned, a favorite Thai mural scene depicts the wife of a Brahman rebelling against her husband/owner's wishes after village women criticize her for undue subservience.[52]

PREGNANCY

Whether marked with minimal ceremony or celebrated as a great spectacle, formal union with a man was simply a prelude for a young woman's transition to motherhood. In a region of historically low populations, rulers were always anxious to promote demographic growth, but a family's preoccupation with pregnancy and childbirth was more immediate and more personalized. It was not just that children were expected to care for aging parents; societies that placed a high premium on genealogical descent were haunted by the possibility of what Sumatran Malays called a "broken lineage." On the island of Nias the feet of a woman who died without children were carved on a memorial bench to show that she had been on earth, since there were no descendants to testify to her existence.[53] For Vietnamese the failure to bear children could be regarded only as evidence of an extreme lack of filial piety. In the fifteenth century, officials thus objected to royal prohibitions of intercourse during the period of paternal mourning, arguing that abstinence could result in parents dying without children to carry out the obligatory ancestor worship.[54] In societies more concerned with the display of masculine virility, men had a vested interest in the pregnancy of a wife or concubine. In Ambon, high-status men even bought female slaves by whom they could father more offspring and the so-called *anak mas* (golden children) born of these unions were said to be greatly valued.[55]

For women the childbearing stakes were much higher, for motherhood was the primary affirmation of a woman's position as an adult member of the community. In the eastern Indonesian island of Tanimbar, for instance, the same word *(fofoli)* was applied to an expectant mother as to a man who had killed his first pig.[56] Although the barren female could occasionally be accorded a privileged "male-like" status, and a widow without heirs had greater access to inherited goods, a childless marriage was viewed as fundamentally incomplete and was virtually always attributed to the wife's inadequacies. A husband was considered quite justified in seeking a divorce in societies where infertility was imputed to sins committed in previous lives. A Burmese law code, dated to 1707 CE but probably a copy of an earlier text, therefore lays down that a wife who fails to bear children can be "put away."[57] Even in death the resentment and spite attributed to such women might plague their relatives. In Vietnam, peasants thus spoke of Ba-Co, an old spinster who had died without children and could return to claim a life.[58]

Such beliefs help explain the female preoccupation with ensuring conception and a safe delivery through careful selection of a mature and responsible mate. A woman and her family might require evidence, for instance, that a young man had undergone circumcision or that he had taken a head in some raid or had completed his novitiate in a monastery or had made a journey to some foreign land. Conception itself remained a matter of such weight that nothing could be left to chance. Prayers and offerings invoked supernatural or divine assistance, while astrological tables or the phases of the moon could determine the most auspicious times for intercourse.[59] Once pregnancy was confirmed, added precautions were necessary. A husband's activities could be restricted almost as rigidly as those of wife, because of fears that he might inadvertently offend the spirits and thus harm both mother and unborn child.[60] Careless or unnecessary use of sharp instruments was regarded as particularly dangerous, and Spanish missionaries in the Philippines remarked that prospective fathers did not cut their hair. The greatest vigilance, however, was required from the pregnant woman herself. Father Francisco Alcina, a Jesuit missionary who spent thirty-five years in the Visayan Islands, supplies much intriguing information. Expectant mothers, he wrote, refrained from eating turtles or fish without scales because this was thought to lead to a difficult delivery; they also avoided eating anything that might cause the birth of twins, such as two bananas joined together.[61]

At a time when her own death as well as that of her child was a very real possibility, a woman would have been anxious to ensure that all necessary rituals had been observed, while aware that the most careful compliance did not guarantee exemption from danger. Thai medical texts, for example, stress that a complicated pregnancy or even a miscarriage could result when an expectant mother was unduly concerned with sensual matters, ate overly spicy food, displayed a bad temper, or used unacceptable language. In any medicinal preparation the most potent ingredients were usually the most difficult to obtain, and in 1642 a Dutch party outside Melaka met a group of aboriginal forest dwellers bringing to market "roots for pregnant women experiencing difficult labor." An even more exotic ingredient, the dried gall of the slow loris, was mixed with rosewater and rubbed on the abdomen of a pregnant woman to assist delivery.[62] Yet even individuals who observed all the prescribed restrictions could be harmed by malignant forces or fall victim to a magic spell. It is likely that the miniature ceramic models of a woman holding a child, produced by the famed Thai Sawankhalok kilns, were specifically used to solicit supernatural aid.[63]

A combination of indigenous texts and ethnographical data illuminates the widespread perception that a pregnant women would be particularly alert to any unusual signs—dreams, omens, her own cravings—that might predict the sex, personality, and character of her child. Prolonged gestation might herald the birth of some future leader, since this was a common characteristic in the lives of great ancestors. A Thai text notes that a ten-month pregnancy, especially among women of noble blood, could indicate that a divine being had descended to be conceived in a human womb. Although undated, this text also provides some insight into evolving ideas about pregnancy and birth: A month and twelve days into pregnancy, the fetus begins developing; if it is female, revolutions are to the left, if is a boy, to the right. After five months it can feel heat and cold, pleasure and pain.[64] The energies of the family or even the entire community could then be marshaled to ensure the birth of a healthy baby. Among the Iban a ritual known as *pelian bejereki* was specifically intended to throw up a wall of protection around the expectant mother: "Let all of us spirit familiars join the festival / Bringing with us precious charms, such as the petrified white gourd / that caused the womb to develop satisfactorily. . . . The Dayak undertake an important task beneath the light of the waning moon / They fence a happy unborn babe whom they cherish."[65]

CHILDBIRTH AND MOTHERHOOD

Early travel accounts from Southeast Asia frequently remarked that pregnancy and delivery represented little disruption in the lives of ordinary women, who did not take to their beds as was customary in much of Europe.[66] While this resilience often became an allegory for "otherness," the comments of outsiders imply that birth was a mundane event and of little significance in a woman's life. Such impressions are belied not merely by the status accorded motherhood in indigenous sources but also by cultural attitudes toward childbirth itself. In the ecotone of eastern Indonesia, where customs often resembled those of New Guinea, a woman gave birth in relative isolation because of the dangerous forces associated with reproduction, and VOC observers reported that among the interior peoples of Ambon (subsumed under the vaguely inclusive term *alifuru*), a woman about to deliver retreated to a forest hut.[67] Modern research, however, indicates that support was usually available to a mother in labor even when solitary birth was idealized. According to early nineteenth-century evidence, husbands commonly served as midwives among small forest-dwelling groups, perhaps because female relatives were in short supply, perhaps because children were so valued. Even when women were regarded as the primary experts in birth procedures, a prospective father would be assigned a range of other duties. Iban men, for instance, were responsible for pounding bark from the *tekalong* tree (a type of breadfruit, genus *Artocarpus*) to make bandages for binding the abdomen after delivery in order to prevent postpartum uterine expansion and hemorrhage.[68] The idea of male-female partnership is evident in the *Adat Raja-Raja Melayu* (Customs of Malay rulers) compiled in 1779 by a mosque official, which mentions the ruler's presence when his consort delivered and confirms other references found in Malay court literature.[69] A similar role described for Balinese husbands contrasts sharply with practices in India, where it would have been unthinkable for a high-ranking Hindu to attend his wife's confinement, since the pollution of childbirth was deemed to be even greater than that resulting from menstruation, sexual intercourse, defecation, or death.[70]

The historically low status of the midwife in northern India and contemporary Bangladesh is also very different from her standing in Southeast Asia, where obstetrics remained one field where skilled women could largely hold their own. Female "doctors" in seventeenth-century Melaka, reputedly able to diagnose illnesses merely by the patient's appearance, were mostly *dayas* (Arabic, meaning "wet nurse" or "foster mother"). Their status is affirmed by a Malay law code, which says that a midwife should be treated as the raja of any house where a birth was in progress.[71] The Filipino midwife, like her regional counterparts, recruited the aid of her spirit colleagues, "the first midwives of the world," and begged, "By your good will, now grant me the favor such that through my help this creature may be born."[72] An example of the kind of ritual such practitioners might oversee comes from the *Adat Raja-Raja Melayu*, which devotes considerable attention to the Malay ritual of "rocking the womb," a two-day ceremony intended to safeguard the unborn child whose body is still forming. When the royal consort is seven months pregnant, the ruler summons four famous midwives. The ritual begins with the application of henna to the consort's hands and the recitation of prayers by leading Islamic officials. On the second day, the actual rocking of the womb begins. The consort lies on a mattress, while a midwife slips a length of cloth under her waist. Holding both ends, the midwives move these to left and right, apparently to position the baby correctly. This rite is repeated seven times, using different types of cloth with different designs. Wearing special clothing, the ruler also participates, and the following day he and his consort are ceremonially bathed. An elderly woman, presumably also a renowned midwife, pours sanctified water over their heads and processes around them seven times.[73]

If celebrations of conception and pregnancy represent the triumph of female sexuality, the darker side was the very real possibility of infant death. When a census was conducted in 1814, the British resident John Crawfurd, questioning 141 elderly women, found that from a total of 1,019 live births, 651 children (around 63 percent) had died before reaching puberty. Early statistics are always problematic, but this figure can be compared with those of western Europe and Tokugawa Japan around the same time, when it is estimated that between 176 and 200 or so of every thousand infants did not survive the first year.[74] Children could of course die of malnutrition and epidemic in temperate zones, but endemic diseases like malaria and dysentery were especially virulent in tropical climates. Smallpox became another widespread cause of infant death as trading contacts reached more remote and previously unexposed populations. Because illness was so readily attributed to the venom of evil spirits or some kind of black magic, parents were ever alert to any measure that might keep their children safe. In Vietnam, where maintenance of the patriline was all-important, elite families even bestowed female names and titles on their sons to divert attention from soul-stealing spirits.[75] Sanctified water and religious texts were among the venerated sources of security, and amulets could take many forms. In 1672 it was reported that children in the hills of west Sumatra were wearing "new double stuivers" on chains around their necks as a protection against harm.[76]

At times, neither supernatural assistance nor the midwife's skills could prevent the birth of an imperfect infant. While the "albinos" and "dwarves" in royal entourages affirm the potency that could infuse physical difference, congenital disabilities were more commonly interpreted as a sign of divine anger, a punishment for past misdeeds, or an ill-timed conception. A *kutika* (calendrical chart) from Makassar bluntly predicts that a child born on the sixteenth day of the month would become insane.[77] Opposite-sex twins were particularly calamitous because of the widespread abhorrence of sexual intimacy between brother and sister. As Father Alcina's reference to food taboos in the Philippines suggests, the sibling incest by which many legendary ancestors successfully defied the natural order was unsupportable in a village family. Parental exile, special purification ceremonies, payment of fines, or appropriate compensation could be necessary to restore cosmic equilibrium following a "wrong birth." For example, Minangkabau customary law lays down that if a woman bears twins, "a boy and a girl, it is *sumbang* (incest). The headman collects followers, fires [*bedil*] on the house, seizes the property of the parents . . . and takes the children into custody. The father has to redeem them, for only thus can disaster be averted." In some cases a solution was found in infanticide; even in modern times some Akha groups in Thailand killed newborn twins, while the parents were temporarily banished and sexual relations between them proscribed for a year. The imbalance caused by this "abnormal" birth could only be restored if the wife went bareheaded like a man, while her husband might be required to wear her headdress and undertake weaving.[78]

It is worth noting that infanticide for economic reasons or because of sexual preference was far less prevalent in Southeast Asia than in neighboring world areas. Studies of Tokugawa Japan have shown that peasants took direct measures to control family size through abortion and the killing of newborns, especially girls, and that domain lords only began to outlaw such practices in the eighteenth century. In this regard a French missionary in Vietnam specifically compared the Chinese to the "Tonkineese," saying the latter did not drown infants they were unable to support, since the desire for children was so great that any unwanted babies could easily be adopted or sold.[79] Nor do we encounter any evidence of Southeast Asian ritual traditions that demanded abortion or infanticide, like those associated with the *arioi* cult in Tahiti.[80] Spanish references to the termination of pregnancies in the Philippines may be related to beliefs in seventeenth-century Taiwan, where female fertility was thought to endanger male hunting and where massage was used to abort births until an expectant mother was in her mid-thirties. Although such practices probably meant children were doubly valued, it does not follow that sons were favored, and the Dutch minister Candidus specifically commented on the care and affection Taiwanese showed to daughters, remarking that parents "love the girls more than the boys."[81] Furthermore, even when a scarcity of resources or other factors made contraception desirable, the sex of the fetus was not a consideration, because of the Southeast Asian preference for prebirth decisions. In this regard, any actions taken were normally situated firmly within the female circle, sometimes in secret defiance of a husband's anxiety to father more children.[82]

Overshadowing miscarriage or infant mortality, the great dread of Southeast Asian women, whatever their class, must have been the possibility of their own death during childbirth. We do not know much about maternal fatalities in premodern times, but infection and postpartum hemorrhage (attributed by a French priest in Tonkin to an abnormal rising and "choking" blood level as well as to premature bathing of the new mother) would have claimed an untold number of lives.[83] The new mother was also considered extremely vulnerable to malign forces, and Filipinos told Spanish missionaries that spirits *(asuang)*, often in female form, would seek out a dwelling where a woman was about to deliver. A mother in labor was protected by men who challenged the *asuang* by climbing on the roof, stabbing at the air with their spears, and exposing their genitals. If their efforts were unsuccessful she might become a *patianac* (related to the Malay term *pontianak*, with derivatives found in other Austronesian languages), the voracious and unsatisfied spirit of a woman who has died in childbed. Similar concepts are found in mainland cultures, where the gruesome custom of burying pregnant women alive at city gateways described in Ayutthaya can be attributed to local beliefs that these predatory beings would direct their ferocity toward the kingdom's enemies. Legendary "green" (premature or violent) deaths could also be co-opted into supernatural ranks to serve as guardians of female fertility, like Anauk Mibaya, the consort of a fifteenth-century ruler, included in Burma's pantheon of "thirty-seven nats."[84] For the most part, however, women who died in childbirth were lost souls, "enemies of men" and envious of living mothers. An illustration by the Malay writer Munshi Abdullah depicts the much-feared birth spirit as a disembodied being with an elongated neck, hovering in the air with her entrails trailing behind as she sought for victims whose blood she could suck. Because her favored targets were pregnant woman and newborn infants, traps were set by hanging cuttings from certain thorny plants around the entryways of houses where a woman was in labor.[85]

By involving themselves in such precautions, communities and families registered their belief that for every pregnancy a woman was gambling with her existence. Christian missionaries in seventeenth-century Vietnam could thus exploit the vocabulary of filial loyalty: "We are indebted to our mothers for conceiving us, bearing us in their wombs for nine months and ten days, giving birth to us in great pain and nursing and feeding us for three years."[86] Munshi Abdullah, whose four elder brothers had died before they reached the age of three, expressed similar emotions as he described his mother's labor: "May Allah pardon all her offences and grant her a place among the elect for the great pain and anguish which she suffered through her confinement. . . . It was as though her life hung by a single hair."[87]

The grim fate awaiting the spirits of those who did not survive pregnancy and childbirth offers a compelling explanation for the rejoicing that followed a successful delivery.[88] Though refracted through the disapproving lens of a seventeenth-century priest, descriptions of the "licentious behavior" during the month-long festivities held in the house of a new Lao mother convey something of the joyous relief when mother and child survived the birth ordeal. On these occasions, said Father Marini, "the whole family is usually gathered to have fun, to dance and to play all kinds of games."[89] In the Philippines, the celebration of baptism, while retaining echoes of pre-Spanish rituals such as the mother's naming of the child, can also signal significant shifts in cultural attitudes. As shown in a description of a Manila christening in 1704, the birth of twins was not a tragedy, as it would have been in many other societies; rather, family and friends rejoiced in the arrival of two new Christians.[90]

Such festivities did not imply relaxation of vigilance against potential dangers to mother and child, and postbirth rituals were less a matter of "purification" after pollution than a means of restoring a woman's strength and inner spirit. Father Marini himself acknowledged that Lao "parties" were primarily intended "to scare away the sorcerers and magicians and to stop them from making the mother lose her milk and from bewitching the child with their charms." Throughout Southeast Asia and northeastern India it was common for a woman to lie close to a fire so that she could breathe in the smoke from certain medicinal herbs and leaves, in accordance, as a Lao text puts it, "with the customary tradition."[91] Special care was given to the disposal of the placenta, always vulnerable to a predatory birth spirit. Careless handling could result in misfortune for both mother and child, since it was thought to have a sibling-like relationship with the newborn baby and even with children as yet unconceived.[92] Rituals marking the atrophy of the umbilical cord, which normally drops off when an infant is around ten days old, were equally important, typically combining ancient practices with symbolism derived from newer religious beliefs. In Gresik, on Java's north coast, the oldest female relative held the infant high in the air while the story of the prophet Yusup (Joseph) was recited. This, it was hoped, would ensure good health and enable the child to rise above misfortune and achieve greatness as Yusup himself had done.[93]

In safeguarding the newborn, most Southeast Asian societies accepted that breast milk (often seen as a mutation of blood) contained extraordinary properties of vitalization and healing; in Burma, for instance, a type of vaccine made by mixing breast milk with pustule discharge had reportedly been used to protect children from smallpox "from time immemorial."[94] The indebtedness incurred by ingesting this life-giving essence underlies Thai beliefs that a Buddhist novice should transfer any merit earned to his mother as the "price of milk" or that a young man should repay his mother-in-law for his bride's "milk and care."[95] However, although the image of the nursing mother is symbolically charged in most cultures, the correspondence between female sexuality and maternal love remained ambiguous. The nurturing women who maintain such a persistent presence in Southeast Asia's legendary heritage (often depicted without male partners) are largely detached from any hint of physical desire. Did wet nurses become well-established in elite Southeast Asian families because of a husband's distaste for intercourse with a lactating woman, as was claimed in Europe? Were they recruited by wives in a polygamous household who were anxious to protect their own position vis-à-vis possible rivals? Or was it simply a concern for infant health?[96] Non-elite women normally nursed their own babies, usually for several years (as the medically qualified Governor Padtbrugge noted in Minahasa), and the resulting amenorrhea would have resulted in a natural spacing of children. Very occasionally, sources reveal the resentment felt by women who were expected to satisfy a man's sexual needs while burdened with child rearing and household maintenance. In Vietnam an eighteenth-century poem invoked the tired wife whose husband demands to "use the dirty silkworm" (a euphemism for intercourse) while her child "demands to suck."[97] At times, too, there are hints of how recurring pregnancies affected the female body. In Burma, Father Sangermano remarked that after childbirth "there are few who do not always suffer from hemorrhage, inflammation of the uterus, diarrhea, and fever," and many "women's medicines" were specifically directed toward postpartum problems.[98] Even the expansion of rice-based agriculture, generally commended as an example of a thriving economy, did not come without cost, for the lifting and bending that field work entailed exacerbated the tendency for postnatal prolapse. It was women's "speedy loss of beauty," Father Sangermano believed, that explained the frequency of divorce in Burma. "While young," he said, "[they] are winning and gay; but after their first childbearing they become so changed and deformed that they can scarcely be recognized."[99]

MIDDLE AGE

In its most positive aspects, female sexuality in Southeast Asia is intimately associated with youthful beauty, and the mutual happiness of young love is the most common literary trope. The ideal of sexual attraction maturing into an affectionate and lasting relationship is also a frequent motif in legends and popular stories, with poor but virtuous couples adopting an abandoned orphan or giving shelter to a disguised prince and ultimately being rewarded for their good deeds. In the words of a *kelong*, a genre of traditional Makassarese poetry: "You and I agree to marry / Let us be like two fishing boats / Fishing together the big shiny fish / Tied together for life's long voyage."[100]

Against these romantic stereotypes was the reality of marital disloyalty and, for women (to a far greater extent than men), the possibility that a spouse would seek sexual satisfaction elsewhere. As we have seen, Southeast Asian legal codes generally condemn adultery for either sex, but married women were held to more rigorous standards than their husbands. Public humiliation, like that reported in Minahasa, where an adulterous woman had her face painted black and was carried around to the beating of drums and the chanting of her misdeeds, was quite typical.[101] A wife was constantly enjoined to be faithful to an absent husband, at least for an agreed period of time, and in the Visayas Spanish lexicographers even recorded the words *bingi* and *bingil*, meaning a woman who had been devoted to one man for her entire life.[102] No equivalent was reported for men, whose absences from home provided many opportunities to engage in extramarital affairs. The words of a queen in the Lao *Rama Jataka* express what must have been a common female concern: "Perhaps you were attached to some young woman in a distant land. Perhaps you took a wife in addition to me . . .

while you traveled through the wilderness. . . . I feared that you would not return."[103] The maintenance of a husband's loyalty, a principal concern for elite women, helps explain an emerging genre in eighteenth-century Javanese court literature known as *piwulang estru* (lessons for women), which provided advice on how to be a submissive wife or co-wife and how to provide sexual pleasure.[104] The widespread female desire to sustain a man's affection also supported a lively market in cosmetics and aphrodisiacs. The court ladies of Ternate, for instance, were said to place great store on moss obtained from the mountain people in Halmahera, which was used to make a poultice that "both cooled and improved the complexion."[105]

There was a fine line between preparations thought to recover a woman's sexual vitality and restore her lost youth, and the magic spells, mantras, and potions that could be employed to secretly stoke a man's passion. Fears among European men that they might become a victim to the "love magic" of native females regularly surface in travel accounts. During his sojourn in Batavia the physician Engelbert Kaempfer (1651–1716) heard numerous stories about old women, specialists in "sexual binding," whose philters could ensnare an unwilling man or induce impotency in unfaithful husbands.[106] Religious authorities unequivocally denounced such practices, and a favorite subject of Thai murals concerns the hell torments to be suffered by "women who give their husbands love potions to incite their desire."[107] With a heightened interest in regulating sexual behavior, rulers and their agents were also anxious to control unapproved magic, and Vietnam's Le Code imposed severe penalties on a wife who resorted to "witchcraft or incantations to arouse love from her husband." Europeans could be even more draconian; the Batavian government handed down punishments such as strangulation or drowning in a barrel for women accused of using poisons to keep their lovers faithful.[108]

Written sources, largely emanating from court environments, reiterate the ideal of male dominance and female subservience that provided the rationale for such punishments. Yet it is hard to ascertain the degree to which (for instance), the "intimidating male voices" of Javanese and Balinese texts were transferred to the marriage chamber, so often likened to a battlefield.[109] It would also be useful to know if Vietnamese doctors were following their Chinese mentors, who emphasized that the mutually pleasurable coupling of yin and yang was necessary to produce a male heir and that women who had unpleasant experiences were unlikely to conceive.[110] Balinese instructions on sexual yoga reminded men to delight a woman with lovemaking skills, and Muslim scholars expressed the same view, sometimes referring readers to Arabic and Malay treatises on the "art of coitus."[111] The acerbic mockery of male sexuality in Ho Xuan Huong's poetry is countered by the writings of other Southeast Asian women who depict their physical relations with men as less exploitative and more enjoyable. The veiled eroticism in a poem by Mae Khwe, prominent in the court of the Burmese king Bodawpaya (r. 1782–1819), is a case in point: "A pipe . . . a puff . . . short as a finger . . . I give you / for smoking. If I do not take it / you will think me crude / If I accept it / you will think I like you / If you want me / to smoke it. Put it near the bed / my dear one."[112]

European travelers in Southeast Asia, accustomed to images of Oriental harems, were often surprised to find that monogamy was the norm among ordinary people, even though marriages were easily dissolved. With access to their own economic resources, women were able to leave a union that was no longer beneficial or agreeable. In one Burmese folk song a drummer, whose performances at neighboring villages meant frequent absences from home, complains: "Things have come to such a pass / I've only but to touch the drum / When she threatens a divorce."[113] As noted earlier, termination of marriage bonds was facilitated when there was little property or personal prestige involved and when religious teachings were sympathetic. Buddhism, for example, presents no impediment to separation, and in Ayutthaya a marriage could end after five or six months if a couple so chose, without any obvious disadvantage.[114]

One of the more insidious shifts associated with "early modernity" was the trend for non-elite men to register social ambitions by taking a second wife or concubine or by acquiring a female slave or dependent as a sexual partner.[115] Women in this socially aspirant cohort, less able to leave an unsatisfactory marriage than their lower-ranking sisters, usually had little choice but to accept public disclosure of their inability to satisfy a husband or their failure to provide him with sons. In an effort to ensure marital harmony, legal codes normally favored the first wife. Cambodian law specified that a junior wife accused by her senior of usurping their husband's affections could be whipped with a leather cord and put on public display with her head covered by a bamboo basket.[116] Customary law could also dictate that compensation be made. In Minangkabau communities of west Sumatra, a wife received a mandatory payment if her husband married again, with the proviso that this be shared among the household's other senior women.[117]

Even if the superior status of the first wife were acknowledged, a second marriage created a situation fraught with tension. Though humiliation could be particularly keen when a rival was a social inferior, normative prescriptions urged women to accept a husband's sexual peccadilloes, however mortifying. As a Khmer *chbab* reminds its audience, "wives in their jealousy" who "hate the female slave" will disturb the society's moral order. One wonders if it was fear of his wife's wrath that led an Ambon man to give a concoction made of crushed papaya kernels, vinegar, and the leaves of the *bunga raya* (hibiscus) to his concubine, causing her to abort a six-month-old fetus.[118]

Aging

The topic of aging is central to any discussions of the relationship between female status and the reproductive cycle, since cross-cultural research has shown that women tend to enjoy greater autonomy as their fertile years come to an end. Despite premature deaths from pregnancies, childbirth, and other illnesses, it seems that premodern women generally outlived men. Female longevity in Europe gradually increased, and by the eighteenth century women's average life expectancy (still short by modern standards) was around thirty-four years, as opposed to thirty-one for men. Demographic samples from East Asia offer a similar pattern. It is unlikely that reliable figures for any Southeast Asian community can be extrapolated from currently available material (although something may be inferred from the Philippine evidence), but there are certainly grounds for arguing that the gender ratio follows trends found elsewhere.[119] While providing no division into age groups, data from three regencies in north-coast Java in the late eighteenth century indicate that the female population (35,193) substantially outnumbered the male (29,508). Men's activities, like military and labor service, could well explain this discrepancy, but some years later Crawfurd recorded that in Jogjakarta there were considerably fewer widowers (1,479) than widows (1,919).[120]

The demographic history of premodern Southeast Asia will remain largely speculative, but differing attitudes toward female aging in other world areas may support arguments of regional distinctiveness. European historians have found "widows" (not necessarily old) relatively easy to locate in the sources because a woman's legal status was redefined when her husband died. Records from trials of "witches" provide another pool of information, since accusations were most commonly leveled against older women, often widows.[121] There is no Asian counterpart to the witchcraft campaigns in Europe, where the notion of pacts with the devil was so clearly linked to Christian ideas of good and evil. Nonetheless, widowhood was a culturally marked category in both Hinduized India and Confucian Asia, partly because a woman's social position was conditioned by her marital state and partly because of beliefs that the ideal wife maintained lifelong fidelity to her husband after his death. Even so, there are qualifications. For example, the Hindu practice of *sati* was associated with the higher castes and was not as common as European travelers would have us believe. Although a Hindu widow may have been socially marginalized or even ostracized, her family usually treated her courteously, and local interpretations of Hindu law could permit her to inherit some property. In China the lot of a young upper-class and childless widow made suicide a tempting option, but those with children could become respected and influential matriarchs. Qing laws also gave widows a degree of freedom unthinkable for other women, such as managing the husband's property on behalf of children. In Japan too, samurai ideals of faithful widowhood were commonly ignored at the village level, and peasant women readily divorced or remarried.[122]

In Southeast Asian studies, questions related to aging have not been a primary concern even among anthropologists interested in gender and sexuality. One reason (hardly peculiar to Southeast Asia) is that the decline of female fertility comes slowly and there is no identifiable equivalent of the menarche. The slide into "old age" would have been even less marked in societies where repeated pregnancies and long periods of breast-feeding meant women experienced infrequent or irregular menstrual periods. Another reason, however, is a relative muting of the "widow" category in Southeast Asian sources. This is not to imply, of course, that the death of a husband was of no importance. The widow's funeral lament, a recognized genre in the region's oral heritage, was intended to be both moving and powerful, a public display of a woman's linguistic skills and her mastery of the formulaic repertoire. In a Makassarese *sinrile* (ritual chant) collected in the nineteenth century, for example, the emotional intensity of such poetry comes through even in translation: "I am like water that has been sprinkled on the ground. Who can unite it once more? I am like a rosary whose string has been broken. Who will thread the beads together again?. . . Your body was still so youthful, my love! Your years were so few in number! You were in the bloom of life! . . . And yet you are already dead, placed below in a wooden dwelling."[123] The death of a man in battle could require even greater displays of loyalty and grief. In Naga villages the widow of a man whose death had been avenged in a counterraid went out to meet the returning headhunters, her chants taunting the captured head (which could as easily be that of a woman or a child) by recalling how in life "he" had danced in triumph when her husband had been killed.[124]

As a number of authors have noted, one reason for the taking of heads and other death-related rituals was to close a widow's mourning period so that she could resume normal activities and, if she desired, remarry. Nowhere in Southeast Asia were ordinary women presented with the concept of "the widow" as a fixed category, even in areas where Indian and Chinese influence was strong. Burmese law codes, for instance, differ markedly from their Indian prototypes, laying down that sexual liaisons with a widow who has borne children should not incur punishment: "There is no fault because she owns her own body and she knows all the consequences."[125] The self-immolation by wives and concubines of highborn men in Hinduized Bali and pre-Muslim Java may have reflected much earlier rituals, but the notion of eternal fidelity was always limited to the elite. The *sati*-like ritual described by one European in early sixteenth-century Tenasserim seems to have been conducted as a celebration among women, who sang and danced around the widow, herself in a state of trance. However, while "those who undergo such a death are the most noble of the land . . . all, in general, do not do this."[126]

In most of Southeast Asia one senses that widowhood initiated a period of new independence. In Hindu-Buddhist Java it was quite possible for senior women, freed from the responsibilities of domestic life, to live alone as ascetics, and there are indications that it was also acceptable for older Thai females to travel around the countryside like wandering monks.[127] Remarriage was generally an option, with endorsement especially strong in Muslim societies because of the Prophet's own example (several of his wives were widows of men who had died in battle) and because Islamic teachings laid down the terms under which a new union could occur. In his *Book of Marriage* the revered al-Ghazali reiterated the injunction that although a woman should be "melancholy in the absence of her husband," it was not necessary to mourn longer than four months and ten days.[128] Christianity was equally amenable to remarriage. Chinese observers were shocked by the speed with which the widows of VOC officials took new husbands, and when Spanish inquisitors interrogated 145 "old" Filipino women accused of involvement in spirit propitiation, their marital state was carefully noted but not a single widow was recorded.[129] Chinese influence explains why the valorization of the "chaste widow" was most noticeable in Vietnam, where a woman whose husband had died was subject to obligations clearly spelled out in law, and where elite norms consistently promoted the ideal of the grieving but faithful spouse. Beyond the Sinicized elite, however, the reality of widow remarriage belied both literary images and official exhortations, and a Chinese Buddhist monk bemoaned the propensity of Vietnamese widows to accept another husband. The four poems that he had composed in honor of a virtuous Cham widow would, he hoped, encourage other women to "discard their vulgar customs [of remarriage]."[130]

Revisiting many of the topics addressed in this book, one can only be struck by the presence of senior females in a range of different activities—as spirit mediums, foster mothers, queen dowagers, brothel owners, palace officials, market traders. In virtually all situations, it seems, one could apply the conclusion reached in contemporary northeast Thailand, where "an older woman's claims to . . . age-based standing are not altered by the death or other loss of a husband."[131] It is well known that female longevity is more likely to occur when elderly women retain specific and respected functions, and in most of Southeast Asia the wisdom and experience accumulated over a lifetime were of immense importance in cultures where book knowledge was confined to the very few. Transversing ethnicities and social class, age was recognized as encoding greater skills, whether the task entailed teaching Balinese temple singers, cutting the metal rods for the necks of Padaung girls, weaving sacred cloths to wrap a corpse, or serving as ritual guardians of the indigo vat. Regardless of social status, a senior woman's extended network of indebted kin made her well-suited to broker marriage agreements, settle family quarrels, and mediate in potentially hostile interactions. In the southern Philippines, for instance, a chief's female relatives were typically deployed to negotiate meetings with Spanish missionaries, and in 1622 a pious Christian convert, the grandmother of the local *datu,* was instrumental in obtaining permission for missionaries to move into a certain area of northern Mindanao.[132] The same kind of patronage networks could also operate to the advantage of a wealthy woman, especially after her husband died. In early modern Vietnam a widow's access to her own resources was in sharp contrast to Chinese and nineteenth-century Vietnamese codes, which deprived the remarrying widow of all property rights. In Christian-controlled cities such as Batavia, Melaka, and Makassar, a new status introduced by European law helps account for the prominence of affluent Eurasian widows in documents filed with VOC notaries.[133] At lower socio-economic levels, years of experience ensured older women a continuing economic role, since advancing age did not preclude involvement in many "female" tasks such as weaving, dyeing, potting, gardening, preparing household food, and caring for animals. The evidence from Tokugawa Japan, which indicates that a woman's life span was lengthened when she was a member of the same household as her daughter, seems especially relevant to Southeast Asia because married daughters so often lived with or near their parents.[134]

While sheer longevity was itself impressive, an older woman's standing was further enhanced because she had entered a sexual zone where perceptions of a dangerous fertility no longer applied. In turn, the mysterious processes that ended a woman's reproductive years and made her more "male-like" opened up a much larger social and ritual space than previously available. For example, one particular pattern among the textiles offered by the Jogjakarta court to Ratu Kidul, the princess of the southern ocean, is so sacred that it can be made only by women after menopause; among the Baduy of western Java the pure white cloth used for shrouds is woven exclusively by old women.[135] The assumption that sexual activity was absent or limited also established a tacit connection with the abstinence thought necessary to channel ritual energies. As Janet Hoskins has shown in relation to indigo dyeing in Sumba, participation in certain activities exclusive to old women (or even limited to widows and older never-married women) could stand as an effective rite of maturity, evidence that a woman had reached the highest point in the female life cycle.[136]

With the end of menstruation, the basic indicator of femaleness, older women, far more than men, were touched by the liminality that constantly surfaces in Southeast Asian cultures. The ambiguity of the "woman who is not woman" would have had deep reverberations in societies where ambivalent forms like the crocodile sliding between land and sea, the legendary half-human and half-bird *garuda,* and the male-female hermaphrodite were regarded with particular awe. This ambivalence infuses the image of the old woman *(nenek kabayan)* found across the Indonesian archipelago as she mediates between two worlds—standing guard at entryways to a nonhuman domain, maintaining watch while heavenly nymphs bathe, or ruling over her kingdom below the sea.[137] Demographers have warned against the use of literary allusions as evidence for the realities of aging. Nonetheless, there is a striking parallel between the *nenek kabayan* metaphor and the widespread perception that older women had a special ability to act as conduits to the spirits. Consequently, they were usually able to maintain a ritual role in births, marriages, and funerals even as religious authority was arrogated by men. Against this background it is hardly surprising that elderly women have been a driving force behind the revival of life-cycle rituals in contemporary Vietnam.[138]

As Merry Wiesner reminds us in regard to Europe, it would be simplistic to view the past as a golden age in which age automatically entitled women to the respect of their families and community. By the eighteenth century and probably earlier, the "poor widow" was emerging in Southeast Asia as a social category, and the differential rate often applied to widows in tax registers is an implicit acknowledgement that they were more likely to be living in straightened circumstances.[139] As in Europe, the destitute widow became a depressing reality in Southeast Asia's expanding urban centers, where aging ex-slaves, far from home and family, were frequently cast upon community charity. In Batavia, nearly three-quarters of the female poorhouse population consisted of older native women who had adopted Christianity.[140] A text from northeast Thailand, recording the destruction of an entire Khmer town for the sin of eating meat, notes that only the "deserted women and widows" were saved; despite their virtuous poverty, they had been excluded from the feasting because they were "considered useless."[141]

Challenges to the stereotype of the wise and generous older woman can also be detected in other areas. The sexually experienced widow or divorcée who snares another's husband or attempts to seduce a young man is a common literary theme, and customary law and written codes frequently include warnings against liaisons between a youth and a mature woman. While those eager to attract a lover, ensure a spouse's constancy, or avenge infidelity could readily see older women as repositories of inherited female lore and esoteric remedies, a reputation for success could also justify accusations of evil intent and collusion with supernatural and malicious forces. In her capacity as a midwife, a woman might be suspected of supplying a stillborn fetus for some secret ritual, or that most powerful of amulets, the finger of a child who had died at birth. Assistance in the termination of a pregnancy also risked the condemnation of state and religious authorities; unlike its Chinese prototypes, the Le Code includes a paragraph imposing penal servitude on any woman who administers or purchases abortifacients.

Buddhist texts go further, threatening the abortionist with rebirth as a naked and hungry female ghost, whose body, swarming with flies, will emit "a strong and revolting odor."[142] The intimate involvement of older women with life and death explains the tendency to engender the arts of "black magic" as female, a tendency that appears most pronounced in communities subject to Christian influence. As Carolyn Brewer has shown so dramatically in the Philippines, Spanish missionaries were particularly prone to see spirit propitiation in terms of witchcraft and devil alliance and to condemn "sorceresses" as the cause of infant death and miscarriage.[143] The powers such women could tap were thought to present the Christian mission with its most serious challenge. A priest working in Vietnam in the late eighteenth century thus recounted how a young Christian woman tried to free herself from a spell that had caused her to be obsessed with a non-Christian man. She went to "a heathen woman, a sorcerer," who gave her small pieces of paper on which red characters, evidently the name of a powerful spirit, were written. Following instructions, she swallowed the paper, but rather than being freed from supernatural manipulation, she had become permanently possessed.[144] Although the status of male shamans and healers was often higher than that of females, missionaries almost invariably saw "witches" as women.

In his authoritative study of early Filipino society, William Scott has contrasted sixteenth-century Spanish beliefs that mortals (mostly women) could develop demonic characteristics with indigenous concepts of misfortune or calamity as the work of malicious spirits in human form. Much feared, these counterfeit humans were normally killed, but the relevant point is that they could as well be male as female.[145] Though women were more vulnerable than men to spiritual overpowerment, they were victims who could be healed rather than maleficents deserving of punishment. This is not to say that the stereotype of potential alliances between women and malevolent forces does not have an indigenous history in Southeast Asia. According to Father Sangermano, "It is impossible to persuade the Burmese that there is no such thing in nature as witches and that they are not extremely malicious and hurtful." He described one type of trial by ordeal: "A suspected woman is placed upon a little bier, supported at each end by a boat, and a vessel full of ordure is emptied upon her. The boats are then slowly drawn from each other, till the woman falls into the water. If she sinks, she is dragged out by a rope of green herbs tied round her middle and is declared innocent; but if she swims she is convicted as a witch and generally sent to some place where the air is unwholesome." Given this quote, the translators were probably justified in gendering a Burmese law of 1785 that refers to the immersion of an individual in water "to find out if [she] is a witch."[146]

The comparative dimension is particularly important in any discussion of "black magic," since studies in Europe, Africa, and New Guinea have demonstrated that witchcraft accusations—commonly directed toward women who are older, widowed, poor, physically handicapped, strangers, or otherwise marginalized—increase during periods of community stress. Feminized witches who appear in historical sources from Southeast Asia may be similarly emblematic of anxieties induced by social and economic change. The uncertainties associated with spreading European influence in nineteenth-century Malaya, for example, may explain claims that "plenty of people" could attest the drowning of "ancient Malay dames" accused of casting spells. Yet as C. W. Watson and Roy Ellen have emphasized, witchcraft has never been considered a major social problem in Southeast Asia, even in Bali, where there is a prevailing belief in the presence of black magic.[147] There was no area equivalent to the central plains of India, where in the early nineteenth century more than a thousand women were killed as witches, far exceeding the number of victims of *sati*.[148] Nor do we encounter any state-sponsored campaign similar to that which occurred in China during the "soul-stealing" panic of 1768, although on this occasion women were considered far less threatening than the stereotyped "treacherous monks" and "disheartened scholars" whose literacy gave them privileged access to the occult.[149]

In Southeast Asian societies the continuing prominence of male shamans and the belief that practitioners of magic could use their skills for good as well as ill dampened inclinations to establish a congruency between women and supernatural malevolence. Involvement in "black" magic was universally condemned, but accusations against individuals were tempered by long-standing tendencies to attribute misfortune to supernatural anger rather than human agency. As one Englishman noted of southern Vietnam: "When an infant dies, the parents are supposed to have incurred the displeasure of some malignant spirit, which they endeavor to please by offerings of rice, oil, tea, money or whatever they may imagine to be acceptable to the angry divinity."[150] Certainly, many of these capricious deities were female, an association that could subvert even the sacrosanct image of maternal nurture; one thinks, for instance, of the ferocious and fickle "spirit lord" mother who dwelt on Mount Poppa in central Burma. Even more formidable is the Balinese spirit-widow Calon Arang (Rangda), whom a sixteenth-century text depicts as capable of annihilating an entire population through an epidemic or some other catastrophe.[151] Yet Rangda (played by a man in dance performance) does have a less frightening male counterpart, and colonial sources show that Bali's most feared sorcerers were often men. Women might be considered more likely than men to invoke malign magic, and men might be considered more capable of withstanding dangerous forces, but trance and spirit possession rendered gender boundaries extremely porous. Both men and women could display an aptitude for accessing supernatural powers, which could be used to accomplish sinister as well as benevolent goals.[152]

PLAYED OUT WITHIN a multitude of contexts, the interactions between cultural expectations about "being female" and a woman's progression through the life cycle are both personally unique and universally applicable. Southeast Asian societies are hardly alone in placing a high premium on procreation while infusing menstruation and pregnancy with ambiguities that do not figure in the male reproductive equivalents of erection and ejaculation. Regardless of whether they are spoken, written, chanted, painted, sung, woven, or carved, the region's historical sources are saturated with contradictory messages about female sexuality. Curving hips and luscious breasts, likened to the lushness of the natural world, could invoke images of amorous delights; equally, the appearance of outward beauty could signal danger to a man, be it as a distraction from physical or spiritual goals, a potential vitiation of maleness, or emotional entrapment. Sexuality could never be completely disassociated from its ultimate goal—conception and the creation of new life—but in relations with their future husbands and partners young women were expected to comply with socially condoned codes of behavior that became increasingly restrictive as they moved up the social scale. Although motherhood could impart meaning and purpose to a woman's life, the attainment of this status reinforced beliefs about the dangerous and unpredictable forces associated with reproduction. Marital fidelity was constantly promoted as a desirable female quality, but younger widows and divorcées were readily credited with an insatiable sexual drive, and inexperienced young men seen as their easy prey. With the end of her reproductive years a woman entered a new stage of greater individual freedom and often enhanced authority in the community, but behind the wise and benevolent grandmother figure lurked the shadowy crone, inherently hostile to her fellow humans and prepared to use her knowledge and experience for evil purposes. The universality of these ambiguities, and the ways in which they are accepted, negotiated, or resisted in different historical and cultural environments, have enormous potential for wider and more inclusive conversations. Engaging voices from Southeast Asia can only render these conversations more interesting and more rewarding.

Conclusion

Repositioning Women in
Southeast Asian History

Grounded in the assumption that regional studies are by their very nature comparative, the arguments I have presented in this book can be divided into three broad areas. From the outset a fundamental concern was the extent to which generalizations regarding the "female position" satisfactorily define a Southeast Asian culture area. A second issue was the nature of the relevant historical sources and whether a "history of women" is justifiable when so many aspects of the past are speculative or simply unknown. A third consideration, implicitly framing the entire project, is the degree to which notions of change embedded in the term "early modernity" (itself derived from the European experience) were relevant to women in this part of the world.

In the first instance, the assertion that male-female relations are relatively egalitarian has been central to arguments affirming Southeast Asia's regional coherence and claiming an identity distinct from South and East Asia. For the most part, however, such arguments have depended on ahistorical clichés that essentialize "Chinese" and "Indian" women and give insufficient attention to shifts over time. In China, for instance, a decline in the female position is more evident from the Song period (960–1279), when the revival of Confucianism served to legitimize a "patrilineal, patrilocal and patriarchal" family system.[1] Regardless of normative values, however, the actual experience of being female differed across regions and most notably between classes. The stereotype of the submissive Indian wife thus ignores the fact that Hindu women from laboring classes were much freer than their wellborn sisters, and in south India widow remarriage among lower castes and celebrations at the menarche recall customs found through much of Southeast Asia.[2] "Southeast Asian" and "Pacific" interpretations of gender are less frequently juxtaposed, but here too generalizations must take into account differences among Pacific island cultures and the continuing refinement of broad categories like "Melanesian" or "Micronesian" women.[3]

A simple overlay of women's status on a map of Southeast Asia can also be challenged because the boundaries that delineate world areas, so often drawn up by colonizers, reflect political interests rather than cultural similarities. In 1788, for example, British authorities in India dispatched a survey team to the Andaman and Nicobar islands (between the Burmese coast and north Sumatra) with the goal of establishing a penal settlement. Despite botanic, linguistic, and ethnic affinities with Southeast Asia, these "wild and sequestered" islands were subsequently incorporated into British India and therefore became part of "South Asia."[4] Contemporary disputes continue to highlight the political nature of "world area" cartography. China ("East Asia") and Vietnam are still determining their common boundary, and the borders of "Oceania" will require redrafting if Palau's claim to three tiny Indonesian islands north of New Guinea is recognized. The influence of world area thinking is apparent even when scholars are describing supranational spaces, allowing for the identification of a "Southeast Asian massif" in the tangled highlands that stretch from northeastern India to southwestern China.[5] One can only imagine how approaches to the borderlands might have changed had Burma retained its hold over Manipur and Assam following the end of the first Anglo-Burmese War in 1826.

Notwithstanding these qualifications, I have argued that inaccessible highlands and mountain ranges combined with stretches of rarely traversed oceans to mark off a region that is far more than an academic or diplomatic convenience. Despite centuries of cultural interaction with Chinese and Indian culture, Southeast Asia was shielded from the territorial and cultural expansion associated with the Mughal emperors and with the Ming and Qing dynasties. In Chinese eyes at least, the differences this created were significant. A Ming map of the imperial territories dated to 1526, for instance, represents the border between southwestern China and "Southeast Asia" as a stylized ocean separating Chinese civilization from barbarians who "valued women and undervalued men."[6] To some extent, divergent historical experiences justify the academic division between "Southeast Asian" and "Pacific" studies, most notably in regard to the Philippines, Spain's only Asian colony. Farther south, even the easternmost areas of the Indonesian archipelago were more subject to incoming economic and cultural influences than were the islands of Melanesia, contributing to a process of differentiation that dates back at least two thousand years.[7]

Within Southeast Asia's porous borders, I have offered a guarded defense of claims that women have historically been "less inferior" to men than was generally the case in "East Asia," "South Asia," "Melanesia," and, to a lesser degree, the Pacific. While recognizing the enormous range of Southeast Asian cultures and societies, it is possible to advance a cluster of reasons that, in combination, provide a very general explanation. Although by no means universal, a widespread pattern of tracing kinship through both male and female lines has endorsed inheritance for daughters and allowed women to maintain a reasonable share of family and community resources. In many societies, female interests have been protected by matrilocal residence, by which a young couple lived with the wife's natal family.

Low population densities and communities where agriculture drew heavily on female labor placed a value on all children, regardless of sex. In bride-wealth societies the birth of a daughter was welcomed because her marriage would eventually enhance a family's resources. The personal income that a woman could obtain through marketing and small-scale peddling further affirmed her contribution to family well-being and added to a sense of inde-pendence in marital relationships. A hierarchy that assumed male superi-ority was implicit in the world religions and in the state structures they sup-ported, but the effects of idealized gender roles were felt primarily among the elite. Even here, however, the model of male authority and female com-pliance was often at variance with the ways in which men and women actu-ally related to each other. A Javanese chronicle from the late eighteenth century, for instance, includes an extraordinary account of how Pakubu-wana III (r. 1749–1788), preparing to take a new wife, fled (without trou-sers) from his infuriated Madurese queen, who had confronted him armed and dressed as a soldier.[8]

The second question focused on the nature of the available evidence and whether this is adequate for investigating a "female past" in Southeast Asia. It is apparent that research prospects are most promising in areas where European material can play off indigenous texts, such as Java and Vietnam. It will be far more difficult to say anything substantial about the innumerable smaller Southeast Asian cultures that lack a literate heritage and rarely if ever enter the written record. Passing references to isolated communities—"sea people," for instance, and "hill tribes"—can raise more questions than they answer. What was the relationship, one wonders, between Nicobar islanders and an old Portuguese woman who in 1686 was reported to have survived a shipwreck thirty years before to become their much venerated "queen"?[9] Details retained in provincial gazetteers and other records permit the tracking of Sinification in China's south and southwest, including the effects on women, but without such data it is vir-tually impossible to do more than suggest how individual communities in Southeast Asia were affected by economic or social change. The commod-ification of bridewealth in places like Timor and New Guinea may indeed mean that "purchased" wives are today treated with less respect than their forbears. On the other hand, the view that this has exacerbated domestic violence must be regarded as a discouraging proposition rather than doc-umented fact.[10]

Given the dearth of written material in so many areas, I recognize that a history of women in Southeast Asia can never be more than partial. I nevertheless believe that new lines of inquiry can be opened up by inter-rogating even well-known sources like the Malay epic, the *Sejarah Melayu*. More generally, the literature produced in the region's great courts, enjoyed by audiences where women were often a majority, appears to be a prime candidate for a gendered analysis. Since most extant texts in Southeast Asia have not been translated or edited, such research must rest with specialists. However, the very fact that scholars without specific linguistic skills must turn to their colleagues for assistance encourages interdisciplinary conversations that can be both provocative and insightful. In women's history some of the more rewarding exchanges have been with anthropologists, long concerned with "female-friendly" matters like kinship and the domestic economy. It is a fitting coincidence that Rosemary Firth was putting the final touches to her manuscript on Malay housekeeping at the very time Coedès was completing his *Histoire ancienne;* the following year, Cora Du Bois published a pioneering work on life cycles (half her informants being women) on the remote Indonesian island of Alor.[11]

In the historical search for evidence of indigenous understandings of relations between men and women, orally based sources like popular legends, proverbs, chants, and instructive stories assume greater salience because they were so often concerned with maintaining amicable relations in the community and in fostering household harmony. In consequence, such material can be extremely helpful in envisaging a "female" environment as a supplement to accounts produced by literate elites. As I suggested in chapter 2, the performing arts represent another archive for investigating the transmission of social norms; one might cite, for instance, a father's lecture about a young woman's duties included in a martial dance-drama from west Sumatra or a moralistic lesson from a *jataka* story acted out for a Thai village audience.[12] In a region of relatively meager documentation, "material culture" can impart tangibility to distant and inchoate female lives. Recovered in archaeological sites, old Javanese lamps decorated with erotic symbols or figurines were silent witnesses to a couple's lovemaking; a baby was once rocked to sleep in a pannier found in the hulk of a ship wrecked off the coast of Vietnam in 1796.[13] At times inanimate objects may offer their own commentaries on long-standing discussions of topics like "localization," such as the terra-cotta figures of dancers unearthed in Thailand that display gestures similar to those in carvings on classical temples in India. Unspoken testimonies can also affirm that Southeast Asian cultures retained their own distinctiveness. For example, textiles featuring imposing female figures produced by Indian weavers were intended not for domestic sale but for export to the lucrative Indies market; among the Toraja of central Sulawesi these impressive pieces became potent ritual items.[14]

A third question that has permeated this book concerns the degree to which "early modernity" (roughly from the fifteenth to the early nineteenth century) can be identified as significant in the history of Southeast Asian women. It is evident that many communities in highlands, distant interiors, and remote islands were hardly touched by new ideologies of gender manifested in coastal settlements, European enclaves, and royal capitals. However, despite undoubted continuities, significant changes were afoot. The spread of imported religions and philosophies, the emergence of more centralized states, the strengthening of class divisions, and expanding links to a global economy all required individual societies to reconsider their expectations of women. Although local responses varied markedly and females were not necessarily disadvantaged, these developments had a direct bearing on constructions of gender in contemporary Southeast Asia. In this sense, "early modern" can be justified as a meaningful period in a regional history of women.

A major theme during these centuries is the location of "femaleness" in male-dominated religious systems, as women were excluded from high ritual positions and men acquired opportunities to advance their knowledge and spiritual status. Illiterate and unschooled women faced new challenges even in the sympathetic realm of spirit propitiation; in the late eighteenth century, for instance, a Vietnamese envoy returned from China after studying a technique known as "spirit writing" that could divine supernatural wishes but was restricted to men.[15] In stressing the behavior expected of "good" women, the newly arrived religions of Islam and Christianity joined Buddhism and Confucianism in presenting forthright and persuasive models of female modesty and submissiveness. Thus, though a VOC employee condescendingly equated the numerous Malay "kings" he met in west Sumatra with mayors of small German towns, their wives still remained indoors in accordance with standards set by Muslim elites in larger centers.[16] Working in tandem with religious authorities, state authorities developed and promoted conceptions of male-female relationships that still resonate today. In particular, the documentation of legal precedent codified ideals that reduced the flexibility of customary law and confirmed men's prerogatives in both the household and the community at large.

Women were also economically marginalized by Southeast Asia's expanding international trade, widely seen as a defining characteristic of the period. Though female entrepreneurs and wealthy court ladies sometimes became important players, men always preferred to deal with other men, especially as Europeans, Chinese, and other Asians acquired a commanding position in local economies. The effects of commercialization could re-gender even that quintessential female skill, weaving. In the eighteenth-century, the Spanish established factory schools for training Filipino apprentices in the production of sailcloth, and a generation later men were actively involved in many aspects of what had been a women's domain.[17] The growth of urban centers created a new environment for female poverty where prostitution was often the simplest means of survival for those without family support. A slave bought cheaply in Batavia because she was "old and ugly," but freed as a reward for faithful service when her master returned to the Netherlands, was very likely to end her days in the poorhouse, where most residents were elderly native women.[18]

"Early modernity," however, is not a metaphor for female capitulation. Despite the erosion of their ritual position, women were still respected conduits for conversations with unseen powers, and ordinary people rarely saw spirit possession as a sign of weakness. Constraints imposed by state and religious ideologies were constantly subverted by social status, by age, and by personal initiative, so that women were well able to establish a reputation for religious piety, as repositories of cultural lore, as skillful mediators, and as leaders knowledgeable in public affairs. The willingness of Java's Amangkurat II to entrust an older princess with responsibility for the kingdom's affairs is not particularly unusual; according to the royal orders of Burma, a chief queen was expected to help her son in administration should the ruler be away from the capital.[19] Nor did changes in economic patterns disrupt basic attitudes toward "female" work, which was still seen as essential for household and community survival. This view is appealingly captured in the biography of a modern Kammu man from Laos: "If there are some elderly women in the family, everything in the house will be in good order; and if there are some young girls in the family, the area underneath the house will be full of firewood, the water containers will be filled with fresh water, and all the baskets will be full of rice."[20] As historical records show, the demands of long-distance trade, warfare, raiding, corvée, and religion contributed to a level of male absenteeism that gave women prime responsibility for food production, and analogies between plant growth and human maturation rendered female participation essential to rituals for crop fertility. The income provided by market sales and occupations like pottery and cloth production continued to be essential to household maintenance, while older women could expect to be treated with respect and their expertise regarded as a valuable community resource.

In sum, I have concluded that a geographically defined "Southeast Asia" largely coincides with a culture area where the position of women was relatively favorable and where "early modernity" encodes a period of great consequence in the evolution of male-female interaction. Regardless of whether my interpretations are accepted, an obvious question for those interested in researching the history of women and gender in Southeast Asia concerns future directions and priorities. In a field where generalizations have typically preceded more detailed analyses, a primary task must surely be the return to subregions as a basis for further analysis. It is in this context that historians can best exploit the skills that have long characterized Southeast Asian scholarship—a deep knowledge of local languages, an ability to see source material in unlikely places, and a commitment to collaborative and cross-disciplinary communication. As the bank of case studies increases, discussions will become more nuanced, the comparative exercise more disciplined, and women's issues more central to regional historiography.

Although there will never be any simple way of depicting the female condition in Southeast Asia, whatever theme we choose to explore, the current academic climate offers new and enticing spaces for reinterpretation and debate. A growing sensitivity to gender can only result in more-textured analyses of the region's past, a past in which the ambiguities of the female condition will remain a recurring theme. To illustrate this point, I turn once more to the story of Ken Dedes, which served, many pages ago, as my departure point. Historically marginalized in the standard texts, the extraordinary attributes of this legendary Javanese queen compel attention. Some might regard Ken Dedes as the quintessential victim, a woman without agency who has no control over her own powers and whose fate lies completely in men's hands. On the other hand, her status as *ardhanariswari*, embodying the perfect balance between male and female, opens up possibilities of different interpretations, remembering that the magnificent sculpture of Prajnaparamita, mother of all buddhas, was commonly believed to be her portrait.[21] In thinking across the borders of world areas, it is worth noting that in India androgyny is associated with Shiva and that similar attributes are rarely attached to a goddess; when a female deity does incorporate male elements, she can be extremely dangerous. While echoes of these ideas can be found in Southeast Asia, we might also recall comments made by the Dutch scholar G. A. J. Hazeu more than a century ago. To a far greater extent than in India, he argued, the female figure as a locus of power in the written and oral mythology of Java and the Malayo-Polynesian world (and, one might add, in Southeast Asia generally) grew out of the experiences of real people.[22] Against this background, the Javanese characterization of Ken Dedes as a self-standing woman who has carved out her own space in the cultural record raises provocative questions about the dynamics of indigenous societies and their accommodation of outside influences. Infusing women's history with a profound relevance, the propositions, uncertainties, and contradictions arising from such discussions will enrich our understanding of the Southeast Asian past and encourage the comparative endeavor that lies at the core of area studies.

Notes

Introduction

1. The phrase "men of prowess" entered Southeast Asian studies in the 1980s through the work of O. W. Wolters. See his *History, Culture, and Region in Southeast Asian Perspectives*, rev. ed. (Ithaca, NY: Cornell University; Singapore: ISEAS, 1999), 18–21.

2. I Gusti Putu Phalgunadi, ed. and trans., *The Pararaton: A Study of the Southeast Asian Chronicle* (New Delhi: Sundeep Prakashan, 1996), 57, 77–81, 89; George Coedès, *The Indianized States of Southeast Asia*, trans. Susan Brown Cowing, ed. Walter F. Vella (Honolulu: East-West Center Press, 1968), 346n157. The oft-cited phrase "de prinses met den vlammenden schoot" is taken from N. J. Krom, *Hindoe-Javaansche Geschiedenis* (The Hague: Nijhoff, 1926), 310.

3. George Coedès, *Histoire ancienne des états hindouisés d'Extrême-Orient* (Hanoi: Imprimerie d'Extrême-Orient, 1944), 7–10.

4. Anthony Reid, *Southeast Asia in the Age of Commerce 1450–1680*, vol. 1, *The Lands below the Winds* (New Haven, CT, and London: Yale University Press, 1988), 6, 146, 162.

5. Shelly Errington, "Recasting Sex, Gender, and Power: A Theoretical and Regional Overview," in Jane Monnig Atkinson and Shelly Errington, eds., *Power and Difference: Gender in Island Southeast Asia* (Stanford, CA: Stanford University Press, 1990), 3; Aihwa Ong and Michael G. Peletz, introduction to Aihwa Ong and Michael G. Peletz, eds., *Bewitching Women, Pious Men: Gender and Body Politics in Southeast Asia* (Berkeley: University of California Press, 1995), 9–10.

6. Victor T. King, "Southeast Asia: An Anthropological Field of Study?" *Moussons* 3 (June 2001): 3–25.

7. Jean Gelman Taylor, *The Social World of Batavia: European and Eurasian in Dutch Asia* (Madison: University of Wisconsin Press, 1983).

8. Victor B. Lieberman, "Transcending East-West Dichotomies," in Victor B. Lieberman, ed., *Beyond Binary Histories: Re-Imagining Eurasia to c. 1830* (Ann Arbor: University of Michigan Press, 1999), 27; Anthony Reid, introduction to Anthony Reid, ed., *Southeast Asia in the Early Modern Era: Trade, Power, and Belief* (Ithaca, NY, and London: Cornell University Press, 1993), 1–19.

9. Joan Kelly, "Did Women Have a Renaissance?" in *Women, History, and Theory: The Essays of Joan Kelly* (Chicago: University of Chicago Press, 1984), 19–51; Merry E. Wiesner, *Women and Gender in Early Modern Europe* (Cambridge: Cambridge University Press, 1993).

10. Thomas A. Gregor and Donald Tuzin, eds., *Gender in Amazonia and Melanesia: An Exploration of the Comparative Method* (Berkeley: University of California Press, 2001), 5; Wolters, *History, Culture, and Region*, 229.

11. Barbara N. Ramusack and Sharon Sievers, *Women in Asia: Restoring Women to History* (Bloomington: Indiana University Press, 1999), xxi.

12. Frank N. Trager et al., *Burma: A Selected and Annotated Bibliography* (New York: Burma Research Project, New York University; New Haven, CT: Human Relations Area Files, 1956), 116.

13. See also R. W. Connell, "The State, Gender, and Sexual Politics: Theory and Appraisal," *Theory and Society* 19, no. 5 (October 1990), 520, 527.

14. Sanjay Subrahmanyam, "Connected Histories: Notes towards a Reconfiguration of Early Modern Eurasia," in Lieberman, *Beyond Binary Histories*, 297.

15. Early but insightful studies are M. Kay Martin and Barbara Voorhoeve, *Female of the Species* (New York and London: Columbia University Press, 1975); and Martin King Whyte, *The Status of Women in Preindustrial Societies* (Princeton, NJ: Princeton University Press, 1978).

Chapter 1. Women and "Southeast Asia"

1. Coedès, *Histoire ancienne des états hindouisés d'Extrême-Orient*.

2. Martin W. Lewis and Kären E. Wigan, *The Myth of Continents: A Critique of Metageography* (Berkeley and London: University of California Press, 1997), 176; Paul H. Kratoska, Remco Raben, and Henk Schulte Nordholt, "Locating Southeast Asia," in Paul H. Kratoska, Remco Raben, and Henk Schulte Nordholt, eds., *Locating Southeast Asia: Geographies of Knowledge and Space* (Singapore: University of Singapore Press, 2005), 1–19.

3. Charles Higham, *The Bronze Age of Southeast Asia* (Cambridge: Cambridge University Press, 1996), 1; Mattiebelle Gittinger and H. Leedom Lefferts Jr., eds., *Textiles and the Tai Experience in Southeast Asia* (Washington, DC: Textile Museum, 1992), 23n2.

4. Victor Savage, Lily Kong, and Brenda S. A. Yeoh, "The Human Geography of Southeast Asia: An Analysis of Post-War Developments," *Singapore Journal of Tropical Geography* 14 (1993): 233.

5. Geoff Wade, "The Bai-Yi Zhuan: A Chinese Account of a Tai Society in the 14th Century," paper presented at the 14th IAHA Conference, Bangkok, May 1996, appendix 2, 8. Used with permission.

6. Patricia Buckley Ebrey, "The *Book of Filial Piety for Women* Attributed to a Woman née Zheng (ca. 730)," in Susan Mann and Yu-Yin Cheng, eds., *Under Confucian Eyes: Writings on Gender in Chinese History* (Berkeley: University of California Press, 2001), 47–69; Susan Mann, preface to Nancy Lee Swann, *Pan Chao: Foremost Woman Scholar of China* (Ann Arbor: Center for Chinese Studies, University of Michigan, 2001; reprint of 1932 edition), ix–x; Sharon Sievers, "Women in China, Japan, and Korea," in Ramusack and Sievers, *Women in Asia*, 166.

7. Claudine Salmon, "Wang Dahai et sa vision des 'Contrées insulaires' (1791)," *Études Chinoises* 13 (Fall 1994): 245; Geoff Wade, "The *Ming shi-lu* as a Source for Thai History—Fourteenth to Seventeenth Centuries," *JSEAS* 31, no. 2 (September 2000): 271.

8. Patricia Ebrey, "Women, Marriage, and the Family in Chinese History," in Paul S. Ropp, ed., *Heritage of China: Contemporary Perspectives on Chinese Civilization* (Berkeley and Los Angeles: University of California Press, 1990), 197–224.

9. Matthew H. Sommer, *Sex, Law, and Society in Late Imperial China* (Stanford, CA: Stanford University Press, 2000), esp. chaps. 5 and 7.

10. Edward L. Davis, *Society and the Supernatural in Song China* (Honolulu: University of Hawai'i Press, 2001), 61–64.

11. Hugh R. Clark, *Community, Trade, and Networks: Southern Fujian Province from the Third to the Thirteenth Century* (Cambridge and New York: Cambridge University Press, 1991), 33; Anne Csete, "The Li Mother Spirit and the Struggle for Hainan's Land and Legends," *Late Imperial China* 22, no. 2 (2001): 102, 105.

12. Delia Davin, "Women in the Countryside of China," in Margery Wolf and Roxane Witke, eds., *Women in Chinese Society* (Stanford, CA: Stanford University Press, 1975), 247–248; for a comparable Japan case, see Toshijiro Hirayama, "Seasonal Rituals Connected with Rice Culture," in Richard M. Dorson, ed., *Studies in Japanese Folklore* (Bloomington: Indiana University Press, 1963), 57–75.

13. Mark Elvin, "Blood and Statistics: Reconstructing the Population Dynamics of Late Imperial China from the Biographies of Virtuous Women in Local Gazetteers," in Harriet T. Zurndorfer, ed., *Chinese Women in the Imperial Past: New Perspectives* (Leiden: Brill, 1999), 149; Jane R. Hanks, "Reflections on the Ontology of Rice," in Stanley Diamond, ed., *Culture in History: Essays in Honor of Paul Radin* (New York: Columbia University Press, 1960), 298–301; Roy. W. Hamilton, "The Goddess of Rice," in Roy W. Hamilton, ed., *The Art of Rice: Spirit and Sustenance in Asia* (Los Angeles: UCLA Fowler Museum of Cultural History, 2003), 261.

14. C. R. Boxer, *South China in the Sixteenth Century* (London: Hakluyt Society, 1953), 149.

15. Wang Ping, *Aching for Beauty: Footbinding in China* (Minneapolis: University of Minnesota Press, 2000), 36; Dorothy Ko, *Every Step a Lotus: Shoes for Bound Feet* (Berkeley: University of California Press; Toronto: Bata Shoe Museum, 2001), 14–15, 103; Evelyn Rawski, *The Last Emperors: A Social History of Qing Imperial Institutions* (Berkeley: University of California Press, 1998), 41.

16. Leong Sow-Theng, *Migration and Ethnicity in Chinese History: Hakkas, Pengmin, and Their Neighbors,* ed. Tim Wright, with introduction by G. William Skinner (Stanford, CA: Stanford University Press, 1997), 50; Jeffrey G. Barlow, "The Zhuang Minority Peoples of the Sino-Vietnamese Frontier in the Song period," *JSEAS* 18, no. 2 (September 1987): 263n88.

17. Richard Von Glahn, *The Country of Streams and Grottoes: Expansion, Settlement, and the Civilizing of the Sichuan Frontier in Song Times* (Cambridge, MA: Council on East Asian Studies, Harvard University; distributed by Harvard University Press,

1987), 16; Norma Diamond, "Defining the Miao: Ming, Qing, and Contemporary Views," in Stevan Harrell, ed., *Cultural Encounters on China's Ethnic Frontiers* (Seattle and London: University of Washington Press, 1985), 94–95, 100.

18. Frank Dikötter, "Hairy Barbarians, Furry Primates, and Wild Men: Medical Science and Cultural Representations of Hair in China," in Alf Hiltebeitel and Barbara D. Miller, eds., *Hair: Its Power and Meaning in Asian Cultures* (Albany: State University of New York Press, 1998), 52, 70n5.

19. N. Diamond, "Defining the Miao," 101–103; John Shryock, "Ch'en Ting's Account of the Marriage Customs of the Chiefs of Yunnan and Kueichou," *American Anthropologist* 36, no. 4 (1934): 535; for details of the albums, see Laura Hostetler, *Qing Colonial Enterprise: Ethnography and Cartography in Early Modern China* (Chicago: University of Chicago Press, 2001), 159–192.

20. Hostetler, *Qing Colonial Enterprise,* 171–174; Shryock, "Marriage Customs of Yunnan," 535; Jacqueline Armijo-Hussein, trans., "'The Customs of Various Barbarians,' by Li Jing (1251–?)," in Mann and Cheng, *Under Confucian Eyes,* 89.

21. Wade, "The Bai-Yi Zhuan," appendix 2, 5.

22. Von Glahn, *The Country of Streams,* 152, 154n28, 256nn33–34; Wade, "The Bai-Yi Zhuan," appendix 2, 6.

23. Von Glahn, *The Country of Streams,* 15; Higham, *The Bronze Age,* 147, 152; Yang Yuziang, "Traditional Rituals of the Rice Cultivation Cycle among Selected Ethnic Minority Peoples of Yunnan Province, Southeast China," in Anthony Walker, ed., *Rice in Southeast Asian Myth and Ritual,* Contributions to Southeast Asian Ethnography no. 10 (Columbus: Department of Anthropology, Ohio State University, 1994), 109; Cholthira Satyawadhna, "A Comparative Study of Structure and Contradiction in the Austro-Asiatic System of the Thai-Yunnan Periphery," in Gehan Wijeyewardene, ed., *Ethnic Groups across National Boundaries in Mainland Southeast Asia* (Singapore: ISEAS, 1990), 90.

24. Claudine Lombard-Salmon, *Un exemple d'acculturation Chinoise: La province du Gui Zhou au XVIIIᵉ siècle* (Paris: EFEO, 1972), 297; Wade, "The Bai-Yi Zhuan," appendix 2, 6.

25. Barlow, "The Zhuang Minority," 256–257; Wolfram Eberhard, *China's Minorities. Yesterday and Today* (Belmont, CA: Wadsworth, 1982), 89; Csete, "The Li Mother Spirit," 96, 117; Edward H. Schafer, *Shore of Pearls* (Berkeley: University of California Press, 1969), 67.

26. Wade, "The Bai-Yi Zhuan," appendix 2, 7; Sun Laichen, "Ming–Southeast Asian Overland Interactions 1368–1644" (PhD diss., University of Michigan, 2000), 192, 228–230; Armijo-Hussein, "'Customs of Various Barbarians,'" 92.

27. John E. Herman, "Empire in the Southwest: Early Qing Reforms to the Native Chieftain System," *JAS* 56, no. 1 (February 1997): 51–59, 69; William T. Rowe, *Saving the World: Chen Hongmou and Elite Consciousness in Eighteenth-Century China* (Stanford, CA: Stanford University Press, 2001), 424; Hostetler, *Qing Colonial Enterprise,* 121–125.

28. William Robert Geddes, *Migrants of the Mountains: The Cultural Ecology of the Blue Miao (Hmong Njua) of Thailand* (Oxford: Clarendon Press, 1976), 22.

29. Shryock, "Marriage Customs of Yunnan," 529, 535.

30. C. Pat Giersch, "'A Motley Throng': Social Change on Southwest China's Early Modern Frontier, 1700–1880," *JAS* 60, no. 1 (February 2001): 88; Elvin, "Blood and Statistics," 156; Lombard-Salmon, *Un exemple*, 225.

31. David K. Wyatt, "Southeast Asia 'Inside Out,' 1300–1800: A Perspective from the Interior," in Lieberman, *Beyond Binary Histories*, 256, 262–263; Richard Davis, *Muang Metaphysics: A Study of Northern Thai Myth and Ritual* (Bangkok: Pandora, 1982), 26.

32. Karl Gustav Izikowitz, *Lamet: Hill Peasants in French Indochina* (New York: AMS Press, 1979; reprint of 1960 edition), 19.

33. Sun, "Ming–Southeast Asian Overland Interactions," 211; for the same process in modern times, see Izikowitz, *Lamet*, 28.

34. Cornelia Ann Kammerer, "Shifting Gender Asymmetries among Akha of Northern Thailand," in Nancy Eberhardt, ed., *Gender, Power, and the Construction of the Moral Order: Studies from the Thai Periphery*, Center for Southeast Asian Studies, Monograph 4 (Madison: University of Wisconsin–Madison, 1988), 33–51.

35. Otome Klein Hutheesing, *Emerging Sexual Inequality among the Lisu of Northern Thailand* (Leiden: Brill, 1990), 33, 181.

36. John E. Wills, ed., *Eclipsed Entrepôts of the Western Pacific: Taiwan and Central Vietnam 1500–1800* (Aldershot, Hampshire: Ashgate, 2002).

37. Leonard Blussé and Marius P. H. Roessingh, "A Visit to the Past: Soulang, a Formosan Village anno 1623," *Archipel* 27 (1984): 73; Laurence G. Thompson, "The Earliest Chinese Eyewitness Accounts of the Formosan Aborigines," *Monumenta Serica* 23 (1964): 173, 180; John R. Shepherd, *Statecraft and Political Economy on the Taiwan Frontier, 1600–1800* (Stanford, CA: Stanford University Press, 1993), 63–66; John E. Wills, "The Seventeenth-Century Transformation: Taiwan under the Dutch and the Cheng Regime," in Murray A. Rubenstein, ed., *Taiwan: A New History* (New York and London: M. E. Sharpe, 1999), 86–102.

38. Csete, "The Li Mother Spirit," 105; Shepherd, *Statecraft and Political Economy on the Taiwan Frontier*, chaps. 5 and 6; Laurence G. Thompson, "Formosan Aborigines in the Early Eighteenth Century: Huang Shuchi'ng's *Fan-su liu-k'ao*," *Monumenta Serica* 28 (1969): 105; Emma Jinhua Teng, *Taiwan's Imagined Geography: Chinese Colonial Travel Writing and Pictures, 1683–1895* (Cambridge, MA: Harvard University Asia Center, 2004), 131, 173–186.

39. Michael DiGregorio, A. Terry Rambo and Masayuki Yanagisawa, "Clean, Green and Beautiful: Environment and Development under the Renovation Economy," in Hy Van Luong, ed., *Postwar Vietnam: Dynamics of a Transforming Society* (Singapore: ISEAS; New York: Rowman and Littlefield, 2003), 171–201; Robert Parkin, *A Guide to Austroasiatic Speakers and Their Languages*, Oceanic Linguistics Special Publication 23 (Honolulu: University of Hawai'i Press, 1991), 90; Insun Yu, *Law and Society in Seventeenth and Eighteenth Century Vietnam* (Seoul: Asiatic Research Center, Korea University, 1990), 1–2.

40. Keith Weller Taylor, *The Birth of Vietnam* (Berkeley: University of California Press, 1983), 74, 77; Eric Henry, "Chinese and Indigenous Influences in Vietnamese

Verse Romances of the Nineteenth Century," *Crossroads* 15, no. 2 (2001): 19; Insun Yu, "Bilateral Social Pattern and the Status of Women in Traditional Vietnam," *South East Asia Research* 7, no. 2 (July 1999): 219–292; Edward H. Schafer, *The Vermilion Bird: T'ang Images of the South* (Berkeley and Los Angeles: University of California Press, 1967), 80, 84.

41. Schafer, *The Vermilion Bird*, 84.

42. Henry, "Chinese and Indigenous Influences," 13.

43. Henri Maspero, *Taoism and Chinese Religion*, trans. Frank A. Kierman Jr. (Amherst : University of Massachusetts Press, 1981), 5–6, 241–243; B. J. Terwiel, "Rice Legends in Mainland Southeast Asia," in Walker, *Rice in Southeast Asian Myth and Ritual*, 30; Davis, *Muang Metaphysics*, 31, 51, 61–62. See, however, Vi Van An and Eric Crystal, "Rice Harvest Rituals in Two Highland Tai Communities in Vietnam," in Hamilton, *The Art of Rice*, 123, 131.

44. C. Eckford Luard, *Travels of Fray Sebastian Manrique, 1629–1643*, vol. 1, *Arakan*, 2nd ser., no. 59 (London: Hakluyt Society, 1926), 92, 329.

45. Richard K. Diran, *The Vanishing Tribes of Burma* (London: Seven Dials, 1999), 7; Matthew H. Edney, *Mapping an Empire: The Geographical Construction of British India, 1765–1843* (Chicago: University of Chicago Press, 1997), 1–16; John Pemberton, *Report on the Eastern Frontier of British India* (Gauhati: Department of Historical and Antiquarian Studies in Assam, 1966; reprint of 1835 edition), 3, 16.

46. B. B. Goswami, "The Mizos in the Context of State Formation," in Surajit Sinha, ed., *Tribal Polities and State Systems in Pre-Colonial Eastern and North Eastern India* (Calcutta: Centre for Studies in Social Sciences, 1987), 310; Lian H. Sakhong, *In Search of Chin Identity: A Study in Religion, Politics, and Ethnic Identity in Burma* (Copenhagen: Nordic Institute of Asian Studies, 2003), 3.

47. Sun, "Ming–Southeast Asian Overland Interactions," 21–22; Than Tun, ed., *Royal Orders of Burma, AD 1598–1885* (Kyoto: Center for Southeast Asian Studies, Kyoto University, 1983–1990), 1:72.

48. Willem van Schendel, *Francis Buchanan in Southeast Bengal (1798): His Journey to Chittagong, the Chittagong Hill Tracts, Noakhali, and Comilla* (Dhaka: Dhaka University Press, 1992), 62, 82; Richard M. Eaton, *The Rise of Islam and the Bengal Frontier, 1204–1760* (Berkeley: University of California Press, 1993), 298–299.

49. Van Schendel, *Francis Buchanan in Southeast Bengal*, 112.

50. Ibid., 28.

51. John Rawlins, "On the Manners, Religion, and Laws of the Cucis, or Mountaineers of Tipra," *Asiatick Researches* 2, no. 12 (1790), 183, 191; Willem van Schendel, Wolfgang Mey, and Aditya Kumar Dewan, *The Chittagong Hill Tracts: Living in a Borderland* (Bangkok: White Lotus, 2000), 93; Eaton, *The Rise of Islam*, 236.

52. David Kinsley, *Hindu Goddesses: Visions of the Divine Feminine in the Hindu Religious Tradition* (Berkeley: University of California Press, 1986), 77–78; Barbara N. Ramusack, "Women in South Asia," in Ramusack and Sievers, *Women in Asia*, 27–38; Katherine K. Young, "Hinduism," in Arvind Sharma, ed., *Women in World Religions* (Albany: State University of New York, 1987), 72–92.

53. Pompa Banerjee, *Burning Women: Widows, Witches, and Early Modern European Travelers in India* (New York: Palgrave Macmillan, 2003), 10, 73–107; Laurens van den Bosch, "The Ultimate Journey: Satî and Widowhood in India," in Jan Bremmer and Lourens van den Bosch, *Between Poverty and the Pyre: Moments in the History of Widowhood* (London and New York: Routledge, 1995), 171; Uma Chakravarti, "Wifehood, Widowhood, and Adultery: Female Sexuality, Surveillance, and the State in 18th Century Maharashtra," in Patricia Uberoi, ed., *Social Reform, Sexuality, and the State* (New Delhi: Sage Publications, 1996), 3–22; Ian Wendt, "The Dharma of Women's Work: Gender, Labor, and Law in the Textile Industry of Early Modern South India," paper presented at the annual meeting of AAS, Chicago, March 2005.

54. Kinsley, *Hindu Goddesses,* 49–50; Susan S. Wadley, "Women and the Hindu Tradition," *Signs: Journal of Women in Culture and Society* 3, no. 1 (1977–1978): 113–128.

55. Rajmohan Nath, *The Background of Assamese Culture,* 2nd ed. (Gauhati: Dutta Baruah and Co., 1978; first published in 1948), 6–7; P. J. Marshall, *Bengal: The British Bridgehead: Eastern India 1740–1828,* New Cambridge History of India, vol. 2, part 2 (Cambridge: Cambridge University Press, 1987), 27.

56. Eaton, *The Rise of Islam,* 103–108, 130.

57. Yasmin Saikia, *Fragmented Memories: Struggling to be Tai-Ahom in India* (Durham, NC, and London: Duke University Press, 2004), 113–130.

58. Edward Gait, *A History of Assam,* 2nd rev. ed. (Calcutta and Simla: Thacker, Spink, and Co., 1926), 73n and 73–77; P. Gogoi, *The Tai and the Tai Kingdoms, with a Fuller Treatment of the Tai Ahom Kingdom of the Brahmaputra Valley* (Gauhati: Gauhati University, 1968), 541–542; Verrier Elwin, ed., *India's Northeast Frontier in the Nineteenth Century* (London: Oxford University Press, 1959), 368; Sayeeda Yasmin Saikia, *In the Meadows of Gold: Telling Tales of the Swargadeos at the Crossroads of Assam* (Guwahati and Delhi: Spectrum, 1997), 194 passim.

59. Nath, *The Background of Assamese Culture,* 9; Saikia, *In the Meadows of Gold,* 194.

60. *An Account of the Burman Empire and the Kingdom of Assam* (Calcutta, 1839), 142; Bani Kanta Kakati, *The Mother Goddess Kāmākhyā; or, Studies in the Fusion of Aryan and Primitive Beliefs of Assam* (Gauhati: Lawyer's Book Stall, 1967; reprint of 1948 edition), 34, 37.

61. Saroj N. Arambam Parratt and John Parratt, *The Pleasing of the Gods: Meitei Lai Haraoba* (New Delhi: Vikas, 1997), 33; Saroj N. Parratt, *The Religion of Manipur: Beliefs, Rituals, and Historical Development* (Calcutta: Firma KLM, 1980), 96–100.

62. Parratt, *The Religion of Manipur,* 147; L. Joychandra Singh, *The Lost Kingdom (Royal Chronicle of Manipur)* (Imphal, Manipur: Prajatantra, 1995), 55; Manjusri Chaki-Sircar, *Feminism in a Traditional Society: Women of the Manipur Valley* (New Delhi: Shakti Books, 1984), 188.

63. Parratt, *The Religion of Manipur,* 59–63; Parratt and Parratt, *The Pleasing of the Gods,* 7–9.

64. Chaki-Sircar, *Feminism in a Traditional Society,* 4.

65. Bertram S. Carey and H. N. Tuck, *The Chin Hills: A History of the People, Our Dealings with Them, Their Customs and Manners, and a Gazetteer of Their Country* (Aizawl, Mizoram, India: Firma KLM, 1976; reprint of 1932 edition), 135.

66. Gait, *A History of Assam,* 144–145; Eaton, *The Rise of Islam,* 77–78.

67. Irfan Habib, "Cartography in Mughal India," in *Medieval India: A Miscellany* (Bombay and Calcutta: Asia Publishing House, 1977), 4:126–127 and map insert; Gait, *A History of Assam,* 144.

68. Jagdish Narayan Sarkar, *The Life of Mir Jumla: The General of Aurangzeb* (New Delhi: Rajesh Publications, 1979), 287, 311; John F. Richards, *The Mughal Empire,* New Cambridge History of India, vol. 1, part 5 (Cambridge: Cambridge University Press, 1993), 167.

69. J. F. Richards, *The Mughal Empire,* 105–106, 137; Saikia, *Fragmented Memories,* 127.

70. S. C. Dutta, *The North-east and the Mughals, 1661–1714* (Delhi: DK Publications, 1984), 116, 234; Sarkar, *The Life of Mir Jumla,* 300–304, 305n4; J. F. Richards, *The Mughal Empire,* 168; Jos Gommans, "Burma at the Frontier of South, East, and Southeast Asia: A Geographic Perspective," in Jos Gommans and Jacques Leider, eds., *The Maritime Frontier of Burma: Exploring Political, Cultural, and Commercial Interaction in the Indian Ocean World, 1200–1800* (Leiden: KITLV Press, 2002), 5.

71. Jadunath Sarkar, "Assam and the Ahoms in 1660 AD," *Journal of Bihar and Orissa* 1, no. 2 (December 1915), 190; Gait, *A History of Assam,* 141–146.

72. Verrier Elwin, ed., *The Nagas in the Nineteenth Century* (London: Oxford University Press, 1969), 73; J. Shakespear, *The Lushei Kuki Clans* (London: Macmillan, 1912), 295.

73. N. E. Parry, *The Lakkers* (London: Macmillan, 1932), 276; T. H. Lewin, *Wild Races of South-Eastern India* (London: W. H. Allen, 1870), 345; Elwin, *The Nagas,* 43, 52; see a recent comment by David Ludden, *Where Is Assam? Using Geographical History to Locate Current Social Realities* (Guwahati: Center for Northeast India, South and Southeast Asia Studies, 2003), 6.

74. Subrahmanyam, "Connected Histories," 297; Swapna Bhattacharya, "Myth and History of Bengali Identity in Arakan," in Gommans and Leider, *The Maritime Frontier of Burma,* 203.

75. Lewin, *Wild Races,* 24, 92, 99, 254.

76. Van Schendel, *Francis Buchanan in Southeast Bengal,* 82.

77. Pamela Gutman, "Vishnu in Burma," in Donald M. Stadner, ed., *The Art of Burma: New Studies* (Mumbai, India: Marg Publications, 1999), 34.

78. Donald M. Stadner, "Pagan Bronzes: Fresh Observations," in Stadner, *The Art of Burma,* 63.

79. Susan Wadley, "The Paradoxical Powers of Tamil Women," in Susan Wadley, ed., *The Powers of Tamil Women* (Syracuse, NY: Maxwell School of Citizenship and Public Affairs, Syracuse University, 1980), 161; George Hart, "Some Aspects of Kinship in Ancient Tamil Literature," in T. Trautmann, ed., *Kinship and History in South India,* Michigan Papers on South and Southeast Asia, no. 7 (Ann Arbor: University of Michigan, 1974), 41–63; Kalpana Ram, *Mukkuvar Women: Gender, Hegemony, and*

Capitalist Transformation in a South Indian Fishing Village (London and Atlantic Highlands, NJ: Zed Books, 1991), xiv; Bina Agarwal, *A Field of One's Own: Gender and Land Rights in South Asia* (Cambridge: Cambridge University Press, 1994), 94; Karin Kapadia, *Siva and Her Sisters: Gender, Caste, and Class in Rural South India* (Boulder, CO: Westview Press, 1995), 69–74; Sherry B. Ortner, "Gender and Sexuality in Hierarchical Societies: The Case of Polynesia and Some Comparative Implications," in Sherry B. Ortner and Harriet Whitehead, eds., *Sexual Meanings: The Cultural Construction of Gender and Sexuality* (Cambridge: Cambridge University Press, 1981), 398.

80. Robert Knox, *An Historical Relation of the Island Ceylon in the East Indies*, ed. H. A. I. Goonetileke (New Delhi: Navrang, 1995; reprint of 1681 edition), 11–12.

81. Elizabeth J. Harris, *The Gaze of the Coloniser: British Views on Local Women in 19th Century Sri Lanka* (Colombo, Sri Lanka: Social Scientists' Association, 1994), 46–48; Joseph Joinville, "On the Religion and Manners of the People of Ceylon," *Asiatic Researches* 7 (1803): 424; Robert Percival, *An Account of the Island of Ceylon* (London: C. and R. Baldwin, 1805), 194.

82. Agarwal, *A Field of One's Own*, 127.

83. Tessa Bartholmeusz, *Women under the Bō Tree: Buddhist Nuns in Sri Lanka* (Cambridge: Cambridge University Press, 1994), 37, 46, 80–81.

84. David Lewis, "The Pacific Navigators' Debt to the Ancient Seafarers of Asia," in Neil Gunson, ed., *The Changing Pacific: Essays in Honour of H. E. Maude* (Melbourne: Oxford University Press, 1978), 63.

85. Toichi Mabuchi, *Ethnology of the Southwestern Pacific: The Ryukyus-Taiwan–Insular Southeast Asia* (Taipei: Chinese Association for Folklore, 1974); Ann Kumar and Phil Rose, "Lexical Evidence for Early Contact between Indonesian Languages and Japanese," *Oceanic Linguistics* 39, no. 2 (December 2000): 219–255; Roxana Waterson, *The Living House: An Anthropology of Architecture in South-East Asia* (Singapore: Oxford University Press, 1990), 15–17; Hokama Shuzen, *Omoro Sōshi* (Tokyo: Iwanami Shoten, 1998; reprint of 1985 edition), 256. Reference kindly supplied by Anna Nagamine.

86. Patrick Vinton Kirch, *The Lapita Peoples* (London and Cambridge, MA: Blackwell, 1997), 80, 103, 260; Ben Finney, "Colonizing the Island World," in Ward Goodenough, ed., *Prehistoric Settlement of the Pacific* (Philadelphia: American Philosophical Society, 1996), 115–116; Thomas Gibson, *And the Sun Pursued the Moon: Symbolic Knowledge and Traditional Authority among the Makassar* (Honolulu: University of Hawai'i Press, 2005), chap. 3.

87. Kirch, *The Lapita Peoples*, 74–75; Francis X. Hezel, SJ, *The New Shape of Old Island Cultures: A Half Century of Social Change in Micronesia* (Honolulu: University of Hawai'i Press, 2001), 10; Geoffrey Irwin, *The Prehistoric Exploration and Colonisation of the Pacific* (Cambridge: Cambridge University Press, 1992), 127.

88. Alexander Spoehr, "Conquest Culture and Colonial Culture in the Marianas during the Spanish Period," in Gunson, *The Changing Pacific*, 247–260, 253, 259.

89. Clive Moore, *New Guinea: Crossing Boundaries and History* (Honolulu: University of Hawai'i, 2003); Andrew Strathern and Pamela J. Stewart, *The Python's Back: Pathways of Comparison between Indonesia and Melanesia* (Westport, CT: Greenwood

Press, 2000); Jelle Miedema and Ger Reesink, *One Head, Many Faces: New Perspectives on the Bird's Head Peninsula of New Guinea* (Leiden: KITLV Press, 2004); Matthew Spriggs, *The Island Melanesians* (Oxford and Cambridge, MA: Blackwell, 1997).

90. Kirch, *The Lapita Peoples*, 47–52, 80, 103, 152, 295n25; Moore, *New Guinea*, 2, 21–43; James J. Fox, introduction to James J. Fox, ed., *The Flow of Life: Essays on Eastern Indonesia* (Cambridge, MA: Harvard University Press, 1980), 1–18; Janet Hoskins, "The Menstrual Hut and the Witch's Lair in Two Eastern Indonesian Societies," *Ethnology* 41, no. 4 (Fall 2002): 317.

91. Irwin, *The Prehistoric Exploration*, 1, 7, 15; Finney, "Colonizing the Island World," 83, 94.

92. David Lewis, *We, the Navigators* (Canberra: ANU Press, 1972), 305–306, 393n16; Richard Parmentier, *The Sacred Remains: Myth, History, and Polity in Belau* (Chicago and London: University of Chicago Press, 1987), 40; William A. Lessa, "An Evaluation of Early Descriptions of Carolinian Culture," *Ethnohistory* 9, no. 4 (Fall 1962): 328–329.

93. Parmentier, *The Sacred Remains*, 36, 39; Kirch, *The Lapita Peoples*, 63, 75; George Keate, *An Account of the Pelew Islands* (London: G. Nichol, 1789), 24–27.

94. Diane Bell, "An Accidental Australian Tourist: Or a Feminist Anthropologist at Sea and on Land," in Stuart B. Schwartz, ed., *Implicit Understandings: Observing, Reporting, and Reflecting on the Encounters between Europeans and Other Peoples in the Early Modern Era* (Cambridge: Cambridge University Press, 1994), 515–519; Alan Walker and David R. Zorc, "Austronesian Loanwords in Yolngu-Matha of Northeast Arnhemland," *Aboriginal History* 5, part 2 (1981): 115; C. C. Macknight, *The Voyage to Marege': Macassan Trepangers in Northern Australia* (Melbourne: Melbourne University Press, 1976), 34–36.

95. Irwin, *The Prehistoric Exploration*, 200.

96. Kalpana Ram and Margaret Jolly, eds., *Maternities and Modernities: Colonial and Postcolonial Experiences in Asia and the Pacific* (Cambridge: Cambridge University Press, 1998).

97. Robert I. Levy, *Tahitians: Mind and Experience in the Society Islands* (Chicago and London: University of Chicago Press, 1973), 130–132; Neil Gunson, "Sacred Women Chiefs and Female 'Headmen' in Polynesian History," in Caroline Ralston and Nicholas Thomas, eds., "Sanctity and Power: Gender in Polynesian History," special issue, *Journal of Pacific History* 22, no. 3–4 (July–October 1987), 145; Nico Besnier, "Polynesian Gender Liminality through Time and Space," in Gilbert Herdt, ed., *Third Sex, Third Gender: Beyond Sexual Dimorphism in Culture and History* (New York: Zone Books, 1994), 291–294.

98. Jonathon Lamb, Vanessa Smith, and Nicholas Thomas, *Exploration & Exchange: A South Seas Anthology, 1680–1800* (Chicago: University of Chicago Press, 2000), 104–106, 136.

99. Hezel, *The New Shape*, 10.

100. Carol E. Robertson, "The Māhū of Hawai'i," *Feminist Studies* 15, no. 2 (1998): 317.

101. Toichi Mabuchi, "Spiritual Dominance of the Sister," in Allan H. Smith,

ed., *Ryukyuan Culture and Society* (Honolulu: University of Hawai'i Press, 1964), 88–89; Douglas Oliver, *Ancient Tahitian Society* (Honolulu: University of Hawai'i Press, 1974), 1:249: Jocelyn Linnekin, *Sacred Queens and Women of Consequence: Rank, Gender, and Colonialism in the Hawaiian Islands* (Ann Arbor: University of Michigan Press, 1990), 15, 38; Nicholas Thomas, "Unstable Categories: *Tapu* and Gender in the Marquesas," in Ralston and Thomas, "Sanctity and Power," 133; Gunson, "Sacred Women Chiefs," 141; Hezel, *The New Shape,* 26.

102. Spriggs, *The Island Melanesians,* 11.

103. Ronald M. Berndt and Catherine H. Berndt, *The First Australians* (Sydney: Ure Smith, 1952), 72–77; Beth A. Conklin, "Women's Blood, Warrior's Blood, and the Conquest of Vitality in Amazonia," in Gregor and Tuzin, *Gender in Amazonia and Melanesia,* 152; Isobel M. White, "Aboriginal Women's Status: A Paradox Resolved," in Fay Gale, ed., *Women's Role in Aboriginal Society* (Canberra: Australian Institute of Aboriginal Studies, 1970), 21–23.

104. For example, Marilyn Strathern, *Women in Between: Female Roles in a Male World: Mt. Hagen, New Guinea* (London and New York: Seminar Press, 1972), ix; Janet Bateman, "Alliance and Antagonism in the Iau Social and Spirit Worlds," in Marilyn Gregerson and Joyce Sterns, eds., *Symbolism and Ritual in Irian Jaya* (Jayapura, Irian Jaya: Chenderawasih University; Dallas: Summer Institute of Linguistics, 1998), 97; R. F. Salisbury, *From Stone to Steel: Economic Consequences of a Technological Change in New Guinea* (London and New York: Melbourne University Press/Cambridge University Press, 1962), 49.

105. A. Haga, *Nederlandsch Nieuw Guinea en de Papoesche eilanden: Historisch bijdrage, 1500–1883* (Batavia/The Hague: Bruining/Nijhoff, 1884), 1:117.

106. Moore, *New Guinea,* 71; D. A. P. Koning, "Eenige gegevens omtrent land en volk der noordoostkust van Ned. Nieuw-Guinea, genaamd Papoea Telandjung," *BKI* 55 (1903): 264.

107. Salisbury, *From Stone to Steel,* 109.

108. Haga, *Nederlandsch Nieuw Guinea,* 1:38; Margaret Jolly, "Damming the Rivers of Milk? Fertility, Sexuality, and Modernity in Melanesia and Amazonia," in Gregor and Tuzin, *Gender in Amazonia and Melanesia,* 181; Moore, *New Guinea,* 77; Spriggs, *The Island Melanesians,* 209–211.

109. M. R. Allen, *Male Cults and Secret Initiations in Melanesia* (London and New York: Melbourne University Press/Cambridge University Press, 1967), 90; M. J. Meggitt, "Male-Female Relationships in the Highlands of Australian New Guinea," in "New Guinea: The Central Highlands," special issue, *American Anthropologist* 66 (1964): 204–222; Gregor and Tuzin, *Gender in Amazonia and Melanesia.*

110. Subrahmanyam, "Connected Histories," 315.

111. John McKinnon and Jean Michaud, "Introduction: Montagnard Domain in the South-East Asian Masif," in Jean Michaud, ed., *Turbulent Times and Enduring Peoples: Mountain Minorities in the South-East Asian Masif* (Richmond, Surrey: Curzon Press, 2000), 2.

112. King, "Southeast Asia: An Anthropological Field of Study?" 12; Wolters, *History, Culture, and Region,* 235.

Chapter 2. Early Modernity, Sources, and Women's History

1. Ashley Thompson, "Introductory Remarks between the Lines: Writing Histories of Middle Cambodia," in Barbara Watson Andaya, ed., *Other Pasts: Women, Gender, and History in Early Modern Southeast Asia* (Honolulu: Center for Southeast Asian Studies, University of Hawai'i, 2000), 47.

2. Marcia-Anne Dobres, "Digging Up Gender in the Earliest Human Societies," in Teresa A. Meade and Merry E. Wiesner-Hanks, eds., *A Companion to Gender History* (Malden, MA: Blackwell, 2004), 213–214; Elisabeth A. Bacus, "Accessing Prestige and Power: Women in the Political Economy of Protohistoric and Early Historic Visayan Polities," in S. Nelson and M. Rosen-Ayalon, eds., *In Pursuit of Gender: Worldwide Archaeological Perspectives* (Walnut Creek, CA: AltaMira Press, 2002), 315–317.

3. Charles Higham, *The Archaeology of Mainland Southeast Asia* (Cambridge: Cambridge University Press, 1989), 77, 139–140; Charles Higham and Rachanie Thosarat, *Khok Phanom Di: Prehistoric Adaptation to the World's Richest Habitat* (Fort Worth and Philadelphia: Harcourt Brace, 1994), 26–31.

4. Cynthia Eller, *The Myth of Matriarchal Prehistory: Why an Invented Past Won't Give Women a Future* (Boston: Beacon Press, 2000), 107; Michael Pietrusewsky and Michele Toomay Douglas, *Ban Chiang, a Prehistoric Village Site in Northeast Thailand,* vol. 1, *The Human Skeletal Remains* (Philadelphia: Museum of Archaeology and Anthropology, University of Pennsylvania, 2002), 22, 260; Nancy Tayles, Kate Domett, and U Pauk Pauk, "Bronze Age Myanmar (Burma): A Report on the People from the Cemetery of Nyaunggan, Upper Myanmar," *Antiquity* 75 (2001): 277, 278.

5. See Miriam T. Stark, ed., *Archaeology of Asia* (New York: Blackwell, 2006).

6. Higham, *The Bronze Age,* 147–157.

7. Claire Holt, *Art in Indonesia* (Ithaca, NY, and London: Cornell University Press, 1967), 26–27; Bob Hudson, "The Nyaungyan 'Goddesses': Some Unusual Bronze Grave Goods from Upper Burma," *TAASA Review: Journal of the Asian Arts Society of Australia* 10 (2001): 4–7.

8. Rasmi Shoocongdej, "Gender Roles Depicted in Rock Art: A Case from Western Thailand," and C. F. W. Higham, "Women in the Prehistory of Mainland Southeast Asia," both in Nelson and Rosen-Ayalon, *In Pursuit of Gender,* 202, 223.

9. Peter Bellwood, *Prehistory of the Indo-Malaysian Archipelago,* rev. ed. (Honolulu: University of Hawai'i Press, 1997), 151, 216, 224, 289; Bacus, "Accessing Prestige and Power," 316; Jan Wisseman Christie, "Weaving and Dyeing in Early Java and Bali," in Wibke Lobo and Stefanie Reimann, eds., *Southeast Asian Archaeology 1998* (Hull, UK: Centre for South-East Asian Studies, University of Hull; Berlin: Ethnologische Museum, 2000), 25.

10. Kirch, *The Lapita Peoples,* 152 and 295n25; Jan Wisseman Christie, "Negara, Mandala, and Despotic State: Images of Early Java," in David G. Marr and A. C. Milner, eds., *Southeast Asia in the 9th to 14th Centuries* (Singapore: Institute of Southeast Asian Studies; Canberra: Research School of Pacific and Asian Studies, ANU, 1986), 80.

11. Michael Vickery, *Society, Economics, and Politics in Pre-Angkor Cambodia: The 7th–8th Centuries* (Tokyo: Toyo Bunko, Centre for East Asian Cultural Studies for UNESCO, 1998), 153, 163–164, 217–220, 280.

12. Coedès, *The Indianized States,* 172; Trudy Jacobsen, "Autonomous Queenship in Cambodia, 1st–9th Centuries CE," *JRAS* 13, no. 3 (2003): 357–375; Sheldon Pollock, "The Sanskrit Cosmopolis 300–1300 CE: Transculturation, Vernacularization, and the Question of Ideology," in Jan E. M. Houben, ed., *Ideology and Status of Sanskrit: Contributions to the History of the Sanskrit Language* (Leiden and New York: Brill, 1996), 220n28; Ian Harris, *Cambodian Buddhism: History and Practice* (Honolulu: University of Hawai'i Press, 2005), 23.

13. N. C. van Setten van der Meer, *Sawah Cultivation in Ancient Java,* Oriental Monograph Series, no. 22 (Canberra: ANU Press, 1979), 94–96; Antoinette M. Barrett Jones, *Early Tenth Century Java from the Inscriptions: A Study of Economic, Social, and Administrative Conditions in the First Quarter of the Century* (The Hague: Nijhoff, 1979), 96–98; J. G. de Casparis, ed., *Prasasti Indonesia* (Bandung, Indonesia: Masa Baru, 1950), 4, 20.

14. Pe Maung Tin, "Women in the Inscriptions of Pagan," *JBRS* 25, no. 3 (1935): 149–159.

15. Michael Aung-Thwin, *Pagan: The Origins of Modern Burma* (Honolulu: University of Hawai'i Press, 1985), 34, 41; A. B. Griswold and Prasert na Nagara, "The Aśokārāma Inscription of 1399 AD: Epigraphic and Historical Studies, No. 2," *JSS* 57, no. 1 (1969): 55.

16. John K. Whitmore, "Gender, State, and History: The Literati Voice in Early Modern Vietnam," in B. Andaya, *Other Pasts,* 217–227.

17. Chou Ta-Kuan, *Notes on the Customs of Cambodia,* translated into English by J. Gilman D'Arcy Paul from Paul Pelliot's French translation (Bangkok: Social Science Association Press, 1967), 26.

18. Ibid., 34; J. V. G. Mills, trans. and ed., *Ying-yai Sheng-lan: "The Overall Survey of the Ocean's Shores" [1433]* (Cambridge: Cambridge University Press for the Hakluyt Society, 1970), 104.

19. Laurence Palmer Briggs, *The Ancient Khmer Empire* (Philadelphia: Transactions of the American Philosophical Society, 1951), 17; Coedès, *The Indianized States,* 37; David Chandler, *A History of Cambodia,* 3rd ed. (Boulder, CO: Westview Press, 2000), 13.

20. Robert Parkin, "Descent in Old Cambodia: Deconstructing a Matrilineal Hypothesis," *Zeitschrift für Ethnologie* 115 (1990): 214; Judy Ledgerwood, "Khmer Kinship: The Matriliny/Matriarchy Myth," *Journal of Anthropological Research* 51, no. 3 (1995): 247–261; Trudy Jacobsen, "Apsarā, Accoutrements, Activists: A History of Women and Power in Cambodia" (PhD diss., University of Queensland, 2004), 22–23.

21. Marshall Sahlins, "The Stranger King: Or Dumézil among the Fijians," in *Islands of History* (Chicago: University of Chicago Press, 1985), 73–103; W. G. Maxwell, "The History of Perak from Native Sources," *JSBRAS* 2 (December 1878): 89–90.

22. M. L. Finot, "Notes d'épigraphie: L'inscription Sanskrite de Say Fong," *BEFEO* 3 (1903): 30.

23. H. Van der Veen, *The Merok Feast of the Sa'dan Toradja, VKI* 45 (1965): 93.

24. N. Peri, "Hariti, la mère de demons," *BEFEO* 17, no. 3 (1917): 77; John Miksic, *The Legacy of Majapahit* (Singapore: National Heritage Board, 1995), 165; J. J. Boeles, "The Buddhist Tutelary Couple Hāritī and Pāñcika, Protectors of Children, from a Relief at the Khmer Sanctuary of Pimai," *JSS* 56, no. 2 (July 1968): 199.

25. Harris, *Cambodian Buddhism*, 15, 17, 21; Nguyen The Anh, "The Vietnamization of the Cham Deity Pô Nagar," in Keith Weller Taylor and John K. Whitmore, eds., *Essays into Vietnamese Pasts* (Ithaca, NY: Southeast Asia Program, Cornell University, 1995), 43.

26. Vickery, *Society, Economics, and Politics*, 142; J. G. de Casparis and I. W. Mabbett, "Religion and Popular Beliefs of Southeast Asia before c.1500," in Nicholas Tarling, *The Cambridge History of Southeast Asia* (Melbourne and Cambridge: Cambridge University Press, 1992), 1:313; Nancy Dowling, "O Great Goddess," *Indonesia Circle* 62 (1994): 70–73; Pauline Lunsingh Scheurleer, "Skulls, Fangs, and Serpents: A New Development in East Javanese Iconography," in Lobo and Reimann, eds., *Southeast Asian Archaeology*, 196–198.

27. Stadner, "Pagan Bronzes," 63; Elizabeth Guthrie, "Outside the Sima," *Udaya: Journal of Khmer Studies* 2 (2001): 7–18. See also John P. Ferguson, "The Great Goddess Today in Myanmar and Thailand: An Exploration of Her Symbolic Relevance to Monastic and Female Roles," in James J. Preston, ed., *Mother Worship: Theme and Variations* (Chapel Hill: University of North Carolina Press, 1982), 286.

28. M. C. Ricklefs, *The Seen and Unseen Worlds in Java 1726–1749: History, Literature, and Islam in the Court of Pakubuwana II* (Honolulu: University of Hawai'i Press, 1998), 278; H. R. van Heekeren, *The Bronze-Iron Age of Indonesia, VKI* 22 (The Hague: Nijhoff, 1958), 61; Holt, *Art in Indonesia*, 26.

29. Peter Worsley, "Narrative Bas-Reliefs at Candi Surawana," in David G. Marr and A. C. Milner, eds., *Southeast Asia in the 9th to 14th Centuries* (Canberra: Department of Anthropology, Research School of Pacific Studies, ANU, 1986), 341ff.

30. Nguyen The Anh, "Vietnamization of the Cham Deity," 44–45.

31. Frank Reynolds and Mani Reynolds, *Three Worlds According to King Ruang*, Berkeley Buddhist Studies Series, no. 4 (Berkeley: Asian Humanities Press, 1982), 132.

32. Stuart Robson, trans., *Désawarnana (Nagarakṛtagama) by Mpu Prapanca* (Leiden: KITLV Press, 1995), 26, 74; Helen Creese, *Women of the Kakawin World: Marriage and Sexuality in the Indic Courts of Java and Bali* (Armonk, NY: M. E. Sharpe, 2004), 69; Barbara Watson Andaya, "Localising the Universal: Women, Motherhood, and the Appeal of Early Theravada Buddhism," *JSEAS* 33, no. 1 (February 2002): 27.

33. Gillian Green, "Indic Impetus? Innovations in Textile Usage in Angkorian Period Cambodia," *JESHO* 43, no. 3 (August 2000): 293.

34. Stephanie W. Jamison, *Sacrificed Wife/Sacrificer's Wife: Women, Ritual, and Hospitality in Ancient India* (New York and Oxford: Oxford University Press, 1996),

10–12; Anne M. Blackburn, *Buddhist Learning and Textual Practice in Eighteenth-Century Lankan Monastic Culture* (Princeton, NJ: Princeton University Press, 2001), 7.

35. Cited in Andrew Huxley, "The Importance of the Dhammathats in Burmese Law and Culture," *Journal of Burma Studies* 1, no. 1 (1997): 2. Michael Aung-Thwin checked the Burmese for me.

36. Robert Blust, "Linguistic Evidence for Some Early Austronesian Taboos," *American Anthropologist* 83, no. 2 (1981): 292; David K. Wyatt, "Relics, Oaths, and Politics in Thirteenth-Century Siam," *JSEAS* 32, no. 1 (February 2001): 33.

37. Michael W. Young and Julia Clark, *An Anthropologist in Papua: The Photography of F. E. Williams, 1922–39* (Honolulu: University of Hawai'i Press, 2001), 180–181.

38. David Collins, *An Account of the English Colony in New South Wales,* ed. Brian H. Fletcher (Sydney: A. H. and A. W. Reed, 1975), 464–466.

39. Panuti H. M. Sudjiman, ed., *Adat Raja-Raja Melayu* (Jakarta: University of Indonesia Press, 1983), 56–57; Nicolaus Adriani, "De Toradjasche vrouw als priesteres," in *Verzamelde geschriften* (Haarlem: De Erven F. Bohn, 1932), 2:180–215.

40. W. W. Skeat and F. F. Laidlaw, "The Cambridge University Expedition to Parts of the Malay Peninsula, 1899–1900," *JMBRAS* 26, no. 4 (1953): 13.

41. For overviews of gender studies in East Asia, see Anne Walthall, "From Private to Public Patriarchy: Women, Labor, and the State in East Asia, 1600–1919," in Meade and Wiesner-Hanks, eds., *A Companion to Gender History,* 448–449; Ramusack and Sievers, *Women in Asia,* 38–41. For *bhakti* writing in India, see Susie Tharu and K. Lalita, eds., *Women Writing in India 600 BC to the Present,* vol. 1, *600 BC to the Early Twentieth Century* (New York: Feminist Press, 1991), 56–115.

42. Reid, *Southeast Asia in the Age of Commerce,* 1:216.

43. Uli Kozok, "On Writing the Not-To-Be-Read: Literature and Literacy in a Pre-Colonial 'Tribal' Society," *BKI* 156, no. 1 (2000): 47.

44. William Chiang, *We Two Know the Script; We Have Become Good Friends: Linguistic and Social Aspects of the Women's Script Literacy in Southern Hunan, China* (Lanham, MD, and New York: University Press of America, 1995), 34–38, 49–50; Cathy Silber, "From Daughter to Daughter-in-law in the Women's Script of Southern Hunan," in Christine Gilmartin, Gail Hershatter, Lisa Rofel, and Tyrene White, eds., *Engendering China: Women, Culture, and the State* (Cambridge, MA, and London: Harvard University Press, 1994), 47–68.

45. Olga Dror, "Doan thi Diem's 'Story of the Van Cat Goddess' as a Story of Emancipation," *JSEAS* 33, no. 1 (February 2002): 63–72.

46. For example, H. van den Brink, *Dr. Benjamin Frederick Matthes: Zijn leven en arbied in dienst van het Nederlandsch bijbelgenootschap* (Amsterdam: Nederlandsch Bijbelgenootschap, 1943), 184; Ann Kumar, *Java and Modern Europe: Ambiguous Encounters* (Richmond, Surrey: Curzon Press, 1997), 52–53.

47. A. H. Hill, trans. and ed., *The Hikayat Abdullah* (Kuala Lumpur: Oxford University Press, 1970), 41.

48. Gerrit Knaap, "Pants, Skirts, and Pulpits: Women and Gender in Seventeenth-Century Amboina," in B. Andaya, *Other Pasts,* 164.

49. Creese, *Women of the Kakawin World*, 5, 36–39, 63; Huynh Sanh Thong, *The Heritage of Vietnamese Poetry* (New Haven, CT, and London: Yale University Press, 1979), 100, 157ff.

50. Khing Mya Tchou, *Les femmes de lettres Birmanes* (Paris: Editions L'Harmattan, 1994), 20–29; G. E. Harvey, *History of Burma* (London: Frank Cass, 1967; reprint of 1925 edition), 104.

51. Mattani Mojdara Rutnin, *Dance, Drama, and Theatre in Thailand: The Process of Development and Modernization* (Tokyo: Centre for East Asian Cultural Studies for UNESCO, 1993), 41–42.

52. Ann Kumar, "Javanese Court Society and Politics in the Late Eighteenth Century: The Record of a Lady Soldier. Part 1, The Religious, Social, and Economic Life of the Court," *Indonesia* 29 (April 1980): 1–46; "Part 2, Political Developments," *Indonesia* 30 (October 1980): 67–111; Kumar, *Java and Modern Europe*, 63.

53. John Balaban, ed. and trans., *Spring Essence: The Poetry of Ho Xuan Huong* (Port Townsend, WA: Copper Canyon Press, 2000), 35; alternative translations are in Huynh, *The Heritage of Vietnamese Poetry*, 100, and Tran My-Van, "'Come On, Girls, Let's Go Bail Water': Eroticism in Ho Xuan Huong's Vietnamese Poetry," *JSEAS* 33, no. 3 (October 2002): 487.

54. P. J. Zoetmulder, *Kalangwan: A Survey of Old Javanese Literature* (The Hague, Nijhoff, 1974), 187–188. See also Creese, *Women of the Kakawin World*, 41–43.

55. Ruzy Suliza Hashim, *Out of the Shadows: Women in Malay Court Narratives* (Bangi: Universiti Kebangsaan Malaysia, 2003), 55; Henry, "Chinese and Indigenous Influences," 7–9.

56. Sachchidanand Sahai, *The Rama Jataka in Laos: A Study in the Phra Lak Phra Lam* (Delhi: BR Publishing, 1996), 1:23n28, 2:25; Garrett Kam, *Ramayana in the Arts of Asia* (Singapore: Select Books, 2000), 151.

57. Nguyen Van Ky, "Rethinking the Status of Vietnamese Women in Folklore and Oral History," in Gisele Bousquet and Pierre Brocheux, eds., *Viêt Nam Exposé: French Scholarship on Twentieth-Century Vietnamese Society* (Ann Arbor: University of Michigan Press, 2002), 87–107; Nhung Tuyet Tran, "Vietnamese Women at the Crossroads: Gender and Society in Early Modern Dai Viet" (PhD diss., University of California, Los Angeles, 2004), 26.

58. Carolyn Brewer, *Holy Confrontation: Religion, Gender, and Sexuality in the Philippines, 1521–1685* (Manila: Institute of Women's Studies, St. Scholastica's College, 2001) [revised as *Shamanism, Catholicism, and Gender Relations in Colonial Philippines, 1521–1685* (Aldershot, Hampshire: Ashgate, 2004)], 376–377.

59. Miguel Loarca, "Relación de las Islas Filipinas," in B and R, 5:121–125; Brewer, *Holy Confrontation*, 74–76.

60. Benedict Sandin, "Mythological Origins of Iban Shamanism," *Sarawak Museum Journal* 32 (1983): 235–250.

61. Donald K. Swearer and Sommai Premchit, *The Legend of Queen Cāma: Bodhiramsi's Cāmadevāvamsa, a Translation and Commentary* (Albany: State University of New York Press, 1998), 42.

62. Ibid., 41–47.

63. C. C. Brown, "Sejarah Melayu or 'Malay Annals,'" *JMBRAS* 25, no. 2–3 (1952), 29.

64. M. C. Ricklefs, *Jogjakarta under Sultan Mangkubumi 1749–1792: A History of the Division of Java* (London: Oxford University Press, 1974), 379–407.

65. Noel Singer, *Burmese Puppets* (Singapore: Oxford University Press, 1992), xi, 2, 8, 62.

66. Margot A. Jones, "*Mua roi nuoc:* The Art of Vietnamese Water Puppetry: A Theatrical Genre Study" (PhD diss., University of Hawai'i at Manoa, 1996), 17.

67. Sahai, *The Rama Jataka,* 1:231.

68. G. L. Koster, "The Soothing Works of the Seducer and Their Dubious Fruits: Interpreting the *Syair Buah-Buahan,*" in C. M. S. Hellwig and S. O. Robson, eds., *A Man of Indonesian Letters: Essays in Honour of Professor A. Teeuw* (Dordrecht: Foris, 1986), 81.

69. Ricklefs, *Seen and Unseen Worlds,* 6; Peter Carey and Vincent Houben, "Spirited Srikandis and Sly Sumbadras: The Social Political and Economic Role of Women at the Central Javanese Courts in the 18th and Early 19th centuries," in Elsbeth Locher-Scholten and Anke Niehof, eds., *Indonesian Women in Focus: Past and Present Notions, VKI* 127 (Leiden: KITLV Press, 1992), 17.

70. See also Barbara Watson Andaya, *Perak, the Abode of Grace: A Study of an Eighteenth-Century Malay State* (Kuala Lumpur: Oxford in Asia, 1979), 190–191.

71. Deborah Wong, *Sounding the Center: History and Aesthetics in Thai Buddhist Performance* (Chicago: University of Chicago Press, 2001), 235–242.

72. Najma Khan Majlis, "Status of Women in Mughal India (AD 1526–1707) as Reflected through Mughal Miniatures." Paper presented at the 14th IAHA Conference, Bangkok, May 1996; Zinat Kausar, *Muslim Women in Medieval India* (New Delhi: Janaki Prakashan, 1992), 182–183.

73. Alec Gordon, "Women in Thai Society as Depicted in Mural Paintings," in Michael C. Howard, Wattana Wattanapun, and Alec Gordon, eds., *Traditional T'ai Arts in Contemporary Perspective* (Bangkok: White Lotus 1998), 175–190; David K. Wyatt, *Reading Thai Murals* (Chiang Mai, Thailand: Silkworm Books, 2004), 33, 75, 76.

74. David Hanlon, "Beyond 'the English Method of Tattooing': Decentering the Practice of History in Oceania," *Contemporary Pacific* 15, no. 1 (Spring 2003): 30.

75. Ibid., 20.

76. Benedict Sandin, *The Sea Dayaks of Borneo before White Rajah Rule* (East Lansing: Michigan State University Press, 1968), plate opposite 36; Geneviève Duggan, *Ikats of Savu: Women Weaving History in Eastern Indonesia* (Bangkok: White Lotus, 2001), 51.

77. Roy W. Hamilton, "Textile Change in 20th Century Ndona, Flores," in Marie-Louise Nabholz-Kartaschoff, Ruth Barnes, and David J. Stuart-Fox, eds., *Weaving Patterns of Life* (Basel: Museum of Ethnography Basel, 1993), 271; Ruth Barnes and Joanne B. Eicher, eds., *Dress and Gender: Making and Meaning in Cultural Contexts* (New York and Oxford: Berg, 1992), 6.

78. Waterson, *The Living House,* 42, 169–197; Rosalind C. Morris, *In the Place of*

Origins: Modernity and Its Mediums in Northern Thailand (Durham, NC, and London: Duke University Press, 2000), 124.

79. *Women in Thai Literature* (Bangkok: National Identity Board, Office of the Prime Minister, 1992), 55–56; Creese, *Women of the Kakawin World*, 27–28, 186–187.

80. Huynh, *The Heritage of Vietnamese Poetry*, 102. Alternative translations are in Balaban, *Spring Essence*, 47, and Tran My-Van, "'Come On, Girls,'" 479.

81. Ann Helen Unger and Walter Unger, *Pagodas, Gods, and Spirits of Vietnam* (London: Thames and Hudson, 1997), 14; Sandin, *The Sea Dayaks*, 78.

82. Daniel Beeckman, *A Voyage to and from the Island of Borneo* (London: Dawsons, 1973; reprint of 1718 edition), preface, 45.

83. Luard, *The Travels of Fray Sebastian Manrique*, 91; Reid, *Southeast Asia in the Age of Commerce*, 1:153.

84. Justin Corfield and Ian Morson, eds., *British Sea-Captain Alexander Hamilton's A New Account of the East Indies (17th–18th Century)* (Lewiston, NY: Edwin Mellon Press, 2001), 359; Th. Salmon, *Hedendaagsche historie of tegenwoordige staat van alle volkeren* (Amsterdam: Isaak Tirion, 1739), 3:165. See also Barbara Watson Andaya, "From Temporary Wife to Prostitute: Sexuality and Economic Change in Early Modern Southeast Asia," *Journal of Women's History* 9, no. 4 (February 1998): 21–22.

85. Cited in Brewer, *Holy Confrontation*, 50, 380.

86. Malcolm Mintz, personal communication.

87. F. Policarpo Hernández, *The Augustinians in the Philippines* (Makati, Philippines: Colegio San Agustin, 1998), 24, 54–57; William Henry Scott, *Barangay: Sixteenth-Century Philippine Culture and Society* (Quezon City: Ateneo de Manila University Press, 1994), 97.

88. J. V. Mills, trans. and ed., *Eredia's Description of Malaca, Meridional India, and Cathay*, MBRAS, reprint 14 (1997): 40–41, 47–49.

89. Rijklof van Goens, *Javaense reyse: De bezoeken van een VOC gezant aan het hof van Mataram 1648–1654*, ed. Darja van Wever (Amsterdam: Terra Incognita, 1995), 75–81.

90. Corfield and Morson, *A New Account*, 359–360; E. M. Beekman, ed. and trans., *The Poison Tree: Selected Writings of Rumphius on the Natural History of the Indies* (Kuala Lumpur: Oxford University Press, 1993), 5.

91. J. V. Mills, "Eredia's Description of Malaca," 40.

92. Antonio Pigafetta, *Magellan's Voyage around the World*, ed. and trans. James A. Robertson (Cleveland: Clark, 1906), 2:169.

93. J. van Iperen, "Beschryvinge van eene blanke negerin uit de Papoesche eilanden," *VBG* 2 (1780): 229–235.

94. William Marsden, *The History of Sumatra* (Kuala Lumpur: Oxford University Press, 1975; reprint of 1811 edition), 47, 261–266.

95. Simon de la Loubère, *A New Historical Relation of the Kingdom of Siam*, ed. David K. Wyatt (Kuala Lumpur: Oxford University Press, 1969), 113; Richard Cushman, trans., and David K. Wyatt, ed., *The Royal Chronicles of Ayutthaya* (Bangkok: Siam Society, 2000), 305.

96. Marijke Barend-van Haeften, *Oost-Indië gespiegeld: Nicolaas de Graaf, een schrijvend chirurgijn in dienst van de VOC* (Zutphen, Netherlands: Walburg Press, 1992), 156.

97. John Bastin, *Lady Raffles: By Effort and Virtue* (Singapore: National Museum, 1994), 37–54; Raimy Ché-Ross, "Syair Peri Tuan Raffles Pergi ke Minangkabau: A Malay Account of Raffles' Second Expedition to the Sumatran Highlands in 1818," *JMBRAS* 65, no. 2 (2003): 51.

98. E. M. Merewether, "Inscriptions in St. Paul's Church, Malacca," *JSBRAS* 34 (July 1900): 11; Bastin, *Lady Raffles*, 70.

99. Susan Morgan, *Place Matters: Gendered Geography in Victorian Women's Travel Books about Southeast Asia* (New Brunswick, NJ: Rutgers University Press, 1996), 10; Florence E. Hewitt, "Dyak Pemali (Restrictions)," in A. J. N. Richards, ed., *The Sea Dyaks and Other Races of Sarawak* (Kuching: Borneo Literature Bureau, 1963), 45–48.

100. Creese, *Women of the Kakawin World*, 239.

101. Luís de Matos, *Imagens do Oriente no século XVI* (Lisbon: Imprensa Nacional —Casa da Moeda, 85), 120.

102. Leonard Blussé and R. Falkenburg, *Johan Nieuhofs beelden van een Chinareis 1655–1657* (Middelburg, Netherlands: Stichting VOC Publicaties, 1987), 61, 85, 89–91, 98n3; Thomas Bowrey, *A Geographical Account of Countries Round the Bay of Bengal, 1669 to 1679*, ed. Richard Carnac Temple (Cambridge: Hakluyt Society, 1905).

103. Sommer, *Sex, Law, and Society*, 17–29.

104. Than Tun, *Royal Orders*, 2:50; John K. Whitmore, "Paperwork: The Rise of the New Literati and Ministerial Power and the Effort toward Legibility in Dai Viet," unpublished paper (cited with permission).

105. Frank N. Trager and William Koenig, *Burmese Sit-Tans, 1764–1826: Records of Rural Life and Administration* (Tucson: University of Arizona Press for AAS, 1979), 168.

106. M. R. Fernando, "The Lost Archives of Melaka: Are They Really Lost?" *JMBRAS* 78, no. 1 (2005): 20.

107. Myra Sidharta, "On the Remnants of the 'Gong Goan' Archives in Jakarta: A Preliminary Study," in Lin Tein-wai, ed., *Collected Essays on Local History of the Asia-Pacific Region: Contribution of Overseas Chinese* (Hong Kong: University of Hong Kong, 1991), 517–518.

108. Remco Raben, "Batavia and Colombo: The Ethnic and Spatial Order of Two Colonial Cities, 1600–1800" (PhD diss., University of Leiden, 1995), 183.

109. Michael Cullinane, "Accounting for Souls: Ecclesiastical Sources for the Study of Philippine Demographic History," in Daniel F. Doeppers and Peter Xenos, eds., *Population and History: The Demographic Origins of the Modern Philippines* (Madison: Center for Southeast Asian Studies, University of Wisconsin, 1998), 282–283; B and R, 48:52–58.

110. Leonard Y. Andaya, *The Heritage of Arung Palakka: A History of South Sulawesi (Celebes) in the Seventeenth Century* (The Hague: Nijhoff, 1981), 160, 203, 300.

111. Wolters, *History, Culture, and Region*, 237.

Chapter 3. Women and Religious Change

1. Corfield and Morson, *A New Account,* 363; Georges Condominas, "Phibun Cults in Rural Laos," in George William Skinner and A. Thomas Kirsch, eds., *Change and Persistence in Thai Society: Essays in Honor of Lauriston Sharp* (Ithaca, NY: Cornell University Press, 1975), 252–257; Wajuppa Tossa, trans. and ed., *Phādāeng Nāng Ai: A Translation of a Thai-Isan Folk Epic in Verse* (Lewisburg, PA: Bucknell University Press, 1990), 65–66.

2. Blust, "Linguistic Evidence," 292–300, and "Early Austronesian Social Organization: The Evidence of Language," *Current Anthropology* 21, no. 2 (April 1980): 215.

3. David Henley, *Nationalism and Regionalism in a Colonial Context: Minahasa in the Dutch East Indies* (Leiden: KITLV Press, 1996), 45. See also David Hicks, *A Maternal Religion: The Role of Women in Tetum Myth and Ritual,* Special Report 22 (De Kalb: Center for Southeast Asian Studies, Northern Illinois University, 1984).

4. Carlos Quirino and Mauro Garcia, trans. and eds., "The Manners, Customs, and Beliefs of the Philippine Inhabitants of Long Ago, Being Chapters of 'A Late 16th Century Manila Manuscript,'" *Philippine Journal of Science* 87, no. 4 (December 1958): 433.

5. Corfield and Morson, *A New Account,* 364; Maurice Durand, *Technique et panthéon des médiums viêtnamiens* (Paris: EFEO, 1959), 22; Father Adriano di St. Thecla, *Opusculum de sectis apud Sinenses et Tunkinenses (A Small Treatise on the Sects among the Chinese and Tonkinese: A Study of Religion in China and North Vietnam in the Eighteenth Century),* trans. and annotated by Olga Dror (Ithaca, NY: Southeast Asia Program, Cornell University, 2002), 149, 168.

6. Shepherd, *Statecraft and Political Economy,* 64; Susan Star Sered, *Priestess, Mother, Sacred Sister: Religions Dominated by Women* (New York: Oxford University Press, 1994), 13, 18–19; Gunson, "Sacred Women Chiefs," 153; Mabuchi, *Ethnology,* 167.

7. Quirino and Garcia, "Manners, Customs, and Beliefs," 441–42; William Scott, *Barangay,* 240.

8. B and R, 33:167–171; Corfield and Morson, *A New Account,* 422–423; Knaap, "Pants, Skirts, and Pulpits," 155.

9. Léopold Cadière, "Une princesse chrétienne à la cour des premiers Nguyên: Madame Marie," *BAVH* 26, no. 2 (1939): 70. For further information, see Barbara Watson Andaya, "Old Age: Widows, Midwives, and the Question of 'Witchcraft' in Early Modern Southeast Asia," *Asia-Pacific Forum* 28 (June 2005): 120–123. See also the contributions to Paul Cohen and Gehan Wijeyewardene, eds., "Spirit Cults and the Position of Women in Northern Thailand," special issue, *Mankind* 14, no. 4 (1984); Davis, *Muang Metaphysics,* 26; Tanabe Shigeharu, "Spirits, Power, and the Discourse of Female Gender: The *Phi Meng* Cult of Northern Thailand," in Manas Chitakasem and Andrew Turton, eds., *Thai Constructions of Knowledge* (London: School of Oriental and African Studies, University of London, 1991), 191.

10. William Scott, *Barangay,* 234; Janet Hoskins, "Doubling Deities, Descent, and Personhood," in Atkinson and Errington, *Power and Difference,* 273–306.

11. Brewer, *Holy Confrontation*, 233–234.

12. Janet Hoskins, "Doubling Deities, Descent, and Personhood," in Atkinson and Errington, eds., *Power and Difference*, 277, 281, 303, 305; Morris, *In the Place of Origins*, 128–134.

13. Corfield and Morson, *A New Account*, 364; St. Thecla, *Opusculum*, 168–169. For a nineteenth-century illustration of men wearing a female-style headdress and cooking and weaving, see Wyatt, *Reading Thai Murals*, 27–28.

14. See L. Andaya, "The *Bissu:* Study of a Third Gender in Indonesia," in B. Andaya, *Other Pasts*, 38–42.

15. Lamb et al., *Exchange and Exploration*, 136; Levy, *Tahitians*, 130–132.

16. Brewer, *Holy Confrontation*, 51; Knaap, "Pants, Skirts, and Pulpits," 155.

17. Nguyen Ngoc Huy and Ta Van Tai, with Tran Van Liem, *The Lê Code: Law in Traditional Vietnam: A Comparative Sino-Vietnamese Legal Study with Historical Juridical Analysis and Annotations* (Athens: Ohio University Press, 1987), 2:115; Nai Pan Hla, trans., and Ryuji Okudaira, *Eleven Mon Dhammasat Texts* (Tokyo: Center for East Asian Cultural Studies for UNESCO, 1992), 582; Bonnie Pacala Brereton, *Thai Tellings of Phra Malai: Texts and Rituals Concerning a Popular Buddhist Saint* (Tempe, AZ: Program for Southeast Asia Studies, 1995), 114.

18. R. Ng. Poebatjaraka, "De Calon Arang," *BKI* 82 (1926): 110–180, esp. 152; Raechelle Rubinstein, *Beyond the Realm of the Senses: The Balinese Ritual of Kakawin Composition* (Leiden: KITLV Press, 2000), 33; Thomas A. Reuter, *Custodians of the Sacred Mountains: Culture and Society in the Highlands of Bali* (Honolulu: University of Hawai'i Press, 2002), 71–72.

19. Cuong Tu Nguyen, *Zen in Medieval Vietnam: A Study and Translation of the Thien Uyen Tap Anh* (Honolulu: University of Hawai'i Press, 1997), 19–21; Minh Chi, Ha Van Tan, and Nguyen Tai Thu, *Buddhism in Vietnam: From its Origins to the 19th Century* (Hanoi: The Gioi, 1999), 113; Harris, *Cambodian Buddhism*, 23–25.

20. Diana Y. Paul, *Women in Buddhism: Images of the Feminine in Mahāyāna Tradition* (Berkeley: University of California Press, 1985), xxvii, 7.

21. C. J. Reynolds, "A Nineteenth-Century Thai Buddhist Defense of Polygamy and Some Remarks on the Social History of Women in Thailand," in *Proceedings, Seventh IAHA Conference* (Bangkok: Chulalongkorn University, 1979), 929–930; Reynolds and Reynolds, *Three Worlds*, 77–79, 149–150.

22. Peter Skilling, "A Note on the History of the Bhikkhunī-sangha (II): The Order of Nuns after the Parinivāna," *WFB Review* 30, no. 4, and 31, no. 1 (October–December 1993 and January–March 1994): 37.

23. Nicolas Gervaise, *Histoire naturelle et politique du royaume de Siam*, trans. as *The natural and political history of the kingdom of Siam* and ed. John Villiers (Bangkok: White Lotus, 1989), 163; de la Loubère, *The Kingdom of Siam*, 113; Peter Skilling, "Female Renunciants *(nang chi)* in Siam According to Early Travellers' Tales," *JSS* 83, no. 1–2 (1995): 55–61.

24. Cushman and Wyatt, *The Royal Chronicles of Ayutthaya*, 305, 424; Thadeus Flood and Chadin Flood, trans. and eds., *The Dynastic Chronicles of the Bangkok Era: The First Reign* (Tokyo: Centre for East Asian Cultural Studies, 1978), 1:178–182.

25. Margaret Cone and Richard F. Gombrich, *The Perfect Generosity of Prince Vessantara: A Buddhist Epic* (Oxford: Clarendon Press, 1977), xxi; Shawn Frederick McHale, *Print and Power: Confucianism, Communism, and Buddhism in the Making of Modern Vietnam* (Honolulu: University of Hawai'i Press, 2004), 156; Alain Forest, *Les Missionnaires français au Tonkin et au Siam XVIIᵉ–XVIIIᵉ siècles: Analyse comparée d'un relatif succès et d'un total échec* (Paris: L'Harmattan, 1998), 3:285–286.

26. Sahai, *The Rama Jataka*, 2:179, 211, 231.

27. Gordon, "Women in Thai Mural Paintings," 181.

28. For references, see B. Andaya, "Localising the Universal," 12.

29. Wyatt, *Reading Thai Murals*, 40–41.

30. Luard, *Travels of Fray Sebastian Manrique*, 227.

31. John S. Strong, *The Legend and Cult of Upagupta: Sanskrit Buddhism in North India and Southeast Asia* (Princeton, NJ: Princeton University Press, 1992), 241.

32. Hans Penth, "Reflections on the Saddhamma-Sangaha," *JSS* 65, no. 1 (January 1977): 273.

33. Aung-Thwin, *Pagan*, 41.

34. Tchou, *Les femmes de lettres Birmanes*, 42; see also B. Andaya, "Localising the Universal," 12–13.

35. Alexandre Agadjanian, "Aspects de la perception du bouddhisme en Europe du XVIᵉ au XVIIIᵉ siècle, d'après les textes des missionaires et voyageurs," in Nguyen The Anh and Alain Forest, eds., *Notes sur la culture et la religion en péninsule indochinoise en hommage à Pierre-Bernard Lafont* (Paris: L'Harmattan, 1995), 123–126; G. F. de Marini, *A New and Interesting Description of the Lao Kingdom (1642–1648)*, trans. Walter E. J. Tips and Claudio Bertuccio, with introduction by Luigi Bressan (Bangkok: White Lotus, 1998), 16.

36. For further references on this topic, see B. Andaya, "Localising the Universal."

37. Skilling, "Female Renunciants," 61n16; Kamala Tiyavanich, *Forest Recollections: Wandering Monks in Twentieth-Century Thailand* (Honolulu: University of Hawai'i Press, 1997), 28.

38. E. H. S. Simmonds, "Siamese (Thai)," in Arthur T. Hatto, ed., *Eos: An Enquiry into the Theme of Lovers' Meetings and Partings at Dawn in Poetry* (London and The Hague: Mouton, 1965), 186–195.

39. Swearer, *The Legend of Queen Cāma*, xxi–xxii.

40. Ang Chouléan, "Le sacré au féminin," *Seksa Khmer* 10–13 (1987–1990): 7–9, 22, and "Recherches recentes sur le culte des megaliths et des grottes au Cambodge," *Journal Asiatique* 281, no. 1–2 (1993): 195.

41. Than Tun, *Royal Orders*, 1:121–122.

42. Brereton, *Thai Tellings*, 114.

43. Knox, *An Historical Relation*, 97; de la Loubère, *The Kingdom of Siam*, 119.

44. Blackburn, *Buddhist Learning*, 131, 153.

45. See chap. 2, n. 27; Guthrie, "Outside the Sima," 8–11; S. J. Tambiah, "The Ideology of Merit," in E. R. Leach, ed., *Dialectic in Practical Religion*, Cambridge Papers in Social Anthropology, no. 5 (Cambridge: Cambridge University Press, 1968), 41–

121; Guy Tachard, *A Relation of the Voyage to Siam Performed by Six Jesuits Sent by the French King to the India and China in the Year 1685* (Bangkok: White Orchid Press, 1996; reprint of 1688 edition), 290.

46. Joan R. Piggott, "Chieftain Pairs and Corulers: Female Sovereignty in Early Japan," in Hitomi Tonomura, Anne Walthall, and Wakita Haruko, eds., *Women and Class in Japanese History* (Ann Arbor: Center for Japanese Studies, University of Michigan, 1999), 31–32; Nguyen Cuong Tu, *Zen in Medieval Buddhism,* 130, 133, 138, 185–194.

47. Huynh, *The Heritage of Vietnamese Poetry,* 19; Nguyen Cuong Tu, *Zen in Medieval Buddhism,* 197–198, 254; J. C. Cleary, "Buddhism and Popular Religion in Medieval Vietnam," *Journal of the American Academy of Religion* 59, no. 1 (Spring 1991): 100–106.

48. Minh et al., *Buddhism in Vietnam,* 22–23; Unger and Unger, *Pagodas, Gods, and Spirits,* 33, 87; Nguyen The Long and Pham Mai Hung, *130 Pagodas in Ha Noi* (Hanoi: The Gioi, 2003), 5.

49. Nguyen Van Huyen, *Le culte des immortels en Annam* (Hanoi: Impr. d'Extrême-Orient, 1944), 11; Joseph Nguyen Huy Lai, *La tradition religieuse spirituelle et sociale au Vietnam: Sa confrontation avec le christianisme* (Paris: Beauchesne, 1981), 266.

50. John K. Whitmore, "The Development of Le Government in Fifteenth Century Vietnam" (PhD diss., Cornell University, 1968), 204–205; Whitmore, "The Literati Voice," 225.

51. Nhatrang Cong Huyen Ton Nu Thi, "The Traditional Roles of Women as Reflected in Oral and Written Vietnamese Literature" (PhD diss., University of California, Berkeley, 1973), 18–24.

52. Minh et al., *Buddhism in Vietnam,* 122–124.

53. Peter C. Phan, *Mission and Catechesis:: Alexandre de Rhodes and Inculturation in Seventeenth-Century Vietnam* (Maryknoll, NY: Orbis Books, 1998), 47; Yu, *Law and Family,* 25.

54. Li Tana, *Nguyen Cochinchina: Southern Vietnam in the Seventeenth and Eighteenth Centuries* (Ithaca, NY: Southeast Asia Program, Cornell University, 1998), 108.

55. Tran Quoc Vuong, "Popular Culture and High Culture in Vietnamese History," *Crossroads* 7, no. 2 (1992): 31–32; Minh et al., *Buddhism in Vietnam,* 142; Chün-Fang Yü, *Kuan-Yin: The Chinese Transformation of Avalokiteśvara* (New York: Columbia University Press, 2000), 129–137.

56. Peri, "Hariti, la mère de demons," 77; Minh et al., *Buddhism in Vietnam,* 130–140; Nhung Tran, "Vietnamese Women at the Crossroads," 141; Chi Lan Do-Lam, *La mère et l'enfant dans le Viêtnam d'autrefois* (Paris: L'Harmattan, 1998), 58–65.

57. Nola Cooke, "Nineteenth-Century Vietnamese Confucianization in Historical Perspective: Evidence from the Palace Examinations (1463–1883)," *JSEAS* 25, no. 2 (September 1994), 284; idem., "The Myth of the Restoration: Dang-Trong Influences in the Spiritual Life of the Early Nguyen Dynasty (1802–47)," in Anthony Reid, ed., *The Last Stand of Asian Autonomies: Response to Modernity in the Diverse States of Southeast Asia and Korea, 1750–1900* (Basingstoke, UK, and London: Macmillan,

1997), 279–280; Philip Taylor, *Goddess on the Rise: Pilgrimage and Popular Religion in Vietnam* (Honolulu: University of Hawai'i Press, 2004), 27–28.

58. Ngo Duc Thinh, "The Pantheon for the Cult of Holy Mothers," *Vietnamese Studies* 131, no. 1 (1999): 23; Phan, *Mission and Catechesis*, 18.

59. Nguyen The Anh, "Vietnamization of the Cham Deity," 47; Dror, "'Story of the Van Cat Goddess,'" 68–69; Dao Thai Hanh, "La deesse Lieu-Hanh," *BAVH* 1, no. 2 (1914): 180–181.

60. Doan Lam, "A Brief Account of the Cult of Female Deities in Vietnam," *Vietnamese Studies* 131, no. 1 (1999): 17; Nguyen Thi Hue, "From Buddha-Mother Man Nuong to Holy Mother Lieu Hanh," *Vietnamese Studies* 131, no. 1 (1999): 87; Dror, "'Story of the Van Cat Goddess,'" 63–72; Forest, *Les missionaires français*, 3:253–254.

61. Nguyen Ngoc Huy and Ta, *The Lê Code*, 1:189; Durand, *Technique et panthéon*, 12.

62. Sered, *Priestess, Mother, Sacred Sister*, 219.

63. John Barrow, *A Voyage to Cochinchina* (Kuala Lumpur: Oxford in Asia, 1975; reprint of 1806 edition), 329.

64. Ludvik Kalus and Claude Guillot, "Réinterprétation des plus anciennes stèles funéraires islamiques nousantariennes: II, La stèle de Leran (Java) datée de 473/1082 et les stèles associées," *Archipel* 67 (2004): 17–36; Hubert Jacobs, ed., *A Treatise on the Moluccas (c. 1544) . . . of Antonio Galvão* (Rome: Jesuit Historical Institute, 1971), 83; Claudine Salmon, "Cults Peculiar to the Chinese of Java," in Cheu Hock Tong, ed., *Chinese Beliefs and Practices in Southeast Asia: Studies on the Chinese Religion in Malaysia, Singapore, and Indonesia* (Petaling Jaya, Malaysia: Pelanduk Publications, 1993), 283, 300n14; Armando Cortesão, ed., *The Suma Oriental of Tomé Pires* (New Delhi: Asian Educational Services, 1990; reprint of 1944 edition), 2:249.

65. Solange Hertz, trans., *Rhodes of Vietnam* (Westminster, MD: Newman Press, 1966), 117–118; J. Noorduyn, *Een achttiende-eeuwse kroniek van Wadjo': Buginese historiografie* (The Hague: Martinus Nijhoff, 1955), 104–106.

66. Barbara Freyer Stowasser, *Women in the Qur'an, Traditions, and Interpretation* (New York and Oxford: Oxford University Press, 1994), 90; Leonard Y. Andaya, "'A Very Good-Natured but Awe-Inspiring Government': The Reign of a Successful Queen in Seventeenth-Century Aceh," in Elsbeth Locher-Scholten and Pieter Rietbergen, eds., *Hof en Handel: Aziatische Vorsten en de VOC 1620–1720* (Leiden: KITLV Press, 2004), 70.

67. Gerret Vermeulen, *De gedenkwaerdige voyagie van Gerret Vermeulen naar Oost-Indien, in 't jaar 1668 aangevangen, en in 't jaar 1674 voltrokken* (Amsterdam: Jan. Claesz., 1677), 38.

68. Barbara Watson Andaya, "Delineating Female Space: Seclusion and the State in Pre-Modern Island Southeast Asia," in B. Andaya, *Other Pasts*, 231–253; Izaak Commelin, *Begin ende voortgangh van de Vereenighde Nederlantsche Geoctroyeerde Oost-Indische Compagnie* (Amsterdam: Theatrum Orbis Terrarum, 1970; reprint of 1646 edition), 1:69; P. A. Leupe, "Schrifteliyck rapport gedaen door den Predicant Justus Heurnius, aangaende de gelengenheijt van 't eijlandt Ende tot het voortplanten van de Christelyke religie, en van wegen de gelengentheijt van Bali in 1638," *BKI* 3, no. 3 (1855): 258.

69. G. W. J. Drewes, *Een Javaanse primbon uit de zesdiende eeuw* (Leiden: Brill, 1954), 13.

70. B and R, 2:138; William Dampier, *A New Voyage around the World,* ed. Albert Gray (New York: Dover Publications, 1968; reprint of 1697 edition), 229, 244.

71. W. L. Olthof, *Babad tanah djawi in proza: Javaansche geschiedenis* (The Hague: Martinus Nijhoff, 1941), 21.

72. Fazlur Rahman, *Health and Medicine in the Islamic Tradition: Change and Identity* (New York: Crossroad, 1987), 29–48; Ustaz Iljas Ismail, *Fundamental Teachings of Islam* (Manila: Islamic Da'wah Council of the Philippines, 1984; reprint of 1974 edition), 42.

73. S. W. R. Mulyadi, *Hikayat Indraputra: A Malay Romance* (Dordrecht: Foris, 1983), 23–24; R. O. Winstedt, ed., *Hikayat Bayan Budiman, or Khojah Maimun* (Singapore: Methodist Publishing House, 1920), 6, 42, 94, 146.

74. Ismail Hamid, *The Malay Islamic Hikayat* (Kuala Lumpur: Universiti Kebangsaan Malaysia, 1983), 64, 86, 90, 119, 177; Ricklefs, *Seen and Unseen Worlds,* 53–61.

75. Russell Jones, ed. and trans., *Hikayat Sultan Ibrahim bin Adham* (Berkeley: Center for South and Southeast Asian Studies, University of California, 1985), 173–175.

76. Camille Adams Helminski, *Women of Sufism: A Hidden Treasure* (Boston and London: Shambhala Productions, 2003); Annemarie Schimmel, *My Soul Is a Woman: The Feminine in Islam,* trans. Susan H. Ray (New York: Continuum, 1997), 34–44, 93–96; Netty Bonouvrié, "Female Sufi Saints on the Indian Sub-Continent," in Ria Kloppenborg and Wouter J. Hanegraaff, eds., *Female Stereotypes in Religious Traditions* (Leiden: Brill, 1995), 111; Margaret Smith, *Rabi'a: The Life and Work of Rabi'a and Other Women Mystics in Islam* (Oxford: Oneworld Publications, 1994), 12, 19ff, 123, 176; Boaz Shoshan, *Popular Culture in Medieval Cairo* (Cambridge: Cambridge University Press, 1993), 12–13; Gavin R. G. Hambly, "Becoming Visible: Medieval Islamic Women in Historiography and History," in Gavin R. G. Hambly, ed., *Women in the Medieval Islamic World: Power, Patronage, and Piety* (New York: St Martin's Press, 1998), 7–8.

77. Peter Riddell, *Islam and the Malay-Indonesian World* (Honolulu: University of Hawai'i Press, 2001), 129; Amirul Hadi, *Islam and State in Sumatra: A Study of Seventeenth-Century Aceh* (Leiden and Boston: Brill, 2004), 84–86, 157–160.

78. Leila Ahmed, *Women and Gender in Islam* (New Haven, CT, and London: Yale University Press, 1992), 98–99, 104, 113–114.

79. Schimmel, *My Soul Is a Woman,* 45–47, 102, 105–114; Cyril Glassé, *The Concise Encyclopedia of Islam* (San Francisco: Harper and Row, 1989), 167, 358; Smith, *Rabi'a,* 183; Ricklefs, *Seen and Unseen Worlds,* 41n45; G. W. J. Drewes and L. K. Brakel, *The Poems of Hamzah Fansuri,* Bibliotheca Indonesica for KITLV (Dordrecht: Foris, 1986), 85–87, 164; P. Voorhoeve, "Three Old Achehnese Manuscripts," *BSOAS* 14 (1951–1952): 340.

80. Schimmel, *My Soul Is a Woman,* 118–138; Richard Maxwell Eaton, *Sufis of Bijapur 1300–1700: Social Roles of Sufis in Medieval India* (Princeton, NJ: Princeton University Press, 1978), 161–164.

81. P. J. Zoetmulder, *Pantheism and Monism in Javanese Suluk Literature: Islamic and Indian Mysticism in an Indonesian Setting,* ed. and trans M. C. Ricklefs (Leiden: KITLV Press, 1995), 170, 287–288.

82. Cortesão, *The Suma Oriental of Tomé Pires,* 2:268.

83. Abdul Wahab Bouhdiba, *Sexuality in Islam,* trans. Alan Sheridan (London: Routledge and Kegan Paul, 1988), 11, 44; Knaap, "Pants, Skirts, and Pulpits," 165; Madelaine Farah, trans., *Marriage and Sexuality in Islam: A Translation of al-Ghazālī's Book on the Etiquette of Marriage from the Ihyā'* (Salt Lake City: University of Utah Press, 1984), 107–108.

84. Cortesão, *The Suma Oriental of Tomé Pires,* 2:267; David S. Moyer, *The Logic of the Laws: A Structural Analysis of Malay Language Legal Codes from Bengkulu, VKI 75* (The Hague: Nijhoff, 1975), 41.

85. Ricklefs, *Seen and Unseen Worlds,* 74–75.

86. Wazir Jahan Karim, *Women and Culture: Between Malay Adat and Islam* (Boulder, CO: Westview Press, 1992), 7, 219; Schimmel, *My Soul Is a Woman,* chaps. 5 and 6; Th. W. Juynboll, *Handleiding tot de kennis van de Mohammedaansche wet volgens de leer der Sjāfiïtische school,* 3rd ed. (Leiden: Brill, 1925), 64; Ito Takeshi, "The World of the Adat Aceh" (PhD diss., ANU, 1984), 211, 231.

87. Sudjiman, *Adat Raja-Raja Melayu,* 56–61, 72–73.

88. L. Andaya, "'A Very Good-Natured but Awe-Inspiring Government,'" 80.

89. *Dagh-Register gehouden int casteel te Batavia* (Batavia and The Hague: Bataviaasch Genootschap; Nijhoff; Kolff, 1887–1931), 1661:79.

90. Creese, *Women of the Kakawin World,* 211–241; Cortesão, *The Suma Oriental of Tomé Pires,* 1:177–177.

91. M. B. Hooker, "The Trengganu Inscription in Malayan Legal History," *JMBRAS* 49, no. 2 (1976): 128; Zakaria Ali, *Islamic Art: Southeast Asia 830 AD–1570 AD* (Kuala Lumpur: Dewan Bahasa dan Pustaka, 1994), 52.

92. Robertus Padt-Brugge, "Beschrijving der zeden en gewoonten van de bewoners der Minahassa . . . 1679," *BKI* 13, no. 1–2 (1866): 325; "Statistieke anteekeningen over de Residentie Menado," *TNI* 1 (1840): 125; Gibson, *And the Sun Pursued the Moon,* 76–77.

93. William Scott, *Barangay,* 25.

94. Lamb et al., *Exploration & Exchange,* 186; Nico Kaptein, "Circumcision in Indonesia: Muslim or Not?" in Jan Platvoet and Karel van der Toorn, eds., *Pluralism and Identity: Studies in Ritual Behaviour* (Leiden: Brill, 1995), 285–302; Knaap, "Pants, Skirts, and Pulpits, 151, 156; Yoneo Ishii, *The Junk Trade from Southeast Asia: Translations from the Tōsen Fusetsu-gaki 1674–1723* (Singapore: ISEAS; Canberra: Research School of Pacific and Asian Studies, ANU, 1998), 60–63.

95. Nicolas Gervaise, *Description historique du royaume de Macassar,* ed. Jean-Pierre Duteil (Paris: Éditions Kimé, 2003), 111; Andrée Feillard and Lies Marcoes, "Female Circumcision in Indonesia: To 'Islamicize' in Ceremony or Secrecy," *Archipel* 56, no. 1 (1998): 339–340.

96. Kumar, *Java and Modern Europe,* 63, 112; Kumar, "Javanese Court Society and Politics," 19.

97. Padt-Brugge, "Beschrijving der zeden," 318.

98. Moyer, *The Logic of the Laws,* 66.

99. Ahmed, *Women and Gender in Islam,* 49–50; Schimmel, *My Soul Is a Woman,* 29–31.

100. E. Netscher, "Verzameling van overleveringen van het rijk van Manangk-abou uit het oorspronkelijk Maleisch vertaald," *Indisch Archief* 3 (1850): 63.

101. A. Kadir Manyambeang and Ambo Gani, *Lontarak Makkatterek dan Ilang-nya Nabi Muhammmad s.a.w.* (Jakarta: Departemen Pendididikan dan Kebudayaan, 1979), 24.

102. Mohd. Taib Osman, "Malay Traditional Beliefs: An Integration of Foreign Elements on a Malay Base," in Rainer Carle et al., *Gava': Studies in Austronesian Languages and Cultures* (Berlin: Dietrich Reimer, 1982), 592; Baroroh Baried, "Sh'ia Elements in Malay Literature," in Sartono Kartodirdjo, ed., *Profiles of Malay Culture: Historiography, Religion, and Politics* (Jogjakarta: Ministry of Education and Culture, 1976), 62, 65; Kassim Ahmad, *Hikayat Hang Tuah* (Kuala Lumpur: Dewan Bahasa dan Pustaka, 1971), 437–442.

103. Thus named because Aisyah joined an insurrection against the Caliphate of Ali, but the fighting died down when the battle lines approached the camel she was riding.

104. For example, Farah, *Marriage and Sexuality,* 32, 34, 104.

105. Riddell, *Islam and the Malay-Indonesian World,* 157.

106. Ann Kumar, "Imagining Women in Javanese Religion: Goddesses, Ascetes, Queens, Consorts, Wives," in B. Andaya, *Other Pasts,* 87–104.

107. Ricklefs, *Seen and Unseen Worlds,* 41–43, 122–125; Peter Carey, ed. and trans., *Babad Dipanagara: An Account of the Outbreak of the Java War (1825–30)* (Kuala Lumpur: MBRAS, 1981), xl–xli.

108. John Carroll, "Berunai in the Boxer Codex," *JMBRAS* 55, no. 2 (1982): 9; Gervaise, *Description historique du royaume de Macassar,* 121; Knaap, "Pants, Skirts, and Pulpits," 158.

109. G. W. J. Drewes, "Further Data Concerning 'Abd al-Samad al-Palimbani," *BKI* 132, no. 2–3 (1976): 279–281.

110. Ibid.; Ricklefs, *Seen and Unseen Worlds,* 110, 137, 210–211, 222–224.

111. Light to Cornwallis, July 30, 1792, Straits Settlements Records, G3R4/5, fol. 65, Oriental and India Office Collection, British Library, London).

112. Thomas Forrest, *A Voyage to New Guinea and the Moluccas from Balambangan* (Kuala Lumpur: Oxford University Press, 1969; reprint of 1779 edition), 20.

113. J. V. Mills, "Eredia's Description of Malaca," 48–89.

114. Adrien Launay, *Histoire de la mission du Tonkin: Documents historiques, 1658–1717* (Paris: Les Indes Savantes, 2000), 57.

115. Christoforo Borri, "Relation de la nouvelle mission à Cochinchine," *BAVH* (December 1931): 392–394; Nola Cooke, "Expectations and Transactions: Local Responses to Catholicism in Seventeenth-Century Nguyễn Cochinchina (Đàng Trong)," paper presented at the 18th IAHA Conference, Taipei, December 2004 (used with permission).

116. Eric Anderson, "Traditions in Conflict: Filipino Responses to Spanish Colonialism, 1565–1665" (PhD diss., University of Sydney, 1977), 69, 100, 218; Brewer, *Holy Confrontation,* 134–145, 159–160, 164–167, 198–199.

117. Shepherd, *Statecraft and Political Economy,* 65.

118. Georg Schurhammer, SJ, *Francis Xavier: His Life, His Times,* vol. 3, *Indonesia and India, 1545–1549,* trans. M. Joseph Costelloe, SJ (Rome: Jesuit Historical Institute, 1980), 3:89–90; Gerrit J. Knaap, *Kruidnagelen en christenen: De Verenigde Oost-Indische Compagnie en de bevolking van Ambon 1656–1696, VKI* 125 (Dordrecht: Foris, 1987), 107–108; Knaap, "Pants, Skirts, and Pulpits," 155.

119. René B. Javellana, "Imagined Villagescape as a Metaphor for Heavenly Realities," in Jose M. Cruz, ed., *Declaración de la Doctrina Christiana en idioma Tagalog* (Quezon City: Ateneo de Manila University Press, 1995), 201; Adrien Launay, *Histoire de la mission de Siam 1662–1811* (Paris: Charles Douniol and Retaux, 1920), 2:63, 62, 133.

120. Nola Cooke, "Missionary Praxis and Christianity as a Healing Religion in Seventeenth-Century Nguyễn Cochinchina," unpublished manuscript kindly provided to author.

121. Hertz, *Rhodes of Vietnam,* 191.

122. Luard, *Travels of Fray Sebastian Manrique,* 196.

123. René B. Javellana, ed. and trans., *Casaysayan nang Pasiong Mahal ni Jesuscristong Panginoon natin na sucat ipag-alab nang puso nang sinomang babasa* (Quezon City: Ateneo de Manila University Press, 1988), 183–184, 208, 213; Vitaliano R. Gorospe and R. Javellana, *Virgin of Peñafrancia, Mother of Bicol* (Manila: Bookmark, 1995), 20, 23.

124. Phan, *Mission and Catechesis,* 220; Alan Cole, *Mothers and Sons in Chinese Buddhism* (Stanford, CA: Stanford University Press, 1998), 133, 176; Nhung Tuyet Tran, "Feminizing the 'Orthodox': Images of Female Sanctity in 17th Century Buddhist and Christian *nôm* Texts," paper presented at the annual meeting of AAS, San Diego, March 2004 (cited with permission).

125. Forest, *Les missionaires français,* 3:198, 286; Hertz, *Rhodes of Vietnam,* 66, 100; Adrien Launay, *Histoire de la mission de Cochinchine 1658–1823* (Paris: MEP, 1923; reprint, Paris: Les Indes Savantes, 2000), 3:346, 350, 356, 359, 360; Launay, *Histoire de la mission du Tonkin,* 304; Monina Mercado, *Antipolo: A Shrine to Our Lady* (Manila: Aletheia Foundation, 1980), 89–90.

126. Phan, *Mission and Catechesis,* 276; Forest, *Les missionaires français,* 3:295, 304.

127. René B. Javellana, *Wood and Stone for God's Greater Glory: Jesuit Art and Architecture in the Philippines* (Quezon City: Ateneo de Manila University Press, 1991), 11; Esperanza Bunag Gatbontan, *A Heritage of Saints* (Manila: Editorial Associates, 1979), 45; Strong, *The Legend and Cult of Upagupta,* 241; Brewer, *Holy Confrontation,* 207–208.

128. Knaap, "Pants, Skirts, and Pulpits," 154.

129. Hendrik E. Niemeijer, "Slavery, Ethnicity, and the Economic Independence of Women in Seventeenth-Century Batavia," in B. Andaya, *Other Pasts,* 184–185.

130. Phan, *Mission and Catechesis*, 47.

131. Cadière, "Une princesse chrétienne," 63–130.

132. Launay, *Histoire de la mission du Tonkin*, 37, 43–44, 49–51, 340; Launay, *Histoire de la mission de Cochinchine*, 3:343, 348.

133. Launay, *Histoire de la mission de Siam*, 1:8, 14, 15; ; Nhung Tuyet Tran, "Les Amantes de la Croix: An Early Modern Vietnamese Sisterhood," in Gisele Bousquet and Nora Taylor, eds., *Le Vietnam au féminin* (Paris: Les Indes Savantes, 2005), 56–63.

134. Launay, *Histoire de la mission de Cochinchine*, 3:341–342.

135. Claudine Salmon, "Tang-Viet Society as Reflected in a Buddhist Bell Inscription from the Protectorate of Annam (798)," in Shing Müller, Thomas O. Hollman, and Putao Gu, eds., *Guandong: Archaeology and Early Texts* (Wiesbaden: Harrassowitz Verlag, 2004), 135; Nola Cooke, personal communication, 11 August 2004; Forest, *Les missionaires français*, 3:143–148; Launay, *Histoire de la mission de Cochinchine*, 1:311.

136. Peter Schreurs, MSC, *Caraga Antigua: The Hispanization and Christianization of Agusan, Surigao, and East Davao, 1521–1910* (Manila: National Historical Institute, 2000), 195–203; Brewer, *Holy Confrontation*, 268–269; Luciano P. R. Santiago, "'To Love and to Suffer': The Development of the Religious Congregations for Women in the Philippines during the Spanish Era (1565–1898), Part I," *Philippine Quarterly of Culture and Society* 23, no. 2 (June 1995): 164–186, and "Part II," 24, no. 1–2 (March–June 1996): 134–140.

137. Santiago, "'To Love and to Suffer'" (1996), 147.

138. Ibid., 144–164; Forest, *Les missionaires français*, 3:145; Nhung Tran, "Les Amantes de la Croix," 63.

139. Phan, *Mission and Catechesis*, 54, 64; Forest, *Les missionaires français*, 3:165–166, 314; Launay, *Histoire de la mission de Cochinchine*, 2:311.

140. Edgar Wickberg, *The Chinese in Philippine Life 1850–1898* (Quezon City: Ateneo de Manila University Press, 2000), 18–20; Greg Bankoff, *In Verbo Sacerdotis: The Judicial Powers of the Catholic Church in Nineteenth-Century Philippines* (Darwin: Centre for Southeast Asian Studies, Northern Territory University, 1992), 41n63.

141. Bankoff, *In Verbo Sacerdotis*, 41n62.

142. Ibid., 13, 22.

143. Hendrik E. Niemeijer, *Batavia: Een koloniate samenleving in de zeventiende eeuw* (Amsterdam: Balans, 2005), 294–300.

144. Pedro Chirino, *The Philippines in 1600*, trans. Ramón Echevarria (Manila: Historical Conservation Society, 1969), 287–288.

145. John Leddy Phelan, *The Hispanization of the Philippines: Spanish Aims and Filipino Responses 1565–1700* (London: University of Wisconsin Press, 1967), 64–65; Brewer, *Holy Confrontation*, 118–119.

146. Phan, *Mission and Catechesis*, 242–244, 246.

147. Knaap, *Kruidnagelen en christenen*, 103, 109; Knaap, "Pants, Skirts, and Pulpits," 171–172.

148. Javellana, *Casaysayan nang Pasiong*, 161.

149. Valerio Valeri, *Kingship and Sacrifice: Ritual and Society in Ancient Hawaii* (Chicago: University of Chicago Press, 1985), 113; V. E. Korn, "Batakse offerande," *BKI* 109 (1953): 32–51, 97–127.

Chapter 4. Women and Economic Change

1. Victor Lieberman, "Mainland-Archipelagic Parallels and Contrasts, c. 1750–1850," in Reid, *The Last Stand of Asian Autonomies*, 27–53.

2. David Sopher, *The Sea Nomads: A Study Based on the Literature of the Maritime Boat People of Southeast Asia* (Singapore: Singapore National Museum, 1965), 301–302; E. C. Godée Mosbergen, *Geschiedenis van de Minahassa tot 1829* (Weltevreden, Netherlands: Government Printer, 1928), 42–43.

3. Annamarie L. Rice, "North Coast of Irian Jaya," in Paul Michael Taylor and Lorraine V. Aragon, eds., with Annamarie L. Rice, *Beyond the Java Sea: Art of Indonesia's Outer Islands* (Washington, DC: Smithsonian Institution; New York: Harry N. Abrams, 1991), 257, 269, 276; William Scott, *Barangay*, 254, figure 12; Agnes Estioka-Griffin, "Women as Hunters: The Case of an Eastern Cagayan Agta Group," in P. Bion Griffin and Agnes Estioko-Griffin, eds., *The Agta of Northeastern Luzon: Recent Studies* (Cebu City, Philippines: University of San Carlos, 1985), 18–32.

4. Knaap, "Pants, Skirts, and Pulpits," 149; see also Renée Valeri, "La position sociale de la femme dans la société traditionelle des Moluques Centrales," *Archipel* 13 (1977): 53–78.

5. Blussé and Roessingh, "A Visit to the Past," 73; Johan Nieuhof, *Voyages and Travels to the East Indies 1653–1670*, with introduction by Anthony Reid (Kuala Lumpur and London: Oxford University Press, 1988; reprint of 1704 edition), 175.

6. *Ikat* is a type of weaving where the warp, weft, or both are tie-dyed before weaving to create designs on the finished fabric. In a number of Iban areas only *pua*, an elaborate cloth of very specific and complicated patterns, could receive the heads of warriors. Gavin Traude, *The Women's Warpath: Iban Ritual Fabrics from Borneo* (Los Angeles: UCLA Fowler Museum of Cultural History, 1996), 70, 92; James Jemut Masing, *The Coming of the Gods: An Iban Invocatory Chant (Timang Gawai Amat) of the Baleh River Region, Sarawak* (Canberra: Department of Anthropology, Research School of Pacific Studies, ANU, 1997), 1:25– 27.

7. Masing, *The Coming of the Gods*, 1:25, 31; 2:119.

8. Margaret Ehrenberg, *Women and Prehistory* (London: British Museum Publications, 1989), 81; Ester Boserup, *Women's Role in Economic Development* (New York: St. Martin's Press, 1970), 35, 172–185.

9. Petrus Goo, "Sago and Sago Larvae in Rituals," in Gunter Konrad and Ursula Konrad, eds., *Asmat Myth and Ritual: The Inspiration of Art* (Venice: Erizzo Editrice, 1996), 93–94.

10. Hans Straver, *De zee van verhalen: De wereld van Molukse vertellers* (Utrecht: Steunpunt Edukatie Molukkers, 1993), 99–100; Anthony Whitten and Jane E. J. Whitten, "The Sago-Palm and Its Exploitation on Siberut Island, Indonesia,"

Principes 25, no. 3 (1981): 98; Tan Koonlin, *The Swamp-Sago Industry in West Malaysia: A Study of the Sungei Batu Pahat Floodplain* (Singapore: ISEAS, 1983), 10.

11. Trager and Koenig, *Burmese Sit-Tans,* 11; F. K. Lehman, *The Structure of Chin Society: A Tribal People of Burma Adapted to a Non-Western Civilization* (Urbana: University of Illinois Press, 1963), 57; Mabuchi, *Ethnology,* 292; Wayne H. Fogg, "Swidden Cultivation of Foxtail Millet by Taiwan Aborigines: A Cultural Analogue of the Domestication of *Setaria italica* in China," in David N. Keightley, ed., *The Origins of Chinese Civilization* (Berkeley, Los Angeles, and London: University of California Press, 1983), 108; James J. Fox, "Genealogy and Topogeny: Towards an Ethnography of Rotinese Ritual Place Names," in James J. Fox, ed., *The Poetic Power of Place: Comparative Perspectives on Austronesian Ideas of Locality* (Canberra: Comparative Austronesian Project, Research School of Pacific Studies, ANU, 1997), 96–98.

12. Han Knapen, *Forest of Fortune? The Environmental History of Southeast Borneo, 1600–1800, VKI* 189 (Leiden: KITLV Press, 2001), 219.

13. Hicks, *A Maternal Religion,* 78–80; James J. Fox, "The Historical Consequences of Changing Patterns of Livelihood on Timor," in Deborah Wade-Marshall and Peter Loveday, eds., *Contemporary Issues in Development* (Darwin: North Australia Research Unit, ANU, 1988), 268–270.

14. H. Overbeck, "Malay Customs and Beliefs as Recorded in Malay Literature and Folklore," *JMBRAS* 2 (1924): 286; Julian Jacobs, *The Nagas: Society, Culture, and the Colonial Encounter* (London: Thames and Hudson, 1990), 38; Jasper Ingersoll, "The Priest Role in Central Thailand," in Manning Nash, Gananath Obeyeseker, and Michael H. Ames, eds., *Anthropological Studies in Theravada Buddhism,* Cultural Report 13 (New Haven, CT: Yale University Southeast Asia Studies, 1966), 60; F. M. Schnitger, *Forgotten Kingdoms in Sumatra* (Leiden: Brill, 1964), 186; Beatriz van der Goes, "Beru Dayang: The Concept of Female Spirits and the Movement of Fertility in Karo Batak Culture," *Asian Folklore Studies* 56 (1997): 388; Cornelia Kammerer, "Gateway to the Akha World: Kinship, Ritual, and Community among Highlanders of Thailand" (PhD diss., University of Chicago, 1986), 112. I am grateful to Dr. Kammerer for allowing me access to this thesis.

15. Roy W. Hamilton, "The Goddess of Rice," in Hamilton, *The Art of Rice,* 261.

16. C. H. M. Nooy-Palm, *The Sa'dan Toraja: A Study of Their Social Life and Religion* (The Hague: Nijhoff, 1979), 2:91.

17. Shepherd, *Statecraft and Political Economy,* 81–83; Agarwal, *A Field of One's Own,* 158; Anne Walthall, "The Life Cycle of Farm Women in Tokugawa Japan," in Gail Lee Bernstein, ed., *Recreating Japanese Women, 1600–1945* (Berkeley: University of California Press, 1991), 57; Toshijiro, "Seasonal Rituals," 65–68.

18. Claudine Salmon, "Wang Dahai and His View of the 'Insular Countries' (1791)," in Ding Choo Ming and Ooi Kee Beng, eds., *Chinese Studies in the Malay World: A Comparative Approach* (Singapore: Times Media, 2003), 44.

19. Lehman, *The Structure of Chin Society,* 49; Elwin, *The Nagas,* 105.

20. Marsden, *History of Sumatra,* 71; Elsbeth Locher-Scholten, "Female Labour in Twentieth-Century Java: European Notions—Indonesian Practice," in Elsbeth

Locher-Scholten and Anke Niehof, eds., *Indonesian Women in Focus: Past and Present* (Leiden: KITLV Press, 1992), 94.

21. Padt-Brugge, "Beschrijving der zeden," 327; Knapen, *Forests of Fortune?* 213.

22. Cheryl P. Claasen, "Gender, Shellfishing, and the Shell Mound Archaic," in Joan M. Giro and Margaret W. Conkey, eds., *Engendering Archaeology: Women and Prehistory* (London: Blackwell, 1991), 276–300; Lisa Marie Leimar Price, "Women's Wild Plant Food Entitlements in Thailand's Agricultural Northeast" (PhD diss., University of Oregon, 1993), 24, 155–170.

23. Gerrit J. Knaap, *Shallow Waters, Rising Tide: Shipping and Trade in Java around 1775* (Leiden: KITLV Press, 1996), 64.

24. Chandler, *A History of Cambodia,* 87.

25. Gervaise, *The Natural and Political History,* 116.

26. John A. Larkin, *The Pampangans: Colonial Society in a Philippine Province* (Berkeley: University of California Press, 1972), 25.

27. B and R, 48:52–58.

28. Remco Raben, "Round About Batavia: Ethnicity and Authority in the Ommelanden, 1600–1800," in Kees Grijns and Peter J. M. Nas, eds., *Jakarta-Batavia: Socio-Cultural Essays, VKI* 197 (Leiden: KITLV Press, 2000), 106–107.

29. Lorraine M. Gesick, *In the Land of Lady White Blood: Southern Thailand and the Meaning of History* (Ithaca, NY: Southeast Asia Program, Cornell University, 1995), 10.

30. Elwin, *India's North-East Frontier,* 363.

31. Claudine Salmon, "Wang Dahai and His View," 44.

32. Eaton, *The Rise of Islam,* 300; Julius Jacobs, *Het familie- en kampongleven op Groot-Atjeh: Eene bijdrage tot de ethnographie van Noord-Sumatra* (Leiden: Brill, 1894), 2:122.

33. Carol Ireson, *Field, Forest, and Family: Women's Work and Power in Rural Laos* (Boulder, CO: Westview Press, 1996), 225; Hoshino Tatsuo, "Wen Dan and Its Neighbours: The Central Mekong Valley in the Seventh and Eighth Centuries," in Mayoury Ngaosrivathana and Kennon Breazeale, eds., *Breaking New Ground in Lao History: Essays on the Seventh to Twentieth Centuries* (Chiang Mai, Thailand: Silkworm Books, 2002), 58.

34. G. J. Knaap, ed., *Memories van overgave van gouverneurs van Ambon in de zeventiende en achttiende eeuw,* Rijks Geschiedkundige Publicatiën, Kleine Serie 62 (The Hague: Martinus Nijhoff 1987), 295.

35. Agarwal, *A Field of One's Own,* 69, 94–97.

36. Joseph Minattur, "The Nature of Malay Customary Law," in David C. Buxbaum, ed., *Family Law and Customary Law in Asia: A Contemporary Legal Perspective* (The Hague: Nijhoff, 1968), 29; Launay, *Histoire de la mission de Cochinchine,* 2:421.

37. Gesick, *In the Land of Lady White Blood,* 10, 39

38. John Bastin, *The British in West Sumatra (1685–1825)* (Kuala Lumpur: University of Malaya Press, 1965), 144.

39. Mai Thi Tu and Le Thi Nham Tuyet, *La femme au Viet Nam* (Hanoi: Éditions en Langues Étrangères, 1976), 31.

40. Nhung Tran, "Vietnamese Women at the Crossroads," 146–176; Truong Huu Quynh, "The Development of Private Landed Property in Vietnam in the XVIIIth Century," paper presented at the 13th IAHA Conference, Tokyo, September 1994, 4, 6; Phan Huy Le, "Ancient Land Registers in Vietnam," *Vietnam Social Sciences* 46 (1995): 25–38; Tran Thi Van Anh, "Women and Rural Land in Vietnam," in Irene Tinker and Gale Summerfield, eds., *Women's Rights to House and Land: China, Laos, Vietnam* (London: Lynne Rienner, 1999), 97–98.

41. John Kleinen, *Facing the Future, Reviving the Past: A Study of Social Change in a Northern Vietnamese Village* (Singapore: ISEAS, 1999), 33–34; Choi Byung Wook, *Southern Vietnam under the Reign of Minh Mang (1820–1841): Central Policies and Local Response* (Ithaca, NY: Southeast Asia Program, Cornell University, 2004), 166.

42. Tran Thi Van Anh, "Women and Rural Land in Vietnam," 97–98; Nhung Tran, "Vietnamese Women at the Crossroads," 173, 176, 178.

43. Trager and Koenig, *Burmese Sit-Tans*, 361; Saito Teruko, "Rural Monetization and Land Mortgage: *Thet-Kayits* in Kon-Baung Burma," in Reid, *The Last Stand of Asian Autonomies*, 167, 173.

44. Gaspar de San Agustin, *Conquistas de las Islas Filipinas: Conquest of the Philippine Islands, 1565–1615,* ed. Pedro G. Galende (Manila: San Agustin Museum, 1998), 489; A. J. E. A. Bik, ed., *Dagverhaal eener reis, gedaan in het jaar 1824 tot nadere voorkenning der eilanden Keffing, Goram, Groot- en Klein Kei en de Aroe Eilanden* (Leiden: Sijthoff, 1928), 78; W. van Hogendorp, "Vervolg van beschrijving van het eiland Timor," *VBG* 2 (1780): 75; John Ball, *Indonesian Legal History 1602–1848* (Sydney: Oughtershaw Press, 1982), 96; Yu, "Bilateral Social Pattern," 227, and *Law and Society,* 83.

45. Bowrey, *A Geographical Account,* 31; Lehman, *The Structure of Chin Society,* 199.

46. Christiaan Gerard Heersink, "The Green Gold of Selayar: A Socio-economic History of an Indonesian Coconut Island, c. 1600–1950: Perspectives from a Periphery" (PhD diss., Free University, Amsterdam, 1995), 40.

47. Bik, *Dagverhaal eener reis,* 33, 78.

48. Geddes, *Migrants,* 57–58.

49. William Scott, *Barangay,* 73; Li, *Nguyen Cochinchina,* 85.

50. B and R, 33:211–212.

51. Christoforo Borri, *Cochin-China* (Amsterdam and New York: Theatrum Orbis Terrarum, 1970; reprint of 1633 edition), n.p.; Judith Jacob, *The Traditional Literature of Cambodia: A Preliminary Guide* (Oxford: Oxford University Press, 1996), 57.

52. Mrs. R. N. Bland, "Malacca Lace," *JSBRAS* 45 (June 1906): 273, 275.

53. Frederick Charles Danvers, *Letters Received by the East India Company from Its Servants in the East* (London: Sampson Low, Marsten, and Co., 1896), 1:21.

54. Elizabeth Moore and U Aung Myint, "Beads of Myanmar (Burma): Line Decorated Beads amongst the Pyu and Chin," *JSS* 81, no. 1 (1993): 58; Charles Hose and William McDougall, *The Pagan Tribes of Borneo* (London: Oxford University Press, 1993; reprint of 1912 edition), 1:83, 226.

55. Alexander Spoehr, *Zamboanga and Sulu: An Archaeological Approach to Ethnic Diversity* (Pittsburgh: Department of Anthropology, University of Pittsburgh, 1973), 199–120.

56. Khoo Joo Ee, *Kendi: Pouring Vessels in the University of Malaya Collection* (Singapore: Oxford University Press, 1991), 1, 3, 31, and accompanying illustrations; Saikia, *In the Meadows of Gold,* 70.

57. Sylvia Fraser-Lu, *Burmese Crafts: Past and Present* (New York: Oxford University Press, 1994), 207.

58. Padt-Brugge, "Beschrijving der zeden," 323; see also Forrest, *A Voyage to New Guinea,* 96.

59. Fraser-Lu, *Burmese Crafts,* 204–211; Donn Bayard, "A Novel Pottery Manufacturing Technique in Western Loei Province, Thailand," *JSS* 65, no. 1 (January 1977), 243; Charlotte Reith, "Comparison of Three Pottery Villages in Shan State, Burma," *Journal of Burma Studies* 1 (1997): 47, 53, 82; author's notes from Leiden Museum, July 14, 2002.

60. Anne Richter, *Arts and Crafts of Indonesia* (London: Thames and Hudson, 1993), 41; Parry, *The Lakkers,* 128; William Scott, *Barangay,* 63, 88; Mick Schippen, *The Traditional Ceramics of Southeast Asia* (London: A. and C. Black Publishers; Honolulu: University of Hawai'i Press, 2005), 12 passim.

61. Hy Van Luong, "Engendered Entrepreneurship: Ideologies and Political-Economic Transformation in a Northern Vietnamese Center of Ceramics Production," in Robert W. Hefner, ed., *Market Cultures: Society and Values in the New Asian Capitalisms* (Singapore: ISEAS, 1998), 293; Nhatrang, "The Traditional Roles of Women," 172.

62. Ravi Mathur, "Ikat and Brocade Weavers of India," in Songsak Prangwattahanakun, ed., *Textiles of Asia: A Common Heritage* (Chiang Mai, Thailand: National Culture Commission, Ministry of Education and Center for the Promotion of Arts and Culture, Chiang Mai University, 1993), 79.

63. Susan Mann, *Precious Records: Women in China's Long Eighteenth Century* (Stanford, CA: Stanford University Press, 1997), 149, 157; Walthall, "From Private to Public Patriarchy," 447–448.

64. E. Netscher and J. A. van der Chijs, *De munten van Nederlansche Indië, beschreven en afgebeeld, VBG* 31, no. 2 (Batavia: Lange, 1864), 189; van den Brink, *Dr. Benjamin Frederick Matthes,* 200; Roy Ellen, *On the Edge of the Banda Zone: Past and Present in the Social Organization of a Moluccan Trading Network* (Honolulu: University of Hawai'i Press, 2003), 107.

65. Adrian Vickers, *Bali, a Paradise Created* (Berkeley, CA: Periplus Editions, 1989), 18; Gittinger and Lefferts, *Textiles and the Tai Experience,* 20.

66. William Wilson, *A Missionary Voyage to the Southern Pacific Ocean Performed in the Years 1796, 1797, 1798 in the Ship "Duff"* (London: Missionary Society, 1799), 371.

67. J. S. Cummins, trans. and ed., *The Travels and Controversies of Friar Domingo Navarrete 1618–1656* (Cambridge: Cambridge University Press for the Hakluyt Society, 1962), 1:109–111; Padt-Brugge, "Beschrijving der zeden," 325; Adriani, "De Toradjasche vrouw als priesteres"; Eija-Maija Kotilainen, *"When the Bones Are Left": A Study of the Material Culture of Central Sulawesi* (Helsinki: Finnish Anthropological Society, 1992), 13, 131–154, esp. 150.

68. Cummins, *The Travels and Controversies of Friar Domingo Navarrete,* 109–111; Padt-Brugge, "Beschrijving der zeden," 327.

69. Bacus, "Accessing Prestige and Power," 307ff; W. H. Scott, "Sixteenth-Century Tagalog Technology from the *Vocabulario de la Lengua Tagala* of Pedro de San Buenaventura, OFM," in Rainer Carle, Martina Heinschke, Peter W. Pink, Christel Rost, and Karen Stadtlander, eds., *Gava': Studies in Austronesian Languages and Cultures* (Berlin: Dietrich Reimer, 1982), 523–535.

70. Masing, *The Coming of the Gods,* 2:396; Julian Davison and Vinson H. Sutlive Jr. "The Children of *Nising:* Images of Headhunting and Male Sexuality in Iban Ritual and Oral Literature," in Vinson H. Sutlive Jr., ed., *Female and Male in Borneo: Contributions and Challenges to Gender Studies* (Williamsburg, VA: Borneo Research Council, 1991), 210; Jill Forshee, *Between the Folds: Stories of Cloth, Lives, and Travels from Sumba* (Honolulu: University of Hawai'i Press, 2001), 34; Barbara Watson Andaya, "History, Headhunting, and Gender in Monsoon Asia: Comparative and Longitudinal Views," *South East Asia Research* 12, no. 1 (March 2004): 31.

71. Gavin Traude, "*Kayau Indu,* the Warpath of Women," *Sarawak Museum Journal* 17 (1991): 1–41; Valerie Mashman, "Warriors and Weavers: A Study of Gender Relations among the Iban of Sarawak," in Sutlive, *Female and Male in Borneo,* 231–263; Ruth Barnes, "Women as Headhunters: The Making and Meaning of Textiles in a Southeast Asian Context," in Barnes and Eicher, *Dress and Gender,* 29–43.

72. David J. Stuart-Fox, "Textiles in Ancient Bali," in Nabholz-Kartaschoff et al., *Weaving Patterns of Life,* 89; Jan Wisseman Christie, "Ikat to Batik? Epigraphic Data on Textiles in Java from the Ninth to the Fifteenth Centuries," in Nabholz-Kartaschoff et al., *Weaving Patterns of Life,* 12–14, 24–26; J. de Rovere van Breugel, "Beschrijving van Bantam en de Lampongs," *BKI* 5 (1856): 345.

73. Anita Spertus and Robert J. Holmgren, *Early Indonesian Textiles from Three Island Cultures: Sumba, Toraja, Lampung* (New York: Metropolitan Museum of Art, 1989), 26; Janet Hoskins, "Why Do Ladies Sing the Blues? Indigo Dyeing, Cloth Production, and Gender Symbolism in Kodi," in Annette B. Weiner and Jane Schneider, eds., *Cloth and Human Experience* (Washington, DC, and London: Smithsonian Institution Press, 1989), 153–154.

74. Duggan, *Ikats of Savu,* 38.

75. J. Hooyman, "Berigten omtrent het katoenspinnen en weven onder de Javanese en Chinezen," *VBG* 2 (1780): 423–425, 426–447; Nhung Tran, "Vietnamese Women at the Crossroads," 83.

76. Toby Volkman, "Our Garden Is the Sea: Contingency and Improvisation in Mandar Women's Work," *American Ethnologist* 21, no. 3 (1994): 565; M. A. P. Meilink-Roelofsz, *Asian Trade and European Influence in the Indonesian Archipelago between 1500 and about 1630* (The Hague: Nijhoff, 1962), 94–96, 161, 214; J. V. Mills, "Eredia's Description of Malaca," 39.

77. Barbara Watson Andaya, "The Cloth Trade in Jambi and Palembang Society during the Seventeenth and Eighteenth Centuries," *Indonesia* 48 (1989): 33; Forrest, *A Voyage to New Guinea,* 39.

78. Gittinger and Lefferts, *Textiles and the Tai Experience*, 160; Ruurdje Laarhoven, "The Power of Cloth: The Textile Trade of the Dutch East India Company (VOC), 1600–1780" (PhD diss., ANU, 1994).

79. Wil O. Dijk, "The VOC's Trade in Indian Textiles with Burma, 1634–80," *JSEAS* 33, no. 3 (October 2002): 500; de Rovere van Breugel, "Beschryving van Bantam," 346; Thomas Forrest, *A Voyage from Calcutta to the Mergui Archipelago* (London: J. Robson, 1792), 79; B. Andaya, "The Cloth Trade," 43; Tchou, *Les femmes de lettres Birmanes*, 19.

80. Peter Boomgaard, *Children of the Colonial State: Population Growth and Economic Development in Java, 1795–1880* (Amsterdam: Free University Press, 1989), 128; Kumar, *Java and Modern Europe*, 275.

81. Matsuo Hiroshi, *The Development of Javanese Cotton Industry* (Tokyo: Institute of Developing Economies, 1970), 1–3, 77; B. Andaya, "The Cloth Trade," 40; Rens Heringa, "The Historical Background of Batik on Java," in Rens Heringa and Harmen C. Veldhuisen, eds., *Fabric of Enchantment: Batik from the North Coast of Java* (Los Angeles: Los Angeles County Museum of Art, 1996), 31–38; Harmen C. Veldhuisen, "From Home Craft to Batik Industry," in Heringa and Veldhuisen, *Fabric of Enchantment*, 40–41; Luc Nagtegaal, *Riding the Dutch Tiger: The Dutch East Indies Company and the Northeast Coast of Java, 1680–1743, VKI* 171 (Leiden: KITLV Press, 1996), 135–136.

82. Barbara Leigh, *Tangan-Tangan Trampil: Hands of Times: The Crafts of Aceh* (Jakarta: Djambatan, 1989), 81; Laarhoven, "The Power of Cloth," 119n49; Maria Loudes Diaz-Trechuelo, "Eighteenth-Century Philippine Economy: Agriculture," *Philippine Studies* (January 1966): 120; de la Loubère, *The Kingdom of Siam*, 13.

83. V. Ball, ed., *Travels in India by Jean-Baptiste Tavernier, Baron of Aubonne*, ed. William Crooke (New Delhi: Oriental Books, 1977; reprint of 1889 edition), 2:220; H. K. Barpujari, *Francis Jenkins: Report on the North-East Frontier of India* (Delhi: Spectrum, 1995), 51–53; Sun, "Ming–Southeast Asian Overland Interactions," 117, 121.

84. Li Tana and Anthony Reid, *Southern Vietnam under the Nguyen: Documents on the Economic History of Cochinchina (Dang Trong, 1602–1777)* (Singapore, ISEAS; Canberra: Economic History of Southeast Asia Project, ANU, 1993), 121; Mann, *Precious Records*, 158; John White, *A Voyage to Cochin China*, ed. Milton Osborne (Kuala Lumpur and New York: Oxford University Press, 1972), 261; Li Tana, personal communication, May 2002.

85. Rens Heringa, "Kain Tuban: Een oude Javanese indigo traditie," in Loan Oei, ed., *Indigo: Leven in een kleur* (Amsterdam: Stichting Indigo, Fibula-van Dishoeck, 1985), 163; see also Hoskins, "Why Do Ladies Sing the Blues?" 150–157; Danielle C. Geirnaert, "The Sumbanese Textile Puzzle: A Comparative Exercise," in Nabholz-Kartaschoff et al., *Weaving Patterns of Life*, 203–228.

86. Trager and Koenig, *Burmese Sit-Tans*, 137–138, 322–323, 341.

87. Diaz-Trechueolo, "Eighteenth-Century Philippine Economy," 98f; M. C. Ricklefs, *War, Culture, and Economy in Java 1677–1726: Asian and European Imperialism in the Early Kartasura Period* (Sydney: Allen and Unwin, 1993), 125; Kumar, *Java and Modern Europe*, 76, 197, 324, 350.

88. A Theo André, *Cultuur en bereiding van indigo op Java* (Amsterdam: J. H. de Bussy, 1891), 239–243; Duggan, *Ikats of Savu,* 32.

89. Anthony Reid, *Southeast Asia in the Age of Commerce 1450–1680.* Vol. 2, *Expansion and Crisis* (New Haven, CT, and London: Yale University Press, 1993), 93.

90. Barbara Watson Andaya, *To Live as Brothers: Southeast Sumatra in the Seventeenth and Eighteenth Centuries* (Honolulu: University of Hawai'i Press, 1993), 80; J. Kathirithamby-Wells, *The British West Sumatran Presidency (1760–1785): Problems of Early Colonial Enterprise* (Kuala Lumpur: University of Malaya, 1977), 71.

91. For references and further detail, see Barbara Watson Andaya, "Women and Economic Change: The Pepper Trade in Pre-Modern Southeast Asia," *JESHO* 38, no. 2 (1995): 165–190.

92. Li and Reid, *Southern Vietnam under the Nguyen,* 17, 125.

93. B. Andaya, "Women and Economic Change," 165–190.

94. Ma. Luisa Camagay, *Working Women of Manila in the 19th Century* (Quezon City: University of the Philippines Press/University Center for Women's Studies, 1995), 5–6.

95. Bik, *Dagverhaal eener reis,* 33, 69.

96. Patricia Spyer, *The Memory of Trade: Modernity's Entanglements on an Eastern Indonesian Island* (Durham, NC, and London: Duke University Press, 2000), 17–18, 137–138.

97. R. Shelford, "An Illustrated Catalogue of the Ethnographical Collection of the Sarawak Museum: Part II, Personal Ornaments," *JSBRAS* 43 (April 1905): 58.

98. Heather Sutherland, "Money in Makassar: Credit and Debt in an Eighteenth Century Settlement," in Edi Sedyawati and Susanto Zuhdi, eds., *Arung Samudera: Persembahan Memperingati Sembilan Windu A. B. Lapian* (Depok: Pusat Penelitian Kemasyarakatan dan Budaya, Lembaga Penelitian, Universitas Indonesia, 2001), 723.

99. Reid, *Southeast Asia in the Asia of Commerce,* 1:162–164.

100. G. W. J. Drewes, *De biografie van een Minangkabausen peperhandelaar in de Lampungs* (The Hague: Nijhoff, 1961), 121.

101. Vincent Loth, "Fragrant Gold and Food Provision: Resource Management and Agriculture in Seventeenth-Century Banda," in Roy Ellen, Peter Parkes, and Alan Becker, eds., *Indigenous Environmental Knowledge and Its Transformations: Critical Anthropological Perspectives* (Amsterdam: Harwood Academic Publishers, 2000), 76; Nguyen Thanh-Nha, *Tableau économique du Viêt Nam aux XVIIe et XVIIIe siècles* (Paris: Éditions Cujas, 1970), 141; Yu, *Law and Society,* 65.

102. Shaun Kingsley Malarney, "Return to the Past? The Dynamics of Contemporary Religion and Ritual Transformation," in Hy Van Luong, ed., *Postwar Vietnam: Dynamics of a Transforming Society* (Singapore: ISEAS; New York: Rowman and Littlefield, 2003), 243–244.

103. Sahai, *The Rama Jataka,* 1:277, 2:250.

104. Micheline Lessard, "Curious Relations: Jesuit Perceptions of the Vietnamese," in Keith Weller Taylor and Whitmore, eds., *Essays into Vietnamese Pasts,* 149; Gordon, "Women in Thai Mural Paintings," 183.

105. Suzanne April Brenner, *The Domestication of Desire: Women, Wealth, and*

Modernity in Java (Princeton, NJ: Princeton University Press, 1998), 146–147; Nai Pan Hla and Okudaira, *Eleven Mon Dhammasat Texts,* 562.

106. G. P. Rouffaer and J. W. Ijzerman, *De eerste schipvaart der Nederlanders naar Oost-Indië onder Cornelis de Houtman 1595–1597* (The Hague: Linschoten-Vereeniging, 1915–1921), 1:112 and illustration facing 110.

107. Nhung Tran, "Vietnamese Women at the Crossroads," 5, 93.

108. White, *Voyage to Cochin China,* 245–246; Trager and Koenig, *Burmese Sit-Tans,* 354.

109. Ann Kumar, "Encyclopedia-izing and the Organization of Knowledge," *BKI* 155, no. 3 (1999): 484–485.

110. Forest, *Les missionaires français,* 3:254.

111. E. H. S. Simmonds, "Francis Light and the Ladies of Thalang," *JMBRAS* 38, no. 2 (December 1965): 217; Peter Carey, ed., *The British in Java, 1811–1816: A Javanese Account* (London: Oxford University Press for the British Academy, 1992), 29; Manuscripts Division National Library, Bangkok: R3/1191/3; R3/1203/91; R3/1204/21, R3/1204/21 (references kindly supplied by Dr. Ken Breazeale, November 23, 1998).

112. Michael Symes, *An Account of an Embassy to the Kingdom of Ava in the Year 1795* (Edinburgh: Constable, 1827), 1:254.

113. Han ten Brummelhuis, *Merchant, Courtier and Diplomat: A History of the Contacts between the Netherlands and Thailand* (Lochem-Gent: De Tijdstroom, 1987), 25; Dhiravat na Pombejra, "VOC Employees and Their Relationships with Mon and Siamese Women: A Case Study of Osoet Pegua," in B. Andaya, *Other Pasts,* 200–211; Corfield and Morson, *A New Account,* 360; see also William Dampier, *Voyages and Discoveries,* ed. C. Wilkinson (London: Argonaut Press, 1931), 40; Alexander Woodside, "Central Viet Nam's Trading World in the Eighteenth Century as Seen in Le Quy Don's 'Frontier Chronicles,'" in Keith Weller Taylor and Whitmore, *Essays into Vietnamese Pasts,* 162.

114. H. Kern, ed., *Het itinerario van Jan Huygen van Linschoten 1579–1582* (The Hague: Martinus Nijhoff, 1955), 74.

115. Christine Dobbin, *Asian Entrepreneurial Minorities: Conjoint Communities in the Making of the World-Economy 1570–1940* (Richmond, Surrey: Curzon Press, 1996), 22. For specific references, see B. Andaya, "From Temporary Wife to Prostitute," 31n37.

116. Li and Reid, *Southern Vietnam under the Nguyen,* 58.

117. Corfield and Morson, *A New Account,* 360, 457.

118. Li, *Nguyen Cochinchina,* 64. See also B. Andaya, "From Temporary Wife to Prostitute," 11–34.

119. Ten Brummelhuis, *Merchant, Courtier, and Diplomat,* 60; Pombejra, "VOC Employees and Their Relationships," 210.

120. Samuel Purchas, ed., *Purchas His Pilgrimes* (Glasgow: James MacLehose and Sons, 1905), 2:446.

121. Ibid., 2:471; see also Leonard Blussé, *Strange Company: Chinese Settlers, Mestizo Women and the Dutch in VOC Batavia,* VKI 122 (Dordrecht: Foris, 1986), 168.

122. Vu Minh Gian, "Contribution to Identifying Pho Hien through Two Stelae," in *Pho Hien: The Center of International Commerce in the XVIIth–XVIIIth Centuries*, Association of Vietnamese Historians, People's Administrative Committee of Hai Hung Province (Hanoi: The Gioi, 1994), 122.

123. Nagtegaal, *Riding the Dutch Tiger*, 119; B. Andaya, *To Live as Brothers*, 54–56.

124. Gordon, "Women in Thai Mural Paintings," 184; Wyatt, *Reading Thai Murals*, 54.

125. White, *Voyage to Cochin China*, 261; Trager and Koenig, *Burmese Sit-Tans*, 132, 200; Skeat and Laidlaw, "The Cambridge University Expedition," 25–26.

126. Nguyen Ngoc Huy et al., *The Lê Code*, 1:267.

127. Mills, "Eredia's Description of Malaca," 40; Claudine Salmon, "Wang Dahai and His View," 53.

128. Mills, "Eredia's Description of Malaca," 48; *Dagh-Register*, 1646:64; Jennifer Sowerwine, "New Land Rights and Women's Access to Medicinal Plants in Northern Vietnam," in Irene Tinker and Gale Summerfield, eds., *Women's Rights to House and Land: China, Laos, Vietnam* (London: Lynne Rienner, 1999), 136; David Craig, *Familiar Medicine: Everyday Health Knowledge and Practice in Today's Vietnam* (Honolulu: University of Hawai'i Press, 2002), 107.

129. W. van Hogendorp, "Beschrijving van het eiland Timor," *VBG* 1 (1779): 290; Van Iperen, "Beschryvinge van eene blanke negerin," 229–235.

130. William Scott, *Barangay*, 239; J. S. Stavorinus, *Voyages to the East Indies*, trans. S. H. Wilcocke (London: Dawsons, 1969; reprint of 1798 edition), 1:247; W. Ph. Coolhaas, ed., *Generale missiven van gouverneurs-generaal en raden aan heren XVII der Verenigde Oostindische Compagnie* (The Hague: Nijhoff, 1960), 2:24.

131. Valerie Hanson, *Negotiating Daily Life in Traditional China: How Ordinary People Used Contracts 600–1400* (New Haven, CT, and London: Yale University Press, 1995), 90.

132. Maya Shatzmillar, "Women and Wage Labour in the Medieval Islamic West: Legal Issues in an Economic Context," in *JESHO* 40, no. 2 (May 1997): 179; Avner Giladi, *Infants, Parents, and Wet Nurses: Medieval Islamic Views on Breast-Feeding and Their Social Implications* (Leiden: Brill, 1999), chap. 3. See also Valerie Fields, *Wet Nursing: A History from Antiquity to the Present* (Oxford: Basil Blackwell, 1988), 36, 37, 53.

133. Hill, *Hikayat Abdullah*, 37.

134. Leonard Y. Andaya, *The World of Maluku: Eastern Indonesia in the Early Modern Period* (Honolulu: University of Hawai'i Press, 1993), 68; idem, *Heritage of Arung Palakka*, 57, 315; idem, "A Village Perception of Arung Palakka and the Makassar War of 1666–67," in Anthony Reid and David Marr, eds., *Perceptions of the Past in Southeast Asia* (Singapore: Heinemann, 1979), 374; B. Andaya, *To Live as Brothers*, 35.

135. Eric Alan Jones, "Wives, Slaves, and Concubines: A History of the Female Underclass in Dutch Asia" (PhD diss., University of California, Berkeley, 2003), 200.

136. Angela Ki Che Leung, "Women Practicing Medicine in Premodern China," in Zurndorfer, *Chinese Women in the Imperial Past*, 103, 112–113; Charlotte Furth, *A Flourishing Yin: Gender in China's Medical History, 960–1665* (Berkeley and London:

University of California Press, 1999), 108–110, 178, 220; Yuki Terazawa, "The Medicalization of the Female Reproductive Body in Late-Seventeenth-Century Japan as Seen through Childbirth Manuals," paper presented at the annual meeting of AAS, Chicago, March 2001.

137. Viggo Brun and Trond Schumacher, *Traditional Herbal Medicine in Northern Thailand* (Berkeley: University of California Press, 1987), 37.

138. Jean Mulholland, *Herbal Medicine in Paediatrics: Translation of a Thai Book of Genesis,* Faculty of Asian Studies Monographs, n.s., 14 (Canberra: ANU, 1989), 56–57; Dhiravat na Pombejra, *Court, Company, and Campong: Essays on the VOC Presence in Ayutthaya,* Occasional Paper 1 (Ayutthaya: Ayutthaya Historical Study Centre, 1992), 29, 33; Ball, *Travels in India,* 2:280.

139. Hoang Bao Chau, Phu Duc Thao, and Huu Ngoc, "Overview of Vietnamese Traditional Medicine," in Hoang Bao Chau, Phu Duc Thao, and Huu Ngoc, eds. *Vietnamese Traditional Medicine* (Hanoi: The Gioi, 1992), 13, 18–22; Richard J. Couglin, "Pregnancy and Birth in Vietnam," in Donn V. Hart, Phya Anuman Rajadhon, and Richard J. Coughlin, *Southeast Asian Birth Customs: Three Studies in Human Reproduction* (New Haven, CT: Human Relations Area Files, 1965), 211.

140. Lance Castles, "Ethnic Profile of Djakarta," *Indonesia* 3 (April 1967): 156; Niemeijer, *Batavia,* 61; Raben, "Batavia and Colombo," appendix 3.

141. Barend-van Haeften, *Oost-Indië gespiegeld,* 157–158.

142. Purchas, *Purchas His Pilgrimes,* 3:440.

143. B and R, 5:145; Rouffaer and Ijzerman, *De eerste schipvaart,* 1:129; Carroll, "Berunai in the Boxer Codex," 14; H. A. van Foreest and A. de Booy, eds., *De vierde schipvaart der Nederlanders naar Oost-Indië onder Jacob Wilkens en Jacob van Neck (1599–1604)* (The Hague: Linschoten-Vereeniging, 1980), 1:225.

144. Blussé, *Strange Company,* 168; Niemeijer, *Batavia,* 187.

145. Lessard, "Curious Relations," 149–150.

146. B. Andaya, "From Temporary Wife to Prostitute," 35; Nhung Tran, "Vietnamese Women at the Crossroads," 125, 128.

147. Aroonrut Wichienkeeo and Gehan Wijeyewardene, trans. and ed., *The Laws of King Mangrai (Mangrayathammasart)* (Canberra: Department of Anthropology, Research School of Pacific Studies, 1986), 74.

148. B. Andaya, "From Temporary Wife to Prostitute," 35.

149. B and R, 2:138; see also Li and Reid, *Southern Vietnam under the Nguyen,* 77; Barend-van Haeften, *Oost-Indië gespiegeld,* 143.

150. Bowrey, *A Geographical Account,* 206–207. For further detail on China, see Sommer, *Sex, Law, and Society,* 351n29.

151. Barrow, *A Voyage to Cochinchina,* 305. For similar comments, see B and R, 5:119; Beeckman, *A Voyage to and from Borneo,* 42.

152. For further details, see B. Andaya, "From Temporary Wife to Prostitute," 26.

153. Ta Van Tai, "The Status of Women in Traditional Vietnam: A Comparison of the Code of the Lê Dynasty (1428–1788) with the Chinese Codes," *Journal of*

Asian History 15 (1981): 116; Than Tun, *Royal Orders,* 2:28; Symes, *An Account of an Embassy,* 1:252.

154. B. Andaya, "From Temporary Wife to Prostitute," 11–34.

155. For case studies, see Jones, "Wives, Slaves, and Concubines."

156. H. E. Niemeijer, "The First Protestant Churches on Java's Northcoast: A Church Report from Rev. J. W. Swemmelaar," *Documentatieblad voor de Geschiedenis van de Nederlandse Zending en Overzeese Kerken* 5, no. 2 (1998): 58.

Chapter 5. States, Subjects, and Households

1. Nguyen Ngoc Huy et al., *The Lê Code,* 1:177–178; Wichienkeeo and Wijeyewardene, *The Laws of King Mangrai,* 42.

2. Kumar, *Java and Modern Europe,* 197.

3. Jacobsen, "Apsarā, Accoutrements, Activists," 128; B. Andaya, *To Live as Brothers,* 76, 130.

4. Wichienkeeo and Wijeyewardene, *The Laws of King Mangrai,* 26.

5. B and R, 5:145.

6. Kumar, *Java and Modern Europe,* 245.

7. Trager and Koenig, *Burmese Sit-Tans,* 137–138, 144, 322–323, 341; William J. Koenig, *The Burmese Polity, 1752–1819: Politics, Administration, and Social Organization in the Early Kon-baung Period* (Ann Arbor: Center for South and Southeast Asian Studies, University of Michigan, 1990), 41, 109.

8. For example, Kraisri Nimmanahaeminda, "An Inscribed Silver-Plate Grant to the Lawa of Boh Luang," in *Felicitation Volumes of Southeast-Asian Studies Presented to His Highness Prince Dhaninivat Kromamun Bidyalabh Bridhyakorn* (Bangkok: Siam Society, 1965), 2:235.

9. Katherine Ann Bowie, "Peasant Perspectives on the Political Economy of the Northern Thai Kingdom of Chiang Mai in the Nineteenth Century: Implications for the Understanding of Peasant Political Expression" (PhD diss., University of Chicago, 1988), 47–53; B. Andaya, *To Live as Brothers,* 77, 129.

10. Victor B. Lieberman, *Burmese Administrative Cycles: Anarchy and Conquest, c. 1580–1760* (Princeton, NJ: Princeton University Press, 1984), 97–98; Li, *Nguyen Cochinchina,* 26, 39.

11. Geritt Knaap, "Head-hunting, Carnage, and Armed Peace in Amboina, 1500–1700," *JESHO* 46, no. 2 (2003): 170–171.

12. Tony Day, *Fluid Iron: State Formation in Southeast Asia* (Honolulu: University of Hawai'i Press, 2002), 254.

13. Drewes, *De biografie van een Minangkabausen peperhandelaar,* 110.

14. Padt-Brugge, "Beschrijving der zeden," 318; Rawlins, "On the Manners, Religion, and Laws of the Cucis," 191.

15. B and R, 5:165; see also B. Andaya, "'History, Headhunting, and Gender in Monsoon Asia," 42ff.

16. Adriani, "De Toradjasche vrouw als priesteres," 196.

17. Ibid.; Leonard Y. Andaya, "The Nature of War and Peace among the Bugis-Makassar People," *South East Asia Research* 12, no. 1 (March 2004): 68, 73–74.

18. Jan Knappert, *Mythology and Folklore in South-East Asia,* ed. Graham Saunders (New York: Oxford University Press, 1999), 98–99.

19. Nai Pan Hla and Okudaira, *Eleven Mon Dhammasat Texts,* 557; Mason Hoadley and M. B. Hooker, *An Introduction to Javanese Law: A Translation and Commentary on the Agama,* AAS Monograph 37 (Tucson: University of Arizona Press, 1982), 196; Wichienkeeo and Wijeyewardene, *The Laws of King Mangrai,* 42; Nguyen Ngoc Huy et al., *The Lê Code,* 1:186.

20. Friedrich V. Lustig, ed. and trans., *Burmese Classical Poems* (Rangoon: U Khin Pe Gyi, 1966), 16; see also the same sentiment in Maung Myint Thien, trans., *Burmese Folk-Songs* (Oxford: Asoka Society, 1970), 54; Knappert, *Mythology and Folklore,* 98–99.

21. See Nola Cooke, "Women, Gender, and Sexuality in 17th Century Nguyễn Cochinchina: New Light from Old Sources," paper presented at the 4th International Convention of Asian Scholars, Shanghai, August 20–24, 2005 (cited with permission).

22. Sun, "Ming–Southeast Asian Overland Interactions," 297.

23. Van Hogendorp, "Vervolg van beschrijving van het eiland Timor," 71; Masing, *The Coming of the Gods,* 2:227.

24. Christie, "Ikat to Batik?" 11–30; Boomgaard, *Children of the Colonial State,* 24.

25. Kumar, *Java and Modern Europe,* 327, 340; see also Trager and Koenig, *Burmese Sit-Tans,* 68, 102; Nguyen Ngoc Huy et al., *The Lê Code,* 1:180.

26. Trager and Koenig, *Burmese Sit-Tans,* 137–138, 144, 322–323, 341; B. J. Terwiel, *Through Travellers' Eyes: An Approach to Early Nineteenth-Century Thai History* (Bangkok: Editions Duang Kamol, 1989), 138.

27. Trager and Koenig, *Burmese Sit-Tans,* 113, 120, 123.

28. Kathirithamby-Wells, *The British West Sumatran Presidency,* 132–133; B and R, 50:199.

29. J. S. Furnivall, "Matriarchal Vestiges in Burma," *JBRS* 1, no. 1 (1911): 21; Trager and Koenig, *Burmese Sit-Tans,* 132, 200, 291, 361; Koenig, *The Burmese Polity,* 41.

30. Trager and Koenig, *Burmese Sit-Tans,* 64, 176, 209, 213–214, 255, 343; Koenig, *The Burmese Polity,* 41.

31. For example, Manuscripts Division National Library, Bangkok: R3/1191/3, R3/1203/91, R3/1204/21. References kindly supplied by Dr. Ken Breazeale, November 23, 1998.

32. Raben, "Batavia and Colombo," 200.

33. Cortesão, *The Suma Oriental of Tomé Pires,* 2:274; see also the illustration of women traders in Nieuhof, *Voyages,* 184.

34. Anthony Reid, "The Origins of Revenue Farming in Southeast Asia," in John Butcher and Howard Dick, eds., *The Rise and Fall of Revenue Farming: Business Elites and the Emergence of the Modern State in Southeast Asia* (New York: St. Martin's Press, 1993), 74–76.

35. Kumar, *Java and Modern Europe*, 245.

36. Eliodoro G. Robles, *The Philippines in the Nineteenth Century* (Quezon City: Malaya Books, 1969), 72–73.

37. Mayoury Ngaosyathn, "Tribal Politics in Laos," in Andrew Turton, ed., *Civility and Savagery: Social Identity in Tai States* (Richmond, Surrey: Curzon Press, 2000), 248–249.

38. Diran, *The Vanishing Tribes*, 140, 218–219.

39. Padt-Brugge, "Beschrijving der zeden," 327.

40. Lieberman, *Burmese Administrative Cycles*, 237.

41. Shawn McHale, "Refashioning the Disturbing Past of Tran Vietnam (1225–1400)," *JESHO* 42, no. 4 (2002): 504–505.

42. Fray Juan Francisco de San Antonio, *The Philippine Chronicles of Fray San Antonio*, trans. D. Pedro Picornell (Manila: Casalinda and Historical Conservation Society, 1977), 147.

43. J. J. Ras, *Hikajat Bandjar: A Study in Malay Historiography* (The Hague: Nijhoff, 1968), 365; Ida Pfeiffer, *A Lady's Second Journey Round the World* (New York: Harper, 1856), 48.

44. Elwin, *The Nagas*, 85; idem, *India's North-East Frontier*, 111.

45. Borri, *Cochin-China*, n.p.

46. Ras, *Hikajat Bandjar*, 264–265; Ricklefs, *War, Culture, and Economy*, 64, 213.

47. Kees van Dijk, "Sarong, Jubbah, and Trousers: Appearances as a Means of Distinction and Discrimination," in Henk Schulte Nordholt, ed., *Outward Appearances: Dressing State and Society in Indonesia* (Leiden: KITLV Press, 1997), 48–49; cf. John Pemberton, *On the Subject of "Java"* (Ithaca, NY, and London: Cornell University Press, 1994), 58.

48. J. Taylor, *The Social World*, 67.

49. Yung-Chung Kim, ed. and trans., *Women of Korea: A History from Ancient Times to 1945* (Seoul: Ewha Womans University Press, 1976), 122; Woodside, "Central Viet Nam's Trading World," 166; Li, *Nguyen Cochinchina*, 87; Li and Reid, *Southern Vietnam under the Nguyen*, 122.

50. Lombard-Salmon, *Un exemple*, 221; Ko, *Every Step a Lotus*, 117.

51. John K. Whitmore, "Note: The Confucian Scholar's View of His Country's Early History," in Kenneth R. Hall and John K. Whitmore, eds., *Explorations in Early Southeast Asian History: The Origins of Southeast Asian Statecraft* (Ann Arbor: Center for South and Southeast Asian Studies, University of Michigan, 1976), 197, 199–200; Nguyen The Anh, "Vietnamization of the Cham Deity," 46; Nguyen Ngoc Huy et al., *The Lê Code*, 1:189.

52. Pombejra, "VOC Employees and Their Relationships," 210.

53. Bastin, *The British in West Sumatra*, 45.

54. B and R, 50:209–210.

55. Knaap, *Kruidnagelen en christenen*, 78.

56. Niemeijer, "Slavery, Ethnicity, and the Economic Independence of Women," 177.

57. B and R, 50:200.

58. Chau Hai, "The Chinese in Pho Hien and Their Relations with Other Chinese in Other Urban Areas of Vietnam," in *Pho Hien*, 212–213.

59. Leonard Blussé, "*Kongkoan* and *Kongsi:* Representations of Chinese Identity and Ethnicity in Early Modern Southeast Asia," in Leonard Blussé and Felipe Fernández-Armesto, eds., *Shifting Communities and Identity Formation in Early Modern Asia* (Leiden: Research School of Asian, African, and Amerindian Studies, Leiden University, 2003), 102.

60. Ibid., 98.

61. Li, *Nguyen Cochinchina*, 33–34, 40.

62. Blussé, "*Kongkoan* and *Kongsi*," 104; Claudine Salmon, "Wang Dahai and His View," 46; Claudine Salmon, "Le rôle des femmes dans l'émigration chinoise en Insulinde," *Archipel* 16 (1978): 165; Claudine Salmon, "Wang Dahai et sa vision," 245; Anne Lombard-Jourdan and Claudine Salmon, "Les Chinois de Kupang (Timor) aux alentours de 1800," *Archipel* 56, no. 1 (1998): 424–425.

63. Day, *Fluid Iron*, 63–78; Sarah Hanley, "Engendering the State: Family Formation and State Building in Early Modern France," *French Historical Studies* 16, no. 1 (Spring 1989): 12, 26–27.

64. E. Reimers, trans., *Selections from the Dutch Records of the Ceylon Government: Memoirs of Ryckloff van Goens* (Colombo: Ceylon Government Press, 1932), 32.

65. Day, *Fluid Iron*, 39; J. Rigby, ed. and trans., *The Ninety-Nine Laws of Perak*, Papers on Malay Subjects (Kuala Lumpur: Government Press, 1929), 85; B. Andaya, *To Live as Brothers*, 31.

66. Nguyen Ngoc Huy et al., *The Lê Code*, 2:115; Connell, "The State, Gender, and Sexual Politics," 507–544.

67. Day, *Fluid Iron*, 85; Haji Mohamed Din bin Ali, "Malay Customary Law and the Family," in David Buxbaum, ed., *Family Law and Customary Law in Asia: A Contemporary Legal Perspective* (The Hague: Nijhoff, 1968), 189; for an alternative version, see M. B. Hooker, ed., *Readings in Malay Adat Laws* (Singapore: Singapore University Press, 1970), 12.

68. Wichienkeeo and Wijeyewardene, *The Laws of King Mangrai*, 21–22.

69. H. J. de Graaf, *De vijf gezantschapreizen van Ryklof van Goens naar het hof van Mataram 1648–1654* (The Hague: Nijhoff, 1956), 145.

70. Quoted in Bastin, *The British in West Sumatra*, 43.

71. Junko Koizumi, "From Water Buffalo to Human Being: Women and the Family in Siamese History," in B. Andaya, *Other Pasts*, 328n16; Nguyen Ngoc Huy et al., *The Lê Code*, 2:5.

72. Nai Pan Hla and Okudaira, *Eleven Mon Dhammasat Texts*, 609–610; Maung Maung, *Law and Custom in Burma and the Burmese Family* (The Hague: Nijhoff, 1963), 13; A. B. Griswold and Prasert na Nagara, "Epigraphic and Historical Studies, No. 17: The Judgements of King Man Ray," *JSS* 65, no. 1 (January 1977)," 156; Marsden, *History of Sumatra*, 218; Rigby, *Ninety-Nine Laws*, 52; Wichienkeeo and Wijeyewardene, *The Laws of King Mangrai*, 31; Reynolds, "A Defense of Thai Polygamy," 933.

73. Boomgaard, *Children of the Colonial State*, 142–143.

74. Donald K. Swearer, Sommai Premchit, and Phaithoon Dokbuakaew, *Sacred Mountains of Northern Thailand and Their Legends* (Chiang Mai, Thailand: Silkworm Books, 2004), 58–60.

75. David Chandler, "Normative Poems *(Chbab)* and Pre-Colonial Cambodian Society," *JSEAS* 15, no. 2 (September 1984), 273; Saveros Pou, "La littérature didactique Khmèr: Les cpāp," *Journal Asiatique* 269 (1981): 459; Nai Pan Hla and Okudaira, *Eleven Mon Dhammasat Texts*, 585, 557.

76. San Antonio, *The Philippine Chronicles*, 167.

77. Wichienkeeo and Wijeyewardene, *The Laws of King Mangrai*, 23, 26.

78. Marsden, *History of Sumatra*, 222.

79. B and R, 5:153–157.

80. Liaw Yock Fang, *Undang-Undang Melaka: The Laws of Melaka*, Bibliotheca Indonesica 13 (The Hague: Nijhoff, 1976), 102–105; Hoadley and Hooker, *An Introduction to Javanese Law*, 189ff; G. A. J. Hazeu, "Tjeribonsch wetboek (pepakem tjerbon) van her jaar 1768," *VBG* 55 (1905): 95.

81. Hoadley and Hooker, *An Introduction to Javanese Law*, 167; M. B. Hooker, ed., *Laws of South-east Asia* (Singapore: Butterworth, 1986), 1:82; Wichienkeeo and Wijeyewardene, *The Laws of King Mangrai*, 26, 30, 40.

82. Kathirithamby-Wells, *The British West Sumatran Presidency*, 110–112; Marsden, *History of Sumatra*, 225–226, 235; L. W. C. van den Berg, *Rechtsbronnen van Zuid-Sumatra* (The Hague: Nijhoff, 1894), 8n23.

83. L. Andaya, *The World of Maluku*, 188.

84. Bankoff, *In Verbo Sacerdotis*, 41n62; Cullinane, "Accounting for Souls," 286.

85. William Howell, "Dyak Divorce," in A. J. N. Richards, *The Sea Dyaks*, 49.

86. Hoadley and Hooker, *An Introduction to Javanese Law*, 164; Nai Pan Hla and Okudaira, *Eleven Mon Dhammasat Texts*, 542, 545.

87. Phün na müang nan lae khao thang müang nan ton chabaphuang khuang [Annals of Nan's paddy fields and routes in Nan: The Huang Khuang Monastery manuscript], transcribed from Muang script to Thai script by Aroonrut Wichienkeeo and Sithana Khampaeng, Document Series 9 (Chiang Mai, Thailand: Chiang Mai Cultural Centre, Chiang Mai Teachers' College, BE 2528 [AD 1985]). Reference kindly furnished by Ken Breazeale, September 1, 2002; Nai Pan Hla and Okudaira, *Eleven Mon Dhammasat Texts*, 557.

88. Rigby, *Ninety-Nine Laws*, 33, 37, 69.

89. Nai Pan Hla and Okudaira, *Eleven Mon Dhammasat Texts*, 557; Hoadley and Hooker, *An Introduction to Javanese Law*, 196; Wichienkeeo and Wijeyewardene, *The Laws of King Mangrai*, 42; Maung Maung, *Law and Custom in Burma*, 73; Liaw, *Undang-Undang Melaka*, 103–105, 131.

90. Nguyen Ngoc Huy et al., *The Lê Code*, 2:111–112, 176; Maung Htin Aung, *Burmese Law Tales: The Legal Element in Burmese Folk-lore* (London: Oxford University Press, 1962), 138.

91. Wichienkeeo and Wijeyewardene, *The Laws of King Mangrai*, 26, 58, 70.

92. Nai Pan Hla and Okudaira, *Eleven Mon Dhammasat Texts*, 574: Knaap, "Pants, Skirts, and Pulpits," 171–172.

93. Nhung Tran, "Vietnamese Women at the Crossroads," 128; Sommer, *Sex, Law, and Society*, 32.

94. Rigby, *Ninety-Nine Laws*, 24, 47, 60, 71; Nguyen Ngoc Huy et al., *The Lê Code*, 2:269–270.

95. Walthall, "The Life Cycle," 51; Merry E. Wiesner-Hanks, *Christianity and Sexuality in the Early Modern World: Regulating Desire, Reforming Practice* (London: Routledge, 2000), 82; Isabel V. Hull, *Sexuality, State, and Civil Society in Germany, 1700–1815* (Ithaca, NY, and London: Cornell University Press, 1996), 70–71; Hanley, "Engendering the State," 11.

96. Armijo-Hussein, "'Customs of Various Barbarians,'" 93; Pierre Lustéguy, *The Role of Women in Tonkinese Religion and Property*, trans. Charles A. Messner (New Haven, CT: Human Relations Area Files, 1954), 128–129; Nguyen Ngoc Huy et al., *The Lê Code*, 1:185, 2:108.

97. Gervaise, *The Natural and Political History*, 80; Nai Pan Hla and Okudaira, *Eleven Mon Dhammasat Texts*, 542.

98. Mohamad Jajuli A. Rahman, *The Malay Law Text* (Kuala Lumpur: Dewan Bahasa dan Pustaka, 1995), 78; Liaw, *Undang-Undang Melaka*, 84; R. O. Winstedt, "An Old Minangkabau Legal Digest from Perak," *JMBRAS* 26, no. 1 (July 1953): 7.

99. Sirtjo Koolhof, "The 'La Galigo': A Bugis Encyclopedia and Its Growth," *BKI* 155, no. 3 (1999): 377.

100. Cf. Nguyen Van Ky, "Rethinking the Status of Vietnamese Women," 99–100; Liaw, *Undang-Undang Melaka*, 391, 396, 536, 541.

101. Nguyen Ngoc Huy et al., *The Lê Code*, 1:208.

102. John Ball, *Indonesian Legal History: British West Sumatra, 1685–1825* (Sydney: Oughtershaw Press, 1984), 68–73; Hazeu, "Tjeribonsch wetboek," 33.

103. Dampier, *A New Voyage*, 269; for further references, see B. Andaya, "From Temporary Wife to Prostitute," 13.

104. Wichienkeeo and Wijeyewardene, *The Laws of King Mangrai*, 37, 58.

105. Frederick Hirth and W. W. Rockhill, eds., *Chau Ju-Kua: His Work on the Chinese and Arab Trade in the Twelfth and Thirteenth Centuries* (New York: Paragon, 1966; reprint of 1911 edition); Hazeu, "Tjeribonsch wetboek," 32, 34; Hoadley and Hooker, *An Introduction to Javanese Law*, 194, 220; J. E. Kempe and R. O. Winstedt, "A Malay Legal Digest Compiled for 'Abd al-Ghafur Muhaiyu'd-din Shah, Sultan of Pahang 1592–1624 AD with Undated Additions," *JMBRAS* 21, no. 1 (1948): 5–6, 32.

106. Nai Pan Hla and Okudaira, *Eleven Mon Dhammasat Texts*, 549–550; Griswold and na Nagara, "The Judgements of King Man Ray," 155; Wichienkeeo and Wijeyewardene, *The Laws of King Mangrai*, 22, 51; Gervaise, *Histoire naturelle et politique*, 76, 80.

107. Liaw, *Undang-Undang Melaka*, 79, 83.

108. Nguyen Ngoc Huy et al., *The Lê Code*, 1:208; 2:8, 10, 233, 238; Li and Reid, *Southern Vietnam under the Nguyen*, 74.

109. Marsden, *History of Sumatra*, 236.

110. Mason C. Hoadley, *Selective Judicial Competence: The Cirebon-Priangan Legal Administration, 1680–1792* (Ithaca, NY: Southeast Asia Program, Cornell University,

1994), 97n5; Blussé, *Strange Company,* 161; Knaap, "Pants, Skirts, and Pulpits," 171; Jones, "Wives, Slaves, and Concubines," 85ff.

111. Bankoff, *In Verbo Sacerdotis,* 10, 13–17, 43n75; Brewer, *Holy Confrontation,* 43.

112. Bankoff, *In Verbo Sacerdotis,* 13, 22.

113. Nai Pan Hla and Okudaira, *Eleven Mon Dhammasat Texts,* 550, 571; Maung Maung, *Law and Custom in Burma,* 11–12; Nhung Tran, "Vietnamese Women at the Crossroads," 131.

114. Anthony H. Johns, "'She desired him and he desired her' (Qur'an 12:24): Abd al-Rauf's Treatment of an Episode of the Joseph Story in Tarjuman al-Mustafid," *Archipel* 57, no. 2 (1999): 111–119.

115. Brewer, *Holy Confrontation,* 93.

116. Reynolds and Reynolds, *Three Worlds,* 98–99; Farah, *Marriage and Sexuality,* 121; Hamid, *The Malay Islamic Hikayat,* 65.

117. William Cummings, *Making Blood White* (Honolulu: University of Hawai'i Press, 2002), 147, 174, 185.

118. Huxley, "The Importance of the Dhammathats," 3; Griswold and na Nagara, "The Judgements of King Man Ray," 148; Nai Pan Hla and Okudaira, *Eleven Mon Dhammasat Texts,* 560, 571; Liaw, *Undang-Undang Melaka,* 82–83; Sarasin Viraphol, "Law in Traditional Siam and China," *JSS* 65, no. 1 (1977): 106; Nguyen Ngoc Huy et al., *The Lê Code,* 1:109, 112.

119. De la Loubère, *The Kingdom of Siam,* 59, 85, 103; John O'Kane, trans. and ed., *The Ship of Sulaiman* (London: Routledge and Kegan Paul, 1972), 41, 121, 126.

120. Ken Breazeale, personal communication, June 16, 2003.

121. Gervaise, *The Natural and Political History,* 76.

122. Yu, *Law and Society,* 60, 63.

123. Th. Salmon, *Tegenwoordige staat,* 2:165.

124. Wichienkeeo and Wijeyewardene, *The Laws of King Mangrai,* 22; see also Nai Pan Hla and Okudaira, *Eleven Mon Dhammasat Texts,* 549–550; Griswold and na Nagara, "The Judgements of King Man Ray," 158.

125. Rigby, *Ninety-Nine Laws,* 24, 60.

126. Hazeu, "Tjeribonsch wetboek," 58.

127. Wichienkeeo and Wijeyewardene, *The Laws of King Mangrai,* 30, 31, 38.

128. Hooker, "The Trengganu Inscription," 128; Nguyen Ngoc Huy et al., *The Lê Code,* 2:55.

129. Hull, *Sexuality, State, and Civil Society,* 81, 99.

130. Wichienkeeo and Wijeyewardene, *The Laws of King Mangrai,* 75; Rigby, *Ninety-Nine Laws,* 53, 85.

131. Hoadley, *Selective Judicial Competence,* 96.

132. Liaw, *Undang-Undang Melaka,* 153; Hazeu, "Tjeribonsch wetboek," 39; see also Griswold and na Nagara, "The Judgements of King Man Ray," 157; Maung Maung, *Law and Custom in Burma,* 17; Htin Aung, *Burmese Law Tales,* 30–31.

133. Cummings, *Making Blood White,* 187.

134. Aroonrut Wichienkeeo, "Lanna Customary Law," in Andrew Huxley, ed.,

Thai Law: Buddhist Law: Essays on the Legal History of Thailand, Laos, and Burma (Bangkok: White Orchid Press, 1996), 38.

135. Th. Salmon, *Tegenwoordige staat*, 672; Nguyen Ngoc Huy et al., *The Lê Code*, 2:176.

136. David K. Wyatt, "The 'Subtle Revolution' of Rama I of Siam," in David K. Wyatt and Alexander Woodside, eds., *Moral Order and the Question of Change: Essays on Southeast Asian Thought*, Monograph 24 (New Haven, CT: Yale University Southeast Asia Studies, 1982), 31.

137. Htin Aung, *Burmese Law Tales*, 44–45.

138. Liaw, *Undang-Undang Melaka*, 165.

139. Hazeu, "Tjeribonsch wetboek," 37, 39; Moyer, *The Logic of the Laws*, 70.

140. Rigby, *Ninety-Nine Laws*, 69.

141. R. C. Majumdar, *Ancient Indian Colonies in the Far East and Champa* (Lahore: Punjab Sanskrit Book Depot, 1927), 91, 97; Nguyen Ngoc Huy et al., *The Lê Code*, 2:109, 111.

142. Nhung Tran, "Vietnamese Women at the Crossroads, 143–146.

143. Unger and Unger, *Pagodas, Gods, and Spirits*, 24–25; U Ba Kyaw, trans., *Elucidation of the Intrinsic Meaning So Named the Commentary on the Peta Stories*, by Dhammapala (London: Pali Text Society, 1980), 38, 73; K. I. Matics, *Introduction to the Thai Mural* (Bangkok: White Lotus, 1992), 10.

144. Winstedt, *Hikayat Bayan Budiman*, 6, 42; Drewes and Brakel, *The Poems of Hamzah Fansuri*, 75–77.

145. L. Andaya, "'A Very Good-Natured but Awe-Inspiring Government,'" 72.

Chapter 6. Women, Courts, and Class

1. Than Tun, *Royal Orders*, 1:75.

2. Furnivall, "Matriarchal Vestiges in Burma," 16.

3. Hoshino Tatsuo, *Pour une histoire médiévale du moyen Mékong* (Bangkok: Duang Kamol, 1986), 39–40; A. B. Griswold and Prasert na Nagara, "A Declaration of Independence and Its Consequences: Epigraphic and Historical Inscriptions, Number 1," *JSS* 56, no. 2 (July 1968): 26n39; see also B. Andaya, "Localising the Universal," 26–28.

4. Robson, *Désawarnana*, 59.

5. Vickery, *Society, Economics, and Politics*, 181.

6. G. W. J. Drewes, *Hikajat Potjut Muhamat: An Achehnese Epic* (The Hague: Nijhoff, 1979), 7, 78–79.

7. Emmanuel Guillon, *The Mons: A Civilization of Southeast Asia*, trans. James V. Di Crocco (Bangkok: Siam Society, 1999), 171–172.

8. Pierre-Bernard Lafont, trans. and ed., *Le royaume de Jyn Khên: Chronique d'un royaume tay loe 2 du haut Mékong (XVᵉ–XXᵉ siècles)* (Paris: L'Harmattan, 1998), xxi, xxii, xxv, xxvii, 106, 116, 119–120.

9. Peggy Reeves Sanday, *Women at the Center: Life in a Modern Matriarchy* (Ithaca,

NY, and London: Cornell University Press, 2002), 34–39, 245n12; Anthony H. Johns, trans. and ed., *Rantjak Dilabueh: A Minangkabau Kaba* (Ithaca, NY: Southeast Asia Program, Department of Far Eastern Studies, Cornell University, 1958), xii; Leonard Y. Andaya, *The Kingdom of Johor 1641–1728: Economic and Political Developments* (Kuala Lumpur: Oxford University Press, 1975), 268–269.

10. B. Andaya, *To Live as Brothers*, 59.

11. Ishii, *The Junk Trade from Southeast Asia*, 122.

12. Annabel Teh Gallop, personal communication, Makassar, June 8, 2003.

13. Riddell, *Islam and the Malay-Indonesian World*, 129; L. Andaya, "'A Very Good-Natured but Awe-Inspiring Government,'" 65–81.

14. Bowrey, *A Geographical Account*, 298–299, 310; L. Andaya, "'A Very Good-Natured but Awe-Inspiring Government,'" 79–80.

15. Bowrey, *A Geographical Account*, 310, 325.

16. Khalid M. Hussain, ed., *Taj al-Salatin* (Kuala Lumpur: Dewan Bahasa dan Pustaka, 1966), 63–64; Marsden, *History of Sumatra*, 449–454; Bowrey, *A Geographical Account*, 313–317; "Translation of the Annals of Acheen," *JIAEA* 4 (1850): 599.

17. P. J. B. C. Robidé van der Aa, "De groote Bantamsche opstand in het midden der vorige eeuw," *BKI* 29 (1881): 62–71.

18. Raja Ali Haji, *Tuhfat al-Nafis (The Precious Gift)*, trans. and ed. Virginia Matheson and Barbara Watson Andaya (Kuala Lumpur: Oxford University Press, 1982), 25–26.

19. John Crawfurd, *History of the Indian Archipelago: Containing an Account of the Languages, Institutions, and Commerce of Its Inhabitants* (Kuala Lumpur: Oxford University Press, 1971; reprint of 1820 edition), 74; see also Thomas Stanford Raffles, *History of Java* (Kuala Lumpur: Oxford University Press, 1965; reprint of 1817 edition), 2: appendix F, clxxxv.

20. Els M. Jacobs, *Koopman in Azië: De handel van de Verenigde Oost-Indische Compagnie tijdens de 18de eeuw* (Zutphen, Netherlands: Walburg Press, 2000), 65.

21. L. Andaya, *The Kingdom of Johor*, 269.

22. Jacobsen, "Apsarā, Accoutrements, Activists," 107; Martin Stuart-Fox, *The Lao Kingdom of Lān Xāng: Rise and Decline* (Bangkok: White Lotus, 1998), 63; Souneth Phothisane, "Evolution of the Chronicle of Luang Prabang: A Comparison of Sixteen Versions," in Mayoury Ngaosrivathana and Kennon Breazeale, eds., *Breaking New Ground in Lao History: Essays on the Seventh to Twentieth Centuries* (Chiang Mai, Thailand: Silkworm Books, 2002), 78; Mayoury Ngaosyvathn, *Lao Women: Yesterday and Today* ([Laos]: State Publishing Enterprise, 1993), 24.

23. Stuart-Fox, *The Lao Kingdom of Lān Xāng*, 115–116.

24. Reid, *Southeast Asia in the Age of Commerce*, 1:168–171; L. Andaya, *Heritage of Arung Palakka*, 32.

25. Griswold and na Nagara, "A Declaration of Independence," 26n39; see also B. Andaya, "Localising the Universal," 27.

26. Cushman and Wyatt, *The Royal Chronicles of Ayutthaya*, 32–34, 50, 51. For Thai murals depicting women in battle, see Wyatt, *Reading Thai Murals*, 54–55.

27. Peter Carey, ed., *The Archive of Yogyakarta*, vol. 1, *Documents Relating to Political and Internal Court Affairs, 1792–1819* (London: Oxford University Press for the British Academy, 1980), 190; Dampier, *A New Voyage*, 250.

28. Keith Weller Taylor, *The Birth of Vietnam*, 41.

29. Ishii, *The Junk Trade from Southeast Asia*, 60–63, 113.

30. A. Teeuw and D. K. Wyatt, eds., *Hikayat Patani: The Story of Patani* (The Hague: Nijhoff, 1970), 1:100–101, 2:173–177.

31. Ricklefs, *Seen and Unseen Worlds*, 71–72.

32. Whitmore, "The Literati Voice," 219–220, 226–227.

33. Lady Mary Wortley Montague, *Letters from the Levant during the Embassy to Constantinople 1716–18* (New York: Arno Press and New York Times, 1971), 129, 157; Leslie P. Peirce, *The Imperial Harem: Women and Sovereignty in the Ottoman Empire* (New York and Oxford: Oxford University Press, 1993), 114–115.

34. Rita Costa Gomes, *The Making of a Court Society: Kings and Nobles in Late Medieval Portugal*, trans. Alison Aiken (Cambridge: Cambridge University Press, 2003), 34.

35. B. Andaya, "Delineating Female Space," in B. Andaya, *Other Pasts*, 231–253; Creese, *Women of the Kakawin World*, 46–48.

36. Corfield and Morson, *A New Account*, 393; L. Andaya, *The Kingdom of Johor*, 258–259.

37. Ricklefs, *Seen and Unseen Worlds*, 69, 110, 137, 138.

38. Tchou, *Les femmes de lettres Birmanes*, 32.

39. Stuart-Fox, *The Lao Kingdom of Lān Xāng*, 87.

40. Frederick de Houtman, *Cort verhael vant' gene wederuaren is Frederick de Houtman tot Atchein enz.* (Gouda, Netherlands: Van Goor, 1880), 18–19; Robert Wessing, "The *Gunongan* in Banda Aceh, Indonesia: Agni's Fire in Allah's Paradise?" *Archipel* 35 (1988): 9.

41. Van Goens, *Javaense reyse*, 75–81, 104.

42. Koenig, *The Burmese Polity*, 166.

43. Gavin R. G. Hambly, "Armed Women Retainers in the Zenanas of Indo-Muslim Rulers: The Case of Bibi Fatima," in Hambly, *Women in the Medieval Islamic World*, 436–443; Van Goens, *Javaense reyse*, 75–81, 104.

44. Carey, *The Archive of Yogyakarta*, 1:190.

45. Chou Ta-kuan, *Notes*, 72–73; H. Jacobs, *A Treatise*, 115.

46. Ito, *"Adat Aceh,"* 26.

47. Cushman and Wyatt, *The Royal Chronicles of Ayutthaya*, 21–27.

48. Ibid., 9; Flood and Flood, *Dynastic Chronicles*, 1:54; 2:80, 94; John Laffin, *Women in Battle* (London: Abelard-Schuman, 1967), 46–47; Wyatt, *Reading Thai Murals*, 55.

49. Nguyen Ngoc Huy et al., *The Lê Code*, 1:183; Choi, *Southern Vietnam under the Reign of Minh Mang*, 55; Anne Crawford, *Customs and Culture of Vietnam* (Rutland, VT: C. E. Tuttle, 1966), 44–45; Hoang Bao et al., *Vietnamese Traditional Medicine*, appendix; Lessard, "Curious Relations," 154; Keith W. Taylor, "The Literati Revival in Seventeenth-Century Vietnam," *JSEAS* 18, no. 1 (March 1987): 19; Sun Laichen, "Eighteenth-Century Sino-Vietnamese Overland Trade and Mining Industry in Northern

Vietnam," unpublished manuscript, 16 (cited with permission); White, *Voyage to Cochin China*, 321–322, and introduction by Milton Osborne, xii, xii n. 1; Yu, *Law and Society*, 132; Launay, *Histoire de la mission du Tonkin*, 55.

50. A. L. Basham, *The Wonder That Was India* (New York: Grove Press, 1954), 172; K. S. Lal, *The Mughal Harem* (New Delhi: Aditya Prakashan, 1988), 56–60; Gavin Hambly, "A Note on the Trade in Eunuchs in Mughal Bengal," *Journal of the American Oriental Society* 94, no. 1 (1974): 128–129; Luard, *Travels of Fray Sebastian Manrique*, 142–144. The Chinese citation from "A Study of the Eastern and Western Ocean" was kindly provided by Dr. Sun Laichen, June 15, 2004.

51. Leonard Y. Andaya, "Aceh's Contribution to Standards of Malayness," *Archipel* 61 (2001): 56–57; Ito, *"Adat Aceh,"* 26, 66, 84; Bowrey, *A Geographical Account*, 299–300, 325–326.

52. Harvey, *History of Burma*, 198; Gordon, "Women in Thai Mural Paintings," 180; Abbé de Choisy, *Journal of a Voyage to Siam, 1685–1686*, trans. and ed. Michael Smithies (Kuala Lumpur: Oxford University Press, 1993), 184; Michael Smithies, *Mission Made Impossible: The Second French Embassy to Siam, 1687* (Chiang Mai, Thailand: Silkworm Books, 2003), 155.

53. Van den Brink, *Dr. Benjamin Frederick Matthes*, 375.

54. Creese, *Women of the Kakawin World*, 44.

55. B. Andaya, *To Live as Brothers*, 103–104, 129; *Dagh-Register*, 1679:84.

56. Li, *Nguyen Cochinchina*, 108, 126.

57. H. Jacobs, *A Treatise*, 115; P. A. Leupe, ed., "Bali in 1597," *BKI* 5 (1856): 266.

58. Pe Maung Tin and G. H. Luce, *The Glass Palace Chronicle of the Kings of Burma* (Rangoon: Rangoon University Press, 1960), 95, 111; Creese, *Women of the Kakawin World*, 48.

59. Van Goens, *Javaense reyse*, 77; Than Tun, *Royal Orders*, 1:53–54.

60. Flood and Flood, *Dynastic Chronicles*, 2:39–41, 96.

61. Luard, *Travels of Fray Sebastian Manrique*, 1:91.

62. Dhiravat na Pombejra, "Princes, Pretenders, and the Chinese Prakhlang: An Analysis of the Dutch Evidence Concerning Siamese Court Politics, 1699–1734," in Leonard Blussé and Femme Gaastra, eds., *On the Eighteenth Century as a Category of Asian History: Van Leur in Retrospect* (Brookfield, VT: Ashgate, 1998), 124.

63. Flood and Flood, *Dynastic Chronicles*, 2:82.

64. Jacobsen, "Apsarā, Accoutrements, Activists," 114; de la Loubère, *The Kingdom of Siam*, 52; Sahai, *The Rama Jataka*, 37; Pieter van der Aa, *Naaukeurige Versameling der gedank-waardigste zee en land-reysen na Oost en West-Indian . . . zedert het jaar 1614 tot 1634* (Leiden: Pieter van der Aa, 1707), 20; Than Tun, *Royal Orders*, 1:30.

65. Koolhof, "The 'La Galigo,'" 375–377.

66. Carey, *The British in Java*, 97.

67. Purchas, *Purchas His Pilgrimes*, 2:545; Kumar, *Java and Modern Europe*, 114.

68. I am grateful to Trudy Jacobsen for these references. Jacobsen, "Apsarā, Accoutrements, Activists," 124; Gervaise, *The Natural and Political History*, 195; Borri, *Cochin-China*, n.p.

69. Stuart-Fox, *The Lao Kingdom of Lān Xāng,* 81; Maha Sila Viravong, *History of Laos* (New York: Paragon Book Reprint Corp., 1964), 59–60.

70. Heersink, "The Green Gold," 40:

71. Flood and Flood, *Dynastic Chronicles,* 1:33; 2:52, 39–41.

72. Anna Leonowens, *Siamese Harem Life* (New York: Dutton, 1954), 10–11.

73. Lee Butler, *Emperor and Aristocracy in Japan, 1467–1680: Resilience and Renewal* (Cambridge, MA.: Harvard University Asia Center, 2002), 52–53; Ruby Lal, *Domesticity and Power in the Early Mughal World* (Cambridge: Cambridge University Press, 2005), 178.

74. Purchas, *Purchas His Pilgrimes,* 2: 471–472; Creese, *Women of the Kakawin World,* 49.

75. Carey, *The British in Java,* 504n509; Ricklefs, *War, Culture, and Economy,* 119.

76. Beeckman, *A Voyage to and from Borneo,* 77–79; Chandler, *A History of Cambodia,* 93; Flood and Flood, *Dynastic Chronicles,* 1:301.

77. Nancy K. Florida, *Writing the Past, Inscribing the Future: History as Prophecy in Colonial Java* (Durham, NC, and London: Duke University Press, 1995), 287n5; Carey, *The British in Java,* 403.

78. Wolters, *History, Culture, and Region,* 229–237. See also B. Andaya, "Localising the Universal," 26–27; Stuart-Fox, *The Lao Kingdom of Lān Xāng,* 111.

79. Van Goens, *Javaense reyse,* 75–81, 104; Nguyen Ngoc Huy et al., *The Lê Code,* 2:83.

80. Flood and Flood, *Dynastic Chronicles,* 2:25, 27, 88.

81. Ricklefs, *War, Culture, and Economy,* 118.

82. Priscilla Ching Chung, *Palace Women in the Northern Sung 960–1126* (Leiden: Brill, 1981), 40; Evelyn Rawski, *The Last Emperors: A Social History of Qing Imperial Institutions* (Berkeley: University of California Press, 1998), 173–174; Schimmel, *My Soul Is a Woman,* 95; Lal, *Domesticity and Power,* 183–196.

83. Giladi, *Infants, Parents, and Wet Nurses,* 35, 38; Ito, *"Adat Aceh,"* 231.

84. See also B. Andaya, "Localising the Universal," 23; Launay, *Histoire de la mission de Siam,* 304; Kumar, *Java and Modern Europe,* 178.

85. Pombejra, "VOC Employees and Their Relationships," 202–203; B. Andaya, *To Live as Brothers,* 129.

86. Carey, *The Archive of Yogyakarta,* 1:150.

87. Pierre Lustéguy, *The Role of Women in Tonkinese Religion and Property,* trans. Charles A. Messner (New Haven, CT: Human Relations Area Files, 1954), 129; Truong, "The Development of Private Landed Property," 4, 6.

88. Harvey, *History of Burma,* 198; Carey, *The Archive of Yogyakarta,* 1:118–122; Ito, "Adat Aceh," 26.

89. Butler, *Emperor and Aristocracy,* 52–53.

90. For example, Nguyen The Long and Pham, *130 Pagodas,* 62–63, 67, 77.

91. Carey, *The Archive of Yogyakarta,* 1:173; idem, *The British in Java,* 16, 29, 87.

92. Reynolds, "A Defense of Polygamy," 937.

93. Joannes Andries Paravicini, "Eerbiedigst rapport . . . over de zaken en belangen van Timor, Rotty, Solor, Sacoe, Sumba en Borneo," *BKI* 8 (1862): 229–239.

94. Mattani, *Dance, Drama, and Theatre in Thailand,* 49–51; James R. Brandon, *Theatre in Southeast Asia* (Cambridge, MA: Harvard University Press, 1967), 195.

95. E.g., Pemberton, *On the Subject of "Java,"* 55.

96. B. Andaya, *To Live as Brothers,* 78; B. Andaya, *Perak, the Abode of Grace,* 234.

97. Simmonds, "Siamese (Thai)," 193.

98. Carey, *The British in Java,* 12.

99. Pe Maung Tin and Luce, *Glass Palace Chronicle,* 135.

100. Borri, *Cochin-China,* n.p.

101. Hamid, *The Malay Islamic Hikayat,* 96.

102. For example, *Lament of a Royal Concubine,* written in *nom* by Nguyen Gia Thieu (1741–1798).

103. Lustig, *Burmese Classical Poems,* 26; Tchou, *Les femmes de lettres,* 33.

104. Flood and Flood, *Dynastic Chronicles,* 2: 96.

105. Dampier, *A New Voyage,* 250.

106. Beekman, *The Poison Tree,* 67.

107. Van Goens, *Javaense reyse,* 81; Ricklefs, *War, Culture, and Economy,* 219.

108. Cushman and Wyatt, *The Royal Chronicles of Ayutthaya,* 391; Flood and Flood, *Dynastic Chronicles,* 2:39; Nguyen Ngoc Huy et al., *The Lê Code,* 1:215.

109. Cushman and Wyatt, *The Royal Chronicles of Ayutthaya,* 373, 391.

110. Jacobsen, "Apsarā, Accoutrements, Activists," 108, 115.

111. Jeremias van Vliet, *The Short History of the Kings of Siam,* trans. Leonard Andaya, ed. David K. Wyatt (Bangkok: Siam Society, 1975), 73; Harvey, *History of Burma,* 179–180.

112. Pe Maung Tin and Luce, *Glass Palace Chronicle,* 133.

113. L. Andaya, *The Kingdom of Johor,* 138.

114. Ito, *"Adat Aceh,"* 26; Algemeen Rijksarchief, The Hague, VOC 1199, Journal of a mission to Aceh, 1636, fols. 1207–1208 (reference supplied by Leonard Y. Andaya).

115. Flood and Flood, *Dynastic Chronicles,* 2:8.

116. J. Jacobs, *Eenigen tijd onder der baliërs: Een reisbeschrijving* (Batavia: Kolff, 1883), 129, 135, 146; Vickers, *Bali,* 88.

117. Megan J. Sinnott, *Toms and Dees: Transgender Identity and Female Same-Sex Relationships in Thailand* (Honolulu: University of Hawai'i Press, 2004), 49–53; Wyatt, *Reading Thai Murals,* 76; Creese, *Women of the Kakawin World,* 50–51; Tamara Loos, "Sex in the Inner City: The Fidelity between Sex and Politics in Siam," *JAS* 64, no. 4 (November 2005): 881–909.

118. Noriah Mohamed, *Hikayat Panji Semirang* (Kuala Lumpur: Dewan Bahasa dan Pustaka, 1992), 55.

119. Thomas M. Hunter, *Blossoms of Longing: Ancient Verses of Love and Lament: Translations from the Old Javanese* (Jakarta: Lontar Foundation, 1998), 3.

120. Cushman and Wyatt, *The Royal Chronicles of Ayutthaya,* 228–229.

121. A. H. Hill, "Hikayat Raja-Raja Pasai," *JMBRAS* 33, no. 2 (June 1960): 84, 90, 143, 150.

122. Lieberman, *Burmese Administrative Cycles,* 57.

123. Cummings, *Making Blood White*, 178; Wichienkeeo and Wijeyewardene, *The Laws of King Mangrai*, 22.

124. Ricklefs, *War, Culture, and Economy*, 120; Than Tun, *Royal Orders*, 5:46.

125. De la Loubère, *The Kingdom of Siam*, 74, 85; Li and Reid, *Southern Vietnam under the Nguyen*, 74.

126. Majumdar, *Ancient Indian Colonies*, 167; L. W. Shakespear, *History of Upper Assam, Upper Burmah, and North Eastern Frontier* (London: Macmillan, 1914), 38. For Melanesia and Polynesia, see Spriggs, *The Island Melanesians*, 191, 210–211, 218; Lamb et al., *Exploration & Exchange*, 186–188, 260–261.

127. Alfons van der Kraan, "Human Sacrifice in Bali: Sources, Notes, and Commentary," *Indonesia* 40 (October 1985): 119; see esp. Creese, *Women of the Kakawin World*, 210–244.

128. Gerald C. Hickey, *Sons of the Mountains: Ethnohistory of the Vietnamese Central Highlands to 1954* (New Haven, CT: Yale University Press, 1982), 89; Tam Quach-Langlet, "La compassion transcendée: l'"Oraison pour le rachat des âmes abandonées,' attribuée à Nguyen Du," in Nguyen The Anh and Forest, eds., *Notes sur la culture*, 148, 148n33.

129. Cortesão, *The Suma Oriental of Tomé Pires*, 1:176; Eaton, *The Rise of Islam*, 166.

130. Cummings, *Making Blood White*, 109–111; see also Reid, *Southeast Asia in the Age of Commerce*, 1:152–153.

131. Dirk van der Cruysse, *Louis XIV et le Siam* (Paris: Fayard, 1991), 104, 392, 447, 448, 450, 456, 457, 465; de Choisy, *Journal of a Voyage*, 184; Gervaise, *The Natural and Political History*, 186.

132. Cushman and Wyatt, *The Royal Chronicles of Ayutthaya*, 323–324, 337–338, 432.

133. Dampier, *A New Voyage*, 250.

134. Brereton, *Thai Tellings*, 128.

Chapter 7. Being Female in "Early Modern" Southeast Asia

1. Mulholland, *Herbal Medicine*, 16; Keith Norman Macdonald, *The Practice of Medicine among the Burmese*, trans. from original manuscripts (Edinburgh: Maclachlan and Stewart, 1879), 53.

2. Robert A. Nye, "Sexuality," in Meade and Wiesner-Hanks, *A Companion to Gender History*, 11–26.

3. Laura W. R. Appell, "Sex Role Symmetry among the Rungus of Sabah," in Sutlive, *Female and Male in Borneo*, 17.

4. S. C. Sardeshpande, *The Patkoi Nagas* (Delhi: Daya, 1987), 35; Walthall, "The Life Cycle," 45, 47.

5. Masing, *The Coming of the Gods*, 2:239.

6. Nhatrang, "The Traditional Roles of Women," 25; Nhung Tran, "Vietnamese Women at the Crossroads," 26; Wajuppa Tossa, *Images of Women in Thai Literature* (Honolulu: Department of Indo-Pacific Languages, University of Hawai'i, 1992), 9.

7. Kate Frieson, "Sentimental Education: Les Sage Femmes and Colonial Cam-

bodia," *Journal of Colonialism and Colonial History* 1, no. 1 (2000), http://muse.jhu
.edu/journals/journal_of_colonialism_and_colonial_history/v001/1.1frieson.html;
Jacob, *The Traditional Literature of Cambodia*, 57; Nhung Tran, "Vietnamese Women
at the Crossroads," 91.

8. Raffles, *History of Java*, 1:409.

9. Blussé and Roessingh, "A Visit to the Past," 73.

10. Mulholland, *Herbal Medicine*, 16.

11. Beekman, *The Poison Tree*, 131.

12. Knaap, "Pants, Skirts, and Pulpits," 163; Margaret Jolly, introduction to Vicki
Lukere and Margaret Jolly, eds., *Birthing in the Pacific: Beyond Tradition and Modernity?*
(Honolulu: University of Hawai'i Press, 2002), 21; Valerio Valeri, "Both Nature and
Culture: Reflections on Menstrual and Parturitional Taboos in Huaulu (Seram)," in
Atkinson and Errington, *Power and Difference*, 237.

13. Knaap, "Pants, Skirts, and Pulpits," 155–156; for a modern account, see
Renée Valeri, "La position de la femme dans la société traditionelle des Moluques
Centrales," *Archipel* 13 (1977): 62–63.

14. G. W. W. C. van Hoëvell, "Lepas kain kadoe," *TNI*, 2nd ser., no. 5 (1876):
399–400.

15. Jennifer W. Nourse, *Conceiving Spirits: Birth Rituals and Contested Identities
among Laujé of Indonesia* (Washington, DC, and London: Smithsonian Institution,
1999), 242n3; Cora Du Bois, *The People of Alor: A Social-Psychological Study of an East
Indian Island* (Minneapolis: University of Minnesota Press, 1944), 102; Douglas W.
Holland and Jane C. Wellenkamp, *The Thread of Life: Toraja Reflections on the Life Cycle*
(Honolulu: University of Hawai'i Press, 1996), 71–72.

16. Forrest, *A Voyage to New Guinea*, 237.

17. John Crawfurd, "Notes on the Population of Java," *JIAEA* 3 (1849): 43.

18. Ang Chouléan, "De la naissance à la puberté rites et croyances Khmers," in
Joseane Massard-Vincent and Jeanine Koubin, eds., *Enfants et sociétés d'Asie de Sud-
Est* (Paris: L'Harmattan, 1995), 162–163.

19. B. Andaya, *Perak, the Abode of Grace*, 171–174; Hashim, *Out of the Shadows*,
171–172.

20. Flood and Flood, *Dynastic Chronicles*, 1:301. A painting of this event is displayed in the National Museum in Bangkok.

21. Hose and McDougall, *Pagan Tribes of Borneo*, 1:252–258.

22. John Jardine, ed., *The Burmese Empire a Hundred Years ago as Described by Father
Sangermano* (Delhi: BR Publishing, 1984: reprint of 1893 edition), 42–43.

23. Creese, *Women of the Kakawin World*, 175–176, 186–187.

24. Edwin P. Wieringa, "A Javanese Handbook for Would-be Husbands: The
Serat Candraning Wanita," *JSEAS* 33, no. 3 (2002): 441.

25. Sahai, *The Rama Jataka*, 1:216, 238.

26. Yu, *Law and Society*, 56, 60; Tran Quoc Vuong, "Popular Culture," 24; Kern,
Itinerario, 80–81; William Scott, *Barangay*, 97.

27. Knaap, "Pants, Skirts, and Pulpits," 152.

28. Vicente L. Rafael, *Contracting Colonialism: Translation and Christian Conver-*

sion in Tagalog Society under Early Spanish Rule (Durham, NC, and London: Duke University Press, 1993), 189. For modern comments on the same tendency, see Nicola Tannenbaum, "Witches, Fortune, and Misfortune among the Shan of Northwestern Thailand," in C. W. Watson and Roy Ellen, eds., *Understanding Witchcraft and Sorcery in Southeast Asia* (Honolulu: University of Hawai'i Press, 1993), 68; Mary Beth Mills, "Attack of the Widow Ghosts: Gender, Death, and Modernity in Northeast Thailand," in Ong and Peletz, *Bewitching Women, Pious Men*, 251–254; Clifford Sather, "The Malevolent *koklir:* Iban Concepts of Sexual Peril and the Dangers of Childbirth," *BKI* 134, no. 2–3 (1978): 336.

29. Kumar, *Java and Modern Europe*, 114.

30. Nhatrang, "The Traditional Roles of Women," 19, 30; Myint Thien, *Burmese Folk-Songs*, 41, 44, 46, 47.

31. Hull, *Sexuality, State, and Civil Society*, 69, 112, 181; Quirino and Garcia, "The Manners, Customs, and Beliefs," 413; Antonio-Ma Rosales, *A Study of a 16th Century Tagalog Manuscript on the Ten Commandments: Its Significance and Implications* (Quezon City: University of the Philippines Press, 1984), 51.

32. Nguyen Ngoc Huy et al., *The Lê Code*, 1:216, 2:248; B. F. Musallam, *Sex and Society in Islam: Birth Control before the Nineteenth Century* (Cambridge: Cambridge University Press, 1983), 16; G. J. Harrebomée, "Eene bijdrage over de feitelijken toestand der bevolking in de Lampongsche Districten," *BKI*, 4th ser., no. 10 (1885): 384.

33. Chou Ta-Kuan, *Notes*, 18–19; Bowrey, *A Geographical Account*, 24; Werner F. Menski, "Marital Expectations as Dramatized in Hindu Marriage Rituals," in Julia Leslie, ed., *Roles and Rituals for Hindu Women* (London: Pinter, 1991), 57.

34. John Winter Jones, ed., *The Travels of Ludovico di Varthema, AD 1503–1508* (London: Hakluyt Society, 1963; reprint of the 1863 edition), 203–204n; Kern, *Itinerario*, 74.

35. Armijo-Hussein, "'Customs of Various Barbarians,'" 91, 98n20; J. S. Cummins, trans. and ed., *Sucesos de las Islas Filipinas by Antonio de Morga* (Cambridge: Cambridge University Press for the Hakluyt Society, 1971), 278; Brewer, *Holy Confrontation*, 47, For a modern example, see Jérôme Rousseau, *Kayan Religion: Ritual Life and Religious Reform in Central Borneo* (Leiden: KITLV Press, 1998), 63.

36. Bradd Shore, "Sexuality and Gender in Samoa: Conceptions and Missed Conceptions," in Ortner and Whitehead, *Sexual Meanings*, 197.

37. Appell, "Sex Role Symmetry," 22–23.

38. Brun and Schumacher, *Traditional Herbal Medicine*, 77.

39. Cortesão, *The Suma Oriental of Tomé Pires*, 1:177; Peter Xenos, personal communication, January 2001.

40. Sahai, *The Rama Jataka*, 1:211.

41. De Rovere van Breugel, "Beschryving van Bantam," 334.

42. Shryock, "Marriage Customs of Yunnan," 536–539.

43. Patricia V. Symonds, *Calling in the Soul: Gender and the Cycle of Life in a Hmong Village* (Seattle and London: University of Washington Press, 2004), 45; Manning Nash and June Nash, "Marriage, Family, and Population Growth in Upper Burma," *Southwestern Journal of Anthropology* 18, no. 3 (1963): 260.

44. Andrew Caldecott, "Jelebu Customary Songs and Sayings," *JSBRAS* 78 (1918): 37. See also chapter 5, n. 67.

45. Walthall, "The Life Cycle," 54–55; Wakita Haruko, "The Medieval Household and Gender Roles within the Imperial Family: Nobility, Merchants, and Commoners," in Hitomi Tonomura, Anne Walthall, and Wakita Haruko, eds., *Women and Class in Japanese History* (Ann Arbor: Center for Japanese Studies, University of Michigan, 1999), 81; Arno Kalland, *Fishing Villages in Tokugawa Japan* (Honolulu: University of Hawai'i Press, 1995), 163; Paola Paderni, "Between Constraints and Opportunities: Widows, Witches, and Shrews in Eighteenth-Century China," in Zurndorfer, *Chinese Women in the Imperial Past*, 275; Patricia Buckley Ebrey, *The Inner Quarters: Marriage and the Lives of Chinese Women in the Sung Period* (Berkeley and Los Angeles: University of California Press, 1993), 236.

46. Yu, *Law and Society*, 56, 60.

47. Borri, *Cochin-China*, n.p.; Li and Reid, *Southern Vietnam under the Nguyen*, 74; Yu, *Law and Society*, 44, 56–57, 60; Nhung Tran, "Vietnamese Women at the Crossroads," 65.

48. B and R, 5:155–157. Some items may have recirculated back to the groom's female relatives; see Sakhong, *In Search of Chin Identity*, 66.

49. Geddes, *Migrants*, 60, 81; see also Yu, *Law and Society*, 70.

50. Straver, *De zee van verhalen*, 137.

51. H. J. de Graaf, "De Regenten van Semarang ten tijde van de VOC, 1682–1809," *BKI* 134, no. 2–3 (1978): 301–302, 308n10.

52. Napa Sirisambhand and Alec Gordon, "Seeking Thai Gender History: Using Historical Murals as a Source of Evidence," *International Institute for Asian Studies Newsletter* (February 2001): 23.

53. Arletter Ziegler and Alain Viro, "Stones of Power: Statuary and Megalithism in Nias," in Jean Paul Barbier, ed., *Messages in Stone: Statues and Sculptures from Tribal Indonesia in the Collections of the Barbier-Mueller Museum* (Milan: Skira Editore, 1998), 76n36.

54. Marsden, *History of Sumatra*, 244, 264; Yu, "Bilateral Social Pattern," 229.

55. Knaap, "Pants, Skirts, and Pulpits," 152.

56. P. Drabbe, *Het leven van den Tanémbarees: Ethnografische studie over het Tanémbareesche volk* (Leiden: Brill, 1940), 222. For an illustration of a new mother dressed in the costume befitting a victorious headhunter, see Ruth Barnes, "Women as Headhunters: The Making and Meanring of Textiles in a Southeast Asian Context," in Barnes and Eicher, *Dress and Gender*, 41.

57. Maung Maung, *Law and Custom in Burma*, 73; Emil Forchhammer, trans., *King Wagaru's Mon Dhammasattham (Text, Translation, and Notes)* (Rangoon: Government Printing, 1963; reprint of 1892 edition), 6.

58. Léopold Cadière, *Croyances et pratiques religieuses des Viêtnamiens*, 2nd ed. (Saigon: Imprimerie Nouvelle d'Extrême Orient, 1953), 9, 18, 73.

59. Creese, *Women of the Kakawin World*, 71, 294n108.

60. Spenser St. John, *Life in the Forests of the Far East: Or Travels in North Borneo* (London: Smith, Elder, and Co., 1863), 1:170; William Howell, "Pregnancy and

Childbirth (Restrictions)," in A. J. N. Richards, *The Sea Dyaks*, 39–44; W. W. Skeat, *Malay Magic: Being an Introduction to the Folklore and Popular Religion of the Malay Peninsula* (New York: Dover, 1967; reprint of 1900 edition), 344.

61. Quirino and Garcia, "Manners, Customs, and Beliefs," 433, 442; F. Landa Jocano, ed., *The Philippines at the Spanish Contact* (Manila: MCS Enterprises, 1975), 27–28.

62. Mulholland, *Herbal Medicine*, 20–29, 31; Mills, "Eredia's Description of Malaca," 23, 40, 49; P. A. Leupe, "De Orang Benuas of wilden op Malakka in 1642," *BKI* 8 (1862): 133; H. N. Ridley, "On the Use of the Slow Loris in Malay Medicine," *JSBRAS* 34 (July 1900): 32.

63. Roxanna M. Brown, *The Ceramics of South-East Asia: Their Dating and Identification* (Kuala Lumpur: Oxford University Press, 1977), 53, 260–261; Holt, *Art in Indonesia*, 26–27.

64. Hamzah Yunus, ed., *Kitab Pengetahuan Bahasa: Iaitu Kamus Lughat Melayu Johor-Pahang-Riau-Lingga*, by Raja Ali Haji (Kuala Lumpur: Khazanah Fathaniyah, 1996), 201–202; Mulholland, *Herbal Medicine*, 17, 27.

65. Cited in Penelope Graham, *Iban Shamanism: An Analysis of the Ethnographic Literature* (Canberra: Department of Anthropology, Research School of Pacific Studies, ANU, 1994; reprint of 1987 edition), 43.

66. This was also true of China. See Teng, *Taiwan's Imagined Geography*, 107.

67. Knaap, "Pants, Skirts, and Pulpits," 163.

68. G. de Vries, *Bij de berg-alfoeren op West-Seram: Zeden, gewoonten en mythologie van een oervol* (Zutphen, Netherlands: W. G. Thierne, 1927), 92; Rosemary Gianno, "'Women Are Not Brave Enough': Semelai Male Midwives in the Context of Southeast Asian Cultures," *BKI* 160, no. 1 (2004): 37–39; Dobres, "Digging Up Gender," 213; Appell, "Sex Role Symmetry," 14; Symonds, *Calling in the Soul*, 5, 81; Sather, "The Malevolent *koklir*," 330; Donn V. Hart, "From Pregnancy through Birth," in Hart et al., *Southeast Asian Birth Customs*, 58.

69. Overbeck, "Malay Customs and Beliefs," 264; Sudjiman, *Adat Raja-Raja Melayu*, 59–60.

70. Santi Rozario, "The *dai* and the Doctor: Discourse on Women's Reproductive Health in Rural Bangladesh," in Ram and Jolly, *Maternities and Modernities*, 149; Katharane Edson Mershon, *Seven Plus Seven: Mysterious Life-Rituals in Bali* (New York: Vantage Press, 1971), chap. 5; see also Hicks, *A Maternal Religion*, 31; Roxana Waterson, "Houses and the Built Environment in Island South-East Asia: Tracing Some Shared Themes in the Use of Space," in James J. Fox, ed., *Inside Austronesian Houses: Perspectives on Domestic Designs for Living* (Canberra: Comparative Austronesian Project, Research School of Pacific Studies, ANU, 1993), 229.

71. Mills, "Eredia's Description of Malaca," 48; Rigby, *The Ninety-Nine Laws*, 27, 60, 78.

72. Brewer, *Holy Confrontation*, 210. For other examples, see Balaban, *Spring Essence*, 59, and Kozok, "On Writing," 34.

73. Sudjiman, *Adat Raja-Raja Melayu*, 56–57. For a modern account, see Carol Laderman, *Taming the Wind of Desire: Psychology, Medicine, and Aesthetics in Malay Sha-*

manistic Performance (Berkeley and London: University of California Press, 1993), 132, 141–142.

74. Crawfurd, "Notes on the Population of Java," 44; O. Saito, "Infant Mortality in Pre-Transition Japan: Levels and Trends," in Alain Bideau, Bertrand Desjardins, and Héctor Pérez Brignoli, eds., *Infant and Child Mortality in the Past* (Oxford: Clarendon Press, 1997), 135–156.

75. Cadière, *Croyances et pratiques religieuses,* 72.

76. Coolhaas, *Generale missiven,* 3:786.

77. William Cummings, "History-Making, Making History: Writing the Past in Early Modern Makassar" (PhD diss., University of Hawai'i, 1999), 77.

78. Winstedt, "An Old Minangkabau Legal Digest," 9–10. For modern attitudes, see Jane Belo, "A Study of Customs Pertaining to Twins in Bali," in Jane Belo, ed., *Traditional Balinese Culture* (New York: Columbia University Press, 1970; reprint of 1935 edition), 3–56; Jane R. Hanks, "The Power of Ahka Women," in Nancy Eberhardt, ed., *Gender, Power, and the Construction of the Moral Order: Studies from the Thai Periphery* (Madison, WI: Center for Southeast Asian Studies, University of Wisconsin, 1988), 19.

79. Ochiai Emiko, "The Reproductive Revolution at the End of the Tokugawa Period," in Tonomura et al., *Women and Class in Japanese History,* 189; Sommer, *Sex, Law, and Society,* 13; Yu, *Law and Society,* 79–81.

80. Oliver, *Ancient Tahitian Society,* 961.

81. William Scott, *Barangay,* 118; Blussé and Roessingh, "A Visit to the Past," 73; Nieuhof, *Voyages,* 176.

82. Du Bois, *The People of Alor,* 109.

83. Forest, *Les missionaires française,* 3:97n39.

84. Hart et al., *Southeast Asian Birth Customs,* 50; Richard C. Temple, *The Thirty-Seven Nats: A Phase of Spirit-Worship Prevailing in Burma* (London: Kiscadale, 1991; reprint of 1906 edition), 53, 59.

85. Mills, "Eredia's Description of Malaca," 49; Hill, *Hikayat Abdullah,* 116–117.

86. Phan, *Mission and Catechesis,* 220.

87. Hill, *Hikayat Abdullah,* 36.

88. Knaap, "Pants, Skirts, and Pulpits," 155; de Choisy, *Journal of a Voyage,* 241; Mills, "Eredia's Description of Malaca," 49; Quach-Langlet, "La compassion," 153; Sather, "The Malevolent *koklir,*" 330–331.

89. Marini, *A New and Interesting Description,* 17; Mills, "Eredia's Description of Malaca," 48.

90. Cullinane, "Accounting for Souls," 292–294; Jan Parmentier and Ruurdje Laarhoven, eds., *De avonturen van een VOC-soldaat: Het dagboek van Carolus Van der Haeghe, 1699–1705* (Zutphen, Netherlands: Walburg Press, 1994), 103.

91. Sahai, *The Rama Jataka,* 1:82; Marini, *A New and Interesting Description,* 17. See also Mulholland, *Herbal Medicine,* 51; Clarence T. Maloney, "Tribes of Bangladesh and Synthesis of Bengali Culture," in Mahmud Shah Qureshi, ed., *Tribal Cultures in Bangladesh* (Dhaka: Institute of Bangladesh Studies, Rajshahi University, 1984), 36; Price, "Women's Wild Plant Food Entitlements," 176.

92. Mulholland, *Herbal Medicine,* 51–52; Sudjiman, *Adat Raja-Raja Melayu,* 60–61; Richard J. Coughlin, "Pregnancy and Birth in Vietnam," in Hart et al., *Southeast Asian Birth Customs,* 242.

93. Kumar, *Java and Modern Europe,* 112.

94. Macdonald, *The Practice of Medicine,* 48n1, 50.

95. E.g., Symonds, *Calling in the Soul,* 41–42; B. Andaya, "Localising the Universal," 21–24.

96. Vanessa Maher, "Breast-Feeding in Cross-Cultural Perspective," in *The Anthropology of Breast Feeding: Natural Law or Social Contract?* (New York: St. Martin's Press, 1992), 14–16; Musallam, *Sex and Society in Islam,* 11.

97. Nhung Tran, "Vietnamese Women at the Crossroads," 123. For Ho Xuan Huong's better-known poem, see Balaban, *Spring Essence,* 73, 124; Tran My-Van, "'Come On, Girls,'" 489.

98. Jardine, *The Burmese Empire,* 170; Oki Akira, "Introduction to the History of Disease and Healing in Indonesia," *Forum of International Development Studies* 6 (December 1996): 108, 119–120.

99. Andrea Whittaker, *Intimate Knowledge: Women and Their Health in North-East Thailand* (Sydney: Allen and Unwin, 2000), 86; Rajadhon, *Life and Ritual in Old Siam,* 126; Jardine, *The Burmese Empire,* 74.

100. J. Gonda, *Letterkunde van de Indische Archipel* (Amsterdam: Elsevier, 1947), 101–105. Krappert, *Mythology and Folklore,* 94.

101. J. G. F. Riedel, "De Minahasa in 1825. Bijdrage tot de kennis van Noord-Selebes," *TBG* 18 (1872): 485, 556.

102. William Scott, *Barangay,* 107.

103. Sahai, *The Rama Jataka,* 1:96

104. Nancy K. Florida, "Writing Gender Relations in Nineteenth-Century Java," in Laurie J. Sears, ed., *Fantasizing the Feminine in Indonesia* (Durham, NC, and London: Duke University Press, 1996), 210.

105. Beekman, *The Poison Tree,* 225.

106. John Z. Bowers and Robert W. Carubba, "Drug Abuse and Sexual Binding Spells in Seventeenth-Century Asia: Essays from the *Amoenitatum Exoticarum* of Engelbert Kaempfer," *Journal of the History of Medicine and Allied Sciences* 33, no. 3 (July 1978): 343; Corfield and Morson, *A New Account,* 383–386.

107. Brereton, *Thai Tellings,* 111, 111n28, 126–128; see also Flood and Flood, *Dynastic Chronicles,* 2:39.

108. Ta Van Tai, "The Status of Women in Traditional Vietnam," 102; Nguyen Ngoc Huy et al., *The Lê Code,* 1:215; Blussé, *Strange Company,* 166–167.

109. Kumar, "Encyclopedia-izing," 479, 481–482; Florida, "Writing Gender Relations," 210; Marcel Bonneff, "Préceptes et conseils pour les femmes de Java," *Archipel* 13 (1977): 211–219.

110. Furth, *A Flourishing Yin,* 188–189.

111. Reid, *Southeast Asia in the Age of Commerce,* 1:149; Jan van der Putten, "On Sex, Drugs, and Good Manners: Raja Ali Haji as Lexicographer," *JSEAS* 33, no. 3

(October 2002): 424; Teuku Iskandar, *Catalogue of Malay, Minangkabau, and South Sumatran Manuscripts in the Netherlands* (Leiden: Documentatiebureau Islam-Christendom, 1999), 54; Helen Creese and Laura Bellows, "Erotic Literature in Nineteenth-Century Bali," *JSEAS* 33, no. 3 (October 2002): 393–397; Wieringa, "A Javanese Handbook," 433.

112. Tran My-Van, "'Come On, Girls,'" 417–494; Lustig, *Burmese Classical Poems*, 1.

113. Myint Thien, *Burmese Folk-Songs*, 48.

114. Gervaise, *The Natural and Political History*, 80.

115. Beekman, *The Poison Tree*, 225.

116. Jean Thierry, *L'évolution de la condition de la femme en droit privé Cambodgien* (Phnom Penh: Institut National d'Études Juridiques Politiques et Économiques, 1955), 90; Nguyen Ngoc Huy et al., *The Lê Code*, 1:184, 232–233.

117. Moyer, *The Logic of the Laws*, 66.

118. Chandler, "Normative Poems," 274; Beekman, *The Poison Tree*, 162.

119. See also B. Andaya, "Old Age," 104–105.

120. Kumar, *Java and Modern Europe*, 327, 340; Trager and Koenig, *Burmese Sit-Tans*, 102; Crawfurd, "Notes on the Population of Java," 43.

121. Wiesner, *Women and Gender*, 73–75, 219–230.

122. Walthall, "The Life Cycle," 61–62; Kalland, *Fishing Villages in Tokugawa Japan*, 60; Paderni, "Between Constraints and Opportunities," 262; Sommer, *Sex, Law, and Society*, 166–209.

123. Van den Brink, *Dr. Benjamin Frederick Matthes*, 327.

124. Christoph von Fürer-Haimendorf, *The Konyak Nagas: An Indian Frontier Tribe* (New York: Holt, Rinehart, and Winston, 1969), 98.

125. Nai Pan Hla and Okudaira, *Eleven Mon Dhammasat Texts*, 587.

126. John Winter Jones, trans. and ed., *The Travels of Ludovico di Varthema*, Hakluyt Society, 1st ser., no. 32 (London, 1863), 207–208; Creese, *Women of the Kakawin World*, 210–244.

127. Tiyavanich, *Forest Recollections*, 282.

128. Farah, *Marriage and Sexuality*, 125.

129. Kumar, *Java and Modern Europe*, 379; Brewer, *Holy Confrontation*, 318.

130. Knappert, *Mythology and Folklore*, 98–99; Liam Kelley, "Vietnam through the Eyes of a Chinese Abbot: Darshan's Haiwai Jishi (1694–95)" (MA thesis, University of Hawai'i, 1996), 83; Nhung Tran, "Vietnamese Women at the Crossroads," 115.

131. Mills, "Attack of the Widow Ghosts," 254.

132. Schreurs, *Caraga Antigua*, 125, 127.

133. Ta Van Tai, "The Status of Women in Traditional Vietnam," 130–132; Niemeijer, "Slavery, Ethnicity, and the Economic Independence of Women," 179.

134. Laurel L. Cornell, "The Deaths of Old Women: Folklore and Differential Mortality in Nineteenth-Century Japan," in Bernstein, *Recreating Japanese Women*, 79; Walthall, "The Life Cycle," 66–67.

135. Judith Schlehe, "Garments for the Goddess of the Sea," in Nabholz-Kartaschoff et al., *Weaving Patterns of Life,* 321; Jet Bakels, "The Symbolism of Baduy Adat Clothing on the Efficacy of Colours, Patterns, and Plants," in Nabholz-Kartaschoff et al., *Weaving Patterns of Life,* 351.

136. Parry, *The Lakkers,* 128; Hoskins, "Why Do Ladies Sing the Blues?" 143.

137. A. Heuting, "Het woord kabayan en de oude vrouw," *BKI* 90 (1933): 142–144; Mulyadi, *Hikayat Indraputra,* 32, 171; see also Anatole-Roger Peltier, *The White Nightjar: A Lao Tale* (Chiang Mai, Thailand: EFEO, 1999), 15.

138. Peter Laslett, introduction to David I. Kertzer and Peter Laslett, eds., *Aging in the Past: Demography, Society, and Old Age* (Berkeley and London: University of California Press, 1995), 40; Malarney, "Return to the Past?" 235.

139. Wiesner, *Women and Gender,* 76; Kumar, *Java and Modern Europe,* 327, 340; Trager and Koenig, *Burmese Sit-Tans,* 102.

140. Richard Wall, "Elderly Persons and Members of Their Households in England and Wales from Preindustrial Times to the Present," in Kertzer and Laslett, *Aging in the Past,* 88; Margreet van Till, "Social Care in Eighteenth-Century Batavia: The Poorhouse, 1725–1750," *Itinerario* 19, no. 1 (1995): 20.

141. Tossa, *Phādāeng Nāng Ai,* 82–88.

142. Chamindaji Gamage, *Buddhism and Sensuality as Recorded in the Theravada Canon* (Evanston, IL: Northwestern University, 1998), 136–138; Reynolds and Reynolds, *Three Worlds,* 98.

143. Brewer, *Holy Confrontation,* chap. 9; Mills, "Eredia's Description of Malaca," 48.

144. Forest, *Les missionaires française,* 3:253.

145. William Scott, *Barangay,* 81; see also Barbara Watson Andaya and Yoneo Ishii, "Religious Developments in Southeast Asia, c. 1500–1800," in Nicholas Tarling, ed., *The Cambridge History of Southeast Asia* (Sydney: University of Cambridge Press, 1992), 1:510.

146. Than Tun, *Royal Orders,* 4:102.

147. Frank Swettenham, *Malay Sketches* (Singapore: Graham Brash, 1984; reprint of 1895 edition), 198–199; Lyn Parker, *From Subjects to Citizens: Balinese Villages in the Indonesian Nation-State* (Copenhagen: Nordic Institute of Asian Studies Press, 2003), 186; for other references, see Morris, *In the Place of Origins,* 82, 129, 178, 264–265; Rajadhon, *Life and Ritual in Old Siam,* 119; Melford Spiro, *Burmese Supernaturalism* (Philadelphia: Institute for the Study of Human Issues, 1967), 25–30; Sather, "The Malevolent *koklir*," 321–324; Watson and Ellen, *Understanding Witchcraft and Sorcery,* 1; Miedema and Reesink, *One Head, Many Faces,* 142.

148. Ajay Skaria, "Women, Witchcraft, and Gratuitous Violence in Colonial Western India," *Past and Present* 155 (May 1997): 110.

149. Philip A. Kuhn, *Soulstealers: The Chinese Sorcery Scare of 1768* (Cambridge, MA: Harvard University Press, 1990), 1–28, 227.

150. Barrow, *A Voyage to Cochinchina,* 331.

151. R. Ng. Poebatjaraka, "De Calon Arang," *BKI* 82 (1926): 110–180; Miguel Covarrubias, *Island of Bali* (New York: Alfred A. Knopf, 1937), 344.

152. Roy Ellen, "Anger, Anxiety, and Sorcery: An Analysis of Some Nuaulu Case Material from Seram, Eastern Indonesia," in Watson and Ellen, *Understanding Witchcraft and Sorcery,* 97; Gregory Forth, "Social and Symbolic Aspects of the Witch among the Nage of Eastern Indonesia," in Watson and Ellen, *Understanding Witchcraft and Sorcery,* 119n2; Parker, *From Subjects to Citizens,* 183–188; Margaret Wiener, *Visible and Invisible Realms: Power, Magic, and Colonial Conquest in Bali* (Chicago: University of Chicago Press, 1995), 219.

Conclusion

1. Patricia Buckley Ebrey, *Women and the Family in Chinese History* (London and New York: Routledge, 2003), 12, 61, 88.

2. Wendt, "The Dharma of Women's Work"; Kalpana Ram, *Mukkuvar Women: Gender Hegemony and Capitalist Transformation in a South Indian Fishing Community* (London: Zed Books, 1991), 80.

3. Hezel, *The New Shape,* 11; Spriggs, *The Island Melanesians,* 265–266, 279–280.

4. Parkin, *A Guide to Austroasiatic Speakers,* 37; Symes, *An Account of an Embassy,* 1:150–165; L. P. Mathur, *Kala Pani: History of the Andaman and Nicobar Islands* (Delhi: Eastern Book Corp., 1985), 194.

5. Michaud, *Turbulent Times,* 1–14.

6. Teng, *Taiwan's Imagined Geography,* 37, 173–177.

7. Spriggs, *The Island Melanesians,* 165.

8. Pemberton, *On the Subject of "Java,"* 40–42.

9. Launay, *Histoire de la mission de Siam,* 1:87.

10. Sarah Garah, "Struggles of Women and Girls—Simbu Province, Papua New Guinea," in Sinclair Dinnen and Alison Ley, eds., *Reflections on Violence in Melanesia* (Sydney: Hawkins Press; Canberra: Asia Pacific Press, 2000), 162. In East Timor the Asia Foundation reported that 32 percent of male respondents believed that violence toward a wife was justified because they paid a bride-price. See Asia Foundation, "Law and Justice in East Timor: A Survey of Citizen Awareness and Attitudes Regarding Law and Justice in East Timor" (2004), http://www.asiafoundation.org/pdf/easttimor_lawsurvey.pdf, 84.

11. Rosemary Firth, *Housekeeping among Malay Peasants* (London: London School of Economics, Athlone Press, 1943); Du Bois, *The People of Alor.*

12. Kirstin Pauka, *Theater and Martial Arts in West Sumatra: Randai and Silek of the Minangkabau* (Athens: Ohio University Center for International Studies, 1998), 61, 64, 79; Mattani, *Dance, Drama, and Theatre in Thailand,* 7–9.

13. Michael Flecker, "The Archaeological Excavation of the 10th Century *Intan* Shipwreck" (PhD diss., University of Singapore, 2001), 108; Do-Lam, *La mère et l'enfant,* 205.

14. John Guy, *Woven Cargoes: Indian Textiles in the East* (London: Thames and Hudson, 1998), 111.

15. Liam Kelley, "Vietnam as a Domain of Manifest Civility (Van Hien chi Bang)," *JSEAS* 34, no. 1 (February 2003): 75.

16. Vibeke Roeper and Roelof van Gelder, *In dienst van de Compagnie: Leven bij de VOC in Honderd Getuigenissen 1602–1799* (Amsterdam: Athenaeum, 2002), 153.

17. Diaz-Trechuelo, "Eighteenth-Century Philippine Economy," 114–115; see the illustrations in Claudine Salmon, "Les dessins industriels philippins d'Antonio D. Malantie: Une commande de la mission de Lagrené en China (1843–1846)," *Archipel* 67 (2004): 65–71.

18. Roeper and Van Gelder, *In dienst van de Compagnie,* 129–130; van Till, "Social Care in Eighteenth-Century Batavia," 20, 22.

19. Ricklefs, *War, Culture, and Economy,* 120; Than Tun, *Royal Orders,* 3:64.

20. Damrong Tayanin, *Being Kammu: My Village, My Life* (Ithaca, NY: Southeast Asia Program, Cornell University, 1994), 81–82, 85.

21. Ann R. Kinney with Marijke Klokke and Lydia Kieven, *Worshiping Siva and Buddha: The Temple Art of East Java* (Honolulu: University of Hawai'i Press, 2003), 147–148.

22. Wendy Doniger O'Flaherty, *Women, Androgynes, and Other Mythical Beasts* (Chicago: University of Chicago, 1980), 236, 317; Robert Wessing, introduction to "The Divine Female in Indonesia," special issue, *Asian Folklore Studies* 56, no. 2 (1997): 205; G. A. J. Hazeu, "Nini-Towong," *TBG* 43 (1901): 67–70.

Selected Bibliography

This bibliography contains only those works that have been cited more than once in the text. Full details for other cited works are given in the notes.

Adriani, Nicolaus. "De Toradjasche vrouw als priesteres." In *Verzamelde geschriften,* vol. 2, 180–215. Haarlem: De Erven F. Bohn, 1932.

Agarwal, Bina. *A Field of One's Own: Gender and Land Rights in South Asia.* Cambridge: Cambridge University Press, 1994.

Ahmed, Leila. *Women and Gender in Islam.* New Haven, CT, and London: Yale University Press, 1992.

Andaya, Barbara Watson. "The Cloth Trade in Jambi and Palembang Society during the Seventeenth and Eighteenth Centuries." *Indonesia* 48 (1989): 26–46.

———. "Delineating Female Space: Seclusion and the State in Pre-Modern Island Southeast Asia." In B. Andaya, *Other Pasts,* 231–253.

———. "From Temporary Wife to Prostitute: Sexuality and Economic Change in Early Modern Southeast Asia." *Journal of Women's History* 9, no. 4 (February 1998): 11–34.

———. "History, Headhunting, and Gender in Monsoon Asia: Comparative and Longitudinal Views." *South East Asia Research* 12, no. 1 (March 2004): 13–52.

———. "Localising the Universal: Women, Motherhood, and the Appeal of Early Theravada Buddhism." *JSEAS* 33, no. 1 (February 2002): 1–30.

———. "Old Age: Widows, Midwives, and the Question of 'Witchcraft' in Early Modern Southeast Asia." *Asia-Pacific Forum* 28 (June 2005): 104–147.

———, ed. *Other Pasts: Women, Gender, and History in Early Modern Southeast Asia.* Honolulu: Center for Southeast Asian Studies, University of Hawai'i, 2000.

———. *Perak, the Abode of Grace: A Study of an Eighteenth-Century Malay State.* Kuala Lumpur: Oxford in Asia, 1979.

———. *To Live as Brothers: Southeast Sumatra in the Seventeenth and Eighteenth Centuries.* Honolulu: University of Hawai'i Press, 1993.

———. "Women and Economic Change: The Pepper Trade in Pre-Modern Southeast Asia." *JESHO* 38, no. 2 (1995): 165–190.

Andaya, Leonard Y. "The *Bissu:* Study of a Third Gender in Indonesia." In B. Andaya, *Other Pasts,* 27–46.

———. *The Heritage of Arung Palakka: A History of South Sulawesi (Celebes) in the Seventeenth Century.* The Hague: Nijhoff, 1981.

———. *The Kingdom of Johor 1641–1728: Economic and Political Developments.* Kuala Lumpur: Oxford University Press, 1975.

————. "'A Very Good-Natured but Awe-Inspiring Government': The Reign of a Successful Queen in Seventeenth-Century Aceh." In Elsbeth Locher-Scholten and Pieter Rietbergen, eds., *Hof en Handel: Aziatische Vorsten en de VOC 1620–1720,* 59–84. Leiden: KITLV Press, 2004.

————. *The World of Maluku: Eastern Indonesia in the Early Modern Period.* Honolulu: University of Hawai'i Press, 1993.

Appell, Laura W. R. "Sex Role Symmetry among the Rungus of Sabah." In Sutlive, *Female and Male in Borneo,* 1–56.

Armijo-Hussein, Jacqueline M., trans. "'The Customs of Various Barbarians,' by Li Jing (1251–?)." In Mann and Cheng, *Under Confucian Eyes,* 85–102.

Atkinson, Jane Monnig, and Shelly Errington, eds. *Power and Difference: Gender in Island Southeast Asia.* Stanford, CA: Stanford University Press, 1990.

Aung-Thwin, Michael. *Pagan: The Origins of Modern Burma.* Honolulu: University of Hawai'i Press, 1985.

Bacus, Elisabeth A. "Accessing Prestige and Power: Women in the Political Economy of Protohistoric and Early Historic Visayan Polities. In Nelson and Rosen-Ayalon, *In Pursuit of Gender,* 307–322.

Balaban, John, ed. and trans. *Spring Essence: The Poetry of Ho Xuan Huong.* Port Townsend, WA: Copper Canyon Press, 2000.

Ball, V., ed. *Travels in India by Jean-Baptiste Tavernier, Baron of Aubonne.* Edited by William Crooke. New Delhi: Oriental Books, 1977. Reprint of 1889 edition.

Bankoff, Greg. *In Verbo Sacerdotis: The Judicial Powers of the Catholic Church in Nineteenth-Century Philippines.* Darwin: Centre for Southeast Asian Studies, Northern Territory University, 1992.

Barend-van Haeften, Marijke. *Oost-Indië gespiegeld: Nicolaas de Graaf, een schrijvend chirurgijn in dienst van de VOC.* Zutphen, Netherlands: Walburg Press, 1992.

Barlow, Jeffrey G. "The Zhuang Minority Peoples of the Sino-Vietnamese Frontier in the Song Period." *JSEAS* 18, no. 2 (September 1987): 250–269.

Barnes, Ruth, and Joanne B. Eicher, eds. *Dress and Gender: Making and Meaning in Cultural Contexts.* New York and Oxford: Berg, 1992.

Barrow, John. *A Voyage to Cochinchina.* Kuala Lumpur: Oxford in Asia, 1975. Reprint of 1806 edition.

Bartholmeusz, Tessa. *Women under the Bō Tree: Buddhist Nuns in Sri Lanka.* Cambridge: Cambridge University Press, 1994.

Bastin, John. *The British in West Sumatra (1685–1825).* Kuala Lumpur: University of Malaya Press, 1965.

————. *Lady Raffles: By Effort and Virtue.* Singapore: National Museum, 1994.

Beeckman, Daniel. *A Voyage to and from the Island of Borneo.* London: Dawsons, 1973. Reprint of 1718 edition.

Beekman, E. M., ed. and trans. *The Poison Tree: Selected Writings of Rumphius on the Natural History of the Indies.* Kuala Lumpur: Oxford University Press, 1993.

Bernstein, Gail Lee, ed. *Recreating Japanese Women, 1600–1945.* Berkeley: University of California Press, 1991.

Bik, A. J. E. A., ed. *Dagverhaal eener reis, gedaan in het jaar 1824 tot nadere voorkenning der eilanden Keffing, Goram, Groot- en Klein Kei en de Aroe Eilanden.* Leiden: Sijthoff, 1928.

Blackburn, Anne M. *Buddhist Learning and Textual Practice in Eighteenth-Century Lankan Monastic Culture.* Princeton, NJ: Princeton University Press, 2001.

Blair, Emma, and James Alexander Robertson. *The Philippine Islands 1493–1898.* 55 vols. Cleveland: Arthur H. Clark, 1903–1909.

Blussé, Leonard. "*Kongkoan* and *Kongsi:* Representations of Chinese Identity and Ethnicity in Early Modern Southeast Asia." In Leonard Blussé and Felipe Fernández-Armesto, eds., *Shifting Communities and Identity Formation in Early Modern Asia,* 93–106. Leiden: Research School of Asian, African, and Amerindian Studies, Leiden University, 2003.

———. *Strange Company: Chinese Settlers, Mestizo Women, and the Dutch in VOC Batavia.* VKI 122. Dordrecht: Foris, 1986.

Blussé, Leonard, and Marius P. H. Roessingh. "A Visit to the Past: Soulang, a Formosan Village anno 1623." *Archipel* 27 (1984): 63–80.

Blust, Robert. "Linguistic Evidence for Some Early Austronesian Taboos." *American Anthropologist* 83, no. 2 (1981): 285–319.

Boomgaard, Peter. *Children of the Colonial State: Population Growth and Economic Development in Java, 1795–1880.* Amsterdam: Free University Press, 1989.

Borri, Christoforo. *Cochin-China.* Amsterdam and New York: Theatrum Orbis Terrarum, 1970. Reprint of 1633 edition.

Bowrey, Thomas. *A Geographical Account of Countries Round the Bay of Bengal, 1669 to 1679.* Edited by Richard Carnac Temple. Cambridge: Hakluyt Society, 1905.

Brereton, Bonnie Pacala. *Thai Tellings of Phra Malai: Texts and Rituals Concerning a Popular Buddhist Saint.* Tempe, AZ: Program for Southeast Asia Studies, 1995.

Brewer, Carolyn. *Holy Confrontation: Religion, Gender, and Sexuality in the Philippines, 1521–1685.* Manila: Institute of Women's Studies, St. Scholastica's College, 2001.

Brink, H. van den. *Dr. Benjamin Frederick Matthes: Zijn leven en arbeid in dienst van het Nederlandsch bijbelgenootschap.* Amsterdam: Nederlandsch Bijbelgenootschap, 1943.

Brummelhuis, Han ten. *Merchant, Courtier, and Diplomat: A History of the Contacts between the Netherlands and Thailand.* Lochem-Gent: De Tijdstroom, 1987.

Brun, Viggo, and Trond Schumacher. *Traditional Herbal Medicine in Northern Thailand.* Berkeley: University of California Press, 1987.

Butler, Lee. *Emperor and Aristocracy in Japan, 1467–1680: Resilience and Renewal.* Cambridge, MA: Harvard University Asia Center, 2002.

Cadière, Léopold. *Croyances et pratiques religieuses des Viêtnamiens.* 2nd ed. Saigon: Imprimerie Nouvelle d'Extrême Orient, 1953.

———. "Une princesse chrétienne à la cour des premiers Nguyên: Madame Marie." *BAVH* 26, no. 2 (1939): 63–130.

Carey, Peter, ed. *The Archive of Yogyakarta.* Vol. 1, *Documents Relating to Political and*

Internal Court Affairs, 1792–1819. London: Oxford University Press for the British Academy, 1980.

———, ed. *The British in Java, 1811–1816: A Javanese Account.* London: Oxford University Press for the British Academy, 1992.

Carroll, John. "Berunai in the Boxer Codex." *JMBRAS* 55, no. 2 (1982): 1–25.

Chaki-Sircar, Manjusri. *Feminism in a Traditional Society: Women of the Manipur Valley.* New Delhi: Shakti Books, 1984.

Chandler, David. *A History of Cambodia.* 3rd ed. Boulder, CO: Westview Press, 2000.

———. "Normative Poems *(Chbab)* and Pre-Colonial Cambodian Society." *JSEAS* 15, no. 2 (September 1984): 271–279.

Choi Byung Wook. *Southern Vietnam under the Reign of Minh Mang (1820–1841): Central Policies and Local Response.* Ithaca, NY: Southeast Asia Program, Cornell University, 2004.

Choisy, Abbé de. *Journal of a Voyage to Siam, 1685–1686.* Translated and edited by Michael Smithies. Kuala Lumpur: Oxford University Press, 1993.

Chou Ta-Kuan. *Notes on the Customs of Cambodia.* Translated into English by J. Gilman D'Arcy Paul from Paul Pelliot's French translation. Bangkok: Social Science Association Press, 1967.

Christie, Jan Wisseman. "Ikat to Batik? Epigraphic Data on Textiles in Java from the Ninth to the Fifteenth Centuries." In Nabholz-Kartaschoff et al., *Weaving Patterns of Life,* 11–30.

Coedès, George. *Histoire ancienne des états hindouisés d'Extrême-Orient.* Hanoi: Imprimerie d'Extrême-Orient, 1944.

Cole, Alan. *Mothers and Sons in Chinese Buddhism.* Stanford, CA: Stanford University Press, 1998.

Connell, R. W. "The State, Gender, and Sexual Politics: Theory and Appraisal." *Theory and Society* 19, no. 5 (October 1990): 507–544.

Coolhaas, W. Ph., ed. *Generale missiven van gouverneurs-generaal en raden aan heren XVII der Verenigde Oostindische Compagnie.* The Hague: Nijhoff, 1960.

Corfield, Justin, and Ian Morson, eds. *British Sea-Captain Alexander Hamilton's* A New Account of the East Indies *(17th–18th Century).* Lewiston, NY: Edwin Mellon Press, 2001.

Cortesão, Armando, ed. *The Suma Oriental of Tomé Pires.* 2 vols. New Delhi: Asian Educational Services, 1990. Reprint of 1944 edition.

Crawfurd, John. "Notes on the Population of Java." *JIAEA* 3 (1849): 42–49.

Creese, Helen. *Women of the Kakawin World: Marriage and Sexuality in the Indic Courts of Java and Bali.* Armonk, NY: M. E. Sharpe, 2004.

Csete, Anne. "The Li Mother Spirit and the Struggle for Hainan's Land and Legends." *Late Imperial China* 22, no. 2 (2001): 91–123.

Cullinane, Michael. "Accounting for Souls: Ecclesiastical Sources for the Study of Philippine Demographic History." In Daniel F. Doeppers and Peter Xenos, eds., *Population and History: The Demographic Origins of the Modern Philippines,* 281–346. Madison: Center for Southeast Asian Studies, University of Wisconsin, 1998.

Cummings, William. *Making Blood White*. Honolulu: University of Hawai'i Press, 2002.

Cummins, J. S., trans. and ed. *The Travels and Controversies of Friar Domingo Navarrete 1618–1656*. Vol. 1. Cambridge: Cambridge University Press for the Hakluyt Society, 1962.

Cushman, Richard, trans., and David K. Wyatt, ed. *The Royal Chronicles of Ayutthaya*. Bangkok: Siam Society, 2000.

Dagh-Register gehouden int casteel te Batavia. Batavia and The Hague: Bataviaasch Genootschap; Nijhoff; Kolff, 1887–1931.

Dampier, William. *A New Voyage around the World*. Edited by Albert Gray. New York: Dover Publications, 1968. Reprint of 1697 edition.

Davis, Richard. *Muang Metaphysics: A Study of Northern Thai Myth and Ritual*. Bangkok: Pandora, 1982.

Day, Tony. *Fluid Iron: State Formation in Southeast Asia*. Honolulu: University of Hawai'i Press, 2002.

Diamond, Norma. "Defining the Miao: Ming, Qing, and Contemporary Views." In Stevan Harrell, ed., *Cultural Encounters on China's Ethnic Frontiers*, 92–116. Seattle and London: University of Washington Press, 1985.

Diaz-Trechueolo, Maria Lourdes. "Eighteenth-Century Philippine Economy: Agriculture." *Philippine Studies* (January 1966): 65–126.

Diran, Richard K. *The Vanishing Tribes of Burma*. London: Seven Dials, 1999.

Dobres, Marcia-Anne. "Digging Up Gender in the Earliest Human Societies." In Teresa A. Meade and Merry E. Wiesner-Hanks, eds., *A Companion to Gender History*, 211–226. Malden, MA: Blackwell Publishing, 2004.

Do-Lam, Chi Lan. *La mère et l'enfant dans le Viêtnam d'autrefois*. Paris: L'Harmattan, 1998.

Drewes, G. W. J. *De biografie van een Minangkabausen peperhandelaar in de Lampungs*. The Hague: Nijhoff, 1961.

Drewes, G. W. J., and L. K. Brakel. *The Poems of Hamzah Fansuri*. Bibliotheca Indonesica for KITLV. Dordrecht: Foris, 1986.

Dror, Olga. "Doan thi Diem's 'Story of the Van Cat Goddess' as a Story of Emancipation." *JSEAS* 33, no. 1 (February 2002): 63–72.

Du Bois, Cora. *The People of Alor: A Social-Psychological Study of an East Indian Island*. Minneapolis: University of Minnesota Press, 1944.

Duggan, Geneviève. *Ikats of Savu: Women Weaving History in Eastern Indonesia*. Bangkok: White Lotus, 2001.

Durand, Maurice. *Technique et panthéon des médiums Viêtnamiens*. Paris: École Française d'Extrême Orient, 1959.

Eaton, Richard M. *The Rise of Islam and the Bengal Frontier, 1204–1760*. Berkeley: University of California Press, 1993.

Eller, Cynthia. *The Myth of Matriarchal Prehistory: Why an Invented Past Won't Give Women a Future*. Boston: Beacon Press, 2000.

Elvin, Mark. "Blood and Statistics: Reconstructing the Population Dynamics of Late

Imperial China from the Biographies of Virtuous Women in Local Gazetteers." In Zurndorfer, *Chinese Women in the Imperial Past*, 135–222.

Elwin, Verrier, ed. *India's North-East Frontier in the Nineteenth Century*. London: Oxford University Press, 1959.

———. *The Nagas in the Nineteenth Century*. London: Oxford University Press, 1969.

Farah, Madelaine, trans. *Marriage and Sexuality in Islam: A Translation of al-Ghazālī's Book on the Etiquette of Marriage from the Ihyā'*. Salt Lake City: University of Utah Press, 1984.

Finney, Ben. "Colonizing the Island World." In Ward Goodenough, ed., *Prehistoric Settlement of the Pacific*, 71–116. Philadelphia: American Philosophical Society, 1996.

Flood, Thadeus, and Chadin Flood, trans. and eds. *The Dynastic Chronicles of the Bangkok Era: The First Reign*. Tokyo: Centre for East Asian Cultural Studies, 1978 (vol. 1), 1990 (vol. 2).

Florida, Nancy K. "Writing Gender Relations in Nineteenth-Century Java." In Laurie J. Sears, ed., *Fantasizing the Feminine in Indonesia*, 207–224. Durham, NC, and London: Duke University Press, 1996.

Forest, Alain. *Les missionnaires français au Tonkin et au Siam XVIIᵉ–XVIIIᵉ siècles: Analyse comparée d'un relatif succès et d'un total échec*. Paris: L'Harmattan, 1998.

Forrest, Thomas. *A Voyage to New Guinea and the Moluccas from Balambangan*. Kuala Lumpur: Oxford University Press, 1969. Reprint of 1779 edition.

Fraser-Lu, Sylvia. *Burmese Crafts: Past and Present*. New York: Oxford University Press, 1994.

Furnivall, J. S. "Matriarchal Vestiges in Burma." *Journal of the Burma Research Society* 1, no. 1 (1911): 15–30.

Furth, Charlotte. *A Flourishing Yin: Gender in China's Medical History, 960–1665*. Berkeley and London: University of California Press, 1999.

Gait, Edward. *A History of Assam*. 2nd rev. ed. Calcutta and Simla: Thacker, Spink, and Co., 1926.

Geddes, William Robert. *Migrants of the Mountains: The Cultural Ecology of the Blue Miao (Hmong Njua) of Thailand*. Oxford: Clarendon Press, 1976.

Gervaise, Nicolas. *Description historique du royaume de Macassar*. Edited by Jean-Pierre Duteil. Paris: Éditions Kimé, 2003. A reliable translation is *An Historical Description of Macasar in the East Indies* (London: Leigh and Midwinter, 1701).

———. *Histoire naturelle et politique du royaume de Siam*. Translated as *The Natural and Political History of the Kingdom of Siam* and edited by John Villiers. Bangkok: White Lotus, 1989.

Gesick, Lorraine M. *In the Land of Lady White Blood: Southern Thailand and the Meaning of History*. NY: Southeast Asia Program, Cornell University, 1995.

Gibson, Thomas. *And the Sun Pursued the Moon: Symbolic Knowledge and Traditional Authority among the Makassar*. Honolulu: University of Hawai'i Press, 2005.

Giladi, Avner. *Infants, Parents, and Wet Nurses: Medieval Islamic Views on Breast-Feeding and Their Social Implications*. Leiden: Brill, 1999.

Gittinger, Mattiebelle, and H. Leedom Lefferts Jr., eds. *Textiles and the Tai Experience in Southeast Asia*. Washington, DC: Textile Museum, 1992.

Goens, Rijklof van. *Javaense reyse: De bezoeken van een VOC gezant aan het hof van Mataram 1648–1654*. Edited by Darja van Wever. Amsterdam: Terra Incognita, 1995.

Gommans, Jos, and Jacques Leider, eds. *The Maritime Frontier of Burma: Exploring Political, Cultural, and Commercial Interaction in the Indian Ocean World, 1200–1800*. Leiden: KITLV Press, 2002.

Gordon, Alec. "Women in Thai Society as Depicted in Mural Paintings." In Michael C. Howard, Wattana Wattanapun, and Alec Gordon, eds., *Traditional T'ai Arts in Contemporary Perspective*, 175–192. Bangkok: White Lotus, 1998.

Gregor, Thomas A., and Donald Tuzin, eds. *Gender in Amazonia and Melanesia: An Exploration of the Comparative Method*. Berkeley: University of California Press, 2001.

Griswold, A. B., and Prasert na Nagara. "Epigraphic and Historical Studies, No. 17: The Judgements of King Man Ray." *JSS* 65, no. 1 (January 1977): 237–260.

Gunson, Neil, ed. *The Changing Pacific: Essays in Honour of H. E. Maude*. Melbourne: Oxford University Press, 1978.

———. "Sacred Women Chiefs and Female 'Headmen' in Polynesian History." In Caroline Ralston and Nicholas Thomas, eds., "Sanctity and Power: Gender in Polynesian History," special issue, *Journal of Pacific History* 22, no. 3–4 (July–October 1987): 139–168.

Guthrie, Elizabeth. "Outside the Sima." *Udaya: Journal of Khmer Studies* 2 (2001): 7–18.

Hambly, Gavin R. G., ed. *Women in the Medieval Islamic World: Power, Patronage, and Piety*. New York: St. Martin's Press, 1998.

Hamid, Ismail. *The Malay Islamic Hikayat*. Kuala Lumpur: Universiti Kebangsaan Malaysia, 1983.

Hamilton, Roy W., ed. *The Art of Rice: Spirit and Sustenance in Asia*. Los Angeles: UCLA Fowler Museum of Cultural History, 2003.

Hanley, Sarah. "Engendering the State: Family Formation and State Building in Early Modern France." *French Historical Studies* 16, no. 1 (Spring 1989): 4–27.

Hanlon, David. "Beyond 'the English Method of Tattooing': Decentering the Practice of History in Oceania." *Contemporary Pacific* 15, no. 1 (Spring 2003): 19–40.

Harris, Ian. *Cambodian Buddhism: History and Practice*. Honolulu: University of Hawai'i Press, 2005.

Hart, Donn V., Phya Anuman Rajadhon, and Richard J. Coughlin. *Southeast Asian Birth Customs: Three Studies in Human Reproduction*. New Haven, CT: Human Relations Area Files, 1965.

Harvey, G. E. *History of Burma*. London: Frank Cass, 1967. Reprint of 1925 edition.

Hashim, Ruzy Suliza. *Out of the Shadows: Women in Malay Court Narratives*. Bangi: Universiti Kebangsaan Malaysia, 2003.

Hazeu, G. A. J. "Tjeribonsch wetboek (pepakem tjerbon) van her jaar 1768." *VBG* 55 (1905).

Heersink, Christiaan Gerard. "The Green Gold of Selayar: A Socio-economic History of an Indonesian Coconut Island, c. 1600–1950; Perspectives from a Periphery." PhD diss., Free University, Amsterdam, 1995.

Henry, Eric. "Chinese and Indigenous Influences in Vietnamese Verse Romances of the Nineteenth Century." *Crossroads* 15, no. 2 (2001): 1–41.

Heringa, Rens, and Harmen C. Veldhuisen, eds. *Fabric of Enchantment: Batik from the North Coast of Java.* Los Angeles: Los Angeles County Museum of Art, 1996.

Hertz, Solange, trans. *Rhodes of Vietnam.* Westminster, MD: Newman Press, 1966.

Hezel, Francis X., SJ. *The New Shape of Old Island Cultures: A Half Century of Social Change in Micronesia.* Honolulu: University of Hawai'i Press, 2001.

Hicks, David. *A Maternal Religion: The Role of Women in Tetum Myth and Ritual.* Special Report 22. De Kalb: Center for Southeast Asian Studies, Northern Illinois University, 1984.

Higham, Charles. *The Bronze Age of Southeast Asia.* Cambridge: Cambridge University Press, 1996.

Hill, A. H., trans. and ed. *The Hikayat Abdullah.* Kuala Lumpur: Oxford University Press, 1970.

Hoadley, Mason C. *Selective Judicial Competence: The Cirebon-Priangan Legal Administration, 1680–1792.* Ithaca, NY: Southeast Asia Program, Cornell University, 1994.

Hoadley, Mason C., and M. B. Hooker. *An Introduction to Javanese Law: A Translation and Commentary on the Agama.* AAS Monograph 37. Tucson: University of Arizona Press, 1982.

Hoang Bao Chau, Phu Duc Thao, and Huu Ngoc, eds. *Vietnamese Traditional Medicine.* Hanoi: The Gioi, 1992.

Hogendorp, W. van. "Vervolg van beschrijving van het eiland Timor." *VBG* 2 (1780): 63–101.

Holt, Claire. *Art in Indonesia.* Ithaca, NY, and London: Cornell University Press, 1967.

Hooker, M. B. "The Trengganu Inscription in Malayan Legal History." *JMBRAS* 49, no. 2 (1976): 127–131.

Hose, Charles, and William McDougall. *The Pagan Tribes of Borneo.* 2 vols. London: Oxford University Press, 1993. Reprint of 1912 edition.

Hoskins, Janet. "Why Do Ladies Sing the Blues? Indigo Dyeing, Cloth Production, and Gender Symbolism in Kodi." In Annette B. Weiner and Jane Schneider, eds., *Cloth and Human Experience,* 141–173. Washington, DC, and London: Smithsonian Institution Press, 1989.

Hostetler, Laura. *Qing Colonial Enterprise: Ethnography and Cartography in Early Modern China.* Chicago: University of Chicago Press, 2001.

Htin Aung. *Burmese Law Tales: The Legal Element in Burmese Folk-lore.* London: Oxford University Press, 1962.

Hull, Isabel V. *Sexuality, State, and Civil Society in Germany, 1700–1815*. Ithaca, NY, and London: Cornell University Press, 1996.

Huxley, Andrew. "The Importance of the Dhammathats in Burmese Law and Culture." *Journal of Burma Studies* 1, no. 1 (1997): 1–17.

Huynh Sanh Thong. *The Heritage of Vietnamese Poetry*. New Haven, CT, and London: Yale University Press, 1979.

Iperen, J. van. "Beschryvinge van eene blanke negerin uit de Papoesche eilanden." *VBG* 2 (1780): 229–244.

Irwin, Geoffrey. *The Prehistoric Exploration and Colonisation of the Pacific*. Cambridge: Cambridge University Press, 1992.

Ishii, Yoneo. *The Junk Trade from Southeast Asia: Translations from the Tôsen Fusetsu-gaki 1674–1723*. Singapore: ISEAS; Canberra: Research School of Pacific and Asian Studies, ANU, 1998.

Ito Takeshi. "The World of the *Adat Aceh*." PhD diss., ANU, 1984.

Izikowitz, Karl Gustav. *Lamet: Hill Peasants in French Indochina*. With addendum by Rodney Needham. New York: AMS Press, 1979. Reprint of 1960 edition.

Jacob, Judith. *The Traditional Literature of Cambodia: A Preliminary Guide*. Oxford: Oxford University Press, 1996.

Jacobs, Hubert, ed. *A Treatise on the Moluccas (c. 1544) . . . of Antonio Galvão*. Rome: Jesuit Historical Institute, 1971.

Jacobsen, Trudy. "Apsarā, Accoutrements, Activists: A History of Women and Power in Cambodia." PhD diss., University of Queensland, 2004.

Jardine, John, ed. *The Burmese Empire a Hundred Years Ago as Described by Father Sangermano*. Delhi: BR Publishing, 1984. Reprint of 1893 edition.

Javellana, René B., ed. and trans. *Casaysayan nang Pasiong Mahal ni Jesuscristong Panginoon natin na sucat ipag-alab nang puso nang sinomang babasa*. Quezon City: Ateneo de Manila University Press, 1988.

Jones, Eric Alan. "Wives, Slaves, and Concubines: A History of the Female Underclass in Dutch Asia." PhD diss., University of California, Berkeley, 2003.

Kalland, Arno. *Fishing Villages in Tokugawa Japan*. Honolulu: University of Hawai'i Press, 1995.

Kammerer, Cornelia. "Gateway to the Akha World: Kinship, Ritual, and Community among Highlanders of Thailand." PhD diss., University of Chicago, 1986.

Kathirithamby-Wells, J. *The British West Sumatran Presidency (1760–1785): Problems of Early Colonial Enterprise*. Kuala Lumpur: University of Malaya, 1977.

Kern, H., ed. *Het itinerario van Jan Huygen van Linschoten 1579–1582*. The Hague: Martinus Nijhoff, 1955.

Kertzer, David I., and Peter Laslett, eds. *Aging in the Past: Demography, Society, and Old Age*. Berkeley and London: University of California Press, 1995.

Kinsley, David. *Hindu Goddesses: Visions of the Divine Feminine in the Hindu Religious Tradition*. Berkeley: University of California Press, 1986.

Kirch, Patrick Vinton. *The Lapita Peoples*. London and Cambridge, MA: Blackwell, 1997.

Knaap, Gerrit J. *Kruidnagelen en christenen: De Verenigde Oost-Indische Compagnie en de bevolking van Ambon 1656–1696. VKI* 125. Dordrecht: Foris, 1987.

———. "Pants, Skirts, and Pulpits: Women and Gender in Seventeenth-Century Amboina." In B. Andaya, *Other Pasts,* 147–173.

Knapen, Han. *Forest of Fortune? The Environmental History of Southeast Borneo, 1600–1800. VKI* 189. Leiden: KITLV Press, 2001.

Knappert, Jan. *Mythology and Folklore in South-East Asia.* Edited by Graham Saunders. New York: Oxford University Press, 1999.

Knox, Robert. *An Historical Relation of the Island Ceylon in the East Indies.* Edited by H. A. I. Goonetileke. New Delhi: Navrang, 1995. Reprint of 1681 edition.

Ko, Dorothy. *Every Step a Lotus: Shoes for Bound Feet.* Berkeley: University of California Press; Toronto: Bata Shoe Museum, 2001.

Koenig, William J. *The Burmese Polity, 1752–1819: Politics, Administration, and Social Organization in the Early Kon-baung Period.* Ann Arbor: Center for South and Southeast Asian Studies, University of Michigan, 1990.

Koolhof, Sirtjo. "The 'La Galigo': A Bugis Encyclopedia and Its Growth." *BKI* 155, no. 3 (1999): 364–390.

Kozok, Uli. "On Writing the Not-To-Be-Read: Literature and Literacy in a Pre-Colonial 'Tribal' Society." *BKI* 156, no. 1 (2000): 34–55.

Kumar, Ann. "Encyclopedia-izing and the Organization of Knowledge." *BKI* 155, no. 3 (1999): 470–488.

———. *Java and Modern Europe: Ambiguous Encounters.* Richmond, Surrey: Curzon Press, 1997.

———. "Javanese Court Society and Politics in the Late Eighteenth Century: The Record of a Lady Soldier. Part 1, The Religious, Social, and Economic Life of the Court." *Indonesia* 29 (April 1980): 1–46.

Laarhoven, Ruurdje. "The Power of Cloth: The Textile Trade of the Dutch East India Company (VOC), 1600–1780." PhD diss., ANU, 1994.

Lal, Ruby. *Domesticity and Power in the Early Mughal World.* Cambridge: Cambridge University Press, 2005.

Lamb, Jonathon, Vanessa Smith, and Nicholas Thomas. *Exploration & Exchange: A South Seas Anthology, 1680–1800.* Chicago: University of Chicago Press, 2000.

Launay, Adrien. *Histoire de la mission de Cochinchine 1658–1823.* Paris: MEP, 1923. Reprint, Paris: Les Indes Savantes, 2000.

———. *Histoire de la mission de Siam 1662–1811.* 3 vols. Paris: Charles Douniol and Retaux, 1920.

———. *Histoire de la mission du Tonkin: Documents historiques, 1658–1717.* 3 vols. Paris: Les Indes Savantes, 2000.

Lehman, F. K. *The Structure of Chin Society: A Tribal People of Burma Adapted to a Non-Western Civilization.* Urbana: University of Illinois Press, 1963.

Lessard, Micheline. "Curious Relations: Jesuit Perceptions of the Vietnamese." In Taylor and Whitmore, *Essays into Vietnamese Pasts,* 137–156.

Levy, Robert I. *Tahitians: Mind and Experience in the Society Islands.* Chicago and London: University of Chicago Press, 1973.

Lewin, T. H. *Wild Races of South-Eastern India*. London: W. H. Allen, 1870.

Li Tana. *Nguyen Cochinchina: Southern Vietnam in the Seventeenth and Eighteenth Centuries*. Ithaca, NY: Southeast Asia Program, Cornell University, 1998.

Li Tana and Anthony Reid. *Southern Vietnam under the Nguyen: Documents on the Economic History of Cochinchina (Dang Trong, 1602–1777)*. Singapore: ISEAS; Canberra: Economic History of Southeast Asia Project, ANU, 1993.

Liaw Yock Fang. *Undang-Undang Melaka: The Laws of Melaka*. Bibliotheca Indonesica 13. The Hague: Nijhoff, 1976.

Lieberman, Victor B., ed. *Beyond Binary Histories: Re-Imagining Eurasia to c. 1830*. Ann Arbor: University of Michigan Press, 1999.

————. *Burmese Administrative Cycles: Anarchy and Conquest, c. 1580–1760*. Princeton, NJ: Princeton University Press, 1984.

Lobo, Wibke, and Stefanie Reimann, eds. *Southeast Asian Archaeology 1998*. Hull, UK: Centre for South-East Asian Studies, University of Hull; Berlin: Ethnologische Museum, 2000.

Lombard-Salmon, Claudine. *Un exemple d'acculturation Chinoise: La province du Gui Zhou au XVIIIe siècle*. Paris: EFEO, 1972.

Loubère, Simon de la. *A New Historical Relation of the Kingdom of Siam*. Edited by David K. Wyatt. Kuala Lumpur: Oxford University Press, 1969.

Luard, C. Eckford. *Travels of Fray Sebastian Manrique, 1629–1643*. Vol. 1, *Arakan*. 2nd ser., 59. London: Hakluyt Society, 1926.

Lustig, Friedrich V., ed. and trans. *Burmese Classical Poems*. Rangoon: U Khin Pe Gyi, 1966.

Mabuchi, Toichi. *Ethnology of the Southwestern Pacific: The Ryukyus-Taiwan–Insular Southeast Asia*. Taipei: Chinese Association for Folklore, 1974.

Macdonald, Keith Norman. *The Practice of Medicine among the Burmese*. Translated from original manuscripts. Edinburgh: Maclachlan and Stewart, 1879.

Majumdar, R. C. *Ancient Indian Colonies in the Far East and Champa*. Lahore: Punjab Sanskrit Book Depot, 1927.

Malarney, Shaun Kingsley. "Return to the Past? The Dynamics of Contemporary Religion and Ritual Transformation." In Hy Van Luong, ed., *Postwar Vietnam: Dynamics of a Transforming Society*, 225–256. Singapore: ISEAS; New York: Rowman and Littlefield, 2003.

Mann, Susan. *Precious Records: Women in China's Long Eighteenth Century*. Stanford, CA: Stanford University Press, 1997.

Mann, Susan, and Yu-Yin Cheng, eds. *Under Confucian Eyes: Writings on Gender in Chinese History*. Berkeley: University of California Press, 2001.

Marini, G. F. de. *A New and Interesting Description of the Lao Kingdom (1642–1648)*. Translated by Walter E. J. Tips and Claudio Bertuccio. Introduction by Luigi Bressan. Bangkok: White Lotus, 1998.

Marsden, William. *The History of Sumatra*. Kuala Lumpur: Oxford University Press, 1975. Reprint of 1811 edition.

Masing, James Jemut. *The Coming of the Gods: An Iban Invocatory Chant (Timang*

Gawai Amat) of the Baleh River region, Sarawak. 2 vols. Canberra: Department of Anthropology, Research School of Pacific Studies, ANU, 1997.

Mattani Mojdara Rutnin. *Dance, Drama, and Theatre in Thailand: The Process of Development and Modernization.* Tokyo: Centre for East Asian Cultural Studies for UNESCO, 1993.

Maung Maung. *Law and Custom in Burma and the Burmese Family.* The Hague: Nijhoff, 1963.

Meade, Teresa A., and Merry E. Wiesner-Hanks. *A Companion to Gender History.* Malden, MA: Blackwell Publishing, 2004.

Michaud, Jean, ed. *Turbulent Times and Enduring Peoples: Mountain Minorities in the South-East Asian Massif.* Richmond, Surrey: Curzon Press, 2000.

Miedema, Jelle, and Ger Reesink. *One Head, Many Faces: New Perspectives on the Bird's Head Peninsula of New Guinea.* Leiden: KITLV Press, 2004.

Mills, J. V., trans. and ed. *Eredia's Description of Malaca, Meridional India, and Cathay.* MBRAS, reprint 14 (1997).

Mills, J. V. G., trans. and ed. *Ying-yai Sheng-lan: "The Overall Survey of the Ocean's Shores" [1433].* Cambridge: Cambridge University Press for the Hakluyt Society, 1970.

Mills, Mary Beth. "Attack of the Widow Ghosts: Gender, Death, and Modernity in Northeast Thailand." In Ong and Peletz, *Bewitching Women, Pious Men,* 244–298.

Minh Chi, Ha Van Tan, and Nguyen Tai Thu. *Buddhism in Vietnam: From Its Origins to the 19th Century.* Hanoi: The Gioi, 1999.

Moore, Clive. *New Guinea: Crossing Boundaries and History.* Honolulu: University of Hawai'i, 2003.

Morris, Rosalind C. *In the Place of Origins: Modernity and Its Mediums in Northern Thailand.* Durham, NC, and London: Duke University Press, 2000.

Moyer, David S. *The Logic of the Laws: A Structural Analysis of Malay Language Legal Codes from Bengkulu.* VKI 75. The Hague: Nijhoff, 1975.

Mulholland, Jean. *Herbal Medicine in Paediatrics: Translation of a Thai Book of Genesis.* Faculty of Asian Studies Monographs, n.s., no. 14. Canberra: ANU, 1989.

Mulyadi, S. W. R. *Hikayat Indraputra: A Malay Romance.* Dordrecht: Foris, 1983.

Musallam, B. F. *Sex and Society in Islam: Birth Control before the Nineteenth Century.* Cambridge: Cambridge University Press, 1983.

Myint Thien, Maung, trans. *Burmese Folk-Songs.* Oxford: Asoka Society, 1970.

Nabholz-Kartaschoff, Marie-Louise, Ruth Barnes, and David J. Stuart-Fox, eds. *Weaving Patterns of Life.* Basel: Museum of Ethnography Basel, 1993.

Nagtegaal, Luc. *Riding the Dutch Tiger: The Dutch East Indies Company and the Northeast Coast of Java, 1680–1743.* VKI 171. Leiden: KITLV Press, 1996.

Nai Pan Hla, trans., and Ryuji Okudaira. *Eleven Mon Dhammasat Texts.* Tokyo: Center for East Asian Cultural Studies for UNESCO, 1992.

Nath, Rajmohan. *The Background of Assamese Culture.* 2nd ed. Gauhati, India: Dutta Baruah and Co., 1978. First published in 1948.

Nelson, S., and M. Rosen-Ayalon, eds. *In Pursuit of Gender: Worldwide Archaeological Perspectives.* Walnut Creek, CA: AltaMira Press, 2002.

Nguyen Cuong Tu. *Zen in Medieval Vietnam: A Study and Translation of the Thien Uyen Tap Anh.* Honolulu: Kuroda Institute/University of Hawai'i Press, 1997.

Nguyen Ngoc Huy and Ta Van Tai, with Tran Van Liem. *The Lê Code: Law in Traditional Vietnam. A Comparative Sino-Vietnamese Legal Study with Historical Juridical Analysis and Annotations.* 3 vols. Athens: Ohio University Press, 1987.

Nguyen The Anh. "The Vietnamization of the Cham Deity Pō Nagar." In Taylor and Whitmore, *Essays into Vietnamese Pasts,* 43–50.

Nguyen The Anh and Alain Forest, eds. *Notes sur la culture et la religion en Péninsule indochinoise en hommage à Pierre-Bernard Lafont.* Paris: L'Harmattan, 1995.

Nguyen The Long and Pham Mai Hung. *130 Pagodas in Ha Noi.* Hanoi: The Gioi, 2003.

Nguyen Van Ky. "Rethinking the Status of Vietnamese Women in Folklore and Oral History." In Gisele Bousquet and Pierre Brocheux, eds., *Viêt Nam Exposé: French Scholarship on Twentieth-Century Vietnamese Society,* 87–107. Ann Arbor: University of Michigan Press, 2002.

Nhatrang Cong Huyen Ton Nu Thi. "The Traditional Roles of Women as Reflected in Oral and Written Vietnamese Literature." PhD diss., University of California, Berkeley, 1973.

Niemeijer, Hendrik E. *Batavia: Een koloniate samenleving in de zeventiende eeuw.* Amsterdam: Balans, 2005.

———. "Slavery, Ethnicity, and the Economic Independence of Women in Seventeenth-Century Batavia." In B. Andaya, *Other Pasts,* 174–194.

Nieuhof, Johan. *Voyages and Travels to the East Indies 1653–1670.* Introduction by Anthony Reid. Kuala Lumpur and London: Oxford University Press, 1988. Reprint of 1704 edition.

Nooy-Palm, C. H. M. *The Sa'dan Toraja: A Study of Their Social Life and Religion.* 2 vols. The Hague: Nijhoff, 1979.

Nourse, Jennifer W. *Conceiving Spirits: Birth Rituals and Contested Identities among Laujé of Indonesia.* Washington, DC, and London: Smithsonian Institution, 1999.

Oliver, Douglas. *Ancient Tahitian Society.* 3 vols. Honolulu: University of Hawai'i Press, 1974.

Ong, Aihwa, and Michael G. Peletz, eds. *Bewitching Women, Pious Men: Gender and Body Politics in Southeast Asia.* Berkeley: University of California Press, 1995.

Ortner, Sherry B., and Harriet Whitehead, eds. *Sexual Meanings: The Cultural Construction of Gender and Sexuality.* Cambridge: Cambridge University Press, 1981.

Overbeck, H. "Malay Customs and Beliefs as Recorded in Malay Literature and Folklore." *JMBRAS* 2 (1924): 280–288.

Paderni, Paola. "Between Constraints and Opportunities: Widows, Witches, and Shrews in Eighteenth-Century China." In Zurndorfer, *Chinese Women in the Imperial Past,* 258–285.

Padt-Brugge, Robertus. "Beschrijving der zeden en gewoonten van de bewoners der Minahassa . . . 1679." *BKI* 13, no. 1–2 (1866): 304–330.

Parker, Lyn. *From Subjects to Citizens: Balinese Villagers in the Indonesian Nation-State.* Copenhagen: Nordic Institute of Asian Studies Press, 2003.

Parkin, Robert. *A Guide to Austroasiatic Speakers and Their Languages.* Oceanic Linguistics Special Publication 23. Honolulu: University of Hawai'i Press, 1991.

Parmentier, Richard. *The Sacred Remains: Myth, History, and Polity in Belau.* Chicago and London: University of Chicago Press, 1987.

Parratt, Saroj N. *The Religion of Manipur: Beliefs, Rituals, and Historical Development.* Calcutta: Firma KLM, 1980.

Parratt, Saroj N. Arambam, and John K. Parratt. *The Pleasing of the Gods: Meitei Lai Haraoba.* New Delhi: Vikas, 1997.

Parry, N. E. *The Lakkers.* London: Macmillan, 1932.

Pe Maung Tin and G. H. Luce. *The Glass Palace Chronicle of the Kings of Burma.* Rangoon: Rangoon University Press, 1960.

Pemberton, John. *On the Subject of "Java."* Ithaca, NY, and London: Cornell University Press, 1994.

Peri, N. "Hariti, la mère de demons." *BEFEO* 17, no. 3 (1917): 1–102.

Phan, Peter C. *Mission and Catechesis: Alexandre de Rhodes and Inculturation in Seventeenth-Century Vietnam.* Maryknoll, NY: Orbis Books, 1998.

Pho Hien: The Center of International Commerce in the XVIIth–XVIIIth Centuries. Association of Vietnamese Historians, People's Administrative Committee of Hai Hung Province. Hanoi: The Gioi, 1994.

Pombejra, Dhiravat na. "VOC Employees and Their Relationships with Mon and Siamese Women: A Case Study of Osoet Pegua." In B. Andaya, *Other Pasts,* 195–214.

Price, Lisa Marie Leimar. "Women's Wild Plant Food Entitlements in Thailand's Agricultural Northeast." PhD diss., University of Oregon, 1993.

Purchas, Samuel, ed. *Purchas His Pilgrimes.* Vols. 2 and 3. Glasgow: James MacLehose and Sons, 1905.

Quach-Langlet, Tam. "La compassion transcendée: l'"Oraison pour le rachat des âmes abandonées', attribuée à Nguyen Du." In Nguyen The Anh and Forest, *Notes sur la culture,* 135–156.

Quirino, Carlos, and Mauro Garcia, ed. and trans. "The Manners, Customs, and Beliefs of the Philippine Inhabitants of Long Ago, Being Chapters of 'A Late 16th Century Manila Manuscript.'" *Philippine Journal of Science* 87, no. 4 (December 1958): 325–449.

Raben, Remco. "Batavia and Colombo: The Ethnic and Spatial Order of Two Colonial Cities, 1600–1800." PhD diss., University of Leiden, 1995.

Raffles, Thomas Stanford. *History of Java.* 2 vols. Kuala Lumpur: Oxford University Press, 1965. Reprint of 1817 edition.

Rajadhon, Phya Anuman. *Life and Ritual in Old Siam.* Translated and edited by William J. Gedney. New Haven, CT: HRAF Press, 1961.

Ralston, Caroline, and Nicholas Thomas, eds. "Sanctity and Power: Gender in Polynesian History." Special issue, *Journal of Pacific History* 22, no. 3–4 (July–October 1987).

Ram, Kalpana, and Margaret Jolly, eds. *Maternities and Modernities: Colonial and Post-colonial Experiences in Asia and the Pacific.* Cambridge: Cambridge University Press, 1998.

Ramusack, Barbara N., and Sharon Sievers. *Women in Asia: Restoring Women to History.* Bloomington: Indiana University Press, 1999.

Rawlins, John. "On the Manners, Religion, and Laws of the Cucis, or Mountaineers of Tipra." *Asiatick Researches* 2, no. 12 (1790): 187–197.

Reid, Anthony, ed. *The Last Stand of Asian Autonomies: Responses to Modernity in the Diverse States of Southeast Asia and Korea, 1750–1900.* Basingstoke, UK, and London: Macmillan, 1997.

———. *Southeast Asia in the Age of Commerce 1450–1680.* Vol. 1, *The Lands below the Winds.* New Haven, CT, and London: Yale University Press, 1988.

Reynolds, C. J. "A Nineteenth-Century Thai Buddhist Defense of Polygamy and Some Remarks on the Social History of Women in Thailand." In *Proceedings, Seventh IAHA Conference,* 927–970. Bangkok: Chulalongkorn University, 1979.

Reynolds, Frank, and Mani Reynolds. *Three Worlds According to King Ruang.* Berkeley Buddhist Studies Series, no. 4. Berkeley: Asian Humanities Press, 1982.

Richards, A. J. N. *The Sea Dyaks and Other Races of Sarawak.* Kuching: Borneo Literature Bureau, 1963.

Richards, John F. *The Mughal Empire.* New Cambridge History of India, vol. 1, part 5. Cambridge: Cambridge University Press, 1993.

Ricklefs, M. C. *The Seen and Unseen Worlds in Java 1726–1749: History, Literature, and Islam in the Court of Pakubuwana II.* Honolulu: University of Hawai'i Press, 1998.

———. *War, Culture, and Economy in Java 1677–1726: Asian and European Imperialism in the Early Kartasura Period.* Sydney: Allen and Unwin, 1993.

Riddell, Peter. *Islam and the Malay-Indonesian World.* Honolulu: University of Hawai'i Press, 2001.

Riedel, J. G. F. "De Minahasa in 1825: Bijdrage tot de kennis van Noord-Selebes." *TBG* 18 (1872): 458–568.

Rigby, J., ed. and trans. *The Ninety-Nine Laws of Perak.* Papers on Malay Subjects. Kuala Lumpur: Government Press, 1929.

Robson, Stuart, trans. *Désawarnana (Nagarakṛtagama) by Mpu Prapanca.* Leiden: KITLV Press, 1995.

Roeper, Vibeke, and Roelof van Gelder. *In dienst van de Compagnie: Leven bij de VOC in honderd getuigenissen 1602–1799.* Amsterdam: Athenaeum, 2002.

Rouffaer, G. P., and J. W. Ijzerman. *De eerste schipvaart der Nederlanders naar Oost-Indië onder Cornelis de Houtman 1595–1597.* The Hague: Linschoten-Vereeniging, 1915–1921.

Rovere van Breugel, J. de. "Beschryving van Bantam en de Lampongs." *BKI* 5 (1856): 309–362.

Sahai, Sachchidanand. *The Rama Jataka in Laos: A Study in the Phra Lak Phra Lam.* 2 vols. Delhi: BR Publishing, 1996.

Saikia, Sayeeda Yasmin. *In the Meadows of Gold: Telling Tales of the Swargadeos at the Crossroads of Assam*. Guwahati and Delhi: Spectrum, 1997.

St. Thecla, Father Adriano di. *Opusculum de sectis apud Sinenses et Tunkinenses (A Small Treatise on the Sects among the Chinese and Tonkinese: A Study of Religion in China and North Vietnam in the Eighteenth Century)*. Translated and annotated by Olga Dror, with collaboration of Mariya Berezovska in Latin translation; with preface by Lionel M. Jensen. Ithaca, NY: Southeast Asia Program, Cornell University, 2002.

Sakhong, Lian H. *In Search of Chin Identity: A Study in Religion, Politics, and Ethnic Identity in Burma*. Copenhagen: Nordic Institute of Asian Studies Press, 2003.

Salisbury, R. F. *From Stone to Steel: Economic Consequences of a Technological Change in New Guinea*. London and New York: Melbourne University Press/Cambridge University Press, 1962.

Salmon, Claudine. "Wang Dahai and His View of the Insular Countries (1791)." In Ding Choo Ming and Ooi Kee Beng, eds., *Chinese Studies in the Malay World: A Comparative Approach*, 31–67. Singapore: Times Media, 2003.

———. "Wang Dahai et sa vision des 'Contrées insulaires' (1791)." *Études Chinoises* 13, no. 1–2 (Fall 1994): 221–257.

Salmon, Th. *Hedendaagsche historie of tegenwoordige staat van alle volkeren*. Amsterdam: Isaak Tirion, 1739.

San Antonio, Fray Juan Francisco de. *The Philippine Chronicles of Fray San Antonio*. Translated by D. Pedro Picornell. Manila: Casalinda and Historical Conservation Society, 1977.

Sandin, Benedict. *The Sea Dayaks of Borneo before White Rajah Rule*. East Lansing: Michigan State University Press, 1968.

Santiago, Luciano P. R. "'To Love and To Suffer': The Development of the Religious Congregations for Women in the Philippines during the Spanish Era (1565–1898), Part II." *Philippine Quarterly of Culture and Society* 24, no. 1–2 (March–June 1996): 119–179.

Sather, Clifford. "The Malevolent *koklir:* Iban Concepts of Sexual Peril and the Dangers of Childbirth." *BKI* 134, no. 2–3 (1978): 310–355.

Schafer, Edward H. *The Vermilion Bird: T'ang Images of the South*. Berkeley and Los Angeles: University of California Press, 1967.

Schendel, Willem van. *Francis Buchanan in Southeast Bengal (1798): His Journey to Chittagong, the Chittagong Hill Tracts, Noakhale, and Comilla*. Dhaka: Dhaka University Press, 1992.

Schimmel, Annemarie. *My Soul Is a Woman: The Feminine in Islam*. Translated by Susan H. Ray. New York: Continuum, 1997.

Schreurs, Peter, MSC. *Caraga Antigua: The Hispanization and Christianization of Agusan, Surigao, and East Davao, 1521–1910*. Manila: National Historical Institute, 2000.

Scott, Joan W. "Gender: A Useful Category of Historical Analysis." *American Historical Review* 91, no. 5 (December 1986): 1053–1075.

Scott, W. H. "Sixteenth-Century Tagalog Technology from the *Vocabulario de la Lengua Tagala* of Pedro de San Buenaventura, OFM." In Rainer Carle, Martina Heinschke, Peter W. Pink, Christel Rost, and Karen Stadtlander, eds., *Gava': Studies in Austronesian Languages and Cultures*, 523–535. Berlin: Dietrich Reimer, 1982.

Scott, William Henry. *Barangay: Sixteenth-Century Philippine Culture and Society*. Quezon City: Ateneo de Manila University Press, 1994.

Sered, Susan Star. *Priestess, Mother, Sacred Sister: Religions Dominated by Women*. New York: Oxford University Press, 1994.

Shepherd, John R. *Statecraft and Political Economy on the Taiwan Frontier, 1600–1800*. Stanford, CA: Stanford University Press, 1993.

Shryock, John. "Ch'en Ting's Account of the Marriage Customs of the Chiefs of Yunnan and Kueichou." *American Anthropologist* 36, no. 4 (1934): 524–547.

Simmonds, E. H. S. "Siamese (Thai)." In Arthur T. Hatto, ed., *Eos: An Enquiry into the Theme of Lovers' Meetings and Partings at Dawn in Poetry*, 186–195. London and The Hague: Mouton, 1965.

Skeat, W. W., and F. F. Laidlaw. "The Cambridge University Expedition to Parts of the Malay Peninsula, 1899–1900." *JMBRAS* 26, no. 4 (1953).

Skilling, Peter. "Female Renunciants *(nang chi)* in Siam According to Early Travellers' Tales." *JSS* 83, no. 1–2 (1995): 55–62.

Sommer, Matthew H. *Sex, Law, and Society in Late Imperial China*. Stanford, CA: Stanford University Press, 2000.

Smith, Margaret. *Rabi'a: The Life and Work of Rabi'a and Other Women Mystics in Islam*. Oxford: Oneworld Publications, 1994.

Spriggs, Matthew. *The Island Melanesians*. Oxford and Cambridge, MA: Blackwell, 1997.

Stadner, Donald M., ed. *The Art of Burma: New Studies*. Mumbai, India: Marg Publications, 1999.

———. "Pagan Bronzes: Fresh Observations." In Stadner, *The Art of Burma*, 53–64.

Straver, Hans. *De zee van verhalen: De wereld van Molukse vertellers*. Utrecht: Steunpunt Edukatie Molukkers, 1993.

Strong, John S. *The Legend and Cult of Upagupta: Sanskrit Buddhism in North India and Southeast Asia*. Princeton, NJ: Princeton University Press, 1992.

Stuart-Fox, Martin. *The Lao Kingdom of Lān Xāng: Rise and Decline*. Bangkok: White Lotus, 1998.

Subrahmanyam, Sanjay. "Connected Histories: Notes towards a Reconfiguration of Early Modern Eurasia." In Lieberman, *Beyond Binary Histories*, 289–316.

Sudjiman, Panuti H. M., ed. *Adat Raja-Raja Melayu*. Jakarta: University of Indonesia Press, 1983.

Sun Laichen. "Ming–Southeast Asian Overland Interactions 1368–1644." PhD diss., University of Michigan, 2000.

Sutlive, Vinson H., Jr., ed. *Female and Male in Borneo: Contributions and Challenges to Gender Studies*. Williamsburg, VA: Borneo Research Council, 1987.

Swearer, Donald K., and Sommai Premchit. *The Legend of Queen Cāma: Bodhiramsi's Cāmadevāvamsa, a Translation and Commentary*. Albany: State University of New York Press, 1998.

Symes, Michael. *An Account of an Embassy to the Kingdom of Ava in the Year 1795*. 2 vols. Edinburgh: Constable, 1827.

Symonds, Patricia V. *Calling in the Soul: Gender and the Cycle of Life in a Hmong Village*. Seattle and London: University of Washington Press, 2004.

Ta Van Tai. "The Status of Women in Traditional Vietnam: A Comparison of the Code of the Lê Dynasty (1428–1788) with the Chinese Codes." *Journal of Asian History* 15 (1981): 97–145.

Taylor, Jean Gelman. *The Social World of Batavia: European and Eurasian in Dutch Asia*. Madison: University of Wisconsin Press, 1983.

Taylor, Keith Weller. *The Birth of Vietnam*. Berkeley: University of California Press, 1983.

Taylor, Keith Weller, and John K. Whitmore, eds. *Essays into Vietnamese Pasts*. Ithaca, NY: Southeast Asia Program, Cornell University, 1995.

Tchou, Khing Mya. *Les femmes de lettres Birmanes*. Paris: Editions L'Harmattan, 1994.

Teng, Emma Jinhua. *Taiwan's Imagined Geography: Chinese Colonial Travel Writing and Pictures, 1683–1895*. Cambridge, MA: Harvard University Asia Center; distributed by Harvard University Press, 2004.

Than Tun, ed. *Royal Orders of Burma, AD 1598–1885*. 10 vols. Kyoto: Center for Southeast Asian Studies, Kyoto University, 1983–1990.

Till, Margreet van. "Social Care in Eighteenth-Century Batavia: The Poorhouse, 1725–1750." *Itinerario* 19, no. 1 (1995): 18–31.

Tiyavanich, Kamala. *Forest Recollections: Wandering Monks in Twentieth-Century Thailand*. Honolulu: University of Hawai'i Press, 1997.

Toshijiro Hirayama. "Seasonal Rituals Connected with Rice Culture." In Richard M. Dorson, ed., *Studies in Japanese Folklore*, 57–75. Bloomington: Indian University Press, 1963.

Tossa, Wajuppa, trans. and ed. *Phādaeng Nāng Ai: A Translation of a Thai-Isan Folk Epic in Verse*. Lewisburg, PA: Bucknell University Press, 1990.

Trager, Frank N., and William Koenig. *Burmese Sit-Tans, 1764–1826: Records of Rural Life and Administration*. Tucson: University of Arizona Press for AAS, 1979.

Tran My-Van. "'Come On, Girls, Let's Go Bail Water': Eroticism in Ho Xuan Huong's Vietnamese Poetry." *JSEAS* 33, no. 3 (October 2002): 471–494.

Tran, Nhung Tuyet. "Les Amantes de la Croix: An Early Modern Vietnamese Sisterhood." In Gisele Bousquet and Nora Taylor, eds., *Le Vietnam au feminine*, 51–66. Paris: Les Indes Savantes, 2005.

———. "Vietnamese Women at the Crossroads: Gender and Society in Early Modern Dai Viet." PhD diss., University of California, Los Angeles, 2004.

Tran Quoc Vuong. "Popular Culture and High Culture in Vietnamese History." *Crossroads* 7, no. 2 (1992): 39–54.

Tran Thi Van Anh. "Women and Rural Land in Vietnam." In Irene Tinker and Gale

Summerfield, eds., *Women's Rights to House and Land: China, Laos, Vietnam*, 95–114. London: Lynne Rienner, 1999.

Truong Huu Quynh. "The Development of Private Landed Property in Vietnam in the XVIIIth Century." Paper presented at the 13th IAHA Conference, Tokyo, September 1994.

Unger, Ann Helen, and Walter Unger. *Pagodas, Gods, and Spirits of Vietnam*. London: Thames and Hudson, 1997.

Vickers, Adrian. *Bali, a Paradise Created*. Berkeley, CA: Periplus Editions, 1989.

Vickery, Michael. *Society, Economics, and Politics in Pre-Angkor Cambodia: The 7th–8th Centuries*. Tokyo: Toyo Bunko, Centre for East Asian Cultural Studies for UNESCO, 1998.

Von Glahn, Richard. *The Country of Streams and Grottoes: Expansion, Settlement, and the Civilizing of the Sichuan Frontier in Song Times*. Cambridge, MA: Council on East Asian Studies, Harvard University; distributed by Harvard University Press, 1987.

Wade, Geoff. "The Bai-Yi Zhuan: A Chinese Account of a Tai Society in the 14th Century." Paper presented at the 14th IAHA Conference, Bangkok, May 1996.

Walker, Anthony, ed. *Rice in Southeast Asian Myth and Ritual*. Contributions to Southeast Asian Ethnography no. 10. Columbus: Department of Anthropology, Ohio State University, 1994.

Walthall, Anne. "From Private to Public Patriarchy: Women, Labor, and the State in East Asia, 1600–1919." In Meade and Wiesner-Hanks, *A Companion to Gender History*, 444–458.

———. "The Life Cycle of Farm Women in Tokugawa Japan." In Bernstein, *Recreating Japanese Women*, 42–71.

Waterson, Roxana. *The Living House: An Anthropology of Architecture in South-East Asia*. Singapore: Oxford University Press, 1990.

Watson, C. W., and Roy Ellen, eds. *Understanding Witchcraft and Sorcery in Southeast Asia*. Honolulu: University of Hawai'i Press, 1993.

Wendt, Ian. "The Dharma of Women's Work: Gender, Labor, and Law in the Textile Industry of Early Modern South India." Paper presented at the annual meeting of AAS, Chicago, March 2005.

White, John. *A Voyage to Cochin China*. Edited by Milton Osborne. Kuala Lumpur and New York: Oxford University Press, 1972.

Whitmore, John K. "Gender, State, and History: The Literati Voice in Early Modern Vietnam." In B. Andaya, *Other Pasts*, 215–230.

Wichienkeeo, Aroonrut, and Gehan Wijeyewardene, trans. and ed. *The Laws of King Mangrai (Mangrayathammasart)*. Canberra: Department of Anthropology, Research School of Pacific Studies, 1986.

Wieringa, Edwin P. "A Javanese Handbook for Would-be Husbands: The *Serat Candraning Wanita*." *JSEAS* 33, no. 3 (2002): 431–449.

Wiesner, Merry E. *Women and Gender in Early Modern Europe*. Cambridge: Cambridge University Press, 1993.

Winstedt, R. O., ed. *Hikayat Bayan Budiman, or Khojah Maimun.* Singapore: Methodist Publishing House, 1920.

———, "An Old Minangkabau Legal Digest from Perak." *JMBRAS* 26, no. 1 (July 1953): 1–13.

Wolters, O. W. *History, Culture, and Region in Southeast Asian Perspectives.* Rev. ed. Ithaca, NY, Southeast Asia Program, Cornell University; and Singapore: ISEAS, 1999.

Woodside, Alexander. "Central Viet Nam's Trading World in the Eighteenth Century as Seen in Le Quy Don's 'Frontier Chronicles.'" In Taylor and Whitmore, *Essays into Vietnamese Pasts,* 157–172.

Wyatt, David. K. *Reading Thai Murals.* Chiang Mai, Thailand: Silkworm Books, 2004.

Yu, Insun. "Bilateral Social Pattern and the Status of Women in Traditional Vietnam." *South East Asia Research* 7, no. 2 (July 1999): 215–232.

———. *Law and Society in Seventeenth and Eighteenth Century Vietnam.* Seoul: Asiatic Research Center, Korea University, 1990.

Zurndorfer, Harriet T., ed. *Chinese Women in the Imperial Past: New Perspectives.* Leiden: Brill, 1999.

Index

Page numbers in **boldface** type refer to maps.

181, 183, 192, 193, 194–195;
sexual morality, 154, 191, 192, 193;
tattoos as punishment, 159;
women's writings, 55, 63

Bali, 75; black magic, 224; childbirth
roles of men, 210; deformities,
179; intermarriage, 146; poetry,
54, 178, 182, 192; premarital sex,
154; *sati*, 67, 194, 219; sexual yoga,
216; textile trade, 118; women's
quarters, 178, 192
Banda, 114, 117, 123, 190
Bangladesh, 24, 210
Banten: doctors, 129; Muslims, 42, 89,
205; royal women, 168, 182, 184;
senior women in rituals, 205;
slaves, 126–127, 130; trade and
commerce, 37, 42, 120, 124
Batavia, 58, 104; Chinese, 68, 125,
146–147; Christians, 98, 101, 144,
157, 159, 222; divorce, 160; dress,
144; gendered labor divisions, 109;
healers, 128; intermarriage, 145,
146–147; poorhouse, 222; sexual
morality, 101, 157, 216; slaves, 98,
115, 130–131, 132, 230; wet nursing, 129; widows, 221; written
sources on, 3, 65–68
beauty standards. *See* body image
Beeckman, Daniel, 63–64
Bengal: Hinduization, 26–28, 29;
Mughal, 26, 30–31, 194; Muslims,
28, 32, 109, 194; physical environment, 24, 25, 31, 32; prostitution,
131, 132–133; textile production,
117
black magic, 19, 62, 211, 223–224. *See
also* witchcraft
blood: childbirth, 26, 117, 210; first
sexual intercourse, 203–204;
menstrual, 26, 72, 88, 117, 197,
200, 204
bloodletting: human sacrifice rituals,
43, 137. *See also* head-hunting;
warfare
Bode, Mabel, 6
bodhisattvas, 13, 76, 82–83, 84, 123,
156

body alterations, 179, 190; circumcision, 90–91, 208; congenital
deformation, 211; foot binding,
13, 17, 20, 22, 144, 147; mothers
after childbirth, 215; tooth filing,
200
body concealment. *See*
modesty/immodesty; seclusion
body image: albinos, 66, 128, 211;
dwarves, 179, 211. *See also* body
alterations; dress and body decoration; third gender
Borneo, 34; Banjarmasin court, 184;
beads, 113; Brunei, 42, 92–93, 113,
130, 137; Dayaks, 31, 64, 105, 146,
209; European chronicles, 63–64;
intermarriage, 146; Kayan, 113,
201; maize, 107; Muslims, 84;
Rungus, 197–198, 204; Sarawak,
63, 122, 142, 201; transgender
figures, 73. *See also* Iban
Borri, Christoforo, 143, 206
Bowrey, Thomas, 67, 131, 168, 178
Brahmans, 26–27, 28, 29, 46, 204, 207
Brewer, Carolyn, 74, 223
bridewealth, 31, 40, 148–151; daughters valued for, 22, 111–112, 228;
Malay, 88–89, 151; Philippine,
100–101, 150, 151, 206–207; premarital sex and, 100–101, 154;
royal, 187; Taiwan, 22
British: Australia, 52; English East India
Company, 66, 110, 120–121, 148,
150; India, 2–3, 25, 31, 226–227;
and intermarriage, 145; Malaya,
53, 206; Sri Lanka, 33; Sumatra,
112, 151; and wellborn women,
167, 172; written sources, 49, 66,
110, 150, 172
Buchanan, Francis, 26, 32
Buddhists: and abortion, 223; celibacy
among monks and nuns, 79, 80,
89; deflowering monks, 204;
deities, 32, 47–48, 75, 77, 80,
82–83, 97; and divorce, 217; and
foster mothers, 186; gender hierarchies, 13–16, 70, 76, 230; hell as
female, 158; indigenous rituals
displaced by, 137; intermarriage,

Coedès, George, 1–2, 11, 229

colonization: Chinese, 16–24; political boundaries created by, 11, 24–25, 33–35, 226–227. *See also* Europeans; state

Confucianism, 230; commerce less valued by, 124; education, 19–20, 22; gender hierarchies, 12–13, 16, 22, 24, 54, 70, 81–82, 143, 144, 145, 226; patrilocality, 206; vs. spirit communication, 74; Vietnam, 12–13, 24, 45–46, 54, 74, 81–84, 143, 144, 145, 159, 165, 172, 206; widowhood category, 218, 219

court life, 165; Bangkok, 176, 181, 184, 185, 188, 190, 200; circumcision, 90–91; diaries, 90–91, 194; dress, 143; eunuchs, 177–178; guardswomen, 55, 125, 176–177; homosexuality, 93; labor, 136, 178–181, 184; literature, 54, 55, 63, 79, 92, 93, 172–173, 188, 189–190; marriage diplomacy, 183; palace occupations, 136, 178–181, 184, 187–189; palaces, 174–178; pregnancy ceremony, 52; royal women, 46, 69, 81–92, 164–196, 228, 230, 231; visual art, 61; warfare effects on family, 138; women's quarters, 172–181, 183–184, 187, 189–196. *See also* Javanese court life; upper class

courts, 158, 159, 162. *See also* law

Crawfurd, John, 211, 218

Creese, Helen, 154, 173–174, 202

Dalton, Edward, 31, 109

Dampier, William, 126, 155, 170, 190

dancing: as body flaunting, 64; court, 60, 188; hermaphrodite, 73; Miao, 18; and prostitution, 127–128; ritual, 27–28, 29, 60, 71; sexual, 202; transvestite, 89

Daoism, 13, 16, 47, 81, 83

daughters: Christian education, 102; incest by fathers, 192–193, 195; inheritance, 110–111; menstruation celebrated, 199–200; mother-

daughter bond, 206; parents guarding chastity of, 203; "play wives," 136; training for women's roles, 198–199; unhappy wives, 207; valued highly, 22, 109, 111–112, 125–126, 212, 228; valued little, 13, 55, 150, 205. *See also* bridewealth

deities: agriculture, 17, 24, 29, 83, 107; black magic, 224; Buddhist, 32, 47–48, 75, 77, 80, 82–83, 97; Daoist, 16, 47, 83; double-gendered, 73, 232; earth goddesses, 24, 28–30, 32, 47–49, 58, 70, 77, 80, 83, 106, 110; Goddess of the Treasury, 123; Hindu, 27–29, 32, 45, 47–48, 56, 75, 232; Khmer goddesses, 45; mother deities, 13, 16, 24, 28–30, 47, 81–84, 96–97, 107, 224; Ratu Kidul, 60, 175, 221; Tanihale, 73

divorce, 151–153, 217; for childlessness, 208; Christians and, 153, 159–160; Hindus and, 29, 152; law, 152–153, 162, 208; Muslims and, 152, 153, 203, 207; Philippine, 74, 153; royal, 178, 194

Doan Thi Diem, 54, 84

domestic economy, 104–133; archaeological findings, 44, 113; commoditization, 129–132, 150–151; male roles, 24, 38, 44, 104–109, 113–123, 210, 230; state revenue collections, 127, 139–140. *See also* agriculture; labor; property; women's roles in domestic economy

domestic violence: bridewealth and, 228; Chinese toward slave-wives, 127; gender hierarchies and, 148; New Guinea, 39; sexual, 191; Taiwanese rebellion over, 22; urbanization and, 130, 133; Vietnamese protections, 206, 207

Don, Le Quy, 172

dress and body decoration, 24, 25; Akha female headdress styles, 21; beads, 113; beauty standards, 13, 17, 142, 200; Chinese, 13, 17, 142,

143, 144, 146, 147; coins, 122; cultural identity, 142–145, 201; Dutch, 143, 144; foot binding, 13, 17, 20, 22, 144, 147; hair-cutting, 185, 208; maturing girls, 200–201; Miao, 18, 142, 144; Muslim, 85, 143; sexually enhancing, 64, 142–143; tattoos, 61–62, 137, 142, 159, 201; wanton women, 23, 64; warfare, 40, 138, 142, 170, 228. *See also* body image; modesty/immodesty; transvestism

Dutch. *See* VOC (Dutch East India Company)

economics, 104–133, 231; Church charity, 97–98; cloth as currency, 115; coinage, 112, 122–123, 160; deflowering services, 204; global developments, 2–4, 42, 70, 104, 122, 130, 133, 229–230; law penalties, 160–161; marriage, 150–152; polygamy, 217; poverty, 32, 97–98, 130, 132–133, 222, 230; royal women, 178–181, 184, 187–189; taxes, 68, 127, 139–141; widows, 208, 218, 221, 222. *See also* bridewealth; domestic economy; labor; property; trade

education: Buddhist, 77; Christian, 54, 102; Confucian, 19–20, 22, 82; sexual, 201–205; women's access to, 13, 54, 77, 82; in women's roles, 197–198. *See also* literacy

English East India Company, 66, 110, 120–121, 148, 150

Eredia, Manoel Godinho de, 65, 117, 128

ethnicity, 21, 68, 141–147, 165, 201; China minorities, 17, 40; Chineseness, 12–24, 142; Christian gender standards and, 99, 101; cross-cultural intermarriage, 20, 21, 126, 133, 144–147

Europeans, 2–3, 25, 33, 34, 42; vs. bridewealth, 151; childbirth, 209; courts, 159; vs. divorce, 153; dress, 143–144; infant mortality, 211; intermarriage, 145–146; labor

exploitation, 104, 109, 135, 136; and law, 155, 157; life expectancy, 218; and "love magic" of native females, 216; nuns, 98; and Oceania, 35, 38, 39–40; prenuptial births, 154; revenue collection, 141; and *sati*, 27, 67, 218; and state-household compact, 148; tattoos witnessed by, 61–62; written and visual records, 3, 5, 49, 51–74, 88, 90, 93, 94, 101, 105, 112–114, 136, 146, 147, 168, 175, 199–203. *See also* British; French; Portuguese; Spanish; VOC (Dutch East India Company)

family relationships, 5, 12–13; avenging women's honor, 191; eunuchs, 177; filial piety, 12–13, 18, 97, 207–208, 213; matrilocality, 18, 22, 33, 38, 109, 151, 206, 227–228; military service and, 136; mother-daughter, 206; mother-son, 13, 97, 185; patrilineality, 19–20, 21, 31, 102, 110, 169, 211, 226; patri-locality, 21, 182–183, 205–206, 226; religious standards, 12–13, 16, 90–91; senior women's networks, 220–221; sex trade and, 131; sister-brother, 39, 58, 181–182, 192–193, 211–212; state-household compact, 147–150, 153–164; warfare and, 137, 138, 170; women's authority in, 13, 19, 26, 206, 212, 220–221; work group and, 198. *See also* children; domestic economy; domestic violence; gender hierarchies; incest; marriage; matrilineality; motherhood

female ritual prominence, 22, 26–29, 31, 70, 102; agricultural, 17, 19, 21, 26–28, 33, 43, 74, 106–107, 231; Christians and, 84, 94–95; fertility, 29, 102, 107, 231; head-hunting, 22, 31, 137; Muslim, 89; senior women, 21, 22, 71–73, 102, 205, 220, 222; textile-related, 116, 117; Vietnam, 83–84; weddings, 205. *See also* nuns; priestesses female spirit communication, 16, 19, 70, 75, 230–231; agricultural ritual, 19, 26, 74; Buddhists and, 16, 74–75, 78, 80; Christianity and, 71, 94–95, 96, 220, 223; dance, 60, 128; healers and midwives, 78, 128, 129, 210, 222, 223; Muslims vs., 74, 93; Naga, 31; Philippines, 71, 74, 95, 220, 223; senior women, 71, 220, 222, 223; Vietnam, 74, 83–84; and warfare, 137. *See also* priestesses; shamanism; witchcraft

female status, 226; aging central to, 218; agricultural role conditioning, 28–29; colonization affecting, 2–3, 16–27; first wife, 217; motherhood determining, 208; relatively equal/relatively high, 12, 31–32, 41, 43, 103, 226, 227–228; Vietnamese higher than Chinese, 81. *See also* class; freedom and independence, female; gender hierarchies; women's authority; women's history

fertility, 33, 202, 213; aging and, 197, 219, 221; agriculture-female links, 17, 19, 27, 43, 107, 137, 205, 231; childlessness/infertility, 133, 207–208, 218; dangerous female, 72, 197, 199, 210, 212, 221, 225; deities, 27, 47, 48, 73, 82–83; head-hunting linked to, 31, 137; hymen breaking and, 203–204; palace garden and, 174; rituals dominated by females, 29, 102, 107, 231; "rocket ceremony," 70; virility/penis displays and, 48, 95, 107, 173, 195–196, 208. *See also* menstruation; motherhood; pregnancy

fidelity: to absent husbands, 151, 163, 215; male infidelity, 126, 215–216, 217; monogamous, 91; royal, 190, 192–194; sexual morality vs. adultery, 76, 87, 88, 101, 155–161, 162, 193, 215; widows, 13, 27, 29, 89–92, 147, 193–194, 218–220; women joining mates in warfare, 138, 170. *See also* chastity

flaming womb, princess of, 1, 58, 232

food production: mother's milk, 56, 128–129, 186, 197, 214–215; state revenue collection and, 140, 141; women's roles, 104–109, 127, 231. *See also* agriculture

food taboos, 30, 39, 90, 200, 208, 211

foot binding, 13, 17, 20, 22, 144, 147

Forrest, Thomas, 94, 200

freedom and independence, female, 103, 218, 228; Arakan Buddhist, 32; Assam, 31; Hindu, 26, 226; in marriage, 206; Miao, 18; Muslim, 94; Sinhalese, 33; slave manumission, 97–98, 132–133, 222, 230; Taiwan, 22; traders, 121, 228; Vietnamese, 54, 206; widows, 218–219, 220; wife exchange and, 182. *See also* rights; women's authority

French, 38, 141, 147; Ayutthaya chronicles, 66, 80, 119, 154, 176–177, 178, 193, 195; Christian missionaries, 77, 90, 94–100, 124, 138, 177, 186, 212

funerals: relative gender equality, 43; ritual mourning, 89, 219; *sati,* 27, 29, 67, 90, 193–194, 218, 219–220. *See also* graves

gender, 2; bodhisattvas, 13, 76, 82–83; genital, 199; labor division, 104–105, 108–109, 115, 121, 210; and life expectancy, 218. *See also* body image; family relationships; fertility; gender hierarchies; males; sexuality; third gender; transvestism; women's roles in domestic economy

gender hierarchies, 39–40, 48, 228; Chineseness, 12–24; daughters' value, 13, 22, 55, 109, 111–112, 125–126, 150, 205, 212, 228; economic, 16–17, 123, 133; religions and, 12–16, 22–31, 44–51, 54, 70–103, 143–145, 167, 205, 226, 228, 230; state-household compact, 147–150, 164. *See also* domestic economy; female status;

Confucian gender standards, 12–13; erotic art, 60; infant mortality, 211, 212; Kabuki actors, 60; life expectancy of women, 221; male Kabuki actors, 60; matrilocality, 206; "needle shops," 198; premarital sex, 154; pre-Tokugawa, 81; rice rituals, 107–108; royal women, 81, 184, 187; and Ryukyu archipelago, 34; textile production, 115; Tokugawa, 53, 60, 154, 198, 211, 212, 221; widowhood, 219; writing by women, 53

Java, 34, 37, 42; Buddhist, 49–51, 75, 220; childbirth, 214; Chinese, 118, 126–127, 141, 146–147; Cirebon law, 161; corvée workers, 135; divorce, 151–152, 207; domestic economy, 44, 45, 108, 109; Hindus, 47–51, 90, 220; home for unhappy wives, 207; inscriptions, 44, 45; intermarriage, 145, 146–147; life expectancy, 218; literacy of women, 54; Mataram, 42, 147, 175; Muslims, 84–92, 146–147, 194; performance, 59–60; senior women's religious roles, 73, 220; sexual morality, 156, 157, 160; state-household compact, 148; tax farmers, 141; textile production and trade, 117, 118, 124, 127, 136, 139, 221; texts, 1, 56, 58, 63, 86, 89, 92, 124, 151–152, 156, 165, 166, 171–172, 182, 186, 202, 216, 228; wife exchange, 182. See also Banten; Batavia; Jogjakarta; Surakarta/Kartasura

Javanese court life: Ken Dedes, 1, 58, 232; male dress, 60, 143; royal women, 55, 92, 93, 165, 166, 170–176, 184–190, 228, 231; sati, 194, 219; servant and slave women, 180; sex performance aids, 216. See also Jogjakarta; Surakarta/Kartasura

Jogjakarta, 185; economics of women, 125, 187, 188; guardswomen, 125, 176; life expectancy by gender, 218; royal residences, 174, 175;

textiles, 221; tooth-filing, 200; wet nurses, 186; wife exchange, 182

Kaempfer, Engelbert, 216
Kelly, Joan, 4
Ken Dedes, 1, 58, 232
Khmer, 23, 51; dress, 143; infidelity of husbands, 217; inscriptions, 45, 49, 162; royal women, 166, 184–185; state-household compact, 149, 162; tooth-filing, 200; training girls, 198; widows' poverty, 222
Knox, Robert, 33
Korea, 12–13, 71, 144
Kuki, 25, 26, 30, 137. See also Chin

labor, 110, 122; corvée, 30, 108–109, 134–136, 177; European exploitation, 104, 109, 135, 136; gender division, 104–105, 108–109, 115, 121, 210; military, 134–139; palace occupations, 136, 178–181, 184, 187–189; textile production, 62, 113, 115–120, 127, 135–136, 221, 230. See also domestic economy; slaves
Lampung, 137, 203
land ownership, 110–111, 187. See also matrilineality; patrilineality
languages: academic facility with, 3, 4, 51–52, 56; Arakan, old Burmese in, 32; Assamese, 28; Austroasiatic, 16, 22–23; Austronesian, 21–22, 34, 35–36, 52, 71; Batak, 53; Han, 16, 20; Indonesian, 56; Laos, 21; Malay, 21–22, 34, 45, 51, 54, 56, 93, 119; oral legends, 64–65; Papuan, 36; "religious" vocabularies, 71, 90; Sanskrit, 45, 51, 56; southern China, 12, 16, 20; Tai, 16, 25, 28; Taiwan, 21–22; Tibeto-Burman, 21, 25, 29; Vietnam, 22–23, 55. See also literacy
Lao: birth celebrations, 213, 214; Christians in Siam, 96; Lan Xang kingdom, 165, 174, 183; marriage diplomacy, 183; royal women, 165, 166, 169–170, 174, 181, 183; sexual knowledge, 202; texts, 56, 59,

90, 208; corvée, 108–109, 134–135, 177; in domestic economy, 24, 38, 44, 104–109, 113–123, 210, 230; dress, 64, 142–143; fear of female powers, 9, 45, 167, 216, 217; healers, 129–130, 223; homosexuality, 37, 61, 93, 173, 192; infidelity, 126, 215–216, 217; life expectancy, 43, 218; men's houses, 35, 39, 62, 198, 199; mother-son relationship, 13, 97, 185; ritual prominence, 39, 60, 75, 223, 230; sex trade, 130–131; sexual performance enhancement, 64, 142–143, 216–217; sister-brother relationships, 39, 58, 181–182, 192–193, 211–212; slaves, 130; transvestism, 29, 38, 57, 60, 73, 89, 93, 94; virility/prowess, 40, 48, 64, 91, 137, 142–143, 173, 195–196, 199, 208; in warfare, 137, 142, 170–171; women as distractions to spiritual growth of, 48, 77–78, 158, 225; writing about or as women, 52–56, 64–66. *See also* gender hierarchies; migration; patriarchy; third gender

Manipur, 24, 25, 28–31, 71, 133, 227

Marini, G. F. de, 131, 213, 214

maritime communications, 24–25, 32–41, 46, 84–85, 104–105, 108, 115. *See also* trade

marketplace, 104, 112–117, 121–127, 133, 228, 231; Assam women, 31; Banda men excluded, 123; Indian bazaar, 26; Manipur women, 29–30; palace women, 187; pepper, 120; southern China, 17, 46; state revenue collection and, 127, 139, 140, 141. *See also* textile production and trade; trade

marriage, 205–207; Balinese priests, 75; brother-sister, 181–182, 192; Buddhist monkhood as preparation for, 79; child brides, 27, 29, 31; Chinese colonies, 18–19, 20, 21, 22, 23; Christian standards, 100, 153, 157; circumcision of males important for, 90; "companions and friends," 33; concu-

binage, 55, 100–101, 145, 157, 174, 175, 183, 189–190, 192, 194; cousins, 18, 46, 206; economics, 150–152; endogamy, 206; exogamy, 206; Hindu, 26–27; intermarriage cross-culturally, 20, 21, 126, 133, 144–147; laws, 158–160; monogamy, 91, 196, 217; Muslim, 85, 88–89, 91, 93; Oceania, 38; "play wives," 136; polygamy, 91, 172, 189–195; rights, 13, 26–27, 150, 156; royal, 181–182, 183, 189–195; state-household compact, 147–150, 153–154; "temporary marriages" of women traders, 125–127, 131; Vietnam, 23, 145, 146, 147, 206; weddings, 205, 206–207; widow remarriage, 22, 27, 82, 116, 164, 219, 220, 221, 226; wife exchange/ marriage diplomacy, 40, 145, 150, 182, 183; "wife-giving/wife-receiving," 36. *See also* bridewealth; divorce; fidelity; matrilocality; patrilocality; sexuality; widows

Marsden, William, 66, 150

matrilineality, 28–29, 31, 110–112, 169, 227; Cambodia, 45, 46; Cham, 82; Melanesia, 40; Minangkabau, 110, 148, 167, 206; New Guinea, 39; Southeast Asia and Oceania, 38; Taiwan, 22

matrilocality, 18, 22, 33, 38, 109, 151, 206, 227–228

Melaka: Dutch, 66–67, 68, 94, 96, 141; healing practices, 209, 210; infant mortality, 67; intermarriage, 145; literacy of women, 54; matrilineal inheritance, 110; Melaka Straits, 34; Muslims, 84, 85, 88–89, 154; oral contests, 202; Portuguese, 42, 65, 67, 94, 95, 104, 113, 128, 141, 145, 167, 202; revenue collection, 141; sexual morality, 154, 156; spirit communication, 128; state-household compact, 162; tax collection, 141; textile production, 113, 117; widows, 221

Melanesia, 35–36, 37, 40, 226, 227

recurring, 215; taboos, 199. *See also* childbirth; fertility

premarital sex, 18, 31, 74, 202–205; children from, 154, 157, 202–203; class and, 154, 203–204; sexual morality vs., 100–102, 154–155, 157; virginity vs., 88, 101–102, 131, 154, 182

priestesses: Assam, 28–29; Java, 73; Manipur *maibi,* 29, 71; Philippines, 22, 71–73, 95; Ryukyu, 34, 71, 84; Taiwan *inib,* 71, 95; Toraja, 53, 137; Vietnam, 84. *See also* female spirit communication

property: beads, 113; of royal women, 187–189; women as, 129, 150, 156; women's rights to, 13, 22, 26, 218, 221. *See also* bridewealth; inheritance; land ownership; slaves

queens. *See* upper-class women, royal; women's authority

Raffles, Sophia, 66–67
Raffles, Thomas Stamford, 49, 54, 66
Reid, Anthony, 2, 4, 53
religions, 3–4, 42, 70–103, 135; Daoism, 13, 16, 47, 81, 83; gender hierarchies, 12–16, 22–31, 44–51, 54, 70–103, 143–145, 167, 205, 226, 228, 230; indigenous, 28–31, 44–48, 70–75, 83, 89, 93, 95, 137, 143, 167, 205, 223; intermarriage between, 146; "religious" vocabularies, 71, 90; royal pilgrimages, 189; royal women's expenditures on, 187–188; state alliance, 80, 93, 143, 203, 228, 230; worldwide spread, 37, 74, 102, 137, 186, 200, 230. *See also* Buddhists; Christians; Confucianism; deities; Hindus; morality; Muslims; rituals; shamanism

Rhodes, Alexandre de, 73, 82, 97, 101
rice farming: China borderlands, 16–17, 19, 21, 24; deities, 17, 24, 29, 107; female prominence in, 16–17, 19, 21, 24, 28, 29, 31, 33, 106, 107–109; India borderlands,

25, 28, 29, 33; male roles, 24, 107, 108, 109; postnatal labor, 215

rights, 159; marital, 13, 26–27, 150, 156; property, 13, 22, 26, 218, 221. *See also* freedom and independence, female; law; property

rituals: bloodletting and human sacrifice, 43, 137; Buddhist, 137; dancing, 27–28, 29, 71; healing, 78, 86, 204, 209, 214; male prominence, 39, 60, 75, 223, 230; Muslim, 89, 137; purity, 26, 44–45, 88, 155; transgender figures in, 73–74. *See also* female ritual prominence; funerals; life-cycle rites; spirit communication

Rumphius, George, 65, 190
Ryukyu archipelago, 34, 39, 71, 84

Samoa, 38, 39, 74, 204
Sangermano, Vincenzo, 201, 215, 223
seclusion, female, 27; childbirth, 210; menstruation, 38–39, 88, 199, 200; Muslim, 85–86, 93–94, 109; palace quarters, 172–181, 183–184, 196. *See also* modesty/immodesty, female

senior women, 13, 218–224; collaborations among, 109; Hindu, 49–51; life expectancy, 43, 218, 220, 221; menopause, 221; Muslim, 89, 91; nuns, 76–77, 220; palace duties, 184–185; pottery production, 115; poverty of freed slaves, 132–133, 222, 230; ritual prominence, 21, 22, 71–73, 102, 205, 220, 222; tutoring girls in women's roles, 198. *See also* widows

Seram, 112
sexuality, 36, 199; Buddhism and, 76, 77, 79, 80, 81, 89; celibacy in religious vocations, 79, 80, 89, 99, 205; circumcision, 90–91, 208; diseases transmitted by, 133; divorce for want of, 152; eunuchs as guardsmen of, 177; female distractions to male spiritual growth, 48, 77–78, 158, 225; homosexuality, 37, 61, 93, 173, 192; knowledge

about, 201–205; masculine virility displays, 40, 48, 64, 91, 137, 142–143, 173, 195–196, 208; Miao, 18–19; Muslim crime and punishment, 90; nursing mother and, 214–215; Oceania women, 38; in oral legends, 57–58; palace, 172–178, 189–195; performance-enhancing aids, 64, 142–143, 216–217; prostitution, 127–128, 130–133; romantic stereotypes, 215; royal marriage, 181–182, 190–195; senior women, 221, 222; tropical climate, 66; in visual art, 60, 61. *See also* fertility; fidelity; gender; marriage; sexual morality

sexual morality, 70, 152–163, 202; vs. adultery, 76, 87, 88, 101, 155–161, 162, 193, 215; Chinese, 13, 23; Christian missionaries and, 57, 63–65, 74, 90, 100–102, 157–158, 203; Hindu, 26–27, 155; law, 26, 88, 132, 152–163, 215, 216, 219; Oceania women and, 38; royal, 191, 192, 193; Thailand, 159, 160, 163, 204–205; Vietnamese, 46, 132, 153–160, 163, 193, 203, 216. *See also* chastity; incest; marriage; modesty/immodesty; premarital sex

shamanism, 16, 102, 116, 137, 223. *See also* animists; spirit communication; witchcraft

Shan, 25, 109, 136

Siam, 25, 42; Christians, 94, 96, 98; intermarriage, 145; prostitution, 131; trade, 16, 118; training girls, 198. *See also* Ayutthaya; Mon; Thailand

slaves, 130–133, 159; debt, 132; dress, 144; high-status households, 178–181, 208; manumission into poverty, 97–98, 132–133, 222, 230; pepper farming and trade, 120–121; royal women marrying, 193; textile production and trade, 115–116, 118, 131; in VOC households, 66, 130; wet nursing, 129; wives, 126–127

sources, 43–69, 228–229; archaeology, 36, 43–44, 108, 113–114, 119, 229; female voice, 45, 52–55, 173–174; oral legend, 55–59, 77, 86–87, 229; performing arts, 59–60, 61, 229; privileged voices in, 7, 52, 61, 102–103, 165, 194–196; trans-textuality, 58–63; tropical climate affecting, 43, 49, 61, 67, 174; visual art, 44, 60–62, 67, 127, 229. *See also* written sources

"South Asia," 33, 226–227

Southeast Asia, 1–2, 4, 11–12, 21–26, 226–227; Asian context, **14–15;** island, **72;** mainland, **50;** and Oceania, 12, 33–41, **35,** 204, 227

southern China, 11, 12, 16–20, 53, 84, 228; Miao, 16, 18–19, 20, 142, 144, 205, 207; Yue, 16, 23; Zhuang, 16, 17, 19

Spanish: vs. bridewealth, 151; coinage, 122; vs. divorce, 153; and intermarriage, 145; Madagascar, 34; Marianas, 35; Samar, 36; and textile production, 119, 135–136; written records, 49, 53, 57, 61, 63, 69, 71–74, 90, 101, 112–113. *See also* Christianized Philippines; Christian missionaries

spirit communication, 16; male prominence, 60, 223, 230; religions vs., 16, 74–75, 93, 220, 223. *See also* animists; female spirit communication; shamanism; witchcraft

Sri Lanka, 11, 32–33, 110, 205; Buddhists, 16, 33, 51, 75, 76–77, 80

state: early modern, 3–4, 36–37, 42, 134, 164, 229–230; ethnicity and authority of, 141–142; religious alliance, 80, 93, 143, 203, 228, 230; revenue collection, 139–141, 177–178; sexual morality regulated by, 153–158; state-household compact, 147–150, 153–164. *See also* court life; Europeans; law; political boundaries

status. *See* female status; hierarchies

Sulawesi, 34, 35, 42; European chronicles, 65, 69; Manado, 90, 105, 142;

VOC (Dutch East India Company), 22, 42, 58, 93, 104, 230; and abandoned children, 133; agricultural tools, 106, 107; Banda, 114; beads, 113; Borneo, 63–64, 113; coinage, 122; corvée labor, 109, 135; and court life, 52, 59–60, 167, 168, 169, 176, 187, 188–189, 191; Cut Nyak Dhien vs. colonial government, 3; and divorce, 153, 159–160; dress, 143, 144; and healers, 128; intermarriage, 126, 145–146; and law, 155, 159–160, 161; New Guinea, 37, 52; Perak, 60, 188–189; pottery, 114; Reformed Church/Calvinists, 68, 94, 97–98, 101, 157; sexual morality, 101, 102, 157; slaves in households of, 66, 130; Sri Lanka/Ceylon, 33, 65, 147; state-household compact, 147, 148, 149; and textile production and trade, 117, 118, 119, 120, 122, 127, 139; wedding ceremonies, 205; and widows, 98, 140, 220, 221; wife exchange, 182; wives in local commerce, 123, 126; written and visual records, 5, 49, 58, 63–69, 73, 93, 105, 114, 136, 146, 147, 168, 175, 199–203. *See also* Ambon; Batavia; Java; Melaka; Taiwan

Wang Dahai, 108, 109, 112, 128, 147
warfare: androgynous beings in, 73–74; Burma-Arakan, 24–25, 32; Burma-Thailand, 136, 138, 170, 174, 185; China-Vietnam, 3, 23, 46, 59, 63, 171; corvée service, 30, 134, 136; dress and body decoration, 40, 138, 142, 170, 228; and gendered division of labor, 108–109; head-hunting, 22, 31, 67, 137–139, 219; indigenous practices, 136–138; Mughal-Assam, 30–31; Vietnam civil war, 42, 136; women in, 3, 59, 138, 142, 164, 170–171, 183
wet nurses, 89, 128–129, 186, 214
widows: Assam hill women, 31; childless, 208, 218; Chinese and, 13, 22, 23, 31; Christianity and, 98, 220, 221; demographic data, 218; economics, 208, 218, 221, 222; fidelity, 13, 27, 29, 89–92, 147, 193–194, 218–220; freedom, 218–219, 220; Hindus and, 27, 29, 218, 219; Muslim attitudes toward, 89–92, 194, 220; nuns, 13, 76, 205, 220; remarriage, 22, 27, 82, 116, 164, 219, 220, 221, 226; royal, 185; *sati*, 27, 29, 90, 193–194, 218, 219–220; tax collecting, 140; taxes on, 139; traders, 121; of warriors, 138
witchcraft, 30, 73–75, 94–95, 214, 216, 218, 223–224. *See also* black magic; shamanism
Wolters, O. W., 5, 69
women's agricultural prominence, 16–17; fertility links, 17, 19, 27, 43, 107, 137, 205, 231; labor, 16–33, 38, 44, 106–109, 120, 121, 215, 228; millet, 107; pepper, 120, 121–122; rice, 16–17, 19, 21, 24, 28–31, 33, 106, 107–109; rice deities, 17, 24, 29, 107; ritual, 17, 19, 21, 26–28, 33, 43, 74, 106–107, 231
women's authority, 26, 43, 44–45, 165; in family relationships, 13, 19, 26, 206, 212, 220–221; guardswomen, 176–177; kings preferred over, 169–172; Muslims and, 85, 89; religious, 13, 33, 66, 76–77, 81, 82, 87, 95, 97, 98, 207, 220; as rulers, 13, 16, 19, 21, 81, 85, 87, 164, 166–172, 195, 230; Southeast Asia and Oceania, 38; state revenue collection, 140–141; in warfare, 138, 164, 170–171, 183; "women of prowess," 1, 116–117, 177. *See also* female ritual prominence; female status; freedom and independence, female; political influence; senior women; upper-class women; women's agricultural prominence
women's history, 2, 5, 6, 10, 11, 128, 226, 228–231; early modern, 4–6, 42–43, 48–69, 70, 133, 221, 226, 229–231; longitudinal, 2–4; pre-

modern, 2, 5, 43–48, 70–75, 205, 212, 218. *See also* female status; sources

women's roles in domestic economy, 26, 103, 104–133, 231; archaeology, 44, 45; collaborations among women, 109; commoditization of, 129–132, 150; corvée, 135–136; elephant drivers, 61, 127; entertainment, 127–128; food production, 104–109, 127, 231; gender division, 104–105, 108–109, 115, 121, 210; girls trained for, 197–199; healers and midwives, 78, 128, 129, 210–211, 222, 223; household goods and services, 127; money-changing skills, 123; in Mughal miniatures, 61, 135; occupational range, 127–129; pottery production, 44, 113, 114–115; price on, 150–151; rights connected to value of, 27; savings accumulation, 122–123; textile labor, 62, 113, 115–120, 127, 135–136, 221, 230; urbanization and, 130–133; wet nurses, 89, 128–129, 186, 214. *See also* marketplace; senior women; slaves; trade; women's agricultural prominence; women's authority

world areas, 11–12, 21, 34–37, 204, 226–227. *See also* political boundaries

written sources, 18, 51–74, 85–94, 228–229; Buddhist, 45, 49, 59, 75–81, 123, 152–153, 158, 196; Burma, 45, 52, 55, 59, 68, 79, 165, 174, 190, 216–217; Chinese, 45–47, 142, 146, 156, 167, 171, 176, 177, 204; court, 54, 55, 63, 79, 90–93, 169–173, 188, 189–190, 194; European chronicles, 3, 5, 49, 51–74, 88, 90, 93, 94, 101, 105, 112–114, 136, 146, 147, 168, 175, 199–203; gender-related guidance, 12–13, 20, 55, 68, 201–202, 216; Hindu *Ramayana,* 27, 48, 56; Java, 1, 56, 58, 63, 86, 89, 92, 124, 151–152, 156, 165, 166, 171–172, 182, 186, 202, 216, 228; Lao, 56, 59, 77, 123, 169, 205, 215–216; Malay, 47, 49, 52–60, 66, 87, 91–92, 110, 158, 164, 171, 192, 210, 228; men's prominence, 52–54; men writing about or as women, 52–56, 64–66; Oceania and, 38; oral legend and, 55–59, 77; Philippines, 53, 57, 63–74, 94, 109; Thai, 56, 58, 63, 77, 80, 149, 159; transtextuality, 58–63; Vietnam, 3, 45, 49, 56, 59, 63, 127, 129–130, 172, 228; by women, 53–55, 63, 66–67, 79, 84, 174, 216–217. *See also* inscriptions; poetry

Yunnan, 12, 17–21, 24, 25, 43, 205

Zhou Daguan, 46, 176, 204
Zoetmulder, Petrus, 56

About the Author

BARBARA WATSON ANDAYA was educated at the University of Sydney (B.A., Dip. Ed.), the University of Hawai'i (M.A.), and Cornell University (Ph.D), and has taught or conducted research in Australia, Indonesia, Malaysia, the Netherlands, Portugal, England, New Zealand, and the United States. Although her specialization is broadly in Southeast Asian history, her particular area of expertise is the western Malay-Indonesian archipelago. Her publications include *A History of Malaysia* (with Leonard Andaya, 1982, 2000), *To Live as Brothers: Southeast Sumatra in the Seventeenth and Eighteenth Centuries* (1993), and most recently numerous articles and essays on the position of women in Southeast Asia. Barbara Andaya is presently professor of Asian studies and Director of the Center for Southeast Asian Studies at the University of Hawai'i at Manoa, as well as president of the American Association of Asian Studies (2005–2006).

Taxonomy of Major Pathogens

NAME MICROBE FEATURES	DISEASE	PAGES	KEY FEATURES OF PATHOGENESIS/VACCINE
Hepatitis B virus			
Enveloped; HBs antigen; hepadnavirus	Hepatitis	360, 513–14, 731–32	Dark urine, fever, nausea, yellowing skin and eyes, weakness; HBs antigen is assayed to detect presence and degree of viral infection; vaccine is available
Herpes simplex virus			
	Cold sores	615–16	
	Keratitis	616, 632–33	
Enveloped; herpes virus family	Genital herpes	615–16, 782–88	Latent forms in neural ganglia
	Encephalitis	783, 813, 820	
	Neonatal herpes	683–84	
Human herpes virus 6			
Enveloped; herpes virus family	Roseola	614	High fever, sometimes febrile seizure, maculopapular rash
Human papillomavirus			
Infects keratinocytes	Warts	593, 617, 781–82	Stimulates hyperplasia of infected host cells; vaccine is available
	Genital warts		
Monkeypox virus			
Enveloped; poxvirus	Monkeypox	618, 892, 918	Zoonosis; similar but less infectious and less deadly than smallpox
Parvovirus B19			
Parvovirus	Fifth disease (slapped cheek syndrome)	363, 610, 613	Lacelike rash
Varicella-zoster virus			
Enveloped; herpes virus	Chickenpox	605–6, 614–15	Primary infection; vesicular lesions; vaccine is available
	Shingles	605, 633	Reactivation infection arising from latent forms of the virus; vaccine is available
Variola major/minor			
Enveloped; poxvirus; eradicated from Earth except for two secure labs	Smallpox	494–95, 617–18	Replicates in cytoplasm; pustular skin lesions; highly lethal; potential bioterror agent; vaccine is available

RNA VIRUSES

NAME MICROBE FEATURES	DISEASE	PAGES	KEY FEATURES OF PATHOGENESIS/VACCINE
Coronavirus			
			Virus is spread by respiratory droplets
Single-stranded; (+) sense; enveloped; coronaviruses; SARS-CoV, MERS-CoV	Cold	648–50	Rhinorrhea (runny nose)
	SARS	889–93	Respiratory failure
	MERS	591, 880	Respiratory failure
Coxsackievirus			
Single-stranded; (+) sense; picornavirus	Hand, foot and mouth disease	617, 692, 819, 821	Complications include myocarditis
	Herpangina		
Ebola virus			
Single-stranded; (−) sense; enveloped; filovirus	Ebola	36, 54, 688, 692, 865–66	Diarrhea, vomiting, excessive hemorrhaging, death; virus is spread by contact with body fluids
Dengue virus			
Single-stranded; (+) sense; enveloped; flavivirus	Dengue fever (breakbone fever)	692	Transmitted by *Aedes* mosquito; endemic in Caribbean, South America, and Asia; high fever; vaccine available (2016)
Hantavirus			
Single-stranded; (−) sense; enveloped; bunyavirus	Hantavirus pulmonary syndrome		Transmitted by inhalation of dried rodent urine or feces
Hepatitis A virus			
Single-stranded; (+) sense; picornavirus	Hepatitis	730–32, 882	Dark urine, fever, nausea, yellowing skin and eyes, weakness; vaccine is available
Hepatitis C virus			
Single-stranded; (+) sense; enveloped; flavivirus	Hepatitis	351–52, 363–64, 733	Dark urine, fever, nausea, yellowing skin and eyes, weakness

Taxonomy of Major Pathogens

NAME MICROBE FEATURES	DISEASE	PAGES	KEY FEATURES OF PATHOGENESIS/VACCINE
Hepatitis D virus			
Single-stranded; (−) sense; circular genome; enveloped; delta virus	Hepatitis	360, 731–32	Dark urine, fever, nausea, yellowing skin and eyes, weakness; needs hepatitis B virus as helper
Hepatitis E virus			
Single-stranded; (+) sense; Hepeviridae family	Hepatitis	733	Dark urine, fever, nausea, yellowing skin and eyes, weakness
Human immunodeficiency virus (HIV)			
	Acquired immunodeficiency disease (AIDS)	376–81, 953–63, 784–86	Transmitted by blood or sexual contact; virus targets T cells; mononucleosis-like symptoms to increased opportunistic infections and cancers
Influenza virus			
Single-stranded; segmented genome; enveloped; orthomyxovirus	Influenza (flu)	372–73, 416–17, 645, 651–54	Cough, fever, sore throat, headache, tachycardia, weakness; antigenic shift and drift aid its pathogenesis; vaccine is available
Measles virus			
Single-stranded; (−) sense; enveloped; paramyxovirus	Measles	611–13	Cough, fever, runny nose, maculopapular rash, Koplik spots
Mumps virus			
Single-stranded; (−) sense; enveloped; paramyxovirus	Mumps	733–34	Swollen, painful salivary glands; vaccine is available
Norovirus			
Single-stranded; (+) sense; calcivirus	Gastroenteritis	722, 730	Outbreaks associated with cruise ships; watery diarrhea
Poliovirus			
Single-stranded; (+) sense; picornavirus	Poliomyelitis	819–21	Vaccine is available
Respiratory syncytial virus			
Single-stranded, (−) sense; enveloped; paramyxovirus	RSV	649–51	Lower respiratory tract; infects children; low-grade fever, cough, difficulty breathing, wheezing
Rhinovirus			
Single-stranded; (+) sense; picornavirus	Common cold	495–96, 591, 648–50	Rhinorrhea (runny nose)
Rotavirus			
Double-stranded; segmented genome	Gastroenteritis	721–22, 729–30	Usually infects children; watery diarrhea; vaccine is available
Rubella virus			
Single-stranded; (+) sense; enveloped; togavirus	Rubella (German measles)	612–13, 619	Eye pain, conjunctivitis, sore throat, headache; vaccine is available
Yellow fever virus			
Single-stranded; (+) sense; enveloped; flavivirus	Yellow fever	45–46	*Aedes* mosquito-borne; endemic in parts of South America and Africa; jaundice; vaccine is available
Zika virus			
Single-stranded; (+) sense; enveloped; flavivirus	Zika fever	819	*Aedes* mosquito-borne; endemic in parts of Africa, South America, and Southeast Asia; usually mild but associated with fetal microcephaly